WARS OF DISRUPTION AND RESILIENCE

STUDIES IN SECURITY
AND INTERNATIONAL AFFAIRS

WARS OF DISRUPTION AND RESILIENCE

Cybered Conflict, Power, and National Security

CHRIS C. DEMCHAK

The University of Georgia Press
Athens and London

© 2011 by the University of Georgia Press

Athens, Georgia 30602

www.ugapress.org

All rights reserved

Set in Electra by Graphic Composition, Inc.

Printed digitally in the United States of America

Library of Congress Cataloging-in-Publication Data

Demchak, Chris C.

Wars of disruption and resilience : cybered conflict, power,
and national security / Chris C. Demchak.

     p.   cm. — (Studies in security and international affairs)

Includes bibliographical references and index.

ISBN-13: 978-0-8203-3834-7 (hardcover : alk. paper)

ISBN-10: 0-8203-3834-6 (hardcover : alk. paper)

ISBN-13: 978-0-8203-4067-8 (pbk. : alk. paper)

ISBN-10: 0-8203-4067-7 (pbk. : alk. paper)

1. Information warfare.

2. Cyberspace — Security measures.

3. Computer networks — Security measures.

4. Cyberterrorism — Prevention.

5. National security — Technological innovations.

I. Title.

   U163.D36 2011

   363.325 — dc22   2011012912

British Library Cataloging-in-Publication Data available

CONTENTS

Preface   ix

Acknowledgments   xvii

CHAPTER ONE. Globalization and Spread of Cybered Conflict   1
    Emerging Uncivil Cybered International System   5
    Challenge to International Relations Theory   22
    Syncretic Reframing: Security Resilience Strategy for a
        Cybered World   33
    Security Resilience Strategy: Linking Framework and Tools   48

CHAPTER TWO. History's Experiments in Security Resilience   80
    Case Studies of City-State Security Strategies   80
    Greek and Italian City-State Wars of Disruption   83
    British and U.S. Small Wars of Disruption   113
    Lessons for Disruption in a Security Resilience Strategy   166

CHAPTER THREE. Challenges in a New Strategy for Cybered Threats   174
    Political Acceptance of Cybered Threat in Democratic
        City-States   176
    Technical Design for Cybered Conflict   183
    Operational Constraints on Implementation of Disruption   198

CHAPTER FOUR. Institutional Design for Cybered Power and
National Security   224
    Honest Joint Consultation — Knowledge Nexus   230
    Comprehensive Data — Privacy in Behavior-Based Adaptations   237
    Collaborative Actionable Knowledge — the Atrium Model   252
    Gathering What Exists Today   266

CHAPTER FIVE. Disruption and Resilience for National Security and Power in a Cybered World 270

    Marks of the New Cybered Age: Sovereignty, Disruption, and Resilience 273

    Inklings of the Future: The Rise of the Cyber Command 277

    Adapting the Social Contract for Cybered Uncertainty 279

Bibliography 291

Index 323

PREFACE

Building on a century of thinking about violent conflict in war, the argument begins with what is different about conflict today in a globalized, highly cybered international system. The emerging system looks more like city-states that never intend to fight each other again surrounded and interpenetrated by dysfunctional regions, or "badlands," whose actors reach easily into the city-states. Arguing that emerging conflict and enemies are necessarily cybered, thus distant, likely hard to reach accurately, and extremely difficult to simply coerce into quiescence, this book offers a globally applicable underlying theory of why groups choose violence against distant strangers using cyberspace.

Cyber power is the national ability to disrupt this obscured bad actor somewhere in the digitized globe, whether nonstate or state, in proportion to its motivations/capabilities to attack with violent effects and yet be resilient against imposed or enhanced nasty surprises across all critical nationally sustaining systems. In this book, cyber power's underlying strategic elements of both disruption and resilience are built piece by piece. History is employed to test the reasonableness of these elements, especially as knowledge-oriented imperatives for success. The case studies emphasize disruption as the harder case to make over destruction and, to a much lesser extent, resilience. The goal is to outline and argue for a national cyber power strategy that is long in time horizon, flexible in target and scale, and practical enough to maintain the security of a digitized nation facing violent cybered conflict.

The underlying approach is syncretic. Syncretism is distinct from synthesis in that it means to make conflicting explanations harmonize, whereas synthesis means to take pieces of each into a new composite. This work hence does not challenge the value or contribution of any relevant established theories of conflict or surprise, nor does it presume to take them apart; rather it seeks to put their insights into a unified strategy that demonstrates the complementarities of their central tenets.

First, to place disruption as a systemic feature of cybered conflict, this work adopts such a syncretic approach to what is already known and codified from the large history of conflict studies by three main (American) schools of inter-national relations. To place violent aims in the conflicts of a cybered world, a syncretic approach incorporates all three of the dominant schools of interna-tional relations into a *theory of (violent) action* usable for disruption of cybered enemies. The three normally distinct subdisciplines of modern American in-ternational relations theory — realism, liberal institutionalism, and construc-tivism — offer three explanations of prospective violence, respectively: power, interests, and knowledge/culture. Within its own parameters, each field of study has provided powerful arguments concerning the willingness to engage in violence demonstrated by initiating violent conflict. All are bound by their origin legacies, however, and focus on nation-states as the major venue for violence (Hasenclever, Mayer, and Rittberger 1996). The three schools are unable individually to consider the domestic side of national security save as a venue for the study of national security decision makers. But an open cybered world requires just such a comprehensive approach.

In a syncretic view, the collective insights of these fields, however, can be usefully reframed into a *theory of action* explaining in generalizable terms across international contexts the emergence of a willingness to act even if the result will inflict violence on others. It also allows an analytical and strategic weighting of motivating drivers that apply to individuals or to cognitively cohe-sive groups such as militaries, leaders in oligarchies, or state-level allies. Thus the approach largely neutralizes the levels of analysis problem between na-tional and domestic security domains and paves the way for a strategic applica-tion of disruption of information and cultural sensitivity, capital and economic facilitation, and coercion against the bad actors' perceptions of legitimacy, need, and confidence in attempting to attack.

Similarly, a syncretic approach helps place resilience as a systemic feature of cybered conflict comparable to disruption. This work adopts a theory of *surprise accommodation* in which unknowns are either knowable, requiring institutional design accommodation, or unknowable as *rogues* requiring timely collective sense-making and action. It combines the central tenets of a theory of surprise in a growing literature on complexity theory with the organizational theories about accommodating disabling surprises in largescale socio-technical systems and complex adaptive social systems research. Complex systems are less likely to have cascading disruption if their design includes redundancy and slack at critical junctions and continuous trial and error to refresh that knowl-edge. Furthermore, such systems can rebound from and innovate beyond the surprise that is inevitable due to the unknowable unknowns when constantly tested processes of rapid collective sense-making and accurate actions are ensured. Thus, the syncretic view here provides the guidance for resilience, for rebounding and surpassing attacks, as much as it does for disrupting attacks before or during their execution.

Knowledge is as critical continuously 24/7/365 for resilience as it is for effective disruption. Both halves of a strategy for national cyber power require three kinds of institutional adaptation: honest consultation of key actors, comprehensive knowledge gathering, and then rapid, collective, and applied knowledge refinement in operations. These requirements are discussed in two ways in this work. First, they are generic requirements used in the rereading of historical case studies as a way to establish the reasonableness, even intuitive nature of this strategy. Second, they are further described at the end of the book in the employment discussion. The strategic goal is challenging: to ensure national-level institutions of a westernized state both recognize and disrupt in tailored operations the emergence of physically violent threats against their citizens by external actors, as well as knowledgeably design and continuously practice rapid, accurate, collective sense-making and action under urgent conditions of surprise.

For that goal, one needs institutions. If one cannot outright eliminate all chronic, violent threats — and so many will be easily among us using distance-eliminating means — one needs to know more, much more, in advance, accurately, and with time to prepare. In particular, cyber power is about knowing both the world's dysfunctional regions and the defending nations' critical systems intimately. For a book on national security that also addresses international relations theory and cyberspace, this book has another unusual aspect. Rather than simply argue for the value of a "security resilience" strategy for the emerging messy, interconnected world, key chapters of the book describe and substantiate the institutional adaptations that are needed. As a globally underlying critical system, the cybersphere reaches deeply into societal and technical systems that historically could be reasonably separated, such as the world of international security and the world of domestic telecommunications. This work honors no disciplinary borders or artificial levels of analysis to stop consideration of any concept, procedure, organizing principle, tool, or insight shown to work broadly and sensibly for the kinds of chronic, violent, gray threats addressed here. That rather inclusive presumption, in what one might call a *unified* approach to security studies, is what prompts a book on strategy to also explain how to make the strategy work in domestic institutional adaptations. This work has theory as guidance for knowledge searches and choices, but it is no abstract discussion of ideal types. Aside from the traditional international relations, military history, and security studies literature, the ideas are drawn from the comparative literatures in domains traditionally seen as unrelated, such as organizational theory, socio-technical studies, complexity, cyberspace, resilience and reliability studies, criminology, cognitive psychology, sociology of group and social movement formation, and the history of economic development.

To link the strategy for cybered conflict to required institutional change, the book presents a discussion of the three institutional requirements in national structures particularly critical for both disruption and resilience: honest consensus, comprehensive data, and actionable insight. Each is necessary and involves institutional adaptations described in brief. First, a rough but clear consensus is built in the normally empty policy space between agencies called the *knowledge nexus,* and in a cybered world, it must be deliberately constructed by the social and technical ties among the nation's stakeholders in security and societal resilience. Second, knowing what distant and embedded bad actors may do requires sifting massive streams of data for evidence using traceable anonymity of *behavior-based privacy* mechanisms. In this approach, privacy is divided into routine components in which personal identity is encrypted but pseudonymous behavior is then available to security services for identifying emerging bad actor patterns. These are relinked only under legal procedures with validation and appeal processes in place for corrections of errors or miscarriages of justice. Finally, the institutions of cyber power themselves, especially the security services, need to use new and tacit knowledge for both disruption actions and resilience, testing hypotheses about bad actors and responses before the crisis occurs. The *Atrium* model of a security organization is explicitly designed for virtual tools and organizational processes that allow every member to develop knowledge by testing their own hypotheses, integrate others' ideas, collaborate in new processes, and form trust connections. All of these steps make the kind of institutional "knowledge development" necessary to face, derail, mitigate, or improvise in the face of chronic, nasty surprises from the intruding globalizing world.

Second, resilience as the second half of the strategy also requires extensive knowledge of how systems operate with what level of criticality for an acceptable social quality of life. Resilience rests on a *theory of surprise accommoda-*

tion in complex largescale socio-technical systems (LTS). Humans experience surprise in part because their essential societal systems are complex. Such complex systems can impose cascades of multiple source failures due to rogue outcomes that occur no matter what was done in advance. But the bulk of the possibly nasty surprises can be known in form or frequency in advance and then accommodated if the socio-technical institutions are sufficiently alert and knowledge oriented. Institutional change similar to that required for effective disruption is necessary to produce the understanding of how to design, establish, and then keep upgrading the redundancy, slack, and collective trial-and-error learning to make national systems resilient to cyber-enabled attacks. Without this component of cyber power, the disruption portion of a strategic response to attacks will be ultimately futile.

Moving from explaining the strategy to history, the book offers a reasonableness test of the disruption concept in particular by investigating some natural experiments of disruption (and some resilience) in history. In the set of premodern and modern cases, a state would not or could not destroy or own its enemies but needed to disrupt the opponent's behaviors. The goal is to use history to explore where a disruption-heavy strategy could have been or was used to effectively dampen the enemy's desire to act for the near or longer term. The middle sections of the book present case studies of disruption and (when relevant) resilience efforts or opportunities missed from ancient, early Renaissance, and more modern eras. These examples range from Athens to Florence to Britain in Africa to the United States to Central America and Vietnam.

Every book has a space and scope limitation. Cyber power is the output of a security resilience national strategy that comprises both disruption of attacks in advance and resilience to attacks at home. However, this book emphasizes the disruption portion of the argument. First, the concern with enemies abroad is a natural arena for national security and enemies. Two of the three functions of what is called computer network operations in the United States already closely involve disruption, though it is not so labeled. These are computer network attack (CNA) and exploitation (CNE). Indeed, current emerging definitions of cyber power are already beginning to be rather narrowly defined as the strength, reach, and defense of a nation's attack capabilities in security organizations. Once those notions are embedded across the national security community, it will be much more difficult to argue successfully for disruption over destruction and a more holistic approach as the proper response until after a major attack succeeds.

Destruction of enemies, however, is not really possible given today's global internet topology. Everywhere there can be easy access to nodes, tools, resources, and information about possible target vulnerabilities. The diverse, dense, undereducated populations of the wider globe will constantly replace the fallen, even if one could reach out and crush an attacker destructively. Hence the security forces need to displace one of their most strongly held preferences for another. On the other hand, resilience is easier for military leaders to understand as it is much like the reason one has logistics, continuity of operations, and rear or flank or overhead guards. For the national security community, the conceptually tough aspect will rather be in deftly accepting and executing a greater direct role in collective knowledge development, sense-making, and rapid action ensuring the wider domestic resilience of the society. The good news is that the institutional adaptations for a strategy emphasizing disruption are the same for a strategy emphasizing resilience in terms of knowledge development and accurate, rapid collective sense-making and action. Thus the book's discussion aims at the hardest transformation issue, disruption, but at all times where necessary makes sure that resilience lessons are in view as well.

The structure of the book therefore is to present the strategic imperatives and responding strategy of security resilience with emphasis on disruption and appropriate reference to resilience. The first chapter introduces the strategy as a whole, the key concepts and theories of disruption and of resilience, and the critical institutional elements necessary for implementation, which are explained further in the chapter on institutional design for surprise in cybered conflict. The second chapter presents natural experiments in history to see the extent to which the strategy's elements are present when disruption was pursued to more or less success. The third chapter addresses cyberspace directly in terms of the challenges it presents, from grievance farming across the global socio-technical environment to acquiring the knowledge necessary in a legal privacy-sensitive fashion, and the possible pitfalls in an application of disruption. The fourth chapter deals with the practical issues of how the nation institutionalizes a security resilience strategy. This chapter recommends three major institutional adaptations for continuous agency collaborative consensus, the systemic legal acquisition of comprehensive bad behavior information, and the critical collective development of timely, actionable, innovative knowledge in anticipation and response to surprise. The final chapter concludes with an overview of the contribution of this enquiry as well as speculative observations and questions for future work.

Policymakers will find the first, third, and fourth chapters of most interest. Here are the descriptions of the strategy, a more in-depth review of cyber threats and challenges, and a brief introduction to kinds of institutional adaptations and tools necessary and feasible. Scholars and students of security studies should find the first, second, and third chapters of particular interest. These chapters present the historical hunt for cases where a disruption strategy was and was not applied, and where resilience is or is not apparent, and the discussion of cyberspace as a modern case of where both disruption and resilience are needed.

It is important to note that the historical case studies are rereadings of history to show that key presumptions in this strategy are realistic and consistent enough with traditional human inclinations to have a solid chance of success. Historical applications demonstrate that the relatively unchanging human ingenuity and perceptiveness could have implemented such a strategy in some key elements long before the current times. These historical natural experiments include premodern case studies (Greek and Italian city-states), posttelegraph European modern case studies (small Victorian wars), and the U.S. small wars case studies. The cases broadly replicate the difficulties westernized nations face today with nonstate actors. In all cases, defenders engage violent foreign threats, and yet, for various reasons, one side or both cannot or choose not to destroy each other completely. Furthermore, the violence is often chronic as well as destructive, a clearly emerging characteristic of cross-border nonstate conflict today.

It should be emphasized what this book is not aiming to achieve. It does not attempt to explore the acknowledged richness of debate in any of the following areas: democratic peace theories; power expansion or hegemony theories or other critical distinctions in international relations theory; military history; any relevant agent, globalization, or quantitative social networking theories; cognitive psychology; or political disagreements in human security, dispersed peoples, religion, or national security policies. If the observations or recommendations of this work are applied to those debates in some useful way, this outcome is so much the better. It does not attempt to replicate an entire literature on surprise in complex systems and on demonstrably useful socio-technical organizational responses to crises. Rather, this book is itself solely about what it says it concerns: how might a largescale, complex, socio-technically interdependent society today prepare to disrupt chronic, violent, cyber-enabled threats and also be resilient to their successful attacks in a sensible and affordable, coherent strategy using the best of what we know, can seek to learn collectively, and apply effectively over the long term.

The book ends in a discussion of the one key hallmark of cybered conflict today: the hidden and ubiquitous nature of cyber threats physically, legally, and reputationally constraining strategic disruption, were it to be the sole emphasis of a national cyber power capacity. The potential attacker is obscured and deeply embedded virtually, possibly within the targeted societies. Yet they are likely to be physically far from detection or our legal sanctions, able to keep using advantages in scale, proximity, and precision to attack national social infrastructures. While today death is still likely to be the collateral effect of most cybered attacks, westernized democratic city-states are digitally integrating exponentially daily with the wider global community and making the possible violent payoff for a big strike in cyberspace grow commensurately. At some point, accidents that historically could have been contained will be enhanced opportunistically by those for whom the resulting violence was the object itself. We certainly must do better than we are doing today to create and sustain national cyber power to meet especially the cybered attacks with violent outcomes. Without a measured, informed security resilience strategy balancing disruption with resilience, we are most likely to do much worse. This book attempts to answer the exceptionally tough question using existing theories, strategies, institutional tendencies, the natural experiments of history, and the logic of human conflict. How might a largescale, complex, socio-technically interdependent society today prepare strategically and institutionally to disrupt chronic, violent, cyber-enabled would-be attackers in advance and to simultaneously be resilient to their successful attacks in a sensible and affordable, coherent strategy using the best of what we know, can seek to learn collectively, and apply effectively over the long term?

ACKNOWLEDGMENTS

To acknowledge everyone who has helped me think through these issues over the years seems an impossible task but absolutely necessary out of professional respect, personal loyalty, and unending gratitude. I cannot, however, fail to thank deeply Michael Gleim, tax attorney and global security thinker, for his unfailing efforts to edit the academic language into common-speak. Other people whose help and enthusiasm pushed this work include my colleagues on the executive boards of the International Security and Arms Control Section of the American Political Science Association, and of the International Security Studies Section of the International Studies Association (ISA), many of whom heard the talks developing these ideas at one point or another and encouraged this work. Special mention must be made of Tom Volgy, senior professor of political science and former head of ISA at the University of Arizona, whose seminar comments and support contributed to the quality of the work. Emily Goldman's particular support in the early short versions was essential to my continuing this effort, and I thank her for all her support over the several years it took to create a book-length manuscript. To Patrick Morgan, I say heartfelt thanks for very early thoughts on this approach, and I thank Stuart Croft for his guidance on restructuring the argument en route. A particular expression of appreciation goes to Peter Dombrowski for his pointed and helpful read of the near-final draft. I also must thank John Miller for his exceptional comments of both the action and the surprise accommodation theory discussions. I wish to thank my students for their support for the usefulness of an early version, awkwardly labeled the "theory of latitude," and so published. Their constant, novel, and sometimes amusing applications of the theory helped stimulate my thinking and resulted in the more generalizable name, "theory of action." To my colleagues in the complexity theory, largescale socio-technical systems research, large public institutional learning, structural contingency research, and surprise theory communities, I owe a great debt for their willingness to consider my particular blend of resilience and security as interesting, provocative, and enlightening. I would be horribly remiss in not specifically mentioning Todd R. LaPorte, Gene Rochlin, Todd M. La Porte, Louise Comfort, Jane Fountain, James Savage, Tom Volgy, Al Bergeson, Terry Terriff, Stuart Croft, Gale Mattox, and Arjen Boin for their support and the wonderful discussions over the years. It is indeed a blessing to have such colleagues. To my colleagues in the computer science field, whether public or private, open or classified, I remain a gardener, not a botanist, in this field of computers and their technical networks, having programmed only in graduate school. Many deep thanks for exceptionally enlightening and just plain fun conversations to Kurt Fenstermacher, John Mallery, Roger Hurwitz, Vinh Nguyen, Herb Lin, Sandro Gaycken, Roby Gilead, Volker Kozak, Brian Pagel, Raphael Brown, and Rich Palk. A special appreciative note to those who simply inspired me at different points in my life to keep on contributing — Pierre Sprey, Otto Rhein, Charles Perrow, and our much beloved Nelson Polsby. Finally one needs to remember those who simply stood behind one in a long process. Deep thanks and love to Devi, Mike, Wendy, and the infinitely patient alpha felines, all of whom tolerated my distraction and encouraged my enthusiasm in equal measure over the production of this work.

WARS OF DISRUPTION AND RESILIENCE

CHAPTER ONE

Globalization and Spread of Cybered Conflict

Cyberspace enables cooperation and conflict in nearly equal measure. In today's open, near-free, digitally enabled globalization, new and old enemies from unempowered individuals to national-level leaders can use easy access to international systems to engage in conflict, or economics, or both. Barriers to entry have particularly fallen for bad actors seeking to exploit distant populations using cyberspace connections. Each set of actors today at their own chosen scale of organization can reach far, deep, and wide into other nations at little near-term physical cost or physical risk to themselves. At their whim, distant or hidden bad actors can also use cyberspace to add to others' attacks for whatever reason or impulse. They may choose to opportunistically worsen natural disasters, expanding or redirecting disruptive cascading outcomes that disable key functions of whole societies, communities, or opposing military forces. In this world of global digital access, without great wealth, land, authority, or comrades in arms, opponents can easily attempt to harm in one big attack or many smaller attacks that can cumulate over time to even more destruction in tightly coupled modern systems. The intended victims may not even know their attackers, who can emerge from seemingly nowhere, whether inside or outside national borders. This new international reality creates the complexity of national security today and the need for a book reframing security strategy for modern democracies enmeshed in globally enabled cybered conflicts.

The power of a modern state to reduce the harm of obscure unknown attackers lies in its ability to recognize emerging sources of surprise and to disrupt or accommodate them. Conflict between human societies has always been about successfully disrupting the opponent, whether that opponent was a raiding party, an army, a city, or a whole nation, to get some desired outcome. As structured social groups began to desire outcomes that could not be achieved without disrupting other similarly sized opponents, organized conflict emerged as a way to be successful in proportion to the need for disruption. War emerged as a violent conflict between armed organizations, the outcome of which was significant for the successful functioning of opposing societies (O'Connell 1989). Since people get up and get well after being hit and may not stop what they are doing if the object of contest is critical enough, the most readily chosen form of disruption became killing, especially of those who could get up to fight again.

Today conflict is more likely to occur in its older, more basic sense: disrupting an opponent to achieve an outcome while ensuring that the opponent cannot succeed in disrupting one's home social group. The difference between most of human history and today is that open global cyberspace has enabled would-be hidden, distant, or smallscale opponents to attempt societal disruption that historically only close neighbors or superpowers could consider. Harnessed to traditional notions of national security, modern democracies struggle to understand the complex critical systems they constructed for economic prosperity. These now enable nonstate as well as state actors to impose harm across the globe seemingly at will. As currently constructed, cyberspace offers malevolent actors anywhere with internet access three extraordinary advantages in conflict: such actors can easily choose the scale of their organization, the proximity of their targets, and the precision of their attack plans. In other words, initially unknown, distant, or hidden actors in, say, Ghana can use the global web to organize from five to five hundred compatriots, to attack from five to five thousand kilometers away, and to target from five to five million people in one or many democratic nations simultaneously.[1]

When globally enabled by open, near-free cyberspace, conflict becomes vastly more complex and surprising. Today what has been seen as the power of nations to defend themselves is in transition. The historically and conceptually easiest response to attackers was destruction, but as a strategy, such destruction is difficult, if not impossible, for organized modern democratic nations to exert effectively when those who might get up to fight again hide among

---

1. If one were to put these attributes in more concrete military operational terms, cyberspace offers an attacking force five characteristics: reach, free fire at will, mass targets, easy stealth, and near instantaneous high-capacity payload.

innocent civilians across the world under another nation's rule of law. The modern international system is consensually characterized by an assumption that borders are immutable and that complete annihilation of an entire social group, let alone a country, is not acceptable. Today modern democracies act more like the democratic city-states: even if one wins a destructive war, the winning forces withdraw to let the defeated state recover as an independent country. Destruction does not produce many tangible gains.

Furthermore, the first cyberspace-enabled attack may be so successful that even if one could physically destroy the perpetrators after the fact, the violent ripples across key systems in the defending social systems could take years to mitigate, recover, and innovate beyond. Destruction in response may be attempted, but the returns would not in any way compensate for the initial disruptive losses. Under such circumstances, the ability of the defending social group to march armies to the border to stop a neighbor or face down a super-power would be a simply inadequate and tardy strategic response.

Today a nation's "power" rests on its capacities to meet the wide range of cybered conflicts, both disrupting in advance and being resilient to systemic surprise imposed by hidden, distant, and difficult to identify enemies, whether they are state or nonstate actors. This strategic combination of disruption and resilience capacities constitutes the cyber power of a modern democratic state. At its most elemental construction, the modern digitized nation-state must be able to disrupt attackers in advance or during the attack in progress before key systems in the home society are disabled in any significant way. Both capacities — reaching out to disrupt and reaching in to ensure resilience — are critical to national power in a world of cybered conflict. Modern nations can no longer sit behind their borders, treaties, alliances, or militaries.

The cybered age taking shape in front of us requires a new framework for national security, one of *security resilience*.[2] Based on a syncretic approach to international theories and to theories of complexity and surprise, such a strategy aims to balance appropriately the national institutional capacities for

---

2. As of this writing, I can find no other scholarly use of the term *security resilience*. I note, however, that a document published in advance of the spring election in the United Kingdom comes very close. See "A Resilient Nation: National Security Green Paper," 2009, http://www.conservatives.com/~/media/Files/Green%20Papers/National_Security_Green_Paper.ashx?dl=true.

disruption of would-be attackers while simultaneously ensuring societal resilience to potentially cascading and disabling surprises in critical national
systems.

For the modern digitized democracies viewed as today's large city-states, the
global, nearly free, deeply intruding access of cyberspace extends the number,
scale, reach, and abilities of potential enemies far beyond history's usual set
of suspects comprising neighbors, roving bandits, and the occasional expanding empire. The nature of "war" moves from societally threatening one-off
clashes of violence between close neighbors to a global version of long-term,
episodically and catastrophically dangerous, chronic insecurities that involve
the whole society. In cybered conflict across a digitally open international
system, traditional strategic buffers of distance or declared borders do not stop
societally critical attacks. The modern equivalents of ancient city-states face
the dilemmas of their predecessors: how to disrupt an attacker that one usually
cannot destroy as well as ensure the attack itself does not disrupt the city's
systems critically. Now, as then, society's security depends on how well the
community institutionalizes its security strategy with knowledge, consensus,
skills, and design. In the post–Cold War era, national security depends on the
dynamic and responsive weighting of disruption and resilience integrated into
a strategy for the inevitably long term in a chronic war against each emerging
surprise attacker or attack from anywhere in the cybered world.

At the end of the day, the central normative concern is with averting violent
harm as a consequence of conflict that is critically enabled by cybered tools.
Because cyberspace is global, nearly free, and easy to use, the Cold War notions of reaching out to destroy an attacker are too narrow, and resilience needs
to be an essential part of disruption. The tools of harm will come from surprising sources, including those previously considered only domestic concerns
such as cyber stealing from wealthier westerners. As an occupation, cyber
stealing seems not much of a national-level threat, but the global community
engaged in this kind of anonymous activity also develops the tools for other
bad actors much more focused on violent harm. While democratic nations
may seek only to disrupt attackers or their attacks, violent harm is the primus
inter pares goal of those hostile to westernized nations. With sufficiently stoked
grievances among the surging youth populations of dysfunctional regions, attacks to achieve this violence will inevitably impose surprise in cybered ways
for the next generation at least.

EMERGING UNCIVIL CYBERED INTERNATIONAL SYSTEM

Before the complexities of globalization began to change the international environment, the strategic borders of rivers, mountains, seas, walls, or armed guards clarified friend from foe. With the emergence of the modern state, nationally threatening enemies did not emanate from both outside and inside the society simultaneously (Tilly 1992). National security missions could be clearly allocated to either domestic or international arenas, specialized and constrained accordingly. In the bipolar Cold War era, that clarity solidified and routinized with only two significant superpower players in global conflicts. Nations singly or allied in blocs were focused on the threats from one or the other major player. Security communities across the westernized world focused on narrow questions such as launch times and counterattack nuclear payload, geographic distances to move through and occupy in rebuffing a military challenge, and peculiarities of a relatively small number of personalities in security-related international or domestic politics (Sagan and Waltz 1995; E. A. Cohen 2004). In many respects due to the clarity of the enemies, the Cold War era's major security dilemmas were defined more like the set-piece division of threats of western Europe in the 1700s. Institutions grew up focused on either national security threats or domestic concerns regarding social well-being, order, organized criminality, or societal service functions (Strachan 1983).

Technologies and the security of the social order of societies are deeply intertwined and interactive. During the 1800s, across Europe's borders, that era's modernization waves roiled societies burdened with the excess farm population. By the late 1840s, Europe saw violent uprisings in most of its capitals (Sperber 2005). Similarly, the Cold War's technological advances and prosperity inconspicuously developed the elements of today's declining ability to secure borders. Its legacies in globally linked dependencies and small lethal packages of lethal weapons continue to arm enemies or friends, to open or close vulnerabilities, and to stimulate or dampen concerns about security (O'Connell 1989). Individuals, groups, or communities recognizing threats inevitably find ways to use new technologies in their security strategy, even if the solution is a new type of boat by which to run away or a long hunting bow redirected to attack other humans.

The cybered world has challenged the broad but neat internal and external distinctions of security cemented in the bipolar era. Modern actors have discovered how to integrate the exceptionally fast and readily available global communications networks in their plans for conflict. Widely connected, unconstrained, and easily accessed global systems routinely undermine three historically critical dampeners on hostilities — long geographical distances, difficulties in organizing and controlling large enough groups of people, and poor knowledge of the target — in order to be sure to attack effectively. Attacks in history, by contrast, were more likely to be local or littoral, where at least knowledge of the target was easier to obtain. Attack organizations were likely to be small and local or very large and controlled by a state-level equivalent leader or oligarchy. Operations were either raids or campaigns big enough to survive the multitude of surprises from what was unknown, unorganized, or too far to reach (O'Connell 1989). These obstacles historically constrained conflict to being local or between state-level entities.

When globalized communications relax the three dampeners on scale, proximity, and precision, offense at a distance is made easier for those with more-limited resources. A digitized community like a modern nation-state is especially more vulnerable to new attackers from distant poorer and semigoverned rogue states, failing cities, or turbulent hinterlands. The advanced civil societies are deeply embedded in global nets. In contrast, the homelands of the potential new attackers may be internally violent, corrupt, or exploitative, but they are also markedly less digitized. The societies of the dysfunctional regions of the world are less easy or productive cyber targets.

The result is a marked divide in security concerns now emerging between two broad communities of the globally cybered world that do not share the same expectations in acceptable individual and collective behaviors, civil governance, normal societal security, and mechanisms of resource allocations. Including not only the westernized nations but also rapidly developing democracies such as India, the first group acts collectively and individually more like history's city-states. While competing strongly economically, they do not engage in violent existential conflict with each other.[3] They share a roughly convergent collective notion of security, which includes stability, rule of law, honesty, transparency, and importantly, a strong dislike for violent behavior, whether by individuals or states. In contrast, the other group of semigovernable

---

3. It is possible that the U.S.-China relationship could emerge more violently as the conflict between two large city-states contesting regional dominance. The likelihood is low, but higher than any chance of such conflict between other westernized nations.

regions, societies, or darker areas of cyberspace are frequently demographically unstable, politically barely coherent, and poorly productive economically. Collectively termed the "badlands" merely as a shorthand in this book, these areas tend to be internally corrupt, secretive, brutal, and accepting of higher levels of violent behavior as normal though regrettable. This group acts often as a spoiler both in its own internal operations and in the wider international system, becoming a source of global turbulence and of a large volume of mobile bad actors sharing few of the social constraints of the more-digitized nations.

Between the two groups, huge digitally enabled flows of information, people, goods, and resources transfer enormous economic benefits but also misperceptions, weapons, targeting data, and reasons for hostility and resentment. There are large demographic and wealth imbalances between the two groups, and not yet fully understood are possibilities for waves of social turbulence likely to come in the not far future. The 2011 upheavals in Egypt and Tunisia are likely to be foretastes of future instabilities from these more-dysfunctional areas. Too many young males in unstable, semigoverned developing societies perceive little hope for a better life. Global transport systems and cyberspace give these likely aggrieved young populations unprecedented access physically or digitally to the more organized, open, wealthy, civil centers of the world. For example, key experts on global radical Islam have argued its newest expression, the leaderless cell jihad often led by career jihadists in and out of prison and orchestrated by cybered methods, will be around at a minimum for the next twenty years (Pluchinsky 2008).

The widespread availability of cyberspace makes it all too possible in densely populated poorer areas to "farm" deprivation or cultural aversion grievances, whether led by a local group, a national leader, or the cadre of an international cult or movement. Because of the low costs of reaching large numbers of people online, appeals that would have died out in prior generations today survive and sometimes even revive. Through the graphics and availability of the global communications networks, an organizer can deliberately stoke hate or misperceptions and educate across a wider audience about how to perpetrate attacks in, through, or merely enabled by cyberspace. Small, otherwise forgettable data can be retained for access and endless reuse and distortion globally. For example, the worldwide neo-Nazi movement was small and isolated when communication could only travel to would-be recruits through mailed pamphlets or wandering promoters. The spread of global networks even in the 1990s allowed promoters located in places like Canada to reach easily and often into the rooms of unhappy, lower-class teenagers in former East Germany or other Eastern European states, producing a boom in supporters by the end of the 1990s (Rochlin 1997).

In the unfettered netted world, global communities of hate acting malevolently are as likely as those of free will and tolerance expanding civility (Rochlin 1997). In 2010 a talk by an American agricultural official was recorded, and several sentences selectively edited were widely replayed and discussed to show that the speaker, an African American, was against Caucasian people. In fact, she had helped the Caucasian farmer she was discussing, but that portion was not included in the widespread distribution of the misleading quotes. The result for the official was not only losing her job, at least temporarily, but also being the target of death threats left on her home phone and sent by email. The difference from even twenty years prior is that all this happened within thirty-six hours of the initial malicious online blog posting (CNN staff 2010).

The evolving surprises from digitally enabled global exchanges challenge the deeply buried assumptions of security in the modern civil societies. Until recently, many nations did not have laws against malicious hackers as the attacks did not seem at first to obviously clash with the social presumptions, legal entitlements, economic distributions, and strategic outlook of the digitized nations. Cyber criminals, however, now routinely develop tools that delve deeply and covertly into public, commercial, and private networks. Not only are these tools for sale to anyone, including other bad actors, but also in many nations buying and using the tools that operated thousands of infected computer networks still remains legal. For example, when the operators of the largest networks of infected computers worldwide were finally caught in Spain, prosecution by law was not possible. That form of attack was not illegal in Spain (Krebs 2010). With the perfect storm of coalescing events and credulous actors, today inchoate panicky feelings fed by imagery and catalyzing symbolic language on trusted websites or phone text messages can in any society rapidly migrate to physical threats and ultimately to organized attacks (Calhoun 1989). In the tumult, the topology and conflict pathways of the international system are changing as well.

Domesticating International System Led by Modern "City-States"

Today the international system is rapidly "domesticating" in major regions. Among the modern, digitized, democratic nations, the world system is increasingly in large part cooperatively transnational in its internal coupling, dependencies, and conflicts. Policies and players accommodate each other across borders of modern democratic nations and share increasingly similar expectations about life, education, income stability, health, government services, and safety. As networked offices and homes pull individuals and groups in the westernized world recognizably closer to each other, the large populations exist in distinct legal systems, but economic, military, and cognitive distances between them are shortening dramatically. The otherwise sovereign modern westernized and democratic nations in particular are exceptionally unlikely to engage in threatening postures and preparations to fight each other. Despite the history of the twentieth century, one cannot today imagine a Germany attacking any westernized nation for any reason. Equally hard is to conceive of the circumstance under which any part of the former Western Europe erupts in violent conflict with any part of North America. For these nations, violence across a national border is more likely to come from outside their communities, from the interpenetrating dysfunctional areas. While the emergent dysfunctional areas of the world express a "new medievalism" suggested by several international relations scholars, among the modernized, more-digitized nations of the world, the old world of state-against-state war as the only dominant and critical form of conflict no longer exists (Booth 1991).[4]

The topology of the international system is evolving in response to these ideologically and economically similar nations acting like city-states within a larger confederation. They create international regimes, norms, and standards and largely observe their own collectively determined rules. Their economic, political, and cognitive world increasingly involves densely integrated, consensually controlled, and cooperative regional structures and similarly managed large transnational institutions.

In particular, these modern city-states manifest a near universal dislike for conquest or externally imposed violence threatening a nation's internationally recognized borders. In the post–World War II decades, states recognized by the United Nations, no matter how dysfunctional, may face subversion, long-range missiles, and economic tragedies, but generally not conquerors. This injunction against cross-border land grabs has been strongly defended

---

4. "The Middle Ages were characterized by a highly fragmented and decentralized network of sociopolitical relationships, held together by the competing universalistic claims of the Empire and the Church" (Friedrichs 2001, 475).

by developed city-states and underdeveloped nations alike. In a truly anarchic world of states, the nations with the largest nuclear missile inventories would be considered potential territorial security threats. Yet neither France nor the United Kingdom is so considered by the United States. Even fig-leaf, internally imposed coups in Eastern Europe orchestrated at the onset of the Cold War by the former Soviet Union preserved the illusion of national independent sovereignty. Rigged elections enabling Soviet-controlled local communists to take over a satellite nation were the only way the former Soviet Union could expand its imperial reach and yet claim modern legitimacy as a state in the international community.

Even when city-states seem to have empires, they differ markedly in control, scale, and purpose from the empires based on territorial gain. As typified by the Italian Renaissance commercial city-states, territorial domination by a city was for the purpose of obtaining raw materials, usually from the surrounding agricultural region or fishing areas (Holmes 1988). Generally such cities attempted to exert physical control only over the surrounding region to ensure a supply of raw materials and often foodstuffs. Even a city-state-based "empire" was rarely considered a major violent threat. The ancient Athenian "empire" was more of a loose network of scattered cities. Many of these cities were established purely for the purposes of sustaining the flow of raw goods into Athens and to provide an outlet for poorer citizens to leave the overcrowded capital city (Freeman 2000). Even in the ancient world, a war that led accidentally to conquest would also see the subsequent devolution of the new property to proxy owners, or sometimes later the original owners, as the Spartans did for Athens in 404 BCE (Martin 1996, 160).

City-states historically do not challenge territorial borders, and the international community of modern states today often does not act even when faced with horrifically and brutally failing states, piously honoring de jure borders that are de facto not functioning. One could reasonably argue that this presumed "fixity" of borders acts to the detriment of the communities involved, and yet the norm of inviolability is widely observed (Krasner 1999). City-states tend to have limited horizons, with stability in their environment as a very high priority. Today it is reasonable to argue that Rwanda controls much of eastern Congo. Yet there is exceptionally limited academic and nearly no international political support for redrawing the outdated and useless borders drawn during Africa's colonial period (Krasner 2004).

Furthermore, while states may maintain clear borders on maps, and occasionally close them completely, city-states strongly support sieved boundaries intentionally kept open to ensure the flow of commerce. If walls are too strong, they inhibit economically sustaining trade. Today's westernized states are not self-sufficient for the level of economic prosperity they enjoy, and their borders are increasingly porous, electronically and physically. Globalization's historically unprecedented international flows of critical goods, capital, information, and people have sweetened the gains to be made by widespread porosity in state borders, along with obscuring the rise in threats from bad actors entering with the normal flows.

Just how intertwined and interdependent major states have become was recently reflected in the lead paint and tainted toothpaste scandals associated with imports from China. Although it seemed objectively clear that Chinese imports were not being scrutinized either on their way out of China or on their way into the United States, no effort was made on the part of the harmed state, the United States, to punish China. Rather, Chinese leverage over major U.S. corporations forced corporate leaders to ascribe poor Chinese workmanship to themselves in order to maintain the lucrative trading arrangements. An exceptional culturally distinct public apology on the part of the American corporate leaders was demanded and given for the shame China felt at the revelations of these flawed goods (Story 2007). Most Western observers found the practice simply curious and even farcical. That American corporate leaders would, in effect, debase themselves and lie publicly for a contract is an indication of the new relationships among globally interdependent trading entities. States in anarchic and largely autarkic systems do not have to put up with such insults, but city-states are largely too dependent on the surrounding system and trade flows to engage in insults or hostilities in response.[5]

In an emerging world of city-states and interpenetrating dysfunctional areas, the civil commerce-oriented societies fall into the categories of friendly, neutral, or merely unreliable trading partners, rather than enemies. Even when a state qua city-state actually has the capability of harming another state's homeland, seldom will the situation be addressed as realists would predict — as a fight to obliterate a potential enemy with threatening capacities. Historically

---

5. It is worth noting that after being traumatized by the excesses of the Vietnam War abroad and at home, the philosopher Bertrand Russell said that his view of the coming centuries was of squabbling city-states with implications for governance, war, and peace (Russell and Russell 1996).

city-state conflicts reflected this disinterest in decisively physical competition. In the two periods best known for their independent city-states with rudimentary democratic participation, ancient Greece and fifteenth-century Italy, cities did "war" with each other in complex and shifting alliances (Lebow and Kelly 2001). But in both eras, without the intervention of external powers (Persia in Greece and the pope in Italy), the city-states over time and through productive trade became simply too evenly matched in wealth, luck, or cultural aversion to carry through a conquest (Manicas 1982; Holmes 1988).

Wars among the city-states, such as they were, dragged on at a low level, creating not just war weariness in the respective citizens but also disinterest and acceptance of low-level warfare as a chronic fact of life (Connor 1988). Sparta's attempt to dominate Greece, especially Athens, went on for forty years in an almost random pattern of sudden Spartan probing attacks on one city or another. Usually the attack was heralded by spies. Next, neighboring cities banded together with Athens to repulse the Spartan marauders, and then the alliance would dissolve (Robinson 2001). In the later era in Italy, many of the wars between the city-states were really long-term feuds between merchant houses. The "war" would fizzle out once one of the central figures died or a cross-merchant house marriage with attendant inheritances would bring the warring sides together (Holmes 1988). Today, similar feuds result in massive hostile takeovers and strategic divorces across continents, but not war. The competition for resources and access among these westernized nations qua massive city-states is ruthless, opportunistic, and even sometimes insulting, but not likely to be violent. Indeed, under the right circumstances, quite sensitive internal data such as financial records will be shared among neighboring states as if all the nations involved belonged to the same overarching confederation (EurActive Network 2010).

This "domestication" of the international political system and the subsequent change in violent threat patterns contributes to confusion in lessons drawn from the literature on the phenomenon of democratic peace (Starr 1992). Democracy is much more a product, than a producer, of civility. An evolution into large entities with city-state features means the pursuit of civil competitive behaviors due more to recognition of the loss of autarky than the rudimentary practices of a democracy (Ember, Ember, and Russett 1992; Russett and Antholis 1992). Rational state-level decision makers cannot afford to be at odds with sister city-states providing essential goods and services. Furthermore the data is murky on which state is or is not really a democracy. Often, especially recently, the label is applied simply when suffrage is universal, and ostensibly free elections are routinely held. Many new, and some older, democracies are hardly sterling representatives of the other civility-inducing aspects often found in thriving trading cities—a rule of law (even if privately enforced) and reliable stability in monetarized means of exchange.[6] Rather, the slow transformation of the international community into city-like entities does not require democracy *pur* to make interstate relations more civil. For example, Singapore's adept rise in economic status and stability was certainly not due to democratic principles; however, the societal stability and civility have at the end produced democracy (Chua 1997).

In the anarchic system, autarkic states may not have to explicitly recognize their sustaining dependencies, but to survive, city-states must. Their national security policies and institutions ignore this recognition only at their peril (Ember, Ember, and Russett 1992; Held 1992).[7] Not recognizing the rise of the city-state community and, importantly, its critical underlying financial linkages has already proven costly in recent years. To the stated astonishment of financial experts across the westernized modern world, the 2008 U.S. domestic mortgage industry meltdown rippled destructively through otherwise unnoticed tightly coupled connections critically enabling the wealth of the international financial system. In a domesticating international system, city-state political leaders should never have been surprised to find their individual societal control of policy outcomes migrate out of previously recognized and expected future paths.

6. Elections do not make a democracy. Educated citizens, tolerance for differences in opinion, lifestyle, and economic advantage, and reasonable expectations of mutuality in respect, civil rights, and access to resources embedded in functioning social systems make a democracy. Unfortunately modern American politicians and many good-hearted internationalists do not understand that distinction between the resulting democracy and this list of prerequisites. The framers of the American Constitution did. See the *Federalist Papers* by Madison for a good example of this clear insight. These documents are widely available online, e.g., http://www.foundingfathers.info/federalistpapers. Many in westernized democracies take for granted that evidence of a functioning democracy is simply having some electoral choice, but many dictators make sure they are elected, at least once. Hitler and Mussolini were both dictators, and both were elected originally in putatively democratic elections.

7. It is worth mentioning that massive, failed cities such as Lagos, Nigeria, can by their scale and dysfunction put their nation in the group of the world's dysfunctional states rather than in the community of city-states (Gandy 2006).

Deeper Security Surprises

Surprise is a hallmark of the emerging globally connected world, especially in its security challenges to modern digitized democracies. With a globally networked world, physical proximity no longer constrains the dysfunctional behaviors of a geographically distant "badlands" as it once did, making modern notions of the highly restricted, externally focused roles of militaries or security forces difficult to apply. Enemies of concern for national security are rapidly changing their frequency, reach, and even form of threat. With exceptionally fewer state-level possible enemies, the bulk of rising national security threats are often diffuse, opportunistic, chronic, semicovert ("gray"), and globally surprising organizations hiding in nations whose leaders may or may not have the ability to control undesirable activities.

Unlike the traditional threats of peer states for which most national security forces today have been designed and socialized, the bad actors emerging in droves in dysfunctional areas do not have — nor need — established weapon-system inventories and ambitions to create a nation with a border. With a cybered world, transnational organizations are emerging as the normal form of a nonstate actor that could pose harm to distant enemies. These organizations do not stay solely in one nation; they also have less need to concentrate resources in any given place. They are in an open cybered world "ungrounded" and much less trackable by anyone's security services. These organizational threats do not need to sustain ties to a home society for resource and psychological support as Italian Mafia historically needed. Rather, they need to learn how or to hire those who know how to use a mass array of high-volume, usually privately owned, long-distance undersea cables linking continents in order to challenge traditional geographical notions of national power and interests (Wriston 1992).

Unlike most social and technical systems known to human history, the global cyberspace cannot be easily observed from the outside, and therefore it cannot be easily monitored for threats as it expands. Unless one "enters" cyberspace, one cannot "see" into it physically. Connecting to the global networks means both opening a door out into the rest of the connected world and a window into one's own part of it. For security services, the world's interconnected networks present a two-edged sword that is particularly challenging. Like trading city-states, one cannot close the borders and still receive any of its benefits. Hence, cyberspace is both freeing and threatening for the structures of society.

This dual-use nature of the increasingly ubiquitous digital connectivity is what makes this topic so difficult to sort out.

To make a violent attack beyond mere cyber vandalism against websites, attackers can use online access to coordinate a more traditional attack of, say, suicide bombers on airlines. They can also operate through the myriad of international networks to transmit an attack on something at a node, say denying the services of a critical system, ideally simultaneously in multiple locations such as water control systems. Or they could attack the World Wide Web directly, disconnecting key areas of the digital infrastructure of society itself. Of the three options, the second is likely to be the most successful and violent. The first involves the movement of humans or goods that use cyberspace as a coordinating mechanism. But it is hampered by logistics. Humans are more inconvenient, traceable, and slower to move around than internet commands. Traditional and newly developed defensive mechanisms are more attuned to stopping human-borne threats. The third option — destroying the international networks in key places — is hampered deliberately by the design of the multiple nodes and packets of cyberspace's underlying networks. The system was set up in the 1960s. Even the loss of a major internet cable, as happened to Iran in 2008, only slows internet communication to a crawl, rather than shutting it off completely (Hafner 1999; Forte and Power 2008).

To pursue the second option, using cyberspace itself as a weapon for major violent effects, generally involves making "internetted" systems critical to the society act badly or stop functioning completely. In this case, the attacker or group steals access to and then takes control of critical applications in the targeted facility or on the central command server of a wider network. An example would be bypassing the physically difficult direct hijacking of airliners and going for covertly hacking into air traffic controls. One might deceive the controllers' computers into reporting false airliner locations and then insert fixes that cause mass collisions simultaneously across an array of airports.[8] While the air traffic control scenario is already being made extraordinarily difficult today in the Western world, the same cannot be said for many other critical digitally connected societal services around the world. The Stuxnet worm that successfully attacked the nuclear reactors of Iran in 2010 would be an example of this second kind of attack. The malicious software successfully

---

8. For the nervous reader, I use this example because of how hard this would be to do (Lemos 2002).

disabled huge centrifuges and stalled the significant nuclear projects of a nation (Sanger 2010).

Attackers can always rely on human inattentiveness as well as faulty, buggy, or older technology. They spend days and months searching for obscure entrance tunnels often overlooked by users and designers amid the vast array of electronically interconnected computers and applications. When attackers finally find the hole and enter the system, the options for violence expand greatly. A malicious actor can order the local server, computer, or even single application to vandalize itself or others connected to it. This bad actor can also order the violated local computer to spy on the host human, group, or other computers and gather information useful later for violent attacks. Or the local computer can be ordered to hide a program and wait for a signal to do something to destroy itself or others connected to it (O'Brien 2003).

The national security threat for society is that these exploited backdoors lead to one's home computer and also to the computers managing massive regional or national electrical systems running elevators, street lights, water plants, and air traffic systems, sometimes at the same time (Knapp and Boulton 2007). No service or firm or home that is more efficiently and effectively run with networked systems is immune. The infrastructure pathways include the electronic brains of packed subway systems and hurtling commuter trains, not to mention the isolation of hazardous material in oil-to-gasoline production plants and the control of toxic chlorine in municipal water filtration and cleaning systems. The sudden dysfunction of any of these major underlying systems in a wide enough simultaneous attack and the difficulty of immediately replacing them would be akin to the destruction of infrastructure witnessed in the devastation of New Orleans in 2006 after a hurricane or northern Japan in 2011 after the tsunami. The difference is that an attack conducted via cyberspace could involve ten major cities at once and the attackers could adapt and return again and again.

If enough cities are hit at once, the limited emergency resources designed for single major failures are likely to be spread too thin or simply be inadequate. For example, a massive unexpected and unusual windstorm in Western Europe during the winter of 2007–8 affected electricity users from Germany to the Ukraine. The effects included the nearly complete stoppage of both trains in Germany and trans-Europe oil-pumping stations (Associated Press 2007). An attack on the central hubs of Europe's disparate electricity transmission network could achieve the same effect, and even worse than very obvious windstorms, malicious code could be sent from thousands of computers held by unwitting owners, making it hard to stop the attack in its tracks.

The rub is that city-states need openness for commerce and wealth, and this need is readily exploited by semicovert or "gray" organizations operating through, around, and in spite of recognized governments.[9] From behind staunchly internationally maintained state borders, these actors can impose violence at great distance and unpredictably because of the easy access to democratic city-state systems afforded to all other states as a matter of international state-state reciprocity. As the international mafia organizations have demonstrated for decades, it is useful for badland threats to maintain dual identities. Not only are these gray organizations emerging on a scale historically never possible, but they pose a particularly pernicious form of threat equally unprecedented for the national security of these city-states. Not only can anyone open up a website today for the entire world to see, but that site can be laden with hidden tools, messages, instructions, and bad intentions for anyone who visits the site and whose computer may then become a tool for an attack. The modern city-state attackers, whether state or nonstate or a combination, easily hide in the volume and complexity of the open access routes offered to all overtly legal transnational organizations and exchanges.

Furthermore, the city-state defenders must deal with the rise of a different kind of threat beyond that posed by transborder subnational groups: the "false front state." Much of the theory of international conflict assumes the survival of the state is recognized as necessary by its political leaders whose gains cannot be realized elsewhere. While early postcolonial authoritarians could, and did, create Swiss bank accounts for themselves, they generally tried to keep

9. The use of the term *gray* to mean "semi-covert" has both intelligence and information sciences provenances. The common understanding is of a class of phenomena neither white (friendly) or black (enemy) in the intelligence field, or neither explicit (published, tagged, and searchable) or implicit/tacit (unpublished, uncatalogued, and untraceable with normal means) in the information sciences field (Correia and de Castro Neto 2002; Jeffery 2000). *Gray* is a more useful term than the recent use of *dark*, as in the "dark web" (Chen, Wang, and Zeng 2004) or "dark networks" (Milward and Raab 2002), because of the colloquial connotation with gray as "something in-between." One might even think of gray organizations as "dual use" in much the same way as technologies are suspected of being usable for both good and ill purposes. In a globalizing world with much greater reach from ill uses, dual-use technologies have caused no end of trouble and confusion in arms negotiations (Stowsky 2004).

some measure of state integrity and health in order to keep reaping wealth and personal reputation. Today, leaders of a low-capacity near failing "state" with digital links to the resources of the westernized city-states can more easily act against their citizens' and their neighbors' security in ways difficult to challenge from a state accepted into the international system as a normal state.

In the freewheeling finances of a cybered world, corruption in semi-governed states rises in importance internationally. In a financially and operationally linked cybered world, the corrupt actors no longer merely enrich themselves in the home nation, but they can operate through the otherwise legal mechanisms of state functions to globally hide their bad behaviors in the legal financial systems of other nations. It has been a long while since any serious scholar believed corruption in developing nations in a cybered world naturally greased the nascent mechanisms of fledgling market economies.[10] However, today corruption can have national security implications far from the failing state. Criminals, states acting by proxy, and transnational bad actors of all flavors can bribe, fool, and coerce national-level officials in a failing state into creating the necessary legal covers for the bad actors to gain entry into critical systems, financial or otherwise, of the westernized nations. City-states' security can be undermined by these corrupted states of convenience whose rights to free passage across the cybered world are unquestioned internationally. These false front states now more easily act in ways inimical to the security of the state and their citizens, as well as to the stability across the wider international community of states. They can vote in the UN, act militarily, change markets, and deceive on a global scale with rippling consequences elsewhere (Thachuk 2005). The tiny Pacific island of Tuvalu, for example, has been a major contributor to spam and cybercrime internationally due to its easily acquired and ungoverned sale of the .tv domain name (Kenny 2007).

While essential for city-state prosperity, the globe's digital capital-flow virtual highways easily enable false front states. Developing nations especially with large, ungovernable, territorial swathes easily contribute to the ranks of the world's badlands. For example, a drug lord in ungoverned Thai jungles can more easily establish and monitor a Swiss bank account, laundering funds as well as purchasing digitally the weapons he needs to control and murder. To

---

10. Nye (1967) argues that corruption as private vice can be positive under some conditions and has probably helped both the U.S. and Russian economies in the past.

the varying likelihoods, these semigoverned nation-states are more likely to host the bad actors seeking to impose a new deleterious surprise on a democracy. Such gray organizations are all the more perplexing to decipher because the visible perpetrators — the state-level leaders — appear to be committing an entirely modern form of long-term economic starvation. The capital flows are so massive and rapid that state coffers can be irreparably emptied to obscured foreign banks without much record in minutes, while the whole transaction is protected by the originating or receiving state's laws on privacy. National economic suicide would have been irrational in previous eras where the corrupt leaders normally had to keep their corruption winnings in the home society to buy off compatriots and keep the flow coming. Certainly the role of the emerging cybered world in encouraging such distortions is difficult for Western states to reconcile and question. There is limited international interest in directly challenging the presumption of statehood expressed in the UN charter, irrespective of the cost to the lives and prosperity of the citizens in one of these corrupted states.

In the cybered international environment of democratic modern city-states and the highly varied turbulent regions, security challenges from a cybered world inevitably involve large amounts of surprise, whether from states, nonstate actors, or some new form of attack. Historically successful city-states had an instinctively developed two-part strategy. First, if they recognized a threat, they tried to disrupt the attackers in the surrounding land or sea narrows before the offensive forces could get to the city gates. But they also knew by experience that their city needed to be able to withstand a siege if the external disruption plan did not succeed. Not only was uncertainty recognized; for those market city-states that survived, surprise clearly needed to be accommodated in advance. Furthermore, the strategy had to recognize the cognitive disabling effects of surprise as well as the concrete disruption possibilities. Pericles, for example, recognized that puzzlement and shock often allow a cascade of negative effects to avalanche into a catastrophe (La Porte 1996). Having patterns that repeat reliably in a complex system matters to human daily functioning because humans have a cognitive need for stability in expectations. They will accept extraordinarily negative circumstances only if the events are predictable in form or frequency. Pericles practiced the evacuation to the city walls by farmers when his spies indicated a coming Spartan attack, as well as storing supplies for a number of months in order to make it automatic (E. E. Cohen

1992). The citizens practicing a solution to surprise is a strategic asset that reduces the sense of extreme mystification at an event that can be paralyzing and often delays appropriate action (Casti 1994).

In the security challenges posed by a world of city-states vulnerable to cyber-enabled attacks from dysfunctional regions, the more tightly coupled the critical structures are within the targeted society, the more likely are accurate mitigating responses by that society to be delayed. For example, a traditionally purely domestic structure — the marginal home-loan market — imploded in the United States in mid-2008. International onlookers were markedly transfixed in surprise. The spreading effects of a lack of confidence in banks ground the world's credit markets to a crawl and even a halt in many states. Not only was the connectivity up to then unnoticed, but so was the potential speed at which the cascading effects forced closures of large banks across westernized digital nations. What took nine months to several years in 1929 looked well into happening within a week in the digitally interdependent cybered world of 2008 (Fortson 2007).

In the cooperative city-states' and dysfunctional badlands' emergent topology of the global international system, most frameworks for national security response in the modern states have not appropriately adapted to the strategic imperatives of cybered conflict. Hindering this reconsideration of security is a dominant view across the westernized world's security communities of a world of independent and well-governed nation-states with defined territories and clear distinctions between domestic and international functions. In this world, leaders face largely separated decisions across domains of foreign policy, domestic needs, and internal versus external security responsibilities. The prevalent models of international relations reinforce this neatly parsed worldview, generally making recommendations for strategy narrowly pitched at the decisions made by leaders in parameters distinguishable between peace or war, between domestic and foreign events, and between military and police missions. Much depends on the assumptions of strategic buffers such as time and distance to give policymakers the space to make decisions. Only in the nuclear era were these presumptions questioned. The solutions, however, involved mainly only two major superpowers, not any number of actors from small groups to whole regions.

The traditional approaches help little in guiding responses to constant but episodic, cascading surprises emerging from the complexities of human perceptions across a globe and the vast array of underlying connections across social systems. For example, while touting the real and theoretical economic benefits of free trade and the spread of unfettered globalization, Western economic models during the last forty years routinely left out any discussion of the social externalities now proving to be crucial to security. Searching the globe to set up widely dispersed corporate profit centers can spread ideas and infrastructure, but also resentment among displaced elites, workers, or communities. A real world example is the globalized breakdown of the international financial system in 2008. It began as a purely domestic crisis in the United States. Yet it spread in a rapid cascade to harm the economies of many nations seemingly unconnected to the United States and its mortgage-backed securities, astounding Western economists, financial advisors, and political leaders alike. The underlying global financial system had grown up under the myriad of linking and relinking decisions of thousands of profit-seeking independent actors. The complexity was used for profit margins, and the risks were not perceived. Societal turbulence and breakdown so apparent on the ground are never seen in macro or international economic theories, any more than buried deep domestic dependencies in critical global systems are discussed in traditional expressions of international relations.

The legacy narrowness of such models individually inaccurately guides policymakers in today's world of sieved borders and chronic violent threats from distant actors with cheap cybered access operating from politically dysfunctional areas. Today policymakers need to see national security more comprehensively. The well-established cognitive and institutional distinctions between national security assets and domestic police forces will give comparative advantage to cyber-enabled attackers anywhere cyberspace reaches in the world. Furthermore future integrated cybered conflicts are likely to emerge outside of war as well as during active hostilities and to involve many more actors than the main combatants. A key characteristic of global cybered conflict is the ease with which others uninvolved in the conflict can "pile on" and attack either or both sides at whim. The clearly emerging relatedness of many multilevel violent threats can no longer be bureaucratically parsed between domestic police forces with limited knowledge while cross-national computer assaults are left to specialized outward-looking national security forces focused on "wartime."

For the political or military leader in these city-states, the task of ensuring national security is made more difficult when no one theoretical approach offers sufficient guidance for the globalizing cross-domain, -scale, and

-border chronic, endemic, serious violent national threats (Hasenclever, Mayer, and Rittberger 1996). The three major schools of international relations (realism, liberal institutionalism, and constructivism) emerged as recognizable fields during the past half century within the generally accepted framework of a world system of nation-states as the main threat actors and the relations between them as the major venue for violence. Not only is each school unable to uniquely address the foreign challenges, but all three approaches are uncomfortable with the domestic side of national security save as a venue for the study of national security decision makers. With the advent of modern networked digital data, however, new threats reach across the previously acceptable international-domestic divide. It is a tall order for both scholars and political leaders (Betts 2007).

If physical destruction of a potential mass casualty threat is not possible, acceptable, or effective, leaders of democracies facing a world of chronic violent gray threats need broad integrated strategic theories to give them other options. Cronin argues the national responses must be both flexible and particularly multifaceted in their exploitation of globalization in order to meet global terrorism as it emerges (Cronin 2002–3). A city-state's national security frameworks and institutions must handle both the enemies and the effects before, during, and after an attack precisely because of bad actor access to the ever more tightly linked critical processes within and among these massive city-states, for even a relatively moderate violent attack produces rippling nasty surprises. Increasingly the formerly separate domains of international relations, economic globalization, and domestic issues are interrelated or "multicausal," and so are the threat profiles (Legro 2005). The prescriptions of the three main approaches of international relations as they are promoted today, however, are not. Each approach — realism, liberal institutionalism, and constructivism — is individually too narrow for the kind of actionable guidance needed today for such complex interrelatedness. Chapter 2 addresses these difficulties, and chapter 3 offers the security resilience strategy in response.

CHALLENGE TO INTERNATIONAL RELATIONS THEORY

Complex puzzles need collective wisdom for resolution. Security with chronic, violent, semipredictable threats requires an array of tools drawn from experience and logic of deliberate violence at all levels of human behavior. Particularly needed are ways to unify the contributions of the three existing main theories of conflict to make them, in sum, flexible as well as multifaceted. Today the collaborative need for collective knowledge is well known and acknowledged in governments and corporate executive offices. "Countering the spread of the jihadist movement will require coordinated multilateral efforts that go well beyond operations to capture or kill terrorist leaders" (National Intelligence Estimate 2006). A number of scholars of international relations (IR) have offered a synthesis across elements taken from two or more of the main IR approaches.[11]

Unfortunately none of these proposals seemed to have flourished and dominated across the three main schools of IR in the United States as the remaining superpower. Perhaps it is because the proposing scholars are prone to reductionism, slicing off preferred aspects of each established approach but leaving too much aside that is emergent today. All three approaches have individual limitations as theory applicable to the emerging world of cybered conflict today.

Realism, Neo- or Otherwise

First, the dominant approach to international relations in the United States, realism, is closely associated with the use of force (power) to solve a state's security dilemmas arising from an anarchic world. This notion that ultimately security is based on the state's use of coercion against otherwise unfettered threats in an anarchic international system permeates the vast literature sustaining the school's long rise from the 1930s onward.[12] In practice, this major explanation of war and security policies reached its apogee of applicable explanatory power for strategic decisions in the bipolarity of the Cold War. Realist scholars had some success in predicting the outcomes of two superpowers competing for primacy ultimately on the basis of the ability to rain mass

11. A comprehensive list of all scholars who have tried to do this exceeds the scope of this book. In principle the pursuit of scholarly publication is intended to further precisely this outcome (Legro 2005).

12. The wide variety of extensions of realism that emerged over the Cold War era and beyond are not addressed here in large part because the scholars considered realists tend to agree on only two major assumptions: actors of importance are states, and the world is anarchic, thus the emphasis on security and power.

destruction from nuclear, ballistic-missile inventories.[13] Misbehaving states, in the eyes of the dominant players of the international community, were not confused about which major state was a patron and which posed a clear physical threat. Although the product of individual actors behaving in their own self-interests and bounded by their attention and comprehension spans, states could be theoretically viewed as unitary actors. Thus, game theory and other forms of rational choice became part of the realist *weltanschauung* making state actions open to probabilities and mathematical prediction (Powell 1987; Achen 2005).

A bipolar world was uniquely suited to realism's strengths, and now, fifty-plus years later, even scholars of more liberal institutional or closeted cultural persuasions will still often use realist metaphors in their work. Identifying who is and is not a realist sometimes becomes more a matter of the emphasis given to force over money in alliance negotiations, engagement strategies, and strategic policy announcements. As a paradigm, realism was and remains so attractively elegant that its assumptions masking the complex realities of security on the ground took on and still retain the patina of greater objectivity and rigor. Even when realist analysis clearly missed major drivers of actual outcomes, the disconnect often was and still is simply overlooked as noise in the system from "lower" levels of systemic analysis. Thus, the looming potential for system change in the radicalization of mass social movements like terrorism and the massive explosion in technologies can be recast by senior realist scholars as either not important or mundane rational trends simply contributing to a country's relative power. Waltz, for example, has argued that technology and its influences are subsystem variables ancillary to the higher-level realist focus on only systemic-level variables. In the not distant past, terrorists have been cast by realist scholars as rational optimizers who were unlikely to promote mass killing for fear of retribution (Sagan and Waltz 1995).

Deterrence as a strategic option, for example, is particularly difficult for realist scholars to both analytically bound and practically employ in the emerging mass-cybered world because westernized notions of identifiable and negotiable "rational interests" are critical here. Some realists have remarked on the wider complexities beyond their theoretical paradigm. For example, two realist scholars do argue that reason may have little to do with the threat or

13. Seminal realist scholars include Waltz (1979), Mearsheimer (1994), and Van Evera (1994).

use of armed forces in deterrence or retaliation. But this acknowledgment of a shortcoming in realism's applicability was married with a blunt endorsement of military force as an enduring aspect of international politics in pursuit of foreign policy goals (Huth and Russett 1984). Deterrence is so critical to the realist prescription of how to ensure security that failures here have sometimes been met with a resort to assertions rather than a reevaluation of the presumed applicability of realism to state security dilemmas everywhere.

Moreover, the realist community's development of a further distinction into defensive and offensive realism heralded a deepening desire to fit the rest of the world's declining civility into a model of human behavior profoundly tied to who has military power (Copeland 2001). In the realist perspective, military force is integral to the overt and clearly stated threats of nations in conflict, and the identity of the attack target involving force must also be clearly defined (Huth and Russett 1984). Even the slightly more social "selective engagement" as a strategy intrinsically falls back on force in all cases. Troops and force are included—as essential tools—in a discussion about persuading allies to help stem the spread of nuclear, biological, and chemical (NBC) weapons (Art 1998–99).

For example, a subtle logical dissonance appears in realism when scholars consider religious terrorism. Terrorists are made to fit within the niche of rational actors even though the authors may explicitly say the religious terrorists are not. Although an author may argue that deterrence "becomes nearly impossible" against the revenge and retribution motivations of religious terrorists, nonetheless rogue states and terrorists are perceived to be similar enough to put into the same targeting group. Furthermore, a last resort to the tactical use of nuclear attacks in response to terrorism is suggested (Art 1998–99).

Realists have great trouble when pressed for policies to help national leaders be good realists in a world of suicide terrorists or widely anonymous cybered attacks. In some cases, critical practical or institutionalized national security functions are treated as noise below the level of the international system. In other cases, the recommendations are a mélange of measures left unconnected by the tenets of realism itself. These include prescriptions to increase budgets in intelligence intended to uncover hidden nuclear and biological weapons developments and to disable those efforts in rogue states or terrorist organizations, all with some reference to the use of military force (Art 1998–99). For example, selective engagement is characterized as the premier grand strategy for the United States, invoking the most appropriate goals for the nation and best employing the nation's military capability for support (Art 1998–99).

Realist explanations cannot account for interstate cooperation, especially among historical, close-proximity adversaries, each independently armed.[14] As Mastanduno indicated:

> During the 1950s and 1960s, however, students of IR came to conceive of statecraft fairly narrowly, primarily as a problem involving the relationship between military instruments and military objective. Economic statecraft and the link between economic and security issues were largely ignored. By the 1970s and 1980s, specialists in IR became far more concerned with economic issues, and the study of IPE [international political economy] moved to the forefront of the discipline. However, the study of economic statecraft, and economic issues more generally, tended to be conducted separately from the study of military statecraft, and national security issues more generally. Rather than integrating these two concerns in the overall study of international politics, security studies and IPE progressed as separate scholarly activities. (Mastanduno 1998, 826)

In particular, the often domestically refracted reasons for individual acceptance of suicide loosely associated with emerging headless, transnational, extremist, social movements have been deemed irrational by realists and, until the mid-2000's, irrelevant for the security interests of major states. Similarly, the use of cybered means to undermine nations with more powerful militaries has been viewed up to recently as irrelevant unless the tools are clearly identified as having been used by major peer states and their military institutions. The focus on force is deeply engrained in the approach indeed.

Yet both the inter-entity cooperation common to cities in large, loose, political systems and the individually pyrrhic bombings in massed public places are major influences on citizen and state behaviors domestically and abroad today. These behaviors do over time cumulate across an increasingly huge global population to change the international system. In short, while most major complexities were observed accurately at one point or another, the realist recommendations as a whole only superficially accommodated the con-

---

14. See Mearsheimer's (1994) argument for the explanatory and logical poverty of other explanations. See also the elaboration of this difficulty by Wendt (1995).

cerns of institutionalists or constructivists. Realist scholars have tended to stay fundamentally in their theoretical comfort zone focused on force. Indeed, Jervis argues succinctly that the initial Bush polices in Iraq were precisely an expression of raw offensive realism and also therefore of a profound inability of the proponents of this paradigm to see the limitations of the paradigm for a post–Cold War era (Jervis 2003).

Even when authors using the realist approach are trying to speak more broadly to situations where force does not actually happen, the use of force is embedded in prescriptions. For example, look closely at the assumptions underlying the following action-response realist parable involving deterrence and note the embedded use of force irrespective of other tools. First officials in an attacking state plan an attack on a state closely tied to a third state that will have to defend the target state. When leaders in the third state recognize the impending attack, they state a threat to retaliate or clearly imply one by moving their military forces in a way to forestall an attack (Huth and Russett 1984). Deterrence and therefore interruption of planned violence is, by realist accounts, achieved by force or its threats, not otherwise. Mearsheimer in his prescient article on the rise of nationalism after the end of the Cold War attributes its rebirth to elements quite unfamiliar to a realism approach, namely, affiliations and socially constructed resentments, as much as he discusses any security dilemma or economic deprivation (Mearsheimer 1990). Despite these observations, Mearsheimer remains wedded to the realist paradigm. Having leveled broadsides for years at the liberal institutionalists for ineffectiveness, only a few years after his nationalism piece, Mearsheimer (1994) castigated the only other intellectual peer competitor, the emerging school of constructivism, for their utopian and impractical approach.

This singular focus on the use of force as the ultimate arbiter has had consequences beyond the Cold War in persuading some leaders to act. For a particularly pressing and troubling example, the U.S. invasion of Iraq in 2003 can reasonably be characterized as a particularly fundamentalist kind of realism adopted by George W. Bush and his political advisers, most of whom were far from experienced internationalists (Jervis 2003). It proved a financial and political fiasco, with only one of three strategic paths open to the United States: simply leave a failing state, leave an intact Iraq under some kind of caretaker national government with international resources to replace the U.S. support, or leave with Iraq divided into ethnic ministates, preferably each with some oil wells outright owned and defended.[15] None of these are realist solutions to a realism-inspired fiasco. Rather, the attack was viewed as a mistake by realists primarily because of the fear induced in other states faced with the United States exhibiting excessive interventionism. The United States thereby increased the risk of hostile alliances among states balancing against it and possibly making it more difficult to sustain U.S. security elsewhere in the world (Layne 2006).

The massive U.S. operational quagmire in Iraq was not explainable as an outcome by realist analysis. Insurgencies are by their very level of analysis irrelevant to the world system of anarchic states. Stalwart realists rarely entertain the less easily defined concerns of constructivists, and they will generally ignore the benefits of institutionalism except as they relate to power alliances.[16] Leaders facing a complex world of chronic violent threats from social movements and cyberspace are not given much guidance if raw force will not clearly do the job. One might say realism offers a shiny tree ornament but no tree on which to hang it that accurately represents the emerging world faced by leaders now.

Liberal Institutionalism

Scholars most associated with the liberal institutionalist subfield are slightly better at incorporating elements of realism and of constructivism into their prescriptions. This broader view is due not only to the approach's early years but also to its resurgence in the post–World War II period. The original institutionalists were focused on using international institutions as a bulwark against interstate war. The League of Nations and later the United Nations were ideals whose origins began with the tireless efforts of scholars such as Woodrow Wilson. Human social relationships and their attendant interests writ large were

15. The third option, the soft partition, is the most institutionally and culturally sensitive outcome. Some scholars and observers have argued that this was the only real option from the outset, given the distribution of ethnic groups, oil fields, and artificiality of the borders of Iraq (Demchak 2006).

16. For example, although "liberal" goals may be included in a discussion presenting selective engagement as the best and most syncretic grand strategy (among seven) for the United States, rarely mentioned are the explicit and central insights of constructivism on the power of belief and cultural deep institutions to channel what actions are considered acceptable (Art 1998–99).

always fundamental to the approach, as was discomfort with, if not explicit rejection of, the international system as anarchic (Legro 2005). Today the modern institutionalist field is more closely associated with the comparative field of international political economy, redefining interests to emphasize capital flows and economic influences in security (Jönsson and Tallberg 2008).

Institutionalists offer perplexed leaders facing the world of chronic violent threats a second shiny tree ornament that has no tree on which to hang it. In this case, the shiny thing is the idea of economic prosperity through internationally cooperative behaviors. The underlying presumption is that civil behavior emerges if economic prosperity is clearly on the rise collectively. Institutionalists reject the realist claims of anarchy in particular due to its lack of ground truth and its role as a fixation on sovereignty that undermines collective regional solutions to otherwise intractable problems. The post–World War II international system was clearly not a state-pursuing-its-own-security free-for-all. The norm of sovereignty and of independent state actors — essential to the realist anarchic international system — has been widely and frequently violated. The realist adherence to preserving sovereignty irrespective of the costs, or of possible alternative societally helpful institutional arrangements, amounts to "organized hypocrisy" (Krasner 1999).[17]

With interests recast as economic resources husbanded by organizations rather than related to power and force, institutionalist inquiries and recommendations run the gamut from mercenaries to Keynes (Avant 2005; Markwell 1995). Underlying their observations, however, is the "peasant as rational economic actor" notion by which agents with violent threats can be made to see — or made to act as if they see — the futility of further threatening behavior or the economic losses that any violence might produce. In this view, political and resource mechanisms of control are more important than power or belief motivations in producing security-relevant outcomes (Avant 2005).

For the institutionalists, therefore, bad behavior is irrational if the proper incentives have been offered to move outcomes to the desired state in group and individual expected-utility curves. Bad actors are in that sense free riders for whom the proper material offers have not yet been collectively discerned,

17. Of course, to the extent that the field is focused on collective cross-cultural resolutions of conflict, this "hypocrisy" may not always be undesirable. The hypocrisy may be a useful coping mechanism often seen in domestic organizations to relieve otherwise paralyzing pressures for conflicting courses of action (Lipson 2007).

refined politically, financed in institutions, and then explicitly made clear. Institutionalists, however, have great difficulty offering political leaders effective
strategic guidance if money in various institutionalized settings is not reducing
threats from actors across the complex globally connected and demographically huge emerging world.

Constructivism

Finally, constructivism suffers from field myopia as well, although more justifiably. The youngest of the three international relations subfields, constructivism, is still defining its focus on the otherwise missing, often ineluctable,
underlying idea or "knowledge expressed as structure" aspects of human social
systems (Wendt 1995; Legro 2005). Unlike scholars supporting the other approaches, these scholars can directly address the consequences for IR of the
behaviors taken as "irrational" by realists and by institutionalists. From 2004
to 2009 the limited, and often transient, local cooperation of Iraqis with U.S.
Allied Forces often was responding to something beyond force and money given
the possible personal consequences for any Iraqi of being caught cooperating.
This difficult-to-quantitatively-define motivation has been identified by cognition scholars as more "primitive and defensive," and it has real behavior consequences (Armstrong 1999). For constructivists, it is "ideas all the way down
(until you get to biology and natural resources)" (Wendt 1995).

Yet, even more than realism and liberal institutionalism, this reborn scholarly sensitivity to the human culture and ideas variables in IR epitomizes the
third beautiful tree ornament that has no strategic tree on which to hang.
While occasionally claiming to embrace the other fields, the emerging field
of constructivism itself has yet to blend its distinctive approach practically with
the force and money central tenets of the other two approaches.[18] Constructivism is based on presumptions that knowledge filtered by a variety of internalized or collectively socially constructed screens drives human decisions and
thence behaviors. Constructivists accept that these screens could be cultural,

18. An early reflection of this desire not to be seen as orthogonally different is found in the
works of one of the seminal authors of the field. While claiming distinctive insights for critical
theorists and specifically the social structural approach of constructivism, Wendt then notes
his constructivist commonality with Mearsheimer's realism to include the anarchy of the
international system and the primacy of states in analysis (Wendt 1995; Mearsheimer 1994).

organizational, circumstantial, or even emotional, and their exact form and implications are open to comparative empirical research. The field does not, however, try to make general one-size-fits-all prescriptions like realism nor to focus on one particular modality such as the institutions aimed at "peace through economic prosperity" preferred by liberal institutionalists.

Furthermore, the immediate precursors to modern constructivism in IR incurred a dismal reputation in strategic circles after the U.S. war in Vietnam in the 1960s. Extensively using the guidance of sociologists and cultural anthropologists, the U.S. military adopted a "hearts and minds" policy that would, in the abstract, be familiar to modern constructivists. Yet this strategy was widely and unfairly castigated for its stunning failures to persuade villagers to support the government and to reject the overtures of the communist guerilla units spread out across the country (Sheehan 1988). The policy was initiated relatively late in the war. Its underlying "rational peasant" concept led the American military to label whole swathes of land containing thousands of Vietnamese still in their home villages as free-fire zones. This logic said that peasants were rational. Those who were offered "better" land elsewhere and yet refused the offer were demonstrating their rationality if they were already in agreement with the Vietcong. Therefore a refusal to move meant the rational peasant was already aligned with enemies. Hence any peasants who stayed in their villages after being warned of impending U.S. strikes were legitimate wartime targets for carpet bombing.

Not taken into account in the Vietnam War until it was too late were the beliefs and structures that channel and reinforce individual and collective behaviors, the aspects of international relations emphasized by constructivists. The peasants who agreed to leave abandoned everything they knew, from their and their ancestors' home to their skills in manipulating the precise conditions of their existing land for good crops. They would have been agreeing to move south to different land, conditions, social structures, and futures, all on the assurances of either corrupt local officials or very foreign U.S. military advisers. By the time the power of these cognitive factors was recognized, it was difficult to persuade peasants to risk yet more in standing up to the often equally intolerant Vietcong, especially after their village and family might have been carpet bombed (J. W. Gibson 1988; B. Palmer 1984).

Despite the shortfalls in implementation, timing, political support, and military understanding demonstrated by the United States in the Vietnam War, the failure to produce solid peasant democrats was eventually blamed on the "hearts and minds" idea itself by the U.S. national security community dominated by realists. Culture as an analytical variable and guiding tool for foreign or any policy was profoundly damaged. Its study outside of area studies languished, devalued for twenty-five years in American political science. The loss in Vietnam was not just strategic in military terms; it was also a strategic loss in the diversity of international relations thinking of America. During the rest of the Cold War era, the reputational costs of studying culture outside of various area studies were daunting to American scholars and practitioners. Until well into the 1990s, it was common to attribute cultural phenomena to largely economic motivations, saying, for example, terrorists were likely to be open to recruitment simply because they were poor (Sageman 2004). During this time, American scholars who took culture to have independent variable characteristics often used acceptable reformulations such as organizational doctrine or socializations, emergent nationalism, or even cognitive international relations theory as legitimizing overlays to avoid the taint of the older "hearts and minds" focus seen to have failed in Vietnam.[19]

Until the mid-2000s, U.S. policy did not explicitly endorse a cultural perspective in any specific foreign policy. The debacle of the unexpected Iraqi insurgency beginning in 2004 forced a bottom-up reassessment by desperate military leaders. In Iraq, as in Vietnam, paying attention to the values and cultural institutions of the local populace came late in the overall theater and strategy, long after coercion and economic plans laden with ignorance and hubris were imposed.[20] U.S. experiences in Iraq from 2004 to 2008 are better explained by constructivist approaches than by the others, but the corresponding solutions are not easily translated from the constructivists' broad concerns to tools providing actionable guidance for the beleaguered leader. For example, in a 2008 document by the U.S. Congress House Armed Services Committee, the authors observed, "The first rule of war is to understand the nature of the enemy; today that would include Al Qaeda's intent to spread fear and our tendency to exaggerate the actual danger" (U.S. Congress 2008). While that

19. Even Posen's (1986) famous work on doctrine would not offend today's constructivist. Fortunately, American political science had the British school to keep the lamp in the window for when we would need it in the post–Cold War period (Copeland 2003; Buzan 2001; Croft 2006).

20. These points are made in the updated preface to Nagl's (2002) book on insurgencies and culture.

formulation is more constructivist than it is not, the panel did not progress far in implementing these observations to fix the patently clear "U.S. institutional weaknesses in the implementation of any security policy."

SYNCRETIC REFRAMING: SECURITY RESILIENCE STRATEGY FOR A CYBERED WORLD

Cyber power is the national ability to disrupt this obscured bad actor somewhere in the digitized globe, whether nonstate or state, in proportion to the actor's motivations or capabilities to attack with violent effects, and yet be resilient against imposed or enhanced nasty surprises across all critical nationally sustaining systems. This enormously complex challenge requires an approach that deliberately reaches across disciplinary boundaries and epistemologies to integrate competing theories and methods (Tremonte and Racioppi 2008). A new framework needs to grow with the new world order, whether or not it is the one envisioned by established scholars (Kolodziej 2005). When the three schools of international relations theory are adequately seen as complementary rather than competing, a path is formed by which scholars and the policy community can more consensually explain how to prepare for the surprises of the emerging interdependent world.

This process of fusion rather than distinction or highlighting is the essence of a "syncretic" approach that aims to harmonize conflicting explanations.[21] It is essential that this fusion emerge with the accelerating globalization, as the new surprises challenge old approaches. First, the *syncretic security* approach incorporates each main IR school in toto as opposed to a synthetic approach that selects parts for inclusion while rejecting other segments. Taken in sum, the embedded paradigmatic emphases of force, money, and culture (respectively, realism, liberal institutionalism, constructivism) may indeed be integrated to provide strategically actionable guidance. With this framework, national leaders can more justifiably adopt one strategic emphasis over the others, but are not required to routinely pick a particular emphasis. Since this approach allies the ground truths of each school and draws upon a much wider array of scholarly discovery, the approach not only allows but also encourages consideration beyond the history of war and foreign policy and mili-

---

21. Syncretism is strongly tied to concepts of religious or symbolic fusions. Hybridity is another similar term (Kraidy 2005).

tary evolution. Also critically relevant are the various sciences of psychological individual and group motivations, especially loss-aversion or risk-avoidance, history and analysis of political or social movements and organizing, studies of national and organizational culture, and finally the study of conflict, crime, social control, and war. Gang warfare studies have relevance in the study of transnational terrorism and here are given a niche by which to make a contribution. Syncretic security embraces all the wisdom of the vast IR literature and molds its lessons for a 360-degree, 24/7 networked world.

Second, the syncretic security approach supports the creation of rapidly tailored and adjustable strategies under circumstances assumed to be surprising. In particular, it underscores the value of a strategy combining disruption and resilience as the most effective response to a complex world of chronic, violent, gray, and cybered threats. It demands knowledge that is continuous, multilevel, and multiscaled. If implemented properly, intelligence and collaborative deliberation will roam freely in collection and application down to the antigang unit of a local police department back up through all the levels of size and breadth-of-purview to the UN Security Council (Legro 2005).

National leaders need a syncretic security approach to distinguish when the tools of realism, institutionalism, or constructivism — respectively in power, interests, and ideas — should be emphasized and for how long over what, in addition to resilience against what where. Being overwhelmed by disabling surprises across many lower-level attacks on critical internal national systems is likely to be more disruptive to a modern nation of linked functions than one major attack of equivalent one-off destruction short of nuclear war (Robinson, Woodard, and Varnado 1998). Since attacks can today arrive from anywhere, surprise overload is a major information vulnerability. A national strategy in response to cybered security threats must develop effective and legal methods of learning enough to act rapidly and accurately before the attack initiates or completes, and after it succeeds. In basic information theory, to keep a system overloaded by inputs functioning, its operations must either reach outward to reduce the overwhelming stream of inputs, reach inward to increase the processing capabilities, or do both (Thomsen, Levitt, and Nass 2005; Galbraith 1977).

A fragmented playbook here is a hindrance. When the possible responses are discordant and range across strategies, doctrines, and positions for international negotiations, armed conflict, foreign policy disputes, and depths of national preparedness, to name a few, mustering the knowledge needed and then using it effectively is beyond hard. It is simply unlikely. National security leaders require a method of bringing evidence to bear on and weight these prescriptions into actionable strategic goals. For the sake of innovation, they effectively need to do this collectively. In this emerging environment, security requires a more systemic assessment across the levels, scale, and modes of threat and having or developing the appropriate knowledge at the moment and location needed for dampening, deterring, destroying, remediating, improvising, or innovating after a successful attack. For example, having a complete backup computer system continuously running in parallel makes recovering from a disruption easy — but it requires a great deal of knowledge invested in advance in the instantaneous recovery applications in order to create that accommodation against surprise.

Information absorbed into the shared daily practices of a group determines a large part of what is viewed as surprising and threatening. These practices also channel what is routinely monitored for change. When recognized, processed, and acted upon, new information allows a new combination of resources by humans as tool-using animals developing resilience to surprise (Novak 1998). As a result, the national security of a democracy tightly intertwined with other westernized democracies comes to rest on how much they holistically seek to know in advance or accurately decipher when surprised by malicious activities coming inside national borders.

Disruption as Strategic Imperative in Cyber Power

If the sure and certain destruction of bad actors is off the policymakers' table, then some way to forestall violent direct or cybered eruptions for the longest possible intervals is the best fallback position. Implementing the fallback, however, is not easy in a largescale, densely populated, globally cybered world. If anything is usually offered to fill the strategy leaders' options list in the United States, it has too frequently come from either the power preferences of realists (Art 1998–99), the promoted international accommodations of institutionalists (Krasner 2004), or the often multiply conflicting social constructions and deep institutions observed by constructivists (Croft 2006; Fountain 2001). Because of the strict theoretical walls and highlighted conflicts between the three existing international relations approaches, the beleaguered policymaker is forced to choose one or the other approach out of faith and then improvise on its implications. The faith can be misplaced if the wrong approach is chosen.

For example, in the fight against global terrorism, American military thinkers have made much of British successes in past insurgencies by using force and persuasion as a standard ranking of policies, a routinized hierarchy of realist and then constructivist approaches. Yet British inspections of their own history show limited successes in the post–World War II era. Furthermore, none of the successes were in dominantly Muslim nations.[22]

In their individual wisdom built from decades of trying to understand the main drivers of conflict, however, the three fields of international relations have collectively identified three main motivators of violent conflict: beliefs about legitimacy of an action, need for a particular outcome associated with that action, and confidence in the actor's ability to perform the action. These three basic insights of IR theory have many names: "God, butter, and guns," "ideas, money, and force," and even "lawyers, money, and guns." A more analytical and alliterative statement would be "culture, capital, and coercion."[23] This set of three motivators also has substantive support in other fields as a basic set of human violence drivers despite their provenance in studies of international conflict for this work (Barkan and Snowden 2008). Research on human cognition and motivation from the individual level up through largescale, highly socialized, and task-focused organizations provides case after case supporting the power and fundamental nature of these three categories of motivators. From psychology to comparative organization theory and fundamentals of sociology, the three IR schools individually have substantial commonality with a wider understanding of human behavior at all levels. The difficulty lies in combining these insights. At the moment, there is no joint tree on which to hang these individual ornaments.

A security resilience strategy offers a way to use all these approaches by providing a statement about violence and a strategic response framework that

22. This comment was taken from a talk given by Dr. Andrew Dorman of King's College, London, at the annual conference of International Security Studies Section of the International Studies Association, October 2006. He noted that his research team had identified about forty-odd British insurgency operations since the 1940s, with around three successes and none in Muslim nations.

23. The use of these three terms, even more often the first two, is widely spread across IR, sociology, economics, and comparative studies, not to mention military and economic history and theory literatures (Frisch 2001; Skaperdas and Syropoulos 2001; Shama 1992; Tilly 1992; Powell 1993).

incorporates the ground observations of each existing approach about conflict. The framework then allows a case-by-case comparison by which to weight the relative appropriateness of each essential strategic recommendation from each IR theory for the particular chronic violent threat. When defense leaders can justifiably reorder the emphases of their existing strategy more rapidly, they can better tailor their disruption operations according to the available tools and to the emerging violent threat profile. In this sense, a major political leader is not forced to characterize (or publicly justify) a change as a major change in strategy. Rather, as dictated by new knowledge of impending violence, the leader can merely decide to pursue a change in emphasis within an overarching and tailored disruption strategy.

The security resilience strategy then is a construct of the concerted cognitive and institutional efforts to exhaustively understand the mix of motivators influencing specific bad actors to commit or prepare to commit violence. The strategy is in essence the response that aims to disrupt the elements motivating violence, especially the biggest or most recently elevated incentive, for as long an interval as possible.

Disruption as a key part of a national strategy to maintain defensive power in cybered conflicts rests on understanding decisions of bad actors to misuse the advantages of the cybersphere to harm others. Disrupting these decisions requires that one develop a theory of action about how such decisions arise. Once one has that, it is possible to develop an appropriate response.

The theory of action begins by recognizing the variations of deliberate violence at all levels of human behavior.[24] No human is in general and in all circumstances willing to do harm to another. Rather there are motivators of varying strength that, if known to defenders, may be open to disruption before or during an attack. The extent, strength, and longevity of these motivators channel the nature and timing of a decision to attempt an attack. The combination of the motivators determines how acceptable, useful, and possible the attack options are in the eyes of the would-be attacker. Strategic disruption begins with the goal of knowing enough about the drivers of violence to derive strategic options. The theory of action proposed here explains how three key motivators produce violence. It connects successful strategic disruption to ac-

---

24. A new framework needs to grow with the new structure of the world system, whether or not it is the one envisioned by established scholars (Kolodziej 2005).

curately targeting these motivators in reducing the likelihood of an attempt to attack.[25]

The decision of an actor to attack involving violence is the result of three motivators: legitimacy, need, and confidence. The theory of action presumes that a decision to act with violent intent emerges when all three motivators have surpassed an action threshold.[26] Not all motivators have equal sustaining weight. Weak drivers are easier to drive below the threshold but, commensurately, may more quickly be reconstituted. That is, a disruption that drives down the weight of a weak motivator will disrupt the entire equation of violence for a shorter period of time than would a disruption that reduces the weight given much larger motivators.

Humans in general are motivated by their perceptions of legitimacy (often called beliefs), needs (usually monetized), and confidence (historically tied to the ability to wield decisive force). These motivators, given the combination of circumstances, are equally powerful and equally limited. Taken out of order, force directly addresses the basic coalescing instinct to fight, flight, or submit for survival that is hardwired into human cognition (Pan et al. 2007). Force and its variants is the common theme of human history. It is difficult to study politics, social evolution, or any field related to human social systems without dealing with the use of force by one group on another.[27]

Beliefs represent the insatiable human tendency to seek a recurring and

25. This concept was originally developed for an essay on how to understand terrorist and later insurgent violence (Demchak 2003, 2006).

26. The domains of the three main schools of international relations in the United States (realism, liberal institutionalism, constructivism) may be roughly summarized according to their basic approaches to prospective violence as, respectively, power, interests, and knowledge/culture. The associated explanations in each community tend to downplay or occasionally ignore the driving forces of the other schools, leaving each approach often too incomplete for actionable guidance for the complex interrelatedness of an emerging globalized world (Tremonte and Racioppi 2008). But complex puzzles need collective wisdom for resolution and a way to make the contributions of the three existing, main IR approaches flexible as well as multifaceted (Cronin 2002–3, 30). The theory of action syncretically reaches across disciplinary boundaries and epistemologies to integrate the ground truths of the otherwise competing theories about conflict drivers. Each main IR school is accepted in toto as opposed to a synthetic approach that selects parts for inclusion while rejecting other segments.

27. For an excellent review of the origin theories and implications of collective violence across venues, see Barkan and Snowden (2008).

reassuring predictability in complex situations for the purposes of protection. Humans are pattern-matching animals and tend to guide personal choices in order to reinforce or derail the perceived patterns across a multitude of other situations, equivalent in all the particulars or not. This tendency to fall back on instinct and beliefs is particularly strong during a crisis (Billings, Milburn, and Schaalman 1980). Furthermore the likelihood of acting increases if a strong framing story that legitimates violence is well established (Dimitrova and Connolly-Ahern 2007). A framing story is an accepted narrative that provides an explanation for what the human observer is seeing (Lutters and Seaman 2007). Some belief systems permit hate to permeate a worldview such that only the perception of the personal opportunity to cause harm stands in the way of sudden violence (Fein 1993).

Money, of course, represents resources to make survival possible. Contributing far beyond basic sustenance to the development of preferred future outcomes, it is also a key component of perceived needs in an acceptable quality of life. Just like force and beliefs, it is difficult to review any aspect of social history without acknowledging the role of resources. The perceived distribution of resources affects what individuals consider desirable in economic, social status, and accrual expectations. Whether or not objectively true, resource disparity viewed with resentment by would-be violent actors is the essence of "relative deprivation" that encourages a human tendency to act violently. Indeed, rising expectations appear to have a strong effect on the sense of loss and grievance when the anticipated resources do not materialize, even if the expectations were never realistic (Chandra and Foster 2005).[28]

Together, these three motivators map to the three major explanations for conflict in international relations: Beliefs are the focus of constructivism best exemplified by Wendt (1995). Money is the focus of liberal institutionalism (Keohane and Nye 1972). Force is the focus of realism (Waltz 1979). For the purposes of scientific validity, and especially the modern search for quantitative respectability, the three main approaches in IR theory have each taken one

---

28. Among non-Western Muslims, those most likely to be radicalized are the educated with expectations that are dashed by reality and those who go abroad to find them again, only to be disappointed. For reputation reasons, they cannot go home and so drift for meaning into the arms of radicalism. See Sageman (2004) for one of the earliest empirical and seminal pieces of work on this pattern.

of these meta-variables (force, money, or beliefs) and made it the singular and dominant explanation of the onset of conflict.[29]

These three motivators, emphasized singly in major theories, never actually operate alone in real worlds, wars, and societies. Each may have been open to abstraction as an independent variable for the purposes of study, but the claim that one of them operates as a dominant factor in all international circumstances has led to an overextension of analytical power in all three schools, especially realism. Today's world is not well explained by the elegant theoretical parsimony of the Cold War's theories of international conflict, nor their isolation from the rich, often domestic-level literature on conflict within states and among organized groups. Scholarly observations made for many other purposes in each subfield support this approach. For example, two realist authors observed in a piece on deterrence during the Cold War that a failure to attack could be either a change in priorities by leaders — a more institutionalist interpretation — or a change in leaders — a more constructionist interpretation (Huth and Russett 1984). Even stalwart realist scholars find themselves perhaps not willingly, but certainly occasionally, seeking a more syncretic interpretation across approaches.

These three meta-variables routinely intertwine and mutually affect each other, especially in the production of the most basic of all human decisions — to commit violence. The decision to attack, which could involve violence, is simply easier with globally accessible cybered means. Synthesizing the three approaches requires a defining statement that incorporates collectively the central aspect of each motivator.

Proposed here is an underlying or meta–*theory of action* that translates the beliefs, money, and force motivators of human behavior identified in constructivism, liberal institutionalism, and realism into legitimacy, need, and confidence to create an "equation" of variably weighted drivers for violent action by individuals or groups. This synthesis may be captured by the following statement:

> *Actors will commit violence if they perceive the acts to be legitimate, regard the outcome as favorably meeting a critical need, and are confident that their own actions will be successful.*

29. During the unusual clarity of world dominance by only two superpowers during the Cold War era, this method of logically highlighting a cause and its effects was not necessarily inappropriate.

ACTION = fn *(Referent Group's + Self Perceived)*
LEGITIMACY & NEED & CONFIDENCE

Figure 1. Notional Theory of Action Equation of Violence

More colloquially phrased, the theory of action states that to commit violence, actors or a cohesive group will give themselves approval to try to produce more favorable quality-of-life outcomes if they think they can succeed.[30] All three elements must be present for violence to occur. Figure 1 formally states the theory.

Violence is a threshold in the theory of action, not automatic in all circumstances or across all individual or group actors. To produce violence, all three drivers must build past the inhibitors in the on-the-spot individual or collective group evaluations of morality, probability of preferred gain, and the likelihood of personal success — as shown in figure 2. Ratcheting above the threshold for violence can happen very fast if supports are in place for all three drivers. If not, actors' violent action profiles will be different, and they will respond differently. Riots exemplify these varying thresholds quite well. Some people walking past an electronics store being looted may have always thought it was acceptable to take something if the store was unsupervised by its owner, and they had felt a personal need for a TV for a long time. However, no looting occurred because they never perceived a way to take the needed item safely. Only now, and suddenly, do these people realize that they can simply take a TV from the now-vulnerable store with little personal risk of arrest. Conversely, other people will walk by without looting, equally able to loot the store, but perceiving this act as inappropriate. Yet others will shrug and walk on by, already having three large TVs at home.

Another interesting historical analogy demonstrates that *all* these variables must push past the threshold for violent action to occur. In the mid-1800s, violent revolution spread to nearly all the capitals of Europe, yet not to London. While the revolution spiraled out of control in other capitals, in England mostly Chartists and Irish nationalists took up the revolutionary call.

---

30. The combination of legitimacy, perceived strong need, and opportunity has been reflected in research on human behavior for many decades (Bruner and Goodman 1947; Fein 1993; Barkan and Snowden 2008).

Figure 2. Drivers of Violence Push Past the Threshold in Notional Referent Group

They could not, however, spread the sense of grievance further and posed no major threat to the national political system (Sperber 2005). The major issue that could have overcome social status inhibitors to violence, the hated Corn Laws, had already been attacked by English Liberals. Their repeal in 1846 was endorsed by the dominant Liberal Party of England, reducing dramatically the need motivator behind continued collective violence (Gurney 2006).[31] The avarice of the British aristocracy was relatively low while the clear rise of the middle class contributed to a dampening of collective violence. In contrast to compatriots on the Continent, industrializing England operated with a much weaker demand on the ordinary worker's resources, with no conscription, no obligatory residency requirements, and much lower taxes than Continental peers (Schonhardt-Bailey 1991). The hard-won and longstanding institution of the British Parliament and the size, wealth, and surging fortunes of an already established middle-income merchant class contributed to a lack of a widespread sense of grievance around which to organize violent responses (Hilton 2006).

In this setting, the legitimacy attached to a class-based sense of one's rightful place was embedded in the society and dampened the local support for action against the existing economic hierarchy (Sperber 2005, 72). Contemporary and later observers pointed to the strong class beliefs held by most classes that restricted the legitimacy of violently attacking the perquisites of upper

31. Interestingly enough, the repeal of the Corn Laws in England had a demonstration effect in the Netherlands, making "democratic political action in a respectable, dignified and effective manner conceivable" (Houkes and Janse 2005).

classes. It helped, of course, that concepts of noblesse oblige to tenants of landholdings were reinforced strongly religiously as well as socially. Thus, in England as opposed to Paris or Berlin, two of the three drivers to violence did not surpass the thresholds that would otherwise have produced, and sustained, revolutionary fervor.

In the cybered world, a myriad of websites offer a wide variety of violent action motivators that have to be understood across potential attackers. These include emotionally or religiously impassioned legitimacy rationalizations, elevated senses of grievance about shortcomings in quality of life, and examples of successful plans, operations, and leaders. In mid-2010 the French intelligence service arrested about a dozen Muslim radicals simultaneously. The French noted in passing that the radicals habitually viewed website videos to sustain their commitment. Any effective strategy designed for cybered conflict must uncover and discern the relative weight of these motivators in order to disrupt them. Such operations must be tailored to the mix of motivators emerging with a set of attackers, a topic discussed in the final section.

Resilience as Strategic Necessity in Cyber Power

Resilience as a national strategy links surprises imposed by international threats to nationally disabling consequences to be endured if the surprise succeeds. Since World War II, resilience has not been strategically linked to national security specifically unless the threat was long-range missiles or the exceptionally unlikely land invasions. The emergence of cyberspace throughout modern societies, however, has meant some surprises will inevitably be successful, making knowledge of the defending nation's critical systems essential to effectively responding resiliently. In a complex socio-technical system such as a modern city-state or the wider global community of states, both the knowledge needed and the response must be collective to ensure its accuracy and effective application in crisis. The knowledge underlying a national strategy employing resilience is neither easy nor necessarily inexpensive to obtain. In many cases, without a strategy of resilience to persuasively frame the need for knowledge across national actors, much of what could be known and accommodated in advance is often neglected by a lack of collective understanding about how to act protectively.

Today critical systems are often left open to nasty surprises because information required to restore functions is not available to those who need it. Often operators, users, owners, or societies relying on an ever more tightly linked critical system do not think they will face surprise from unexpected sources. Public and quasi-public organizations vary greatly in their sense of urgency about the need to understand the surprises possible in these systems and then to act on that knowledge in concert. They neglect to test for key shortfalls in what might be helpful to know in advance. They frequently delay in integrating reliability-improving designs and processes meant for security. The savings in linking more and more to a digital network are rarely then spent on making sure the negative effects of dependence on that network are understood. Thus, a successful attack can travel from one neglecting operational node to two more to three more, and so on. The lack of knowledge sought in advance easily means it could be impossible to initially dampen the disabling ripples as they spread across the network's connected systems and the people depending on them. These ripples can be devastating for a system that survives the first major event, much like aftershocks from an earthquake.

Complexity automatically produces *surprise* in networked, precision-dependent systems (Casti 1994; Demchak 1992). The mass of varying relationships in a complex system can undermine even the most careful programming of every component (Waldrop 1992; Perrow 1984). The more tightly coupled the system, the more cascades of minor variations sum unpredictably into an unforeseen outcome that is as likely to be undesirable as desirable (Kahn 1966; Hofstadter 1999). This point in the evolution of the system has been called the "threshold point" in the general systems literature or the "edge of chaos" in the chaos literature (Gleick 1997). For humans in — or dependent on — the system, this system behavior invokes feelings of being surprised[32] and unprepared for the event(s) (La Porte 1975).

Up to a certain point, the importance of complexity in any system is relative to the critical knowledge available about the system by those who must run and repair it (Boin et al. 2005; Weick and Roberts 1993). In complex systems, for each level of complexity, there is a universe of unknown outcomes that are

32. This work adopts the approach of socio-technical ensemble theory as a useful integrating approach. This perspective represents a middle ground linking technology and society (or organizations) in highly coupled, interdependent, heterogeneous ensembles. Arising from technical, organizational, social, political, and economic elements, these ensembles pose societally significant control, risk, and social-shaping dilemmas. A particular expression of this theory is found in the literature on largescale technical systems (LTS) (Mayntz and Hughes 1988; LaPorte and Consolini 1991).

deleterious. These outcomes vary on two dimensions: from knowable (with sufficient research) to unknowable, and from accommodated (involving deterrence, dampening, mitigation, or reconstitution in place) to unaccommodated (forcing us to endure the events).

First, the relative *knowability* of possible event outcomes in a complex system range along an axis from knowable to unknowable according to the level of complexity. At a base level, outcome warnings may be knowable in either form or frequency, and preferably both. These are the *knowable unknowns*. Irrespective of how much research is performed, however, some subset of outcomes will remain unknowable in advance, because a system cannot evaluate itself accurately (Hofstadter 1999). Every system has some small number of *unknowable unknowns* (Gomory 1995). The larger this number is among a large number of components, the greater the likelihood of improbable events — "deviant amplitudes" — rippling through the system and producing an unpredictable outcome (or "dynamic instabilities") (Sproull and Kiesler 1992). More complexity tends to produce more unknowable unknowns in general. Thus, with more complexity comes a greater likelihood of events rippling throughout the system.

Second, outcomes also range along an axis in the extent of systemic accommodation of unknowns through human decisions about acceptable levels of risk, the costs in time and resources to research missing knowledge, and the cost and benefits of applying knowledge to forestall, diminish, dampen, mitigate, and compensate for bad outcomes. Sometimes efforts to accommodate a knowable outcome inadvertently also take care of an unknowable outcome. A humane trap set for packrats in a riverside warehouse could also secure, as well as save from death, an illegal and escaped imported river mongoose sniffing around for the rats. While it was foreseen that other small animals could inadvertently land in this trap, capturing the mongoose, which could devastate a local ecosystem, is a benefit unforeseen.

The axes discussed above capture the four general types of unknown outcomes grouped according to the complexity designed into the system (knowable and unknowable) and the responses of the system to the risks (accommodated and unaccommodated). Deleterious outcomes that are foreseeable and accommodated are *tolerable* at least and *serendipitous* if accommodated without foreknowledge. Outcomes that could be known in either form or frequency, but are not accommodated, are *neglected*. The unaccommodated and unknowable outcomes are *rogues* in the profound sense of surprise humans feel when negative outcomes emerge out of nowhere to cripple important operations. All societies have a notion of rogue outcomes, often attributed to an "act of God."

Across these ideal types, knowledge is critical. It is whatever is needed at precisely the moment and place of the undesirable events (i.e., the *point of surprise*) to mitigate, compensate, or possibly reverse the effects. More than just information carried by an individual or contained in human learning, knowledge can be embedded in design, operation, parts, and processes as well as manuals and skill levels across groups of humans involved in the socio-technical system at risk. If the appropriate knowledge is present when the surprise disables functions, but the outcome was not foreseen, then what would have been a rogue outcome becomes a serendipitous one. If only form or frequency is knowable, but it is researched and then accommodated, then a neglected outcome becomes a tolerable one. Figure 3 demonstrates the result.

Thus, knowledge and surprise are directly related to resilience.[33] Surprise is due to a knowledge shortcoming. It strikes hard when our models of reality — our knowledge inventory and structures — diverge from our experience of reality itself (Casti 1994, 268).

Resilience depends on having a theory of surprise accommodation, and that begins with the relationship between complexity and surprise and the ways humans accommodate both in modern societies. Surprise is greater in complex systems because the proportion of the unknowable outcomes is higher than in simple systems. The more structurally intricate a system is, the more that needs to be known in order for it to function according to some desired pattern

---

33. The literature on complexity is incomplete. Examples of conceptual difficulties with complexity and surprise in their various guises exist even in some of the better works. One well-known author observes that size and wealth decrease internal and external uncertainty for militaries without much explanation as to how this intuitively problematical outcome can be true (Posen 1993, 49). A second author suggests that a war without chaos can exist if it is solely between machines — no surprises or uncertainty (Lanir, Fischhoff, and Johnson 1988). Even Perrow (1984), in an otherwise excellent book, seems to muddle the concept of complexity by linking it to a loose coupling and, indirectly, to both greater and lesser redundancy. The operational difficulties are obvious. Complex systems produce the unexpected with annoying regularity, but the fragmented set of approaches has often produced inconclusive research and little broadly applicable guidance. For example, redundancy is either a cure for or a cause of complexity, depending on the author chosen (Landau 1969). The situation is exacerbated by the tendency of complexity to vary in its significance across systems (Roe 1998).

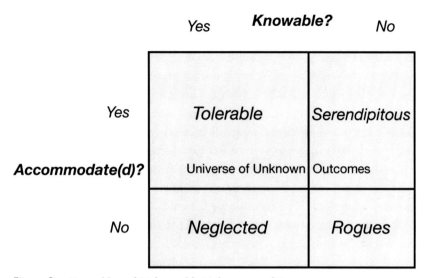

Figure 3. Knowable and Unknowable Unknowns and Rogues

(DeSanctis and Poole 1994). If many types of disturbances are possible and these can be amplified due to tight coupling, then the cost of acquiring the needed knowledge to make predictions about knowable unknowns multiplies exponentially.[34] Many organizations react to such a world by focusing on lo-cally predictable outcomes and ratcheting up their control of local deviations, but this unfortunately tightens the coupling of the organization over time (Weick and Roberts 1993). If this organizational behavior is not accommo-dated, tighter coupling creates a positive feedback loop in which managers react to produce conditions for more surprise.

Modern digitizing city-states unwilling to face and accommodate surprise, perhaps through expense avoidance or wishful thinking, become iteratively more vulnerable to attackers and exploitive actions as their critical systems

34. Modesty and realism require a reminder that every good innovation is always at best an 80 percent solution. While that is an old adage, it has some basis in mathematical fact and physical experiences. One set of industrial risk scholars used complex systems repair data to conclude the following: for a highly complex system, 80 percent of the repairs would take one to two days to solve and complete, while the remaining multiple source failures could take three days to infinity. That is, complexity that is normal for global social systems will always have a remaining 10–20 percent of sheer incomprehensible outcomes labeled *rogues* in this book (Casti 1994). Surprise is discussed more fully in the resilience chapter 5.

become more tightly coupled and complex. Resilience requires efforts in advance to discern and accommodate the knowable unknowns often neglected in existing largescale systems across societies. Accommodation also means finding the knowable shortfalls in the existing array of social trust mechanisms necessary for rapid collective response. Only greater knowledge lessens the effects of neglected or rogue outcomes from exploits by attackers. The goal of resilience is, on one hand, to reveal in advance the form or frequency of some previously unknown outcome in order to ensure having the knowledge to move from neglect to toleration. On the other hand, the goal of resilience can be to simply reduce the automaticity of the coupling so as to dampen the cascades long enough that unknowable knowledge can become knowable.

Humans have a cognitive need for stability in expectations. They will accept extraordinarily negative circumstances and act collectively and accurately only if the events are predictable in form or frequency (Demchak 1991). Resilience rests on acquiring, collectively making sense of, and acting on routine information, and ultimately absorbing this information into the shared daily practices of a group (Comfort, Boin, and Demchak 2010). Effective strategies for establishing national power in cybered conflicts must involve extensive knowledge collection and collective sense-making in advance. Otherwise, critical redundancies in critical knowledge and functions and widely dispersed slack in time are unlikely to buffer critical national systems against attackers and nasty surprises (Bar-Yam 2003; Demchak 1992). When recognized, processed, and acted upon, new information allows a new combination of resources by humans as tool-using animals to ensure developing resilience to surprise across the whole set of critical national systems (Novak 1998).

SECURITY RESILIENCE STRATEGY: LINKING FRAMEWORK AND TOOLS

A national security strategy combining disruption and resilience strategy is necessary precisely because the future, mass-casualty, violent threats to westernized states will be cybered at critical junctures and likely involve nonstate actors as much as the usual set of state suspects. National security in the emerging world neither starts nor stops at the geographic borders when a myriad of globally cybered connections so easily passes across them. If a bad actor living abroad can make a critical system, such as the water-filtering system of New York City serving ten million people, fail suddenly and dramatically, then the successful digital attack is no longer bloodless. People will sicken; some will die; costs will be staggering, and society will be harmed. In 1999 a disgruntled former consultant to a Queensland, Australia, water company managed to break into the sewage control systems and release one million liters of raw sewage into the local water supply (Lemos 2002). Had the attacker been less bitter and more dedicated, the release could have been larger, or he could have sold the knowledge to others to be used in a more sophisticated, larger-scale attack.[35] In 1999 David Copeland built bombs using the infamous Terrorist Handbook that he downloaded from the web; 2 people died and 139 were maimed in London (Forest 2005). Just as cyberspace is the progenitor of both the reach and influence of globalization, it also has spawned a growing set of chronic, violent capabilities available worldwide.

Cyber power emerges when the nation's strategy aims both at disrupting the attacks that can flow in from anywhere in the world and at preparing to collectively easily endure the attacks that get through anyway. The security resilience strategy rests on four main processes: flexible weighting of actions based on theory of action analysis, honest joint consultation, comprehensive relevant data about actors' behaviors and motivations, and collaborative actionable knowledge development. These processes are aimed at generating knowledge for the nation's disruption of and resilience to incoming attacks. The first process more specifically involves a set of strategic tools distinctly tied to disruption, while the latter three processes sustain both disruption and resilience strategic objectives.

Strategic Tools of Disruption: Information, Capital, and Coercion in Tailored Amounts

If together the three motivators of action (legitimacy, need, and confidence) push an individual or group past a threshold into deciding to act with violent outcomes, then the goal of a disruption and resilience strategy is to keep one or more of the motivating drivers below the violence threshold. Armed with knowledge of the weighted motivators supporting an emerging violent action,

---

35. The EPA after 2001 removed from websites the exact locations and roads associated with much of the U.S. domestic water supply as part of the agency's mission to ensure safe drinking water. Likewise engineering drawings of commercial nuclear power plants were belatedly removed from Nuclear Regulatory Commission websites after 9/11 (McDermott 2003).

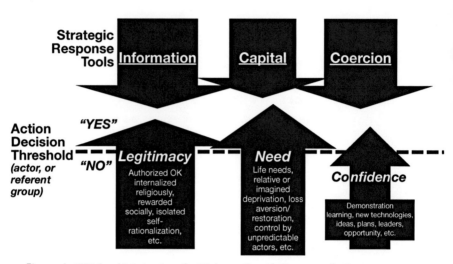

Figure 4. Weighted Motivations for Violence Provide Leverage for Response

national security organizations may have the ability to customize the strategy according to what motivates a particular set of bad actors given the circumstances. Such strategies may choose to "mirror the mix" and emphasize long-term effects by disrupting the stronger violence motivators, or they may go for a short-term respite by simply "messing with the mix," aiming for the one element of the mix that is easiest to push below the violent action threshold. Usually that is the last and least strongly embedded motivator.

By correctly tailoring their strategic tools, national security leaders would have flexibility to choose across a variety of responses to disrupt potential attackers. Three strategic tools map directly to an attacker's motivators: information (beliefs/ideas), capital (resources/quality of life interests), and coercion (force/power) can be targeted, with varying emphases, at the legitimacy assessments, major need perceived, and confidence felt, respectively, by any given set of bad actors. Each of the three main schools of international relations theory promotes one of the strategic tools and offers a wealth of analysis about its use. The depth of research across these approaches can be combined to help the overall success of tailored disruption activities, as shown in figure 4. Acceptable contrary information streams undermine the legitimacy or social constructions of potential bad actors. Appropriate resources or capital meet or redirect perceptions of need. Historically, coercion best undermines confidence built on technology, visions, leaders, and violent organizations.

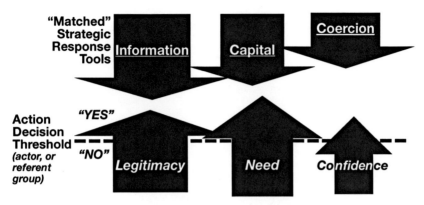

Figure 5. "Mirroring the Mix" of Violence Drivers = Accurate Response Encourages Longer-Term Dampening of Upsurges in Violence

If the theory of action were widespread as a strategic approach, every democracy facing chronic violent cybered threats would have a portfolio of disruption and resilience strategies tailored for particular threats. Any given actionable strategy could vary over time as a threat ebbs and flows. One threat portfolio may heavily emphasize massive social marketing while secondarily funding a wide variety of capital flows with minimal coercive presence. Another may be "hot" with forces on the ground followed by social marketing and cultural reciprocities, without much capital infusion. Such strategies do require intensive efforts to know and to be able to reach into the turbulent regions outside of the modern functioning states. In a cybered world, such weighted strategies may involve exploiting the same scale, proximity, and precision opportunities used by would-be bad actors.

The three motivators are present in varying strengths, and a disruption strategy should emphasize either the strongest or the least embedded motivator. The strongest driver endures well over time as a given. Strategy focused on undermining the strongest driver is more likely to disrupt violent actions over the longer term as well. A strategy emphasizing the least embedded or usually the most recent motivator to pass the threshold is likely to disrupt more quickly but for a shorter period of time. The former policy matches strength for strength and is called "mirroring the mix" as shown in figure 5. It usually is the most demanding in intelligence and range of resources but is generally more effective in disruption over the long term.

A strategy focused on the least embedded driver means merely messing

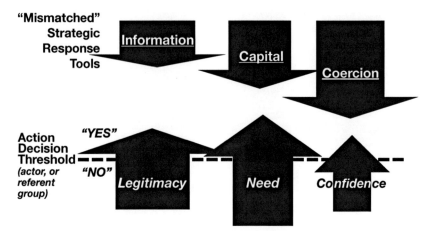

Figure 6. "Messing with the Mix" = Short-Term Response Encourages Chronic Violence

with the violence equation for a short time. But the weakness of the motivation means it can be more easily built up again, producing an episodic character to the profile. For example, a weak confidence motivator could be the sudden emergence of a charismatic leader when legitimacy and need are both strong and longstanding. If the leader is killed, it is easier for another leader to emerge who can simply use the existing strength of the other motivators. If the remote access points are suddenly closed, the attacker is only temporarily stalled. The strength of the other drivers mean they will use the next open access point they perceive. When the action profile and strategic tools differ in emphasis, the variation is called "messing with the mix," as shown in figure 6. It is generally cheaper per event and faster, but it is more short term in effects and requires more frequent returns to disrupt again.

Choosing to strategically emphasize one or another strategic tool directly affects the likely duration of the disruption in violence. For some circumstances, the violence may be such that one wants simply to disrupt it for the short term. A single spontaneous riot is likely to have confidence as its final driver past the threshold. Police in force using coercion can usually dampen or destroy the riot. However, if the other drivers are ethnic hatred and large inequities in income distribution, it is likely that one of these is a stronger driver. Riots will spark relatively often as confidence surges up over the threshold with each new opportunity or motivating leader that emerges. Another example is the gang phenomenon in urban America. Research on U.S. gangs emphasizes their role as substitutes for family and protection for their members; therefore need is the greatest driver, not the emergence of any given leader or of some legitimizing explanation for the gang's action. Too often the police focus is on confidence, using coercion to remove leaders. Equally often this choice is driven by the need for a timely fix and a lack of resources to do anything more than the simple disruption strategy. However, messing with the mix by removing the gang leader only puts the gang's violence on hold until another leader shows up. American research in criminology and sociology supports the notion that widespread quality programs to meet the missing needs of gang members are slower and more costly but ultimately have a greater effect on reducing the violence.

At the end of the day, a disruption strategy must be tailored according to the action motivation profile of the likely attackers and the time and resource needs of the systems that one is trying to protect from those attacks. In particular, continuously developed knowledge must support the weighting of the advantages and disadvantages of the strategic tools of information, capital, and coercion against the strength of the motivator they are most likely to affect. The rest of this chapter discusses the varying challenges and needs associated with choosing to emphasize each of the strategic tools of information, capital, and coercion.

First, conflicting information can reduce the legitimacy of the attack or even its intended outcomes, but only if it is accepted by the would-be bad actor. Information as a tool is powerful only when it resonates productively through the social constructs of its recipients. For example, before the rise of Shaka Zulu in the early 1800s, southern African tribes could not mass into armies for religious reasons. Each man who killed another had to appease the dead man's spirit on the spot by immediately going away for ritual cleansing. As a result, the pattern of conflict was a rough parity and continual raiding with low lethality. Shaka Zulu changed the knowledge framework by showing a way for a man who had killed to put off cleansing for many days or avoid it altogether. He persuaded large portions of Zulu clans' sons (and daughters) to kill without guilt (Jolles and Jolles 2000).

This new information reformulated by Shaka Zulu profoundly changed the conflict equation in Africa just as the colonialists were about to arrive in droves. After dispensing with the death spirits, Shaka Zulu could organize whole regiments and march them on neighbors who were used to the old, relatively non-lethal way of conflict (Mahoney 2003). The defending clans that lacked this new religious understanding were killed, enslaved, or driven out without their cattle. The survivors ran away north, causing a significant disruptive migration of populations northward in the early 1800s, as each small society fled in turn. European colonial powers arrived and exploited the exceptional turbulence in land ownership, stability, and social cohesion that significantly reduced the native population's abilities to fight back (V. D. Hanson 2001).

New information is especially powerful when it is "legitimated," that is, recognized, accepted, translated, and valued. Information may be rapidly incorporated into local practices if it acceptably fits somewhere in the known scheme of things. Changing a social construct is generally difficult but much easier if a valued source offers a plausible logic. For example, Western female business executives should have great difficulty doing business as women in Saudi society. Instead, they are treated as honorary males, and the problem goes away. The logic is that since Allah would not allow women to be in positions such as these, these westerners must not actually be women (Hodgetts and Luthans 2006). In Japan, for example, such expatriate, usually Caucasian, female managers are referred to as the third gender in order to deal with the clash of legitimacy in having women in positions of authority (Tung 2004). While females are this third gender in their business setting, when they leave that setting they are considered female and are no longer free to make their own choices (Doumato and Posusney 2003). Business goes on smoothly precisely because these redefinitions are available.

Legitimacy consists of two acceptability tests, both from the standpoint of the observer: the "rightness" of the action and the appropriateness of the entity performing the action. Information contributes to legitimacy assessments if it connects to cognitive "hooks" in the existing scheme of things (Mueller and Landsman 2004). To be accepted, new information must be deemed possible. Second, the source of the information must be from those whose observations about reality are held to be accurate and valued. Illegitimate information, like illegitimate actions or actors, is disdained or ignored, and it is rarely if ever acted upon (Curtin and Meijer 2006). For example, the classic parable about the boy who cried wolf is a traditional statement about a way that a legitimate source can be made illegitimate. Slowly the source of the information (the boy) is less and less seen as accurate, even though the action (the wolf arrives) is still deemed to be possible.

Changing a group's or community's shared daily actions is often the key to altering legitimacy assumptions and associated receptivity to incorporating new information over time (Burghardt 1982). Strongly held beliefs about actions or actors are difficult for new information to supplant if little else in the environment changes. When other key indicators of predictability in the environment change, individuals recalibrate, usually by consulting with sources of cultural guidance in order to make an acceptable logic embracing the new items in the environment. Thus as a culture evolves in general, the legitimacy profiles for a wide array of actions change as well (Hofstede 1999).

In more structured settings such as organizations, internal culture adapts when leaders or other circumstances change the members' shared daily actions. Because organizations are bounded-cognitive collective systems, they often can alter their cultures more easily than their surrounding community. In practical terms, redirecting an institution's culture requires dramatic, steady, and frequent pressure on the kinds of critical cues humans use to determine their next steps. In turn, the deep institutions of an organized or emergent group may be altered, albeit over time (Fountain 2001). Institutional cultural change is information dependent because organizations constantly refresh their role maps, expectations, and experience lessons. In both neutral and affective communication societies, information shared or developed in practice is critical to the maintenance or evolution of the existing cognitive and authority structures of the organization.[36]

This characteristic of organizations is fortunate for applying a disruption

36. The concept of *communities of practice* (COP) and the advancement of knowledge developed in part from the observations on the power of shared discourse in making change acceptable or not. Ford and Ford (1995) argue not only that organizational change is linguistically based (due to speech as a performative feature), but also that deliberate communication directly facilitates change. Most research on organizational change, however, is derived from Western *neutral* (or *instrumental*) cultures in which the message is more important than the effect it has on the listener. In Western normally lower-context cultural settings, information can come in many nonhuman or persuasive graphical contexts (email) and still be incorporated into legitimacy calculations. However, since roughly 80 percent of the world communicates *affectively* (concerned about the effects of the message on the speaker), and they prefer face-to-face or high-quality imaging communications, the importance of how and to whom legitimacy-related information is conveyed is much more critical than merely the message itself. The amount of scholarly research on non-Western communication styles and the variety of organizational implications lags significantly from that done on Western organizations (Ronen and Shenkar 1985). There is currently a burgeoning literature on international management as well (Meeuwesen et al. 2006).

strategy because changing the legitimacy of violence among attackers cannot wait on the slow change of a whole society's culture. Rather, it is helpful if the attacker's affiliations are more affected by organized groups. At a minimum, changing the legitimacy components in an organization's culture requires the very public promotion of a new logic by senior authorities and the wide distribution of publicly well-rewarded change agents. As these agents are visibly rewarded as a direct result of closer implementation of the logic of the vision, both the actions of these agents and the agents themselves become more socially accepted and thus more legitimate (General Accounting Office 1992).[37] The developing world's greater emphasis on authority-imposed guidance makes the role of a cue-giving authority even more powerful and effective if harnessed to a process aimed at disrupting the legitimacy of violence.

Humans have instinctively rejected the *other* throughout human history. The *other* is anyone not considered to be within the observer's referent group and thus not subject to the social restrictions on in-group violence (O'Connell 1989). This tendency is so pervasive and persistent that even in modern universities students in experiments will consistently exhibit deep responses to faces unlike their own. They are more likely to exhibit empathy for pain when they can see the individual in pain. The imposition of a wall or distance often is sufficient to remove human empathy and desensitize the victimizer to the victim's distress (Frith and Frith 2006). One term for this process of making such distinctions is "aversive discrimination" (Mummendey and Otten 2004). Research shows that aversion generally begins with anger if the out-group target is seen to be acting illegitimately or aggressively. Violence then can emerge as a "subjectively justified payback" if it is characterized by social mores or other legitimating cue givers (Mummendey and Otten 2004).

However, it is still the extraordinarily rare individual who can get to know his or her victims as humans and still kill them point blank without considerable cognitive dissonance about what is happening. Violence tends to require "elaborate and substantial justifications" on the part of the violent actor

---

37. It is important to note that one may not like something that one nonetheless considers legitimate. Often the term is too loosely used for actions that individuals do not like, rather than actions they deem illegitimate. The perennial American debate about dissent and patriotism is an excellent example of the tendency to confuse the two (Berkowitz 2004).

(Mummendey and Otten 2004). Hence, it helps ensure that violence is a possible choice if individuals or groups that are to be physically coerced are consistently portrayed as the *other* and as less moral or more inherently illegitimate by cue givers throughout the society.

For example, so powerful is the need to apply all illegitimate acts worthy of disdain to out-group actors that many in the Middle East believe that the attacks of 9/11 could not have been done by a Muslim. Commonly stated is the belief that all Jews were absent from the buildings on that day as confirming "objective" evidence. Thus, the violence was legitimate because it had nothing to do with Muslims, and its horror could thereby only be the work of some organization dark and evil, such as perhaps the Israeli Mossad, with the intent of blaming or victimizing Muslims (Goldberg 2004). With such circular logic, the promoters of these rumors are able to continue their resentment against an out-group (Jews). With the lack of Jewish victims as "proof" circulating over and over, the fact that the list of names includes Jewish names is forced into the logic as well — explained by the notion that these were added later. That this story is objectively wrong is beside the point.

The deliberate use of out-group hate is historically ancient. Armies have long employed out-group hate. Would-be war leaders made much of clan, race, religious, linguistic, or physical differences in order to have their soldiers know who the enemy was. Distinctive armor and coverings made those differences even clearer. When wars were pursued by neighbors with much in common, out-group distinctions had to be encouraged, especially if the religion and language were the same. Generally wars among such cousins were more limited or "intraspecies," usually developing rules of engagement (O'Connell 1989). Annihilation attacks became more likely when major distinctions like religion or language are added into the calculus. For example, one of the best ways to assure casual brutality in coercion is to have different languages between the opponents. The lack of a communication method, much like not looking at the victim, enables the perpetrator to ignore normal social restrictions. The pitiful mother pleading for her baby is heartbreaking to the person who speaks that language, but to someone who does not, it has little impact. If the person is already seen as subhuman and an enemy, their chances of not being harmed grow slim indeed. For example, much about the horrific brutality of the Serb actions against the Kosovar Albanians in the 1990s can be attributed to an inability of Serbs to speak Albanian or relate to being

Albanian.[38] In another example, it is common today to blindfold hostages continuously, often specifically forbidding guards to look at a kidnapped victim or speak with them other than commands to avoid developing empathy that could abet escape attempts (M. A. Wilson 2000).

Since much violence emerges as an opportunistic expression of a long-standing resentment against an out-group, dampening the choice to attack requires understanding that particular resentment. Tailoring the information-emphasis disruption strategy would mean providing, via legitimated sources, compelling information about shared human traits or struggles to deflate the negative image of the out-group. Information on the common humanity of a target is more powerful if portrayed often and validated by cue givers in a social setting (M. A. Wilson 2000). The goal is to dislodge (or undermine) the anger- or fear-inducing portrayal of the other as immoral or aggressive. Work on violence among ethnic Irish Catholics concluded that it was essential to reduce the positive moral assessment of violence against the other in order to disrupt the legitimacy of a decision to act violently (Ascher 1986). In more recent years in the Balkans and the Middle East, many international peace programs aimed at having warring sides get to know one another in incongruent settings. The type of information provided is deliberately emotional, induced either by spending time together to see one another as friends, or by commiserating over common problems aside from the violence-prone dispute at hand (Olson 2002).

Under some circumstances, disruption of the legitimacy of violence against an *other* is more probable if the strategy delegitimizes, not the likely attacker's beliefs directly, but the sources of accepted legitimating information, such as cue givers in the would-be violent actor's world. Organized and deliberate efforts by attacking groups often require continuous nurturing to ensure an automatic rejection of the *other* in the face of more positive contact (Dennen 1995). Disrupting that nurturing process ripples through to reduce the automaticity of the rejection, making it harder for the organized group to consolidate willingness to act. Research on East German versus West German in-group rejection of immigrants shows a clear pattern in which contact in

38. This analysis is by no means glossing over the incredible violence within societies if the rules of social restraint are lifted and the victim is a stranger. Rather, this discussion is about the strategic uses of the other to enable violence.

daily practices reduces the rejection of the other (Wagner et al. 2003). Today's suicide bombers are often deliberately isolated from contrary evidence, sent to locations where they do not know the victims, and made to detonate their bombs quickly. Much time is spent persuading these individuals that the victims are the *other*, and not really human, in order to justify the actions. If the bombers spent time with the victims, many would simply be unable to act (Bloom 2005).

Disrupting legitimacy requires considerable effort. Well-tailored information strategically delivered needs understanding and mechanisms in place well before they are required to target specific actors. The lead time for impacting legitimacy can often be decades. For example, the United States benefited for some time from its Cold War policy of having foreign military officers study in U.S. military installations. An interesting natural experiment here occurred with Pakistan, where officers were trained in the United States until such exchanges were stopped for nearly two decades in retaliation for Pakistan developing nuclear weapons. Thus, while the senior cohort of Pakistani officers has positive views of the United States, the junior cohort without human-to-human contacts or accepted sources of persuasive information on common interests with Americans is suspicious of, if not actively hostile to, the United States (Cohen 2007)

These mechanisms must be supported by knowledge that is continuously and comprehensively updated. Unlike need and confidence, legitimacy often involves emotional connections. De-legitimizing successfully what was once strongly accepted encourages a feeling of betrayal that takes time to repair. It is powerful and must be intensely knowledge based to be successful. Undermining insurgent legitimacy of violent acts was the genesis for the "hearts and minds" strategy in Vietnam, but in this case it was poorly supported with little understanding of the legitimacy factors on the ground (Mack 1975).

Having the institutional tools to pursue a strategic emphasis on disrupting the legitimacy of violence requires continuous and deliberate effort in the development of knowledge. If left unnurtured by strategy and resources, these skills atrophy in the defending nation. For example, after forty-odd years with the comfortably bipolar Cold War, the large U.S. defense community was exceptionally slow to recognize the different security responses needed for a culturally heterogeneous world. The initial American timetable and objectives for the 2003 Iraq invasion did not reflect the likely economic and legitimacy reactions of a Muslim nation being invaded by a western secular nation, irrespective of the dictator toppled in the process.[39]

A disruption strategy emphasizing information in all its contributions to legitimacy must focus on facts. For example, for some years after 9/11, the prevailing American view was that Muslim jihadists were poor and religious zealots.[40] An analysis of the demographics of jailed Islamic terrorists, however, concluded that the core global Islamists around Osama bin Laden were actually disillusioned, better-educated expatriates, linked by intense, family-clan loyalties that they often developed after meeting by accident in radical mosques in Europe. This suggests a strategy designed to disrupt the violence-legitimating role of the few radical mosques in Europe would be better than trying to simply kill each of the global jihadists as they emerge (Sageman 2004).

One may employ either indirect or direct means to provide legitimated, alternative data. Changing the rightness and appropriateness of an action or target are direct effects in information operations, while believability and trustworthiness are indirect effects. Direct effects are generally simpler to conceive of than indirect; more direct operations using information tend to be more easily detected by those promoting the legitimacy of violent actions. Indirect effects channel perceptions less overtly and are often not as easy to attribute

39. As a result of the rediscovery of culture and beliefs, developers of new concepts and tools shifted from the common term *information warfare* to *information operations* as a way to recognize the use of information outside the clear confines of military-on-military wartime information tactics. In the process, though, the tools stayed much the same, very focused on tactical environments, on tracking, theft, interdiction, or deception in distorting short-term information. Often there is not a commensurate intense discussion of the nonwar strategic use of information tools save in the context of tracking the financial, movement, or marketing activities of Islamic jihadists. The knowledge base is not developed well enough. Only a much smaller group of authors in the information operations literature discuss operational options in having information as the main emphasis strategically and in aiming at the cultural supports for violence as a legitimate individual act (Allen 2007).

40. In the years since the attack on New York in 2001, a publishing flood has occurred in books on Islamic terrorism, its origins, and Western options to counter their activities. Most works are based on secondary sources, while a few are more empirical and also anecdotal, such as the personal experiences of journalists and the autobiographical discourses of moderate Muslims (Bergen 2001). Some portion is also the writings of deeply affronted Christian authors seeking to demonstrate inherent failings in Islam to explain terrorism (Spencer 2002). Very little is systematic and well enough integrated for current use in a disruption and resilience strategy emphasizing information.

to the organizations behind the information operations (Allen 2007). If the information undermining legitimacy in violence comes indirectly through others, there is "consensual validation" without any apparent action by the opponent, and thus those promoting the violence will have to increase their persuasive pressure given the diminishing support (Berger et al. 1998, 379). A subtle disruptive de-legitimating operation is more difficult to counter for both sides because confirming information is more difficult to acquire. It takes more time and resources. The obverse, using obvious means to directly attack violent action as less legitimate, may be simpler to plan and less prone to distortions when successful; however, it is easier to counter given its obvious origins and intent.[41]

An information-heavy disruption strategy can work if legitimacy is determined to be the strongest motivator. It must be given the same initial value and attention as coercion or need, however. As the insurgency in Iraq in 2004 grew rather than diminished over time, only belatedly did the U.S. defense leaders acknowledge the need for legitimacy along with oil revenues and militarized hunts for foreign terrorists. The occupying Americans struggled to develop the knowledge collection, integration, and implementation tools for disrupting this emphasis on legitimacy in the decision to engage in conflict (Petraeus 2006). Although relatively successful at this writing, the traditional focus on coercion as the automatic first choice tragically cost the United States and the Iraqis many lives and resources. The good news is that if legitimacy is the strongest motivator, it is harder for would-be attackers to build legitimacy back up once it is seriously disrupted. Only extensive knowledge of the would-be attackers can determine which method is more likely to be successful.

Second, capital as a strategic tool is best adapted to delinking the bad actor's need, usually expressed in quality-of-life economic terms, from an attack. For example, the Mongols camped outside the walls of Vienna, but after realizing the siege would take them well beyond their desired time frame for rampag-

---

41. Wartime propaganda could indeed be considered direct efforts to delegitimize the willingness of the enemy's population to fight, i.e., act violently against the friendly side. There is exceptionally little evidence that this kind of cross-cultural engagement in information operations had any positive effect at all. Rather, there are more reasons to believe its main purpose was to create a cover for the transmission of coded messages to resistance or spies. In any case, such propaganda was believed at the time to be what nations did, and it was pursued irrespective of any demonstrable value. An excellent discussion of propaganda, radio or otherwise, as persuasive devices can be found in Jowett and O'Donnell (2006).

ing, they became more interested in negotiating a bribe than in spending the time to take the fortified town. Realizing this stronger need, the city fathers generously paid the Mongols not to commit violence, and off the would-be attackers went, at least for another year (D. Morgan 2007). Using capital to bribe an attacker not to attack is as old as the stories written in the Bible and before (Ginzberg and Szold 1998). The success of this disruption strategy has always been dependent on knowledge — for example, knowing whether to negotiate over the land on which one stood or tribute.

The vast majority of needs for which violence is perceived as a remediation involve economic deprivation. Even the desire for repatriation to the landholdings of one's grandfather often found in diasporic violent movements is often driven by a lack of economic options in the new environment rather than a desire to return to the old lands. A consistent fact of human history is the tendency for migrants to stay in the new places if stable economic lives can be constructed. Few will return to the old places, despite nostalgic rhetoric, if their economic security no longer lies solely in dreams of return.

For example, Palestinian youth of poor parents who are persuaded that their grandparents once owned beautiful olive groves are more likely to sacrifice themselves in harsh economic times. In fact, most Palestinian grandfathers would have been tenant farmers to absentee landlords living in Cairo or Damascus before the state of Israel was formed. This harsh fact is not shared with these struggling young people in part because of the prestige the grandfathers would lose in their eyes (Stein 1984; Rowley and Taylor 2006). This buried economic fact continues to be problematic today when a radical Jewish settlement in the middle of an Arab town starts with the legal, if not public, purchase of the land from an Arab, usually through anonymizing middlemen. Then security concerns force a widening of the settlement and the unjust displacement of neighbors who had no voice in the original sale. Equally important is the poor compensation to local Arab neighbors for the subsequent land takings to ensure the security of the settlers. The sense of grievance is magnified by the lack of sustaining compensation (Oren and Newman 2006).

In addition to buried economic facts, there are complexities in the need motivator for which knowledge is essential if capital infusions are tailored well. Often enough capital infusions are seen as less expensive alternatives to coercion using military force. For example, persuading Afghan farmers not to grow poppies or Colombian farmers not to grow coca can mean fully compensating them for the income lost in growing less valuable crops. The intangible disruption benefits for the expense, however, are fewer sons leaving the farm as new recruits to the ranks of bad actors (Rubin 2007). But there may be an additional expense beyond farm subsidies that only greater knowledge development can help target. Farmers with many sons may use the wealth to free more sons from farming so that they can study far from home at a madrassa. There, instead of learning a trade, they could learn jihad and how to use cybered means to conduct attacks. Complex economic systems have considerable leakage and many surprises in cumulative effects that need to be pursued to emphasize capital as a strategic disruptor (Robinson and Torvik 2005).[42]

There is considerable research to show that "relative" or "subjective" deprivation is more often at the core of a need-based motivator to action (Snow and Oliver 1995). This assessment of need may not be grounded in what one would normally use as a comparative economic statistic, but it operates nonetheless to diminish the value of what is currently held or attainable, and what is viewed as likely to be held or attained if only the object of likely violence or sense of grievance were not in the way. Once the sense of deprivation is framed to include a targetable source of loss, the need motivator is much more likely to be operating and exploitable by social peers, the social movement cadre, or even the wider emergence of a justification for acting such as a religious call to action. Such framing is necessary if the need is indeed less concretely obvious, and if collective violent action is heavily associated with actors able to establish the cognitive connections (Benford 1997; Carragee 2004).

In this work, a strategic response emphasizing capital in turn emphasizes the more concrete connections between need reduction and violence. A successful capital emphasis uses mechanisms or processes chosen to reduce the violence associated with the need in ways that can be publicly observed. That is, the response has to have an effect on why violence is perceived as an effective way to mitigate the need. The strategic response emphasizing capital thus acts more on the listeners' receptiveness to a violent frame than on the framing, and even more on the characteristics of the listeners themselves.

For example, modern young males are known to peak biologically in their

---

42. This uncertainty of outcomes is one reason that capital infusions were often seen as secondary to coercion during the heyday of American military in the Cold War (Mastanduno 1998).

need for vigorous activities at around age twenty-five.[43] It is not by accident that young men constitute the major initiators of violence in the world, whether in armies, gangs, terrorist groups, domestic crime, or social vandalism, including internet destructiveness (Hesketh and Xing 2006). This reality is particularly troubling in an era in which in the largest countries, India and China, the sex ratio is skewed toward males in historically unprecedented numbers without a plague or war. This imbalance, up to 20 percent in China, occurs just as a massive youth bubble has emerged in Middle Eastern nations that may be unable to provide this generation reasonable opportunities for education and employment (Boer and Hudson 2004; Fuller 2003; Jacoby 2005). The historically common way of dealing with excess males in a society was to organize them into militaries and go to war. In that way, one could at least occupy them in attacking foreigners rather than making demands on the home nations. The importance of successful management of younger males is explicitly addressed by many institutions dealing with large numbers of young men in close quarters. For example, the modern British Army has a long history of using Fridays both as a housekeeping day (duties to maintain the camp) and as a vigorous sports day intentionally devoted to dissipating energy and maintaining social control of often unstable, testosterone-enhanced emotions (Demchak 1994).

Many cultures have developed physically challenging competitions for young men as a way to keep their violent tendencies under control, while also often training them with skills usable elsewhere. Mongolia developed elaborate horse-archery competitions while American native peoples used raiding competitions to keep social control of otherwise energetic young warriors (Tomikawa 2006; Adelman and Aron 1999). In the United States, dancing contests between rival gangs have been used to change the perceptions of need among younger and newer gang members receptive to leaving the group (Everett, Chadwell, and McChesney 2002; Short 2001).

Keeping a great number of young males in largely urbanized areas of the turbulent, poorer, densely populated developing regions from using cybered means to safely attack others at a distance requires a great deal of knowledge about the quality-of-life needs of these cohorts. A successful disruption strategy using capital to effectively disrupt violence in youth might incorporate the lessons from such programs and seek cultural equivalents (Zuhur 2005).

43. Not surprisingly, this is said to be a function of the peak in testosterone production until a small resurgence when males are in their forties (Hau 2007).

In particular, the strategy must consider the surrounding organizations that frame notions of relative deprivation and the use of violence for these young would-be attackers. Organizations often function as redoubling forums, making and reinforcing the connections for individuals between violence and the major deprivation. Organizations often sustain "violent cultures" in resource-poor, imbalanced societies or regions.[44] Indeed, individuals often fail to make the grievance connection without the organized efforts to connect the dots. Furthermore, capital flows in economic systems are almost always channeled by organizations. Farmers, herders, factory workers, and civil servants use middleman associations to transport goods, themselves, their money, and the lessons about success given the wider local or global economic system. Gangs, fraternities, social movements, militaries, and socially restrictive communities all contribute to the conceptions of deprivation and grievance, and especially to the identification of the source.

With sufficient knowledge, a disruption strategy targeting these important organizations could distinguish between those deliberately or inadvertently encouraging a heightened sense of grievance and strengthening the association of need with violence. For example, in the early 1960s, Western economists with exceptionally limited understandings of social systems, but a great belief in the power of concentrated national capital stocks, attempted to rapidly industrialize newly independent African nations. It was thought that if only the leaders of these nations would force all farmers to sell their goods to a single, national farm purchase organization, then the nation could reap the profit of its agricultural product directly and rationalize the use of these monies to build industrialization rather than having farmers and middlemen squander it less efficiently. The result was massive corruption in the state-owned agriculture bureaucracies, rampant price abuse of farmers, extraordinary black market diversions of products, and the wholesale loss of agricultural productivity as farmers' children ran away to cities from the declining farms (Englebert 2000).

Violent political instability was absolutely inevitable with this relatively ignorant meddling in other social contexts. With all significant economic capital channeled through the government ministries, the tolerance possible

---

44. For a particularly enlightening and concrete discussion of what happens when energetic young males in violence-accepting social groupings strike out to establish their claims to the resources of adult males, see Barker (2005).

in westernized states that separate economic power from political power, at least constitutionally, was instantly lost. With state productive revenue forced to channel through party-held and -controlled organizations, losing an election meant all one's relatives lost their incomes. Either they had jobs in the ministries due to nepotism, or they lived by grace of their clansman's ability to use corruption to amass sufficient funds for the whole clan. It would not be unusual to have twenty-plus people dependent on one civil service job in postcolonial Western Africa, where violence and barbarous election and coup behaviors have been common since the 1960s.[45]

If one seeks to successfully design capital inserts through or even around organizations to specifically reduce a violence-related need, the literature available for guidance drops dramatically in number and in empirical validity. Nonetheless, experts in certain fields are likely to discuss useful tools, even if violence reduction is not their focus: social economists, social anthropologists, political area studies specialists, and historians of economic and political development. In actionable strategic terms, the response must be built by backward mapping from the outcome intended along all the possible paths and distortions as individuals perceive and try to mobilize resources to their personal benefit.

For example, it has proved of little use and, indeed, has shown negative effects for the United States to have funneled millions of dollars in development aid into corrupt ministries of the rump post-2003 Iraq government, while loudly discussing the massive flows of money before the population. Much of the funds expended have been simply lost to corruption, and for security reasons, much has not even been dispersed. The local population, however, only sees the resulting lack of action and assumes it is due to *all* of the money having been stolen. If the ministries had remained being perceived as poor and struggling and trying to little avail, the government might at least have had some sympathy. Instead, the U.S. method of declaring large aid amounts but having no ability to assure its use beyond the centralized institutions has

45. The World Bank's Western-trained non-African economists were largely responsible for this mess. Only in the early 1990s, in an otherwise largely unremarked change in policy, did the World Bank officially remove its support for state-owned agricultural boards. Perhaps it could happen only when the original economists retired. In any event, by then per capita income had literally halved for most subcontinent Africans from its peak in the mid-1960s, and a lack of violence and political stability are nowhere assured on the continent (Theobald 1994).

added to profound distrust of the new government and resentment that unde-serving people in government ministries are stealing the money that would have helped the jobless (Billon 2005). Resentment breeds exceptionally rap-idly and can more easily be mobilized against such clearly identifiable targets for this anger, that is, centralized ministries holding economic reins. The result is violence against those institutions — not to mention others viewed as getting away with undeserved largesse as well. Asserting that, for example, electricity levels are actually greater in the rural areas than they were under the dictator Saddam Hussein does not deter resentment much if the rural areas expected better and the city areas now know they are losing to the rural areas.

A disruption strategy emphasizing capital must address corruption and its obviousness in order to be successful. One of the drawbacks of imposing a fully free press and portals to cyberspace in the interests of furthering democ-racy and education is that average poorer individuals are able to see in detail wealth and a high quality of life seemingly easily available for others but not for themselves. The corruption of the wealthy in Saudi Arabia and other Arab states compared to the modesty enjoined in religious teachings has often been used historically to develop grievances from inchoate dislike to violent col-lective action. Osama bin Laden was only the latest in a longer line of even-tually embittered reformers of their society who used corruption to explain deprivation, in one fell swoop showing both the source and the consequences (Al-Rasheed 2007). In a failing state such as Russia, the newly wealthy under-stood democracy to mean they could flash their resources without social con-trols. So blatant were these displays of money and ease of life, and so strong was the developing blowback among ordinary Russians, that President Vladimir Putin orchestrated the very public downfall of several of the most exhibition-ist new billionaires. He took steps that clearly would never work in a Western democracy adhering to a consensually observed rule of law in order to reach out and humble these potential social destabilizers (Shevtsova 2007). He was rewarded with political stability and electoral support from an otherwise re-signed and frustrated population (Schmidt 2007).

In short, capital cannot be used indiscriminately as a strategic tool to disrupt violence. It has, however, considerable power when properly aligned with the specific circumstances in which need dominates. Knowledge of the actors and the organizations that sustain the resentment associated with attacks would de-termine what different applications of capital as a strategic emphasis are likely to be more successful in pushing the need motivator below the threshold.

Third, coercion is the historically most direct and effective way to diminish an attacker's confidence that his or her participation in an attack will succeed as perceived. War historically reflects the emphasis of coercion over the other strategic disruption responses. The objective is the opponent's confidence because, unlike destroying belief systems or erasing a quality-of-life need, failure can be more easily demonstrated to the opponent's fighters.[46] Confidence is based on a belief that a course of action will succeed, not about what the preferred outcome is or how right or wrong it is. Confidence is the closest to a testable hypothesis of the motivators. Many concrete pieces of data can disprove its likely success. Confidence therefore tends to be much more opportunistic in its hold on the attacker, not the outgrowth of the attacker's life experiences up to that moment. It rises or falls with demonstrations of likely success much more easily than legitimacy or need. Confidence is, in a sense, more fragile, least strongly embedded, and more often the final motivator past the threshold for action.

The history of war is about how necessary organizations are to create and maintain confidence associated with violent outcomes, especially if the would-be actor faces harm if the action fails. Since individuals generally do not like to act violently against other humans, certain prior conditions have proven to be necessary. The first condition is a belief in the efficacy of the tools, leader, plans, or access at hand to achieve the goal of action; the second is a belief that the person contemplating acting is personally capable of success in that act; and the third is having the opportunity to use these tools (O'Connell 1989).

For these three conditions to be met, it has normally taken an organized group to be involved, generally a military (O'Connell 1989). Some militaries have achieved extraordinary levels in their creation and maintenance of the individual soldier's confidence. For example, the British Army of the 1700s and 1800s was particularly successful in keeping the line of soldiers marching in the direct face of fire. Unflinching cohesion while comrades fall around one is historically extraordinary. Even the Romans had shields to maintain confidence, and the infamous foxhole of modern war serves the same purpose. This achievement of the British Army was excruciatingly hard to achieve. It required a harsh regime of strict discipline, endless drill, constant cohort so-

46. It is recommended that the interested reader not acquainted with the history of war read in particular O'Connell (1989) and Adams (1998). Both are excellent introductions to war, its tools, its odd characteristics as employed by humans, and its modern expressions.

cialization (pride in unit victories, young male attachment to unit along with families), and isolation from the lure of running home by frequent deployment overseas (Home 2000).

Using coercion to disrupt an attacker's confidence involves targeting the individual's evaluation of the three components of confidence. Sometimes disrupting an opponent's confidence entails directly working on the individual, that is, destroying the morale of soldiers. Sometimes it means eliminating the leaders, destroying their tools, or demonstrating the lack of success in their plans. Military organizations have provided centuries of trial-and-error experiments in how to destroy the confidence of other organizations' members because coercion was generally the preferred strategic emphasis for disruption of an opponent.

As a constant learned by military organizations over centuries of history characterized by a lack of connectivity and accurate exchange of timely knowledge, coercion was easier organizationally than trying to disrupt legitimated beliefs or erase quality-of-life grievances. Most wars, most armies, and most conflicts had experienced or knew of battles in which one side's soldiers seemingly suddenly lost their confidence and abandoned the violence; they ran away. Even if the immediate use of coercion might have negative longer-term effects as cautioned by military theorists such as Tacitus, Jomini, Clausewitz, and Du Picq through multiple military theorists of the 1900s, political leaders often simply chose it first. Frustrated, angry, or ignorant leaders were often happier to destroy the whole village and "let God sort it out," rather than acquire the knowledge to target only the mechanisms that tend to build confidence in the efficacy of violence.[47] Ironically, jihadists are no less likely to adopt this view when it seems too hard to select targets. Often, suicide bombers will state that they expect God will sort the innocent Muslims they killed and reward them in heaven, thus satisfying their need not to have killed unjustly but also saving them the difficulty of sorting victims in advance (Maikovich 2005).

Despite the likelihood of overkill or sheer destruction of assets, coercion used rapidly had and still has the advantage of making the violence happen too

---

47. A common paraphrase of guidance to "kill everyone; God will sort it out" was attributed to a papal envoy during the Albigensian Crusade, responding to a request for the legitimate way to distinguish between heretical Albigensians and their nonheretic fellows during the crusade (Friedman 1999).

fast for reflection by all the participants. Quickly moving to action means less time for actors to test the course of action against likely success, or the natural disinclination of actors against killing or being killed. Actual battles were often completed in one day because in the darkness of night, many soldiers on both sides would simply vanish, having lost their confidence (Keegan 1978).

Coercion is the right response to a strong confidence driver, but history shows it to be often overused, producing a cyclical "bubbling" of violence rather than longer-term disruption. The reason is that if confidence is the weakest motivator, it is also the easiest to push back across the threshold as well. As readily as confidence is undermined, it can be supported, albeit weakly. In this case, a coercive disruption is never very long in effect. This pattern is particularly visible in small-group, collective violence. For example, U.S. gangs are violent but in punctuated patterns. All too often the security strategy by domestic police has emphasized the removal of the current leader. Violence then subsides only until the rise of another leader restores the dispirited group network to its fighting and violence.[48] If accurate information is missing about how strong a motivator confidence is in a particular situation, applying coercion to dampen the weak confidence of a threat actor may also produce other threat actors in a cycle of hit-revenge-revenge-revenge. Like spores, each then vigorously expands its smaller gang, increasing the overall crime and violence as they fight each other for control. Survivors spend time developing deep resentments and then burst forth when the right tool, leader, plan, or opportunity pops up (Carley 2004).

When coercion seems easiest to apply and even appears to work initially, but then results in a longer-term chronic resurgence of attacks, critical knowledge is missing about the action profile of the attackers. In responding to cybered attackers, in particular, coercion is particularly difficult to apply. Striking at the computers that seem to be involved in a devastating attack could result in the damage of many innocent computers being used as proxies, along with the critical systems on which those innocent middlemen rely. Coercion in cybered conflict also tends to attract the attention of otherwise uninvolved third

48. The consequences of dismantling teams by removing leaders are excellently explored by Carley (2004) in virtual experiments whose results are congruent with studies of gangs and small feudal wars. See also the work by Manuel Castells (1997) in putting this pattern of bubbling, unresolved other motivations for violence into a broader context of modern societies.

parties. In a cybered world, they have the ability to attack if the opportunity emerges, especially if defenders are distracted elsewhere. These third parties can easily choose to pile their attacks onto the attacker's efforts and can choose to do so at their whim without harm to themselves. For example, during the 1999–2001 Israeli-Palestinian hacker war, Brazilian hackers spontaneously joined in, attacking all sides, including innocent organizations in the United States (Allen and Demchak 2003).

Coercion might be the last choice in disrupting a threat in a cybered conflict if the desire is to disrupt attackers for the longest period of time possible. On the other hand, there are, and have been, solid cases where a coercion-heavy disruption and resilience strategy was precisely the right response — for example, the war against Hitler in World War II. Hitler above all had confidence in his ability to win and inspired the same in his followers. There is a growing body of literature about criminal hackers, including those hired by Russian security services as state proxies, and their obsessive concern for their personal physical safety. For them, the strongest driver probably is need, but a very close second is confidence. If one pushes the confidence down, they will return to the attacks. However, if the coercion is sufficiently traumatic in its effects, then many of these hackers, called black hat hackers, immediately turn into white hat hackers working as overt and legal security consultants (Nuwere and Chanoff 2002).

In cybered conflict in particular, focusing on disruption, often called computer network attack, and getting the strongest motivator wrong means less time and resources are available to accurately develop equally critical strategic resilience. In Steinbruner's formulation, the knowledge development processes in the responding nation not only question the knowledge and tests of assumptions supporting coercion but also reevaluate the tests before acting (Steinbruner 2002). Strategic disruption efforts, whether accurately tailored for the long or short term, will in globally complex systems inevitably fail to stop some significant attacks, leaving the nation's security resting on what it has done to ensure the second half of cyber power, resilience.

Resilience's Strategic Tools: Collective Sense-Making and Rapid Action Capacity

Resilience as an element of strategy is actually, if more narrowly, well known to the national security community under different terms such as *continuity of operations.* But national security leaders are rarely aware of or able to benefit from the wider literature on resilience in nonmilitary, largescale, societal systems involving humans and networked machines. The designers of military campaigns intuitively engage (without knowing the terminology) in the precautionary steps analyzed in Sunstein's "Irreversible Harm Precautionary Principle" and "Catastrophic Harm Precautionary Principle" (Sunstein 2006). Militaries offer a rich history of organizations and leaders both fearing surprise and taking steps in advance to nullify its effects. In recent decades, modern armies and navies have altered their organizational structure, socialization, knowledge focus, information content, training, technology, and employment practices to prepare for — and respond to — rippling surprises while operating. Societies have not. However, the leaders of a nation's conflicts generally do not apply the same notions of resilience beyond the battlefield or campaign, especially during peacetime.[49]

The lessons of surviving well against a thinking, malevolent enemy ultimately must involve being prepared nationally at home for nasty surprises if a modern state is to be increasingly dependent on large complex, sociotechnical, cybered systems. Critical to a nation's application of resilience is the expectation that surprises will come as long as the complex systems exist and are critical. Surviving well means providing the necessary knowledge for collective sense-making on the spot and for rapid, accurate, corrective, and innovative action.

In complex systems especially, resilience is a rough and broad summary measure of the appropriateness of the accommodations of surprise that exist in the system — the "system's fit." The better the resilience is, the more accommodated the system is against knowable unknowns and the more likely it has serendipitously accommodated to unknowable unknowns. Whether an uncertainty concerns the specific form or the actual frequency of an occurrence will have an effect on the nature of the accommodation required. For example, if the undesirable outcome is destruction of grain in a warehouse, and if the rogue outcome is either marauding rats or deer that will only come at foreseeable intervals, then obstacles or deterrents that work at least once against each and can be replaced easily are necessary. If, however, the outcome is more likely to be rats, but they could arrive unexpectedly, then the

---

49. For all the obvious reasons associated with living below sea level, the Netherlands is a major exception to this rule.

obstacles or deterrents will have to be tailored to rats and reinforced for multiple, unforeseeable attacks.

It is, of course, most difficult to accommodate undesirable outcomes when both the form and frequency are unknown. If the form is known, then redundancy in the inventory of knowledge relevant to those outcomes is preferred. If only the frequency of disruptions is known, then slack — which entails loosening the coupling among elements and may include redundancy — is preferred as an initial accommodation mechanism.[50] The more resilient nationally critical systems are, the more likely they exhibit the necessary redundancy, slack, and continuous trial-and-error learning essential to collectively make sense of disabling surprises and then act rapidly and accurately in response.[51] A nation seeking credible levels of cyber power requires these attributes of resilience to be well established and maintained; they are not optional.

As a strategic tool of resilience, *redundancy* is about meeting the need for speed in knowledge available on the spot. The great tragedy of the massive, unprecedented American oil spill in the Gulf of Mexico in 2010 was the clear lack of redundancy in preparation for surprise. In misplaced support for a key critical industry, the U.S. government did not assure itself the knowledge it would need if the oil company in charge was surprised in its drilling. British Petroleum (BP), for reasons of cost control, ignored the possibility that it could be surprised, despite drilling so deeply and so expensively into a large oil field. At the moment needed, only BP had the expertise of drilling and could determine how fast and what was attempted. The failure to be redundant in knowledge on the spot produced a spill unprecedented in cost, extent, and likely harmful ecological impacts in the United States and its waters.

A redundant system is resilient in that the knowledge needed to accommodate surprise is on the spot from multiple sources and formats, rather than merely duplicating everything involved. For largescale systems, it is a collective attribute in which the knowledge of many systems, individuals, and tools can immediately be brought to bear when surprised, in both collective sense-

50. There is a vast literature on sensitivity analysis and complexity (Gleick 1988).

51. For heuristic purposes, an intuitively appealing measure of resilience is the parametric multiplication of redundancy by slack. Intuitively appealing, the term rises or falls as the combination of redundancy and slack rises and falls. If system A has high slack and low redundancy and system B has low slack and high redundancy, then it is clear that both could have the same level of resilience as long as the knowledge burden is met for each system's unknowns.

making and then rapid collective action (Comfort, Boin, and Demchak 2010). In the oil spill example, the U.S. government could have developed its own expertise in deep-water well capping before BP was allowed to attempt the well on its own. Redundancy can be designed across critical systems ranging from multiple sources of clean municipal water flows (in case one source is poisoned or blocked) to the design of networks in which each packet can travel through multiple pathways to its destination. For example, in a different kind of accommodation, it used to be the policy of the U.S. Army to staff its units at 125 percent under the calculation that, in a battle, about a quarter would be lost to death, disease, or mistakes (Weigley 1973).

Redundancy often involves multiple pathways rather than coalescing things at any one location. In particular, resilience elsewhere in the complex system can be undermined when a single node, expert, application, dataset, or user is required for necessary and critical operations. When surprise emerges, missing knowledge can be cobbled together more easily across the multiple access points. NASA's space program routinely used five backup computer systems programmed by different groups of scientists to assure near certainty in computer operation, calculating that any conceivable shortfall would not cripple five systems in a row.[52]

As a strategic tool of resilience, *slack* is about having the time to collectively make sense of the unexpected circumstances about which one cannot be sure to have the needed knowledge in advance right where it is needed. Slack is often located in the selective positioning of "air gaps" so that automatic processes or transactions cannot occur without a human or a completely different system making a decision to keep the chain of events going. In principle, the gap allows humans or other sensor systems to recognize the emerging indicators of undesirable events and to act to stop the processes before the system is harmed. In the above example of the oil disaster of 2010, the U.S. government could have required BP to have multiply redundant capping systems previously tested and in place. In that way, the cascading effects of an explosion on the drilling platform, however unlikely a surprise, could have been avoided. Antivirus quarantine functions, for example, in our computer networks are, in effect, slack elements designed to stop apparent malevolence at the entrance

---

52. One series of cascading failure is reported to have come very close, however, with four of five systems going down (Shooman 2002).

to the computer while seeking updated knowledge to discern if the quarantine was appropriate or not.

Slack often involves decoupling links in a critical system to reduce the need for speed in providing knowledge. Slack becomes a preferred element of resilience when the likelihood of crippling, system-wide rogue outcomes rises. The more possible those bad outcomes lacking any form or frequency knowable in advance are, the more necessary are ways to slow the advance of the harm by selectively decoupling links that could move the harm along very rapidly.

Beyond redundancy and slack is understanding and knowledge development — that is, having as much knowledge uncovered in advance as possible. Key to strategic resilience in a world of cybered conflict is the continuous use of *trial and error* in collective, widely engaged, dynamic, high-fidelity simulations. The key is having the individuals involved in the accommodation of the surprise included in advance in routinely anticipating surprises and innovating possible responses in processes, tools, structures, interpretations, and even policy changes. Galbraith (1977) noted that in any situation of rising critical information flows, the organization or socio-technical system has only two theoretically possible options to avoid being overwhelmed: pursuing slack to reduce the inflow or redundancy to increase one's internal processing power, or both. However, these elements can be inappropriately implemented, or equally often, they can drift away from being effective if not continuously tested and adapted as needed. Scholars of largescale, socio-technical systems have shown that only high-fidelity trial and error consistently conducted, interpreted, and retested can indicate where to use redundancy and slack for resilience. Furthermore, the results of these tests need to be collectively absorbed and integrated into the development of capacity for rapid action, especially if bad actors anywhere can discover how to exploit them.

In a cybered world, conflict will ripple through complex systems in unpredictable ways unless many trial-and-error events reveal at least what can be known in advance. Having such events to develop knowledge alone is not sufficient if structures, practices, people, locations, tools, and expectations are not also adapted and retested. Ironically, the modern democratic nation's militaries are well versed in the need for exercising their battlefield preparations, but these exercises are expensive, infrequent, and often scripted events designed to justify the existing structures and tools as appropriate for the enemies seen and expected. In recent years, major exercises scaled for national cybered conflicts have been conducted in the United States, but the chances for integrating these lessons have been lost due to the classification of the results (Clarke and Knake 2010). The U.S. government is developing a military cyber command to defend its military networks, while assigning the coordination of the defense of all other government networks to its ungainly Department of Homeland Security (DHS). Individual citizens and firms are left to their own resources in providing sufficient resilience to their critically important needs. If these national-level cyber exercises show that this fragmented topology is not likely to provide adequate resilience, keeping the results classified undermines the need for trial and error to be a strategic learning tool. If those left outside the cyber-command or DHS nexus do not see the test results, then the lessons of trial and error will not be integrated cognitively among individuals and institutionally among nongovernmental players. Redundancy and slack cannot be accurately developed and updated without system-wide trial-and-error learning across all actors.

Institutional Adaptation for Strategic Knowledge

Cybered conflict requires a uniquely modern, highly informed, rapid way of fighting that accommodates the topology developing across the increasingly digitized international system. Success in the face of surprise in large, dispersed, complex systems is crucially based on knowledge at the right moment, in the right form, and used in the most accurate and timely way. It is not sufficient to simply have a strategy of disruption; without resilience, the surprises of the cybered world will achieve what the attackers seek at some point simply due to the complexity of the environment. Florence as a city-state, for example, subscribed solely to disruption by hired armed forces. Since its security strategy lacked a resilience component, Florence survived the recurring attacks from its neighbors only by sheer luck (Rinaldi 2005).

At the end of the day, an effective security resilience strategy for a nation requires three particularly knowledge-enhancing institutional adaptations beyond just incorporating the theory of action and of surprise accommodation as a framework in national thinking. Resilience and disruption implemented as strategy require a deliberate institutionalization of three processes: cross-actor consensus, comprehensive systemic information sources, and continuous knowledge development. Put in other words, national security processes need to be better at using cybered means to both outwit and, as necessary, robustly endure the surprises. That goal requires better ways of conducting nurtured interstate and interagency institutionalization of cooperation; of routinely acquiring a masked but searchable broad collection of international and domestic behavior data; and, of sustaining unflagging innovative, even virtual collaborative refinement of patterns into collectively wise strategic foreign policy and domestic security options. Failure to disrupt over the long or short term, or to adequately accommodate nasty surprises can, naturally, come from the many unpredictable convergences of dynamic, complex social systems. These include the infamous "sheer damn bad luck" or, on a lesser scale, the friction of operating in complex turbulent environments. Not doing one's homework, however, virtually assures the responding actor a tougher time in figuring out the threat's violence equation in advance or during the attack, and in already being prepared with a response (Comfort, Boin, and Demchak 2010).

What organizations know about their enemies determines the emphases placed in their national strategic choices. In cybered conflict as in war, each side is trying to reduce its own internal uncertainty, while imposing as much uncertainty as possible on the other via surprise. First, organizations try to expand in the direction of their greatest contingency in order to control it (Thompson 1967). To protect themselves, military organizations traditionally try to gather as much knowledge as they can in advance or to acquire such forces or weapons that nearly all surprises thrown at them are unlikely to succeed. The ancient phalanx, with its close step and overlapping overhead shields, is a method of restricting the possible outcomes in battle. While moving forward, the uniform strict phalanx rules made the unit nearly impossible to break unless the shields could be made to drop by the sheer weight of the opposing phalanx or its long spears leveled straight in through the shield barriers. Thus the phalanx was a way to control the possibility of soldiers dropping their shields and running.

The second organizational constant is that organizations will constantly try to weaken or work around their constraints after having moved against the contingencies (Thompson 1967). A well-trained enemy phalanx becomes a constraint for the opposition, one best weakened by besieging the camp, surprising through trickery or betrayal in the night, or attacking on the march. Knowing that, capable Roman officers in particular always had a wide array of scouts and spies moving ahead of and parallel to the main columns of forces (Russell 1999).

What the organization knows from study or experience normally drives how it prepares for surprise. Each organization has an underlying guiding theory — an internalized image and the channeling deep institutions — about what is important to know to protect one's institution (G. Morgan 2006; Fountain 2001). If that understanding is too narrow, limited, or biased, then bad outcomes that could have been known in advance can nonetheless travel along the otherwise ignored information channels to become catastrophic surprises (Steinbruner 2002). For example, if one thinks that only the deliberate use of long-range weapons, nuclear arsenals, or deployed mechanized armies can hurt the nation in important ways, then one does not collect information on or prepare strategies for dealing with accidents, biological threats, massive currency fraud, or even hostile social movements with air travel access into the nation (Sagan 2004). The critical societal systems of westernized states are at exceptional risk without agreement, data, and corrected interpretations in national security strategies, decision making, and action organizations. Without these processes intact and operating robustly, cybered surprises are simply more likely to be successful and brutally disabling with the further intensity of globalization.

A security resilience strategy rests on an institutionalized and long-term comprehensive and consistent knowledge development. The need to collectively consult routinely is already recognized in most westernized nations, although its implementation varies widely in its formality, breadth of purview, and apparent effectiveness. Required is some institutionalized form of a *knowledge nexus* to support the collective social and technical consultation requirements of all national-level security communities playing a role in devising and implementing any national-level strategy. In the modern state, the key communities across the levels of society include the normally insular domains of intelligence, police, and military agencies. To date, a number of nations are nominally encouraging such interagency consultations, but the results so far have had limited successes, especially in incorporating all three domains of police, military, and intelligence (Demchak and Werner 2007a).

Effective security resilience strategy requires more, however, than a mere well-intentioned effort to share. Without sufficiently broad inputs of usable information on potentially violent threats and also the ability to creatively refine the data into guidance, the intention will fail to produce effective strategies. But both are hard to do. Democracies are especially difficult places to collect mass amounts of data if the citizens feel the collection itself is threatening. The section on *behavior-based privacy* addresses the paradox of needing data on the behavior of all citizens in order to filter for emerging bad-actor violence and yet being unable today to protect those individuals from abuse or seemingly irremediable error. Both national and domestic security agencies struggle with the ability of bad actors' activities to blend in. Finding the bad actor requires knowing something about all residents to sort out innocent civilians in a way to protect privacy as well. A behavior-based privacy offers this compromise (Demchak and Fenstermacher 2004).

Finally, a third institutional adaptation is ensuring a full picture wisely interpreted and continuously updated and tested. Even if the data is provided by behavior-based privacy and by consensual sharing across national and domestic policymakers, however, successful diminution of a security threat depends on knowledge development processes structured inside and linked across security institutions. For this requirement, the Atrium Organizational Model offers a means of continuously integrating and developing tacit knowledge across social and virtual levels. Needed to massage the mass of data that has to be interchanged throughout the various systems and agencies responsible for security, this proposed socio-technical structure builds on existing institutional forms but is specifically designed for meeting surprising chronic threats. It is the final of the essential components underlying the effective development of a national strategy of disruption and resilience discussed in chapter 4.

Fortunately the adaptations are reasonable and feasible even in the near term. Several exist in embryonic or isolated forms across the national security structures of westernized nations from the various central homeland security organizations to the councils of advisers to prime ministers to intelligence and police agencies. One way to measure reasonableness of proposals is to compare the functions proposed with history. If these institutional adaptations can provide the knowledge needed for the surprises of a cybered world, then similar structures would have provided better outcomes in roughly similar circumstances in the past. That is, one may reread history for natural experiments in preparedness for the surprises demonstrated by city-states aiming to disrupt surprises from attackers. The goal of the next chapter is to establish how leaders instinctively implemented elements of a security resilience strategy in order to achieve security resilience in their eras.

CHAPTER TWO

History's Experiments in Security Resilience

History does not offer directly equivalent examples of the open-cybered world. If all those appropriate, legal, and sensible institutional responses to multifaceted surprise were in place and nurtured properly, one can argue that a given set of allied city-states would be at about the best place one can be to disrupt and be resilient against threats to tightly linked critical systems inside their respective borders. This discussion seeks to show the reasonableness of a security resilience strategy by rereading historical case studies. The intent is to see to what extent successful and unsuccessful leaders instinctively employed elements of a security resilience strategy in small wars among city-states. The focus is on disruption because these histories concern wartime leaders who for reasons of preference or constraint could not engage in destruction of enemies. Resilience in those eras meant survival, but often at levels that would be unacceptable for modern leaders. In this historical review, resilience is considered in the discussion apart from disruption only to the extent that the evidence suggests exceptional efforts were made to ensure a heightened level of resilience against surprise.

CASE STUDIES OF CITY-STATE SECURITY STRATEGIES

The evidence presented from the following case studies is intended to test the broader theoretical model with the actions of history (Blatter and Blume 2008). The historical case studies are few because they must abide by the two main requirements of the modern city-state under threat. First, neither side intends to be, or is constrained from being, able to occupy the other permanently. Second, the respondent does not intend to be, or is constrained from being, able to annihilate the attacker for various reasons including international or domestic expectations and legitimacy.

The discussion of lessons to be learned from history about security in city-states under threat covers both premodern cases before the development of the telegraph changed military communications and several more modern cases. Modernity is defined by the advent of the telegraph due to its trend-changing effects in organizational control and potentially critical intelligence data for military and political leaders. The focus is on ground forces unless naval organizations are explicitly discussed. The modern cases almost always involve a larger state that is in principle equipped to annihilate an attacking organization, even occupy its territory permanently, but chooses not to do so.

Case Selection

The criteria for assessing the lessons of these historical cases arise from the four requirements of a successful security resilience strategy: flexible theory of action (and possibly surprise accommodation), honest joint consultation, comprehensive relevant data about enemies' behaviors and motivations, and collaborative actionable knowledge development such as is possible through an Atrium organization. In each case, historical hindsight gives us the outcomes by which to look at what leaders sought to know and then what they did about it. The rereading of history permits the highlighting of likely drivers of the threat (weighted legitimacy, need, and confidence) and the emphasis in strategic response across information, capital, and coercion, as well as the levels of unknowns that were or were not accommodated by the leader's actions.

Selective bias is virtually unavoidable in military history simply because the number of nations tends to determine the number of militaries. Wars also tend to come singly and sequentially, making absolutely contemporaneous comparisons exceptionally difficult. This work uses exemplar cases from the era to indicate the best (or worst) practices of the era. The selection of cases is also driven by the likelihood of sufficient evidence of what might be motivating the threat organizations and what might be known by the responding organizations. The further back in history one looks, the less data at this level of detail is available. Lessons of previous ages mostly are to establish the long-term applicability of a weighted theory of action and the critical role of employing knowledge correctly over time to chronic threats. To a lesser extent, the lessons also allow consideration of the theory of surprise accommodation and are so noted where relevant.

Method

Grounded theory is particularly suited for this kind of combinatorial research. One has a framework, that is, a structure of how the world works, and then one explores the available data to see what emerges to force refinements. In this work, inspecting the case studies helps confirm that such an approach is not ahistorical and that the elements of such a strategy (especially the emphasis on disruption over destruction) have been logically necessary to success in other eras (Glaser 2001). The method is to contrast and compare the cases, first assessing for each case the particular correlation between the drivers, the strategic response in disruption (and resilience if present), and the outcome. Then the extent to which the elements of a successful security resilience strategy were or were not present is interpreted from the correlation in a counterfactual technique.[1] In particular, I look at the ebb and flow of conflict before and during the strategy's application period. The analysis posits that the elements of a disruption-led security resilience strategy would have provided success and asks to what extent it was present in the unwitting efforts of the contemporary defenders.

A decade is the marker for the start of a disruption strategy period. By and large, if a disruptive strategy is to work, ten years is historically sufficient to significantly change the trends in manageable social systems. It is half a traditional twenty-year generation. Its midpoint is well within the memories of elders present at the outset. The end of the decade is likely to see a whole crop of newly risen midlevel leaders raised with the decade-long realities of a response to a chronic violent threat.

In systematic qualitative analysis, it is essential to say why one has chosen

---

1. The counterfactual technique is a form of qualitative sensitivity analysis. The method involves altering key elements of a known sequence of events and following through the most likely outcomes of the new sequence (Maldonado 2002). This method assembles as much of the known process as possible to know, assumes some confounding variables and yet attempts to show both qualitatively and quantitatively that X event could not have happened unless Y occurred first (Pearl 1999).

the questions employed in analysis (Strauss and Corbin 1998). The preceding material postulates that the combination of a theory of action and a theory of surprise accommodation with the three institutional adaptations would produce better outcomes in disrupting chronic violent threats and in being resilient to surprises to critical systems. Hence, for these cases, the analytical questions address the presence and efficacy of equivalent elements for a security resilience strategy. That is, is there evidence of some sort of theory of action (and of surprise accommodation), joint honest consultation of key actors, comprehensive knowledge gathering, and then rapid, collective, and applied knowledge refinement in operations? Table 1 lists the questions used to extract the lessons from the historical case studies. Column one lists the question as a heading. Column two elaborates on what is sought in the historical evidence.

GREEK AND ITALIAN CITY-STATE WARS OF DISRUPTION

For the purpose of having historical cases with elements most like the modern threat-respondent circumstances, the history of war is not convenient. Wars intended to physically eliminate the enemy are not appropriate for a disruption strategy analysis. However, two kinds of wars do present some lessons. This first set of case studies addresses peer city-states responding to attacks from another city-state. The different outcomes were strongly influenced by the varied degrees of understanding of the attacker's motivations and surprise capabilities, of honest consultation, of comprehensive data collection, and of knowledge development before and during the conflicts.

Greek City-State (Second Peloponnesian) Archidamian War (431–421 BCE)

In principle, Sparta was the aggressor nation and Athens the attacked responding nation over the ten-year period 431–421 BCE. Sparta and Athens were long-time competitors, but in previous eras they were only two among a jumble of constantly warring peninsular and island-based Greek city-states. The period chosen is an example of a city-state using elements of what could be seen as a premodern disruption-led security resilience in the first ten years of the Second Peloponnesian War, the so-called Archidamian War of 431–421 BCE.

Table 1 Querying History for Evidence of Disruption (and Resilience)
Strategic Choices

Did the strategic response to the threat succeed in long-term disruption or in accommodating surprise by correctly and strategically mirroring the attack motivation profile; and if possible to discern, did the response also prove resilient to systemic surprises?

Evidence of a Theory of Action or Surprise Accommodation	To what extent did leaders seem to have a weighted framework of their options to disrupt the violence of an enemy organization? To what extent did the same leaders demonstrate anticipation of surprise and deliberately seek redundancy, slack, trial and error, and double-loop learning into their home system?
Evidence of Honest Consultation	To what extent did key actors across military and civilian communities consult before, during, and after the conflict on the issues relevant to the violent threat?
Evidence of Comprehensive Data	To what extent did leaders seek before, during, and after the conflict the necessary comprehensive relevant data on the contemporary attributes of the enemy and the origins of the threat posed?
Evidence of Collaborative Actionable Knowledge Development	To what extent did learning before, during, and after the conflict incorporate sought or emergent data in operations to disrupt the threatening violence?

This period was named by contemporary observers for the aging Spartan king who began the war and died early on in 427 BCE. During this period, Athens attempted to stop Spartan assaults and intrigues by making them costly in the homeland of Sparta while avoiding pitched land battles, a Spartan advantage. The two enemies eventually ended the period by negotiating a peace treaty in 421 BCE that kept the Spartans out of the farmlands around Athens for almost a decade (to BCE 413). However, as the strategic application of disruption was not well matched to the Spartan action profiles, the "peace" simply displaced rather than disrupted many other proxy battles (Freeman 2000).

Athens when led by Pericles demonstrated an ability to understand, disrupt, and, under normal circumstances, be resilient to the chronic attacks led by Sparta, especially in the first ten years after Spartan-led attack in 431 BCE. Unfortunately for Athens, the disruption was not long term. The Athenian response led by Pericles was aimed primarily at Sparta's poverty in manpower, secondarily at its confidence in being able to win on a battlefield, and only lastly on the legitimacy motivator. The Spartan violence equation, in contrast, was led by its exaggerated sense of its own legitimacy, then by its confidence, and finally by its need for rapid wars using fewer soldiers. The mismatch in disruption strategy to the violence equation of the threat was worsened over time by the rise of young, arrogant Athenian leaders. They increasingly embraced a rather incoherent and radical democratization ideology as the key to peace and prosperity in the future (Connor 1992). They and the fickle, emotional Athenian assembly led the city to unwise refusals to negotiate peace with Sparta. The operational results were disastrous democratizing expeditions far from a focus on the main threat in Sparta and its allies (Sinclair 1988).

The chronic threat by Sparta was consistent for the era. What is called the First Peloponnesian War of 461–446 BCE was a confused, multistate, fifteen-year melee of many states. Battles were staged, more or less, as a handful of briefly allied democracies or semidemocracies on one side met to battle a handful of ephemerally friendly oligarchies or former democracies on the other. The war season was fall, not spring and summer, in order to "ravage" the opposing town by burning down its food crop just as it was ready for gathering. If the rampage did not enrage the city's defenders to march out and face the attackers, then a siege of relatively short duration ensued. If a town held out even though starving by then, the attackers marched off, feeling at least satisfied at the distress they had caused to their enemy (for the moment). If they did get the defenders and their allies to meet them on a plain, each side formed a line of eight-by-eight-man square phalanxes, and armed with heavy shields and spears, the farmer-citizen-hoplite soldiers lumbered en masse at each other in slow arcs led by the right side. The spears were not very sharp, and it was hard to get past the shields. The impact literally broke the will of one or another phalanx, and the melee that ensued was bloody but not as fantastically lethal as later irregular wars would prove (Adcock 1957).

Up through the early days of the Second Peloponnesian War, there were rules of engagement in conflict that were largely observed. City-states could be subjugated and forced to pay tribute, recompense, or land, but they were rarely razed or annihilated. Before a battle, civilians were offered the chance of leaving all their goods behind but departing safely. If they refused, all bets were off, and losers were enslaved. But executing all the males en masse was not normal prior to this war. Traditional battle had rules as well. Fleeing soldiers were not pursued and murdered from behind. Wounded were permitted to be collected for treatment; dead bodies were returned for soldiers' funerals, though their expensive armor often was not. Navies had rules as well. Athenian citizens expected their triumphant triremes to bring home the bodies of Athenian citizen rowers if possible. The Athenian assembly greatly punished admirals who allegedly left rowers behind. Beyond the rules, wars consisted of poking, stabbing, and slashing however one could with seventy pounds of armor in the close quarters of a hot fall battle plain. Sometimes the phalanxes would be blinded by dust and end up stabbing their own forces in other phalanxes (V. D. Hanson 2005).

Information collection also had its protocols and its season. Elite prisoners could be questioned and held for ransom, but not executed unless some particular reason was offered to justify this deviation. Diplomats were given protection and immunity; couriers were divested of their documents but not killed. Spies could always be killed, but they were not continuous intelligence sources. Most city-state leaders waited until the onset of the war season to get serious about information collection on probable attackers and their routes. Land armies took some time to march out, and so only immediate neighbors needed early warning of armies on the move. If one were not the marching city-state's immediate neighbor, one tended to wait for the urgent plea for help from that or other neighbors for an indication of a threatening march and its likely target (Russell 1999).

After a peace treaty was signed in 446 BCE meant to last for thirty years, Athenian command of the trade routes and access to wealth from the east all around the Aegean Sea led Athens in particular to prosper fantastically. This was the Athenian Golden Age led in large part by the governance of Pericles (or Perikles) under whose guidance massive public funds were expended in major civic monuments and, importantly, in infrastructure. In particular, he built the long wall that ensured Athens access to its seaports even if under attack from the land. Athens grew to a hegemon. Its wealth was admired widely, as well as envied and feared.

Athens ended up with a loose collection of allied states sometimes called an empire because Athenian triremes were wont to visit if an allied state decided to change sides.[2] Athens planted colonies around the Aegean Sea to provide some protection for its trade routes and a weak form of intelligence collection against threats. Importantly, these colonies were a resilience measure to relieve population pressures in Athens and grow friendly future city-states around key Athenian trade routes. The poorer citizens of the burgeoning, cramped main city were offered land in new locations and yet could keep their highly valued citizenship as Athenians. As such they could call upon the loyalty of Athens for protection when needed, as often enough it was. And Athens had a neighborhood of coastal states to provide certainty in the form of goods, greater trade route protection, and the possibly critical information of spies (Freeman 2000).

The peace treaty of 446 BCE stood for just fifteen years rather than the thirty negotiated. During those years, larger oligarchic Corinth, a closer neighbor to Athens than Sparta and a would-be naval competitor, was resolutely a bitter enemy of Athens. It was unable to win against the Athenian Navy. Fearing the growing wealth of Athens, Corinth wanted a fight on land with Sparta's invincible might defeating Athens, and Corinth slipping around to finish off the Athenian Navy once the city was taken. Corinth had spent the fifteen years of peace constantly arguing to the Spartans that as Athens became more rich and powerful, Sparta would be more irrelevant to the wider Greek universe. Corinth frequently urged the Spartans to break the peace treaty of 446 BCE.

The grayer heads in Sparta did want the support of the only naval power of

2. Switching sides usually produced punitive raids and even regime change forced onto local oligarchs. Athenian triremes with their marines sailing into a port were feared by local oligarchs and welcomed by the poor. Many oligarchs found themselves under stress from their own poor to become more democratic and, by definition, more pro-Athenian (Rich and Shipley 1995).

any note apart from Athens, yet only after considerable pushing by Corinth did the Spartans vote to fight in fall 432 BCE. It took even more effort to get them to actually move the following year. For six months the Spartans sparred with Athens through envoys while their Theban ally besieged the small Athenian city of Plataea. In the end, only the fear of losing honor after loudly rattling sabers at Athens and of having to apologize for their Theban ally's unacceptable violence propelled King Achidamus to actually leave the barracks (V. D. Hanson 2005). Sparta broke the truce for real in summer 431 BCE and precipitated the Archidamian War.

Unfortunately for Athens, an unknowable rogue outcome struck Athens, changing eventually the course of Greek civilization. Pericles and the city-state's huge population were crammed into Athens for protection from the annual Spartan attack during the hot, fall war season. With origins and nature still under dispute today, a strange, massively powerful plague arrived from Africa. It was extremely virulent; the effects cascaded through Athens and its allies. The virus spread for the next few years wherever Athenians including sailors went, but only if the recipient location was also crowded (Cunha 2004).

Within a year, Athens lost to this and related diseases between 25 to 30 percent of its soldiers, sailors, wives, children, and servants. The societal loss in social capital in both knowledge and demographic growth was massive (Smallman-Raynor and Cliff 2004). None of these communities were large. Pericles and most of his family died. Losing so many so suddenly ripped society's expectations apart, undermined the willingness to sacrifice for civic virtue, and lowered the expectations of survival. Contemporary observers noted that many survivors, especially young new leaders, no longer believed in building infrastructure for the future since at any time the plague could return to wipe out the rest of their family, fortune, and prospects (Thucydides [431–404 BCE] 2006). The city's defense forces (ships, navy, professional solders) did not recover for well over a decade (V. D. Hanson 2005).

Athens was on its knees, and only Sparta's lack of good information saved the city from a worse fate. Nonetheless Sparta appeared not to know how to respond to this opportunity. Just as the Spartans came back for the second fall of the war, again trying to burn their way across Attica to Athens, they saw the massive funeral pyre smoke. They did not exploit the evident weakness of Athens. Spartan leaders simply assiduously avoided attacking areas including Athens that had a good chance of having the plague.

Sparta's action equation and its ability to impose cascading surprise on

Athens were led by legitimacy, followed by confidence. Both mattered more than need in the chronic attacks on Athens and its allies. Rhetorical pomposity, occasional bold rashness, and calculating cravenness combined to characterize Sparta as both a threat and an ally during the 400s and 300s BCE. Surrounded by unhappy, indentured, ethnically different, and much larger populations, Sparta's small citizen elite ruled an increasingly poorer, agrarian, serf-supported, conservative, and militaristic city-state. Sparta depended for survival on its reputation for never losing in a fight and never allowing a rebellion to succeed. As Athens expanded, democracies began to emerge from the oligarchies that had been, in a pinch, friendlier to Sparta than Athens. The Athenian Navy with its expensive fleet of triremes made sure any individual loss of a potential Spartan ally was nearly permanent (V. D. Hanson 2005).

Legitimacy as a warrior was everything for which the Spartan elite male lived and, if possible, gloriously died. For Sparta, its most prized item was its personal and widely self-promoted image of the incorruptibility and invincibility of its warrior class. It was unthinkable that a Spartan would ever surrender, especially to an effeminate Athenian (Cartledge 2003). Athenian persuasion of island oligarchs away from the Spartan sphere, thus ringing Sparta with democracies, was an affront. More than a hegemonic power challenge, it challenged Sparta's claim to importance, relevance, and automatic respect as soldiers (V. D. Hanson 2005).

The looming specter of slow attrition to poverty for Sparta suggests need could easily have been the greatest driver, as it might be in a more modern or less parochially insular city-state. Nonetheless Sparta resisted breaking the original thirty-year truce for some time. While poorer, it was indeed not destitute. Furthermore, the odd and viciously enforced Spartan notion of civic virtue made envious comparisons to Athenian wealth dishonorable to discuss. For the elite, the greatest shortage was their own numbers. They knew they were few, but the solution indicating a recognized sense of resilience — that is, stay home more from wars or ten months per year of military training in order to have more babies — was never pursued. They could and did have babies out of wedlock that were adopted into the elite families, but there was always some question associated with their true Spartan lineage, even if they were generals like Lysander (Cartledge 2003).

In late 424 BCE, planning to attack an Athenian outpost but fearing the Athenian Navy, Spartan military leaders decided to build a garrison on a small neighboring island. They thought to use the small Spartan fleet operating out of this island to cut off a nearby port the Athenians had recently built on the coast of Spartan territory. Instead, the Athenian Navy returned, drove off the Spartan fleet, and landed troops to clear off the Spartan garrison. The attacking Athenian admirals inadvertently burned down brush cover and then saw the vulnerabilities of the hastily constructed fort containing 400 or so Spartan warriors and attendants. After the Athenian marines attacked, the 120 Spartan warriors who survived included some of Sparta's most esteemed elite warriors. They surrendered, an unthinkable act for Spartans, violating their cult of invincibility and the reputation and honor of the entire nation (V. D. Hanson 2005; Cartledge 2003). To lose one's honor destroyed one's reputation as a warrior entitled to legitimately use violence.

This fixation on honor to justify violence played a central role in Spartan notions of survival. The evidence for the strength of this driver is the Spartan leadership's response to the possibility of having these 120 captured elite Spartan hoplites taken to Athens and executed. Spartans at home reeled in horror and followed the act of surrender with an equally unthinkable, but telling, decision. They chose to unilaterally stop annually directly attacking Athenian farmlands (Attica). They eventually left the captured hostages in Athens for ten years and during that period did not invade the Attica farmlands surrounding Athens. Nor did Sparta further attack the small outpost at Pylos that began this battle (V. D. Hanson 2005). Only when the captured Spartans were returned in 413 BCE after an Athenian disaster in Sicily did Sparta resume its marches on Attica (Cartledge 2003).

The evidence in the field of Spartan confidence to match their self-image suggests it was at best a secondary driver. Confidence as a driver was always present in the Spartan internal and external dialogue. For all that the Spartans were convinced they could not be beaten in battle, however, they also were extremely sensitive to making sure they were always seen to win. If there was a serious chance of losing, the Spartan kings and councils often hesitated to deploy their soldiers. Hence, Sparta would aperiodically show inexplicable lapses during which they would simply not show up in time for a major fight. For all their presumed confidence, the Spartans would on and off again wait to see how the battle would go before joining. Potential Spartan allies would often learn that relying on Sparta to save them in a tough spot with Athens was unrealistic, though they did ask (Whitby 2002).

At times Spartan governing councils tried to inveigle the neighboring large Persian empire into supporting them with skills, ships, or interventions against the Athenians. At the outset of the Second Peloponnesian War, for example, Sparta was the aggressor but not as a hothead just waiting to break the Athenian dominance by force. Rather, it was by the beginning of this war a garrison state closer to a police force, able to muster perhaps four thousand true Spartans or "Peers" while keeping tens of thousands of lesser-status males from the surrounding ethnic groups or "Helots" in bondage and humiliation (Cartledge 2003). Toward the end of the period, like so many other societies under simultaneous demographic and war stress, Sparta began freeing select slaves contingent on their serving as loyal soldiers. The goal was to boost failing numbers of proper Spartan warriors (Brown and Morgan 2006). As a motivator of violent acts, this city-state's confidence had strong limitations in reality, if not in rhetoric.

The way the war began in 431 BCE provides further evidence that legitimacy was a greater motivator than confidence for Sparta. With the exception of some generals like Brasidas, who was considered more of a useful thug in Sparta itself (killed at the battle of Amphipolis 422 BCE), Sparta's collective confidence tended to crack and repair slowly from a major defeat, more like a schoolyard bully than a strategic thinker (Cartledge 2003). It would withdraw to be more cautious the next time, a fact the rest of the Greek world knew and tried to use. Sparta could be goaded or goad itself into reckless wars, but it often preferred to have big friends and a sure thing before marching. Its history was littered with intermittent dallying with the Persians in order to gain advantage in the Greek homelands, especially over Athens.

Pericles, the Athenian leader at the outset of the war, almost certainly had an instinctive command of both disruption and resilience. His actions suggest he had a particularly strong understanding of the differing motivations of the Spartan leaders. He clearly weighted the motivations of the Spartan threats and the form if not frequency of an attack. He deliberately responded with a knowledge-oriented set of practices that both increased the resilience of his city and the likelihood of driving off the Spartans from sheer frustration. Due to spies and scouts maintained by the Periclean defense plans, Athenians usually had advance knowledge a few days before an attack. Protecting property was rehearsed in advance so rural farmers knew what to do when attacks came. Pericles knew, as the Spartans apparently did not, that Attica surrounding Athens was nearly the largest farmland belt around any of the city-states, almost a thousand square miles of highly redundant food stocks. With even half of these cultivated into vineyards and orchards, ravaging Athenian foods stocks by cutting or burning would take years and still not hurt Athens. This enormous resource base meant Athens did not have to meet the Spartan hoplite forces mano-a-mano in the time and place of Sparta's choosing (E. E. Cohen 1992). Archidamus's normal attack plan focused on areas with more traditionally high-value targets as a way to provoke Athens, not harm it. That meant that the Athenian cavalry could focus on harrying and killing ravagers in those areas, not on having to cover the entire thousand square miles (Spence 1990).

In terms of elements of disruption efforts, Pericles clearly emphasized some Spartan motivations over others in his strategic response. In particular, he used Athenian advantages in capital against the well-known Spartan shortage in numbers of elite warriors. Sparta could not simultaneously defend its homeland and successfully attack Athens. Spartan attacks were meant to ravage quickly and force the Athenians to come out to fight a ground war rapidly. The goal was to win before the traditional revenge attacks of the Athenian Navy on the Spartan rear could force the Spartan army to rush home to avoid losing honor in defeat at home.

In terms of resilience, Pericles planned for a short war season. His plans were predicated on a temporary housing of the massive rural population inside the city for a month or less. There would be enough food. While it would be upsetting and disruptive to have Attica farmland burned around the city, it would not be possible to burn that much in one season (Foxhall 1995). Furthermore, the city could use its well-constructed long wall to the port and then trading ships to supplement in the case of shortages. So Pericles set about making the attackers' ravaging even more risky with the cavalry, waiting out the season with rural populations inside the city and also using the Athenian Navy to provoke attacks near the Spartan homeland to make Archidamus break off the attack and rush home (Spence 1990).

Honest consultations on any systematic scale about security threats long before the threat is imminent and by any leader among other peer leaders are not evident in the various sources on ancient Greek city-states in this period. In so intense a political environment as majority-rule-led Athens, revealing too much in order to consult might have been political and literal suicide. Having a successful disruptive strategy for the threat, but not a 24/7 political strategy for dealing with the histrionics of the Athenian assembly, meant personal disaster at home for all Athenian generals or admirals. During the war, no Athenian general or admiral — successful or not — escaped being demoted, reprimanded, or sometimes executed due to often farcical allegations or the mass persuasiveness of those simply envious. With no judiciary or any individual civil rights, a demagogic attack could turn the majority of the assembly against a general, admiral, or even a military success in minutes, with disastrous results.[3] One leader in particular, the orphaned nephew of Pericles, Alcibiades, successfully managed his political survival, as well as impressive command of the navy, and yet was exiled twice by the assembly (Forde 1989).

Pericles, one of the senior leaders for thirty years before his death from plague in 430 BCE, had a remarkable ability to sway the senior Athenians to convene the assembly — or not — on his schedule. As a result, up to and through the start of the Achidamian War, Pericles successfully imposed his disruption and resilience elements of strategy against Spartan attacks by essentially not consulting. He avoided the fractious, emotional, and often irrational moblike decisions of the assembly that might have countermanded his decisions (V. D. Hanson 2005).

By contrast, after Pericles' death early in 430 BCE amid the devastating plagues of 430–429 BCE, arrogant younger leaders were good orators but not able to see the value of a well-targeted strategy of both disruption and resilience. Rather, their consultation appeared to stoke an intense desire to eliminate Spartan and other oligarchic pretentions in the region. Indeed, just as Athens returned to levels of prosperity approaching its pre-plague heights and endured more than ten years of small wars all over the Greek territories, these leaders embraced an even more radical desire to spread democracy by force in dramatic expeditions. There is little evidence of a solid, experience-led, weighted assessment of the likelihood of succeeding in the large and disastrous naval expeditions sent well beyond Sparta into Sicily during this period. Rather, nationalist slogans drove not only the initial decisions but also the bitter recriminations afterward. At the end of the day, the mostly failed realpolitiklike forays would empty the treasury in recurring disasters (Pritchard 2007).

After the loss of Pericles, comprehensive data collection on Sparta by Athenians was episodic at best. The city normally had patchy preparations for

---

3. This uncertainty was the reason the urban wealthy in most cities outside of Athens leaned toward oligarchy for fear of the mob, and the poor loved democracy. It was why all Athenian admirals and generals were politicians from the outset and throughout their tenure. The difficulty of this kind of mass township rule was also why other city-states went in and out of democracy as power centers migrated among prominent clans, developing something called semidemocracy (Hanson 2005).

war, especially after the loss of Pericles (Freeman 2000). Traumatized by the plague, the surviving Athenian majority-ruled assembly did not demonstrate any support for a system of protective information collection either on Sparta or on their own vulnerabilities (Van Doren 1991). At the time Greek culture as a whole did not engage in full-time surveillance of possible enemies or sources of disabling surprise (Russell 1999). Pericles was unique as a leader across the Greek world because he did both.

In general, collecting information on other states, allies or enemies alike, was not pursued by the city-states in peacetime. Greek intercity warfare is filled with many surprise attacks as peacetime cities do not see the threat coming at them until too late. This casualness was somewhat understandable in that constant collection, continuous invasion route surveillance, reliable home guards, and disaster preparations were as expensive then as they are today (Russell 1999). Many states would not see anything like an attack for five years at a stretch. Even then, the attack might come not because the city was of interest but rather because the attacker could not take on its first choice. This is what happened to the small town of Plataea that became the object of extreme Spartan ire when the plague in Athens made a second season of ravaging too risky (V. D. Hanson 2005). Furthermore, in the traditional warfare, one side won and the other side died or ran away. Right after a victory, no enemy was normally left to pose any threat. It was easy to drop intense support of the scout and surveillance networks after the victory, and hard to put them back together if no threat was imminent (Russell 1999).

Spartan parochialism may have gotten in the way of its data collection, but Athenian hubris routinely interfered in its responder's data accumulation. For example, knowing that the tiny Spartan elite sat atop a massive population of servants who were said to be willing to eat their masters raw if need be, one younger Athenian general, Demosthenes, entrepreneurially tricked the Athenian Navy en route to Sicily to detour and take the small port of Pylos on the Spartan headland in 425 BCE. He also sweet-talked the marines into building a garrison and kept a few hundred defenders with him as the navy then sailed away. The goal was to provide a magnet for the escaping thousands of downtrodden Helots, thereby sparking hope and general insurrection at the bottom of Spartan society. He hoped to cause endless trouble for — and the eventual collapse of — the complex Spartan hierarchy (Strassler 1990). The only problem was that critical information suggesting how unlikely this scenario would be was not sought. Pylos survived as a thorn in Sparta's side for about seventeen years but never achieved the intended goal of sparking revolts (Wylie 1993).

Collaborative actionable knowledge development in Athens occurred only initially and under the tutelage of Pericles. By the outbreak of the war, Pericles had ensured that Athens did not need its own farmlands to feed its people any longer, and all the rural folk knew what to do if surprised by military attacks. Greek warring states in general, however, learned on the job, battle by battle, enemy by enemy. At the outset, the Spartans were slow in grasping the difference between this war and all previous wars, especially with regard to the resources of Athens. Spartan generals had no understanding of the capabilities of a powerful seaport trading nation. In this case, Sparta also found itself surprised by the vast expanses of newly founded Athenian vineyards, orchards, and other massive impediments to an army on the move (Platias 2002). The attack slowed to a crawl for the first season, proving Pericles correct that the indirect response would deflect them (V. D. Hanson 2005).

However, none of the younger and postplague Athenian leaders demonstrated any evolution in their understanding of Spartan motivations for these recurring attacks, even after the experience of capturing the 120 Spartan warriors. Had the Athenians developed that information accurately, more Athenian resources would have been directed to capturing other such hostages, and those captured would never have been returned. The lack of ability to learn from this war eventually led to the loss of the set-piece certainty and the destructive, fragmenting rise of the nonprofessional irregular soldier in all Greek city-state armies.

Medieval Italian City-States: Florence and Milan, 1423–1433

During the period 1423–33, the democratic trading city-state of Florence faced chronic violent threats from one of the five major Italian city-states: Milan under Duke Filippo-Maria Visconti. Florence's preferred and consistent security resilience strategy always began with disruption based on capital and legitimacy-related concessions. Over the period, neither this strategic emphasis nor resilience saved Florence, only luck. Not particularly attentive to threats strategically, Florentine leaders managed usually to simply delay anticipated attacks on Florence while the city-state's highly political debates and chosen leaders tried to figure out what it would cost to change the behavior of the threatening individual. Usually only when the threat was at the borders of Tuscany, the region surrounding Florence, did the guild leaders of Florence move to consider coercion, and only if the former options overwhelmingly seemed likely to fail shortly (Fratianni and Spinelli 2006).

In routinely mistaking the conflict motivations of Milan to be amenable to bribes, Florence acted consistently with its era. Conflict among neighboring Italian city-states in the 1400s usually featured temporary alliances, betrayals, and murders similar to the Greek city-states. Like the "war season" of ancient Greece, "wars" in this era were slow-moving, drawn-out campaigns with short, nearly bloodless battles. Actual armed conflicts were intermittent affairs more like set-piece battles between mercenary armies during the war season (not winter).[4] They ebbed and flowed throughout the years, intermixed with much more interesting episodes of sieges, treaty negotiations, false assurances, and much treaty violating.[5] Often opposing commanders, all mercenary professionals with their own companies of soldiers, would suddenly withdraw if they thought their side would lose, the fight would be too costly to their hired soldiers, or they would achieve more pay from their employer by delaying the end of the conflict.[6] In any given conflict, the two mercenary captains and their armies might oppose each other from one campaign season

4. In the modern era, campaigns are parts of wars, but in the era of marching on foot a war could be decided by the army who in one campaign simply kept going. In the discussion for this case, unless a distinction matters, the terms will be used interchangeably.

5. On the other hand, while battles themselves were relatively bloodless, the pillaging of a losing city or citadel afterward was not so kind to its citizens. The prospect of being unleashed to forage, rape, and destroy at will in someone else's city was the true pay bonus keeping mercenary troops in the employ of their captains. Furthermore, prisoners were more useful (for ransom) than deaths of soldiers (Denison 1913). Even lower classes could be extorted for the return of their sons. For example, one study of the petitions from the rural areas after the first duke's rampages on Tuscan territory show a number of requests for financial help to families who had been impoverished in ransoming their prisoners taken either as soldiers or as abducted civilians (Cohn 1999).

6. One famous battle at Zagonara described by Machiavelli in his *Florentine History* is a good example of the relative bloodlessness of these mercenary-led campaigns. "In this *great defeat*, famous throughout all Italy, no death occurred except those of Lodovico degli Obizi and two of his people, who having fallen from their horses were drowned in the morass" (Machiavelli 1906; emphasis added).

to the next, with each having switched employers in the interim (Dupuy and Dupuy 1970).[7]

Florentines and other non-autocratic city-states particularly preferred to pay instead of fight. Their leaders routinely assumed there would always be slack time to buy one's way out of an attack. The use of mercenaries made war expensive both in pay and in the sudden transfer of loyalties. In the midst of what promised to be a major battle, opponents schemed deceptively to pay for results without actual battle (Dupuy and Dupuy 1970). The intrigues and campaigns of the first half of the 1400s in Italy are so numerous and irrelevant that most military and political histories of the period simply call the conflicts the "wars" of Florence and Venice against Milan (Rosse 1859; Montrose 1944; Ruggiero 2005). Often the disruption and resilience efforts of a city-state only succeeded because of the self-preservation tendencies of both sides' expensive, even extorting, and almost certainly arrogant mercenary captains.[8]

Much like democratic Greeks, the Italian republic city-states faced chronic threats from autocratic and princely rulers and similarly tried to reduce the expenses of defense.[9] Democratic city-states in general routinely did not keep standing armies, especially not within city limits. Like merchants, they negotiated armies on retainer, kept far from the city, but in principle always available to be rapidly called into service as needed (Baron 1953). The Italian city-states led by chronically aggressive aristocrats would episodically show up relatively

7. In the 1300s, the princes still tended to use German mercenaries, but by the 1400s and the development of professional Italian heavy cavalry mercenary industry, nearly everyone tried to employ the more famous and successful of the captains and their private armies. The development of these mercenaries was unique and different from the chivalric revival taking place in the rest of Europe. There are a number of good discussions of this "company of adventurers" (Williams 1908; Simone de Sismondi 1847; Mallett 2003; Caferro 1996).

8. A famous late-1300s non-Italian mercenary, Walter of Montreal, led his army of seven thousand lances and two thousand crossbowmen in his "Grand Company" on a long march around Tuscany to force cities to pay him not to pillage their town (Montrose 1944). He was not alone, but the gradual professionalization of the Italian condottierri by the 1400s made defenders more able to meet such extortion with an Italian mercenary company in lieu of just money (Williams 1908).

9. These rulers included cardinals and legates who were de jure and in fact princes, willing to hire mercenaries to shed blood where they could not by papal decree. An archbishop of one town might also be a princely ruler in another, complicating the roster of friends, enemies, and wavering neutrals (Chambers 2006).

suddenly to try to seize, encircle, or strangle the major commercial city-state republics for their wealth. Fortunately, however, the autocrats no less than city republics needed to reserve their merchant classes to produce tax revenues (Mallett 2003). They also tended to keep out of their cities those warriors who could overthrow them, since every city hired from the same pool of duplicitous mercenaries (Williams 1908, 241).

By the beginning of the 1400s, battles of any note involved several or all five major city-state actors: Florence, Milan, Venice, Naples, and the pope in Rome (Papal States).[10] The five were owners, and hence protectors, of many smaller city-states. Those remaining cities that could not afford to retain their mercenaries at high prices or did not want to be taken under control, like Lucca near Florence, tried to be quietly and largely ignored, but that was rarely possible. Most cities were at one point or another of interest to someone better armed, and most were taken under ownership or into the recognized sphere of influence by one of the five large city-states.[11]

Florence, a staunch republic in the upper middle of Italy, lay in the center of productive Tuscany. It competed with Venice as the wealthiest of the five city-states and was the least likely to have territorial designs beyond access to ports (Plumb 1961).[12] Milan to the north, however, was an aristocratic city-

10. There were, of course, several very independent exceptions like Lucca as well as many small, politically irrelevant, isolated, and poor cities. Most only survived as long as an aggressor was willing to support them; otherwise they fell. Furthermore, if they played the external aggressor card too often, the city that eventually absorbed them would kill or permanently exile the families of the nobility or merchants who arranged the external support. Hence, many cities ended up trying to negotiate limited sovereignty or even ownership by the pope as a way out of being pillaged or having their elites beheaded (Williams 1908).

11. As a complicating note, small cities would sometimes cede themselves in toto to a particularly large neighbor such as France or to the pope to save themselves from conquest by a neighboring large state. It was a calculated risk that the larger state was far enough away and would not want to actually manage the city. Sometimes this worked, and other times the acquiring state resold the now helpless city to someone else. The sad tale of Pisa's ceding control to Milan via Genoa and then to France as a way to keep out of Florentine control is a good example of the riskiness of this defensive strategy (Simonde de Sismondi 1847).

12. Not always involved in the disputes with Florence were Venice and the Papal States tied to the pope. Venice to the northwest was an oligarchic, merchant-seagoing, semidemocratic republic with a number of coastal colonies around the bend of the Adriatic Sea to its east. Until the fifteenth century, Venice was more likely to fight with the Turks for those

state, a dukedom bought by the Visconti family in 1328 from Kaiser Ludwig of Bavaria. As in other autocratic Italian states, the duke was called a tyrant, meaning simply a single, unelected ruler.[13] Over the course of the 1400s, Milan under various autocrats spread out over — and was forced to withdraw from — most of the cities of the northern Lombardy plain (Gosman, MacDonald, and Vanderjagt 2005).

During the period 1398–1441, Florence defended itself against three major multiyear campaigns, first by Gian Galeazza of Milan, then King Ladislaus of Naples, and finally Gian's son, Duke Filippo-Maria Visconti of Milan.

By 1420, Filippo-Maria of Milan wanted to expand his suzerainty over neighboring and wealthier lands to the south, in part to regain lands his father had lost in a defeat to Venice and Florence twenty years earlier and in part to reach for the ultimate prize, Rome. Only Florence in Tuscany stood in his way to marching south, city by city, to own most of Italy. Prone to using tricks and then force to win, in 1420 Filippo-Maria sent emissaries and well-paid promoters to Venice to convince the Venetians of his lack of interest in regaining the cities lost after the death of his father. He then also negotiated a mutual non-interference treaty with Florence. He extensively used emissaries, flowery and sincere oaths, and covert propagandists to promote a treaty among the civic rulers of Florence. After intense internal disputes, given a recent nearly lost war with Naples, Florence decided to sign the treaty.[14] In doing so, the Florentines

---

colonies and sea trade routes than to be interested in continental Italy to the west. In the early 1400s, Venice saw opportunities to garner some useful buffer cities belonging to Milan and turned to continental wars (Plumb 1961). Naples to the far south was a hereditary city-state kingdom with continually unfolding aristocratic claims west over to Sicily as well as north to Rome and surrounding lands (Plumb 1961). While its actual holdings varied, it was a kingdom. The Papal States as a group varied by year. They were technically church holdings in the form of cities, and their surroundings were ruled by a legate assigned to each city. Sometimes the cities were given to the pope by their nominal overlord. Other times cities gave themselves to the pope as a last hope to stop imminent pillage and conquest by someone else (Chambers 2006). Under other circumstances, with a hired mercenary army, a pope would claim some neglected right and just assert his ownership to a city (Henderson 1986).

13. In cities with no hereditary rulers, this single ruler, called the *signor*, was often someone of a merchant or mercenary background who took or was given the city to own as a fiefdom (Plumb 1961).

14. Only the death of King Ladislaus by plague saved Florence eight years earlier. A similar act of disease had saved Florence and Venice against the first Duke of Milan in 1402.

abandoned any small republics lying above the demarcation line of the treaty, permitting Milan to simply take them. No other efforts were apparently made to ensure Milan's honesty (Machiavelli 1906).

Upon hearing the treaty was signed, Filippo-Maria Visconti immediately took neighboring cities. In particular, he advanced on the port city-state of Genoa, part of the several critical sea outlets that Florence, an inland city-state, needed to maintain its commerce. Milan used both threat and propaganda to persuade the citizens of Genoa to give up their republic to him. Trying not to void the treaty but also to give the Genovese civic leaders the resources to resist Milan's army, in 1421 Florence suddenly bought the port of Leghorn from Genoa. But Genoa fell anyway in 1422, and the duke then turned to owning the land corridor between Venice and Florence, the region of Romagna (Baron 1953). Filippo-Maria needed to avoid another Florence-Venice alliance such as the one that had defeated his father's forces when the plague struck. If he could control Romagna, he would be able to move south without directly threatening either merchant city-state and formally violating the treaty with Florence or the assurances given Venice. Filippo-Maria used a trick playing off the obsession with contracts of both Florence and Venice. Many of the Romagna cities had given themselves (or were given) to the control of the pope as a way to avoid takeover efforts. In 1422 in response to an appeal by one of three popes, the one actually in Rome, Filippo-Maria marched into Romagna to "help" recover some papal control of a city. While in the area, however, he declared that a recently dying signor of a Romagna city halfway between Venice and Florence had a deathbed request for the duke of Milan to "tutor" the signor's infant son, and in 1423 Filippo Maria's mercenary commander crossed the line of demarcation to take the small city-state for Milan (Simonde de Sismondi 1847).

By the end of 1423, the fractious guilds of Florence finally had a majority of voting citizens who accepted that Visconti Filippo-Maria had violated the treaty and furthermore threatened not only Florence but all of Italy. Florence finally decided that only force of arms would stop the threat and voted to go to war. It took a great deal of oratory and behind-the-scenes arranging to finally achieve the vote to hire the mercenaries needed (Simonde de Sismondi 1847).

Those arguing for the treaty in 1420 noted, however, that twice before Florence had been saved by disease, and many had begun to believe it more than coincidental (Machiavelli 1906).

The early battles were disasters due to not only poor leadership but also logistics and betrayal (Denison 1913). In February 1425, Florence lost its best army yet, composed of four of the best *condottierri* available in Italy. One actually died in battle, and the other three were captured by Milan. A new, desperately raised Florentine army checked the advance of Milan, but Florence later was decisively defeated at Altopascio in 1425 (Kohn 1986, 264). In his castle in Milan in the summer of 1425 Filippo-Marie Visconti, Duke of Milan, was presented with the very real possibility that Florence had no resilience left and might not be able to hold out against Milan one more time.

At the same time, the neighboring city-state of Lucca, in friendship if not outright alliance with Milan, began ravaging and taking Tuscan farmlands, coming within ten miles of Florence. An independent autocracy between Florence and Milan, Lucca had refused Florentine control several times in the past. It was a major competitor to Florence's emerging silk trade and routinely had good relations with the dukes of Milan. Furthermore, Lucca had been for a generation the home to wealthy aristocrats from Pisa who fled Florentine suzerainty of their home city. When Milan marched, the elites of Lucca opportunistically ravaged Tuscan territories both during the initial Florentine war with Milan twenty years earlier and again in 1424. They were undefeated by the Florentine forces sent to punish them in the earlier war, and it looked like they would again be undefeated (Kohn 1986, 264). For everyone, the losses were enormous (Edler 1930). Florence was losing years of agricultural and craft productivity in paying for mercenaries to battle Milan as well as respond to the raids and slow the march of the tyrant of Lucca.

Luck saved Florence again, but this time it was neither a timely death nor disease, but rather the pathologies of the secretive, isolated, and suspicious Duke of Milan. Filippo-Maria Visconti feared the success of his commanders as much as defeat (Simonde de Sismondi 1847, 178). Despite innumerable spies and multiple webs of intrigue, Filippo-Maria had difficulty verifying what unctuous exiles or jealous subordinates might tell him because he never traveled to the battles. For example, he had been assured by Florentine exiles that the peasants of Tuscany were oppressed, and that by merely showing his forces at the borders of Tuscany he would inspire the Florentines to take up arms against their oppressors (Plumb 1961, 81). When that did not happen, Filippo-Maria gave in to his natural suspicions and jealousy of the very successful captain who had led his forces so well. Despite having knighted the captain and made him a son-in-law, Filippo-Maria recalled him to the Milanese court under a pretext in late 1425. Having undoubtedly seen this pattern before, Captain Carmagnola left quickly and traveled through Switzerland to warn Venice.

Inadvertently, the arrival of the cast-off successful captain of Milan created the turning point in Venice. His direct knowledge and valuable skills allowed a new generation of humanist-inclined younger leaders to listen to yet another Florentine delegation asking for a renewed mutual defense league of republican city-states including Venice (Kohn 1986, 488). In 1425, Florence and Venice signed an agreement for a mutual defense league against Milan, each paying half the costs. *Condottieri* hired by Carmagnola along with forces from Siena, Ferrara, Savoy, and Mantua slowly defeated every Milanese stronghold by late 1426, innovating the use of artillery along the way. Even the duke's famous and skillful future son-in-law mercenary captain, Francesco Sforza, was captured. Recognizing the losses, Filippo-Maria Visconti brokered the terms of a treaty called the Peace of Venice through Pope Martin V at the end of 1426. In the treaty he gave the city of Brescia and its lands to Venice and returned any territories back to the Duke of Savoy and to Florence, respectively. Filippo-Marie Visconti also agreed not to intervene in any state between Milan and Rome and retired his remaining forces back to their garrisons, retrieving his mercenary captain and future son-in-law Sforza as well (Kohn 1986, 488).

However, the Duke of Milan's confidence was only rattled, not disrupted for the long term. By 1427, he had tried to assassinate Carmagnola in an ambush, along with the now Venetian mercenary captain's two hundred personal retainers and guards. Even in failure, such an attack was not a minor midnight event and revealed the lack of sincerity in the duke's assurances of peace and in his disinterest in further aggression. Filippo-Marie Visconti resumed warfare on Venice by rearming his fleet on the Po River, but Florentine-Venetian forces under Carmagnola took Cremona and in October 1427 produced yet another victory at Maclovio (Holmes 1988, 260). Consistent with the pattern of quickly withdrawing from a reversal to consider another approach, Filippo-Marie Visconti suddenly agreed to yet another peace treaty, the Peace of Ferrara, vigorously promoted by Florence, which was struggling in spring 1428 with draining bank accounts and constant local losses to ravaging raids from neighboring city-state Lucca (Kohn 1986, 488). Both Florence and Venice reacquired lost lands and cities (Proctor 1844, 147).

By the end of 1428, Florence had signed three peace treaties in eight years, and Milan had already abrogated two of them.[15] On this occasion, instead of withdrawing to commerce as it normally did, however, Florence voted to coercively punish neighboring Lucca for its opportunistic and expensive ravaging of Tuscan countryside each time Milan attacked. Florence had not shown exceptional military skill in its choice of commanders, and Venice firmly held the contract for Carmagnola. Nonetheless, led by a particular family with interests in Lucca's resources and able to overcome the hesitation of major Florentine merchant families in 1430, a war-weary Florence with much smaller public coffers turned to punishing Lucca for the land and revenue losses of the recent opportunistic wartime pillaging. Prior to this assault, the signore of Lucca, Guinigi, had already decided to sell Lucca to the Florentines. Unfortunately for Florence, he was overturned when his people learned of the betrayal, and they revolted to create a new republic. Its new leaders appealed to Filippo-Marie Visconti for help, and so Florence would have to take the city-state by force.

In 1429 Lucca's struggles with Florence provided Milan with a new opportunity at an apparently minimal cost to declare that Florence had broken the treaty, although Lucca was not a party.[16] As long as Filippo-Marie Visconti could arrange to keep Venice out of the conflict, it was likely Florence again would militarily falter as it had always done on its own, and would have no resilient plan as a backup. Over the next two years, Filippo-Maria would send troops under a treaty of neutral passage en route to Naples into Tuscany and then turn the troops to other uses, the first to lift a Florentine siege of Lucca,

15. If the whole house of Visconti is counted, four treaties were signed and three were broken in roughly twenty-five years.

16. There is evidence that the further the duke's reach got from his home in Milan, the less reliable his sources were, especially when it came to the politics of Florence. He apparently did not understand the ebbs and flows of great families, or their bitter political deceptiveness. He is said to have believed the exiled Albizzi family exiles at his court that merely showing up at the gates of Florence would inspire the population to rise up, as so many had in other cities when faced with being plundered, and overthrow the civic rulers led by the Medicis. It is not clear how accurate this explanation is because losers do not write history, and this family was particularly secretive. Nonetheless Occam's razor logic suggests he must have had intelligence difficulties to believe the Florentines would fall for the innocent "passage of arms" request by allies of Milan not once but twice (Machiavelli; Simonde de Sismondi 1847).

and the second to aid Lucca again under punitive attacks by Florence. Each time Florence would militarily fail, rescuing itself by bribes and luck. In the first instance Florence bribed the Duke of Milan's famous son-in-law and skilled mercenary captain, Francesco Sforza, who accepted a bribe of fifty thousand florins to withdraw back to Milan (Hibbert 1975, 42). In the second instance, in 1431, Florence's hapless mercenary captain inadvertently flooded his own camp while attempting to redirect a river into washing away Lucca's walls (Becker 1976, 253).[17] Florence withdrew after even failing to successfully ambush the arriving Milanese in a nearby pass, defeated by arriving late (Proctor 1844, 148). Fortunately for Florence, however, in 1431 the latest Milanese transgression occurred nearer to Venice and reignited Venetian concern and considerable military expertise, distracting Milan from its success against Florence. Venetian leaders agreed to renew the Florentine-Venetian alliance in 1431 against Milan. They again hired the successful Carmagnola and deployed the feared Venetian fleet. The war wound down to a grinding series of minor wins and losses. In 1433, Milan and Lucca signed a new Peace of Ferrara with Florence, Siena, and Venice. The treaty formalized the holdings and positions just as they stood at the signing (Kohn 1986).

For Florence and its exhausted treasury, this treaty ended serious Milanese threats to the city-state by displacing the machinations of Milan onto Venice. After 1433, Filippo-Maria moved to conduct more aggressive operations at sea largely against Venice. Only after the Treaty of Cremona of 1441 and the acquisition of the successful commander Sforza as a son-in-law, did Filippo-Maria Visconti's behavior suggest recognition on his part that his confidence in his Milanese forces operating south of Lombardy's borders was misplaced. Sforza then acted to negotiate yet another peace treaty in November 1441; through the friendship of Sforza and the Medicis of Florence, Milan eventually became an ally of Florence by 1454.[18]

17. Italian mercenary captains may have been professionally good at cavalry charges, but apparently they were not as well versed in moving large bodies of water or in setting sentries on the dams. The defenders of Lucca rushed out and pulled down the dams in the night, diverting the rushing water into the camp of the besiegers instead. A bribe could explain this unusual oversight, but I can find no evidence of who paid whom in this case (Hibbert 1975, 43).

18. Florence had quietly been getting wealthier but was increasingly under the backroom control of the Medicis. They did concern themselves with the resilience of Florence in the form of marriages and intrigue to avoid the need for overt disruption of enemies. The head of

By 1433, however, Florence had spent ten years getting the motivations of the duke wrong and paying heavily for the lack of understanding and analysis. Capital infusions would not disrupt for long a threat led by legitimacy and later sustained by growing confidence if initial forays were successful. Filippo-Marie Visconti was initially motivated by a sense of aggrieved legitimacy. Over the ten-year period before he attained the ducal title, the holdings of the Milanese duchy had largely disintegrated into various autocratic city-states under former mercenaries, independent republics, and other cities now controlled by Venice, Florence, or France. For the new and relatively impoverished young duke, regaining his patrimony meant survival, and that required both respect and resources. All he had for certain was the unrecognized title "Duke of Milan," consisting largely of only the actual city of Milan and the army he had inherited by marrying (and then murdering as an adulterer) the wife of his guardian (Plumb 1961, 81).

For this duke, need was a secondary motivator initially, a requirement to have wealth at one's easy disposal in order to sustain the fight for respect. To be a prince, one must have extensive lands to fund self-promotion, spies, traitors, and large mercenary armies. In regaining their domains, Filippo-Maria demonstrated an interest in acquisition by any means. By the time he turned to physically threatening Florence, he would endeavor to control all the Italian territory around the city either to the north (minus Venice and its lands to the east) or to the south (including Rome) of Tuscany (Browning 2001). Other than to fund his future forces or undercut his allies, at no point would Florentine bribes have worked for long to disrupt this attacker's plans.

During this early threat period focused on regaining or retaining territory normally associated with their titles, confidence was the least and third motivator during his early forays. Like his father, Filippo-Maria simply found it quite difficult to marshal enough reliable forces to take over all the fragmented bits of Italy. Not only was the terrain not conducive to the heavily armed cavalry preferred by the mercenary forces (60 percent of the land consisted of hills, little valleys, and marshes), but a good failure or two usually prompted

---

the Medici family, Cosimo, was a personal friend of Francesco Sforza. From this peace treaty to the final treaty of Lodi in 1454, Florence would steadily become, not the object of chronic violence by Milan, but eventually an ally through the loyalty between Cosimo Medici, the careful banker, and Francesco Sforza, the mercenary captain turned husband of the Duke of Milan's daughter (Mallett 2003).

abandonment or betrayals among the forces needed to conduct battles successfully. Filippo-Maria was more secretive and suspicious than his father, refusing to physically meet any emissary, even a visiting emperor (Plumb 1961, 81). Filippo-Maria conducted all of his intrigues and campaigns from behind his castle walls surrounded by an enormous and well-paid guard, a fact that tended to build both lag and bias into his knowledge and decisions. He was known to brood on a reversal and to suddenly sue for peace, only to break the treaty soon after while trying to portray the betrayal as a small technicality or misunderstanding (Baron 1953; Machiavelli 1906).

However, once his hereditary title was no longer denied him and lands around the target (in this case, Florence) were secured, Filippo-Maria seemed to grow more confident. Florence consistently would have waited too long to realize the rise in his confidence and would continue to attempt bribes to disrupt his activities. At that point, only coercion would disrupt him, but as confidence was only a tertiary and tenuously rising motivator, the effect was to merely mess with the violence profile. The disruption was always for the short term. Florence never demonstrated any consistent command of a knowledge-led theory of action or of surprise accommodation. In particular, no Florentine process of decision making or knowledge collection accurately analyzed the Duke of Milan's motivations until the rise of the Medicis and the decline in democracy by the 1430s. Until the enemy was clearly aiming for Tuscany itself, Florence's response strategy always led with capital payments, usually embedded in a treaty declaring years of harmony to follow. Even when the enemy was at the borders of Tuscany, and as mercenary armies were being hired to march into battle, the preference was so strong that a last-minute treaty would be proffered or accepted (Mallett 2003).

The tendency was so profound that the elites in Florence in particular had developed a rationale for attempting to pay first and for not personally serving in any army. The first was an honest assessment of what usually worked with mercenary armies. It is not that the Florentines were necessarily cowardly, though they valued the mind over brawn. It was simply that money worked in most cases (Fratianni and Spinelli 2006). In one rare instance of Florentine collective acknowledgment of a need to have some resilience, the city bought the city of Pisa, twice. In 1398 Duke Gian Galeazza Visconti of Milan persuaded the seaport of Pisa via its connections to Genoa to shut off Florentine access to ports needed to export goods. After the duke died, it was clearly seen in Florence that at least one port, Pisa, could no longer be allowed to ally itself with Florence's enemies if Florence was to stay secure. Hence it was one of the few times that Florence had to take a city no matter what (Edler 1930). Florence began by trying to buy it from the dead duke's natural son. When the town revolted against the son and his coconspirator, a French marshal sent with troops to sustain the son's claim, Florence ended up in 1404 paying for a town it could not enter due to the rebellion. Reluctantly, Florence then sent a besieging military force. However, before anyone was hurt, a quiet but large side payment to a rebellion leader provided an open side gate to the city during the night. In 1406 Florence finally owned Pisa. Despite earning the enduring enmity of neighboring Lucca to which aristocratic and anti-Florence Pisan exiles had fled, Florence had a secure port for its goods for nearly a generation.[19]

A second reason payment was emphasized by the merchants of Florence was that their notion of sacrifice was to provide what they were best at providing — money.[20] Merchants were not considered good candidates for soldiers in any case. No sensible autocrat or city magistrate wanted armed, organized, trained citizens experienced in war living inside cities. To become a soldier meant leaving the city of one's birth and likely never being allowed to come back to live there. Mercenaries generally bought themselves holdings outside of other cities (Dean 1988). Florentines by this period had such a heightened

19. Unfortunately Florence also had to keep on paying to maintain a very poor city that was now half empty and sadly neglected under Milan's control. Most of its skilled families had run for non-Florentine city-states like Lucca. They feared reprisals but were also largely the anti-Florentine elite of long standing in Pisa. For the next several years, Florence advertised all over Italy to pay skilled labor to move to Pisa and join as citizens. This policy was characterized as one of generosity to rebuild the port and maintain it as a good steward (Simonde de Sismondi 1847, 174). Or, from more modern eyes, it could also be seen as making facts on the ground to ensure the anti-Florentine clans that left could not return. The former is not an unreasonable explanation given the exceptional rise of civic pride and willingness to sacrifice personal wealth for city advancement that developed in Florence by the beginning of the 1400s. If the latter was the true reason, then it was not widely discussed beyond some central actors who used the more generous explanation to justify the payments (Kent 2004, 183).

20. This philosophy was nowhere as evident as in 1427 when the Florentines voted to make taxation fairer by increasing the tax burden on the wealthy and more politically powerful elite in order to defend the city, rather than conscripting sons or instituting a standing army (Kent 2004, 183). This novel fiscal innovation, called the *catasto*, even included penalties for nonpayment of back taxes by the wealthy (Herlihy and Klapisch-Zuber 1985).

sense of city pride that living in another city or abandoning Florence as home was considered a step down. Even seeking a bride outside the city or at least Tuscany was viewed as suspect and disgraceful behavior in more prominent families (Hibbert 1975, 115). Furthermore, the civic rulers and upper class of Florence had passionately embraced a revival of the ancient Roman polity with its learned citizenry, debates, and mass persuasions to policy. This embrace included an interest in rule by the "middle people," not too wealthy or too poor. Even the Florentine judicial system had begun to reflect this interest in tolerance for the middle classes while strongly suppressing lower-class insurrections and "patrician political violence" (Becker 1976). Since neither males nor females of these families would consider themselves worthy unless able to read and quote passages from Roman classics, the rather boring profession of riding around in heavy armor on dusty plains was viewed with particular aesthetic distaste, in addition to being financially unattractive (Sobek 2003).[21]

In addition, Florentine merchants would rarely have long before, once again, a Florentine council of war and its hired forces would prove incapable of conducting a winning strategy of coercion either in its timing or its variation for any length of time. Even if battles could be won, often surprise and indignation rather than knowledge developed by analysis of experience or data collection drove Florence's selection of commanders, timing of force deployments, ideas, and follow-through. Campaigns dragged with little accurate information, and as months would pass with no action, the military operation would lose popular attention and interest. For example, at one point, the threat from Lucca was exceptionally close to home, right up to a few miles from the city itself, yet no competent Florentine commander emerged with any strategy to end the rampages of a bitter enemy.

Only luck would save the city when the otherwise brilliant Lucchese leader died from disease. In keeping with the times, he had no ready and reliable suc-

---

21. The vast literature on the Italian Renaissance has a peculiarly Florentine bias in large part because of this particular emphasis on classical revivalism and its societal effects on art, literature, and cultural developments for a hundred years (Najemy 2004; Plumb 1961, 39). Unsurprisingly, mercenaries tended to come from well-to-do rural families able to afford to outfit the son to join one of the mercenary companies. Moving to a town for the rural elite meant being viewed with suspicion and being excluded from political participation. Captains like the famous Braccio often came from the more martial titled families with declining resources or prospects (Mallett 2003).

cessor to hold together his winnings, thus losing all the gains Lucca had made against a weak and inattentive Florence.

A lack of honest consultation was not the source of Florentine difficulties in disrupting enemies; rather, it was a lack of accurately informed citizens involved in the discussions. In highly institutionalized and public settings involving electing a new set of administrators and councils every two months, Florentines met and met again. The councils and their various family and guild networks consulted before, during, and after conflicts involving a violent threat and held loud debates filled with impressive oratory reportedly reminiscent of ancient Rome. Particularly charismatic harangues would sway the audience and their votes on one issue. Two months later, a new council might make a new argument and change the policy completely (Mallett 2003).

The Florentine system had been designed a hundred years earlier to reduce the power of patriarchal privilege and the disruptive tendencies of the mob, which it did to a large extent and at the cost of public administrative skill or knowledge. Florentine citizens were enthusiastic about this system, and it became synonymous with the independence of the Republic itself. As a democratic process making longer-term decisions such as policies about strategic alliances, however, the Florentine system was both unusual and difficult to emulate.[22] It took enormous skill and even more resources to keep it consistent and effective, as the Medicis would discover after 1441, and the Treaty of Cremona put Cosimo Medici in virtual control.[23] Even the Medici operated to control the city from behind this system, only discarding it in the early 1500s

22. The leaders of the "Ambrosia Republic" in the rump Milan after the death of Duke Gian Galeazza attempted to use the Florentine system, with disastrous results (Sobek 2003).

23. Consulting with an ever-changing set of representatives from underlying and rigid social structures was incredibly grueling. For example, it has been argued that the slow decline of the Medici banking dynasty over the next century was due directly to the draining and distracting effect of the family head trying to maintain the family corporation along with political control of Florentine politics from behind the scenes (Plumb 1961, 137). Machiavelli's descriptions exhaustively illuminate the constant jockeying for advantage in internal games of deliberately mixed signals among the supporters of the regime, former incumbents of the leading positions, and representatives of the various branches of government, not to mention the various lottery-chosen councils (McLean 2005, 640 n5). One of the problems the otherwise bright Medicis faced was the distraction from the family banking business over time due to the draining effects of political intrigue and an intergenerational gradual move to excess in consumption and art (Parks 2005).

with the formal installation of a hereditary Duke Medici of Tuscany (Hibbert 1975). Nonetheless the level of knowledge developed about threats was consistently poor.

Furthermore, with the public consultations on decisions so fragmented and turbulent, voting for war was particularly difficult, while voting to bribe someone was much easier in comparison (Hibbert 1975). Smaller city-states often lost their freedom by frantically investing mercenary or deceptive leaders with last-minute wartime powers that were never given back to the republic in question. In Florence, even the system for conducting war was instituted to keep one family or guild from absconding with either the city's treasury or its liberty. A declaration of war required assembling a *balia* to nominate a "Ten of War" to deal with the war on a daily basis, but this was not done behind the scenes. This election of the *balia* was to be done publicly with every man above the age of fourteen marching in under their guild banners to form a mass parliament. After making sure they had a quorum of at least two-thirds of the eligible male population, this group then selected the Ten of War (Henderson 1986).

In so many ways, there was an excess of consultations in Florence on large issues whose details no one could keep or personally use to advance their family, and insufficient consultation on the critical operational choices. The Florentine system churned its institutional policymakers so often that the true stability in policies was tied resolutely to the traditional groups defined by families, marriage, and guild loyalties (Martines 1968). In this case, the transition to a modern state so necessary for honest, stable, and consistent consultation was still some years away and would occur only with the eventual takeover of Florence from the inside by the Medicis (Kent 2004).[24]

Comprehensive data collection was not demonstrated by Florentines before, during, or after a threat emerging from Milan or any other city-state during this period. Successful merchants collect data instinctively — on customers, on suppliers, on competitors, on product qualities, prices, and substitutes, and on their political environment. However, a merchant maintaining such volumes

---

24. To be fair, however, the raucous, turbulent system, when focused on a threat that everyone accepted as devastating, would on occasion produce an innovation worthy of Florentine conceit. In this case, it was the increase in taxes voted on themselves by the wealthy in 1427 as a way to be more financially prepared for violent threats (Najemy 2004, 183). The sacrifice was real at the time, and the contribution to later modern forms of relatively equitable taxation was significant.

of information for his or her own gain is quite different than paying to have this done for the public good. The natural spying on competitors of the rival merchant city-states produced, at least minimally, a tendency to keep spies on retainer or acquire information through bonds of loyalty. The size of this effort to collect information varied inversely with the scale and distance of the autocrat likely to be a threat (Kent 2004).

Only during an active conflict was data consistently sought. After a peace treaty, the city council usually abandoned efforts to keep the data flow current and detailed. All cities sent minders along to observe the battles and the relative vigor of their mercenary employees (Mallett 2003). Other sources of near real-time data were harder to assure. The mercenaries themselves on occasion could not tell who had won or lost, or been hurt or routed. Simonde de Sismondi describes a battle not so unusual in either its confusing conduct or its indeterminate outcome due to independent decisions to withdraw suddenly in the face of obscuring dust, heat, or approaching darkness (Simonde de Sismondi 1847, 181). Only the slow pace of most campaigns made the real-time data shortcoming less threatening to city-state survival.

Once a treaty was signed, a calming bribe executed, or a war won, not only did Florence send off its mercenaries, but the intrigues turned inward, and what the public was allowed to know declined precipitously. Unlike Milan or even Venice with their more autocratic and stable rulers, the historical discussions of Florentine preparedness for the next conflict suggest the city's rulers abandoned the active and wider net of spies almost every time the imminent attack disappeared, along with any other efforts at resilience (Mallett 1994, 232).

During the period 1423–1433, Florentines were often surprised and then indignant when a threat emerged not far from their doorstep, but most threats were ones they could have foreseen, had they sought the information in advance (noted in particular by Machiavelli 1906). Most of the data Florence needed for better public decisions would have required an institutionalization of data collection as well as public discussion. In large part, scattered across the merchant families was a trove of data that merchants accrued as a normal part of their import and export activities. For example, the Florentine council was able to determine quietly and act upon knowledge that the tyrant of Pisa would take a bribe, for how much, and for what action, all without publicly hunting for data. Clearly it had been in someone's private interest to collect that data and store it. Also, clearly that person was reachable by members of the council. In contrast, Venice expressly expected every citizen who traveled abroad to spy for the city informally. The kinds of data to be provided were to include assessments of personalities, apparent wealth, contingencies, and imminence of change (Plumb 1961, 39).

Finally, even with the data that could be gathered at the last minute in Florence, there was little collaborative knowledge development until the rise of the Medicis. With little accurate data before and during conflict, and no institutionalized way to collect or develop data into knowledge, biases dominated and distorted the inferences drawn from fragmented and outdated information. Both attackers and defenders often drew inaccurate conclusions, especially about enemies and battles (Simonde de Sismondi 1847). At one moment, Florentine orators would consistently interpret nearly bloodless battles as successes when they accomplished nothing. On other occasions, orators would interpret the same sort of battles as grand defeats when they did not miraculously chase the threat away. Often enough, critical data would not be sought or contested, because one dramatic argument in the council so persuaded the multitude of one course of action that further data was not considered necessary. For example, despite good and available evidence that one single influential Florentine family wanted for purely personal reasons to go to war with Lucca, great oratory and little knowledge development produced unanimity in pursuing a punitive war that very nearly ended with Florence broke, defeated, and pillaged (Simonde de Sismondi 1847).

Florence more often messed with rather than matched the action equation of the Duke of Milan. Its resilience was particularly low and at best ad hoc. For the Duke of Milan, confidence was ultimately his strongest motivator, and emphasizing coercion ultimately would have been a better long- and short-term disruptive response from Florence. Capital would not have been enough, had the massed enemies reached the city-state. Over this period, Florence displayed characteristics later echoed during the height of the Cold War by the anticommunists of the American defense administration. Florentine leaders did not demonstrate an overarching understanding of either weighted motivations or surprise accommodation, and their very public consultation, data collection, and knowledge development was inadequate, easily biased, and largely unchallenged internally.[25]

---

25. Even the largest peasant rebellion in Tuscany in 1402–3 caused considerable anxiety among Florentine civic leaders for a short period about the security of the rural hills. But aside from no deaths, many new poorly maintained defensive bastions, and innumerable

BRITISH AND U.S. SMALL WARS OF DISRUPTION

The advent of the telegraph provided historically unprecedented speed and reach in military operations by the 1850s. The spread of telegraph lines also offered the possibilities of enormous increases in knowledge of distant events, enemies, targets, and environments before and during any armed operations. Yet use of such data in a process of disruption and — even less so — resilience was not common among the militaries of the era for some years. Indeed, simply destroying enemies or ignoring those considered too strong or irrelevant was preferred for clarity of the operations.[26] Most Victorian or colonial expeditions were wars of conquest or operations aimed at the annihilation of the enemy's supporting population. Wars against rebellions in the overseas colony or the occasional one-port bombardments often conducted by the British Navy during the 1800s were either associated with prior conquest or meant as one-off gestures intended to support the extractive activities of expatriate entrepreneurs in a developing country.

Few Victorian or colonial "wars" thus qualify as good examples of disruption or resilience-heavy strategies. Nearly none have enough in common with today's threat profiles and cybered world. To be a case study involving elements of a disruption strategy in this framework, the threat must first be perceived as a violent one aimed at the respondent state. Second, both threat and responder must have either no chance or no desire to conquer the other. In a strategy emphasizing either disruption or resilience, one cannot just march in and murder.

Furthermore, up to and through the twentieth century, "limited" wars by westernized states were often characterized by an arrogance that makes them poor exemplars of either disruption or resilience in a national strategy, save in a tediously long list of negative lessons. Often the responders violated minimal

---

intrigues with Milanese enemy forces, the threat to Florence's food supply stimulated no longer-term plan for accommodating any future surprises, not even so much as some simple redundancy in critical crops as Pericles had done (Cohn 1999, 198).

26. Much of this casually destructive behavior began to diminish when the telegraph connected the diplomats and, especially, journalists to their respective home office more rapidly. For example, the behavior of British military men in Asia began to be more circumscribed after the cables connecting London with Beijing were constructed in the 1870s (Knuesel 2007). The telegraph had a number of institution-changing effects not foreseen at the outset of its use (Kieve 1973; Beauchamp 2001).

knowledge requirements for even a basic military strategy acknowledging possible surprise. The commanders often marched in with the largest force that could be mustered and transported. They had little to no understanding of why the "threat" acted as it did. The military leaders rarely planned in advance what to do if their battle environment proved crippling and lethal. In general, the hubris of the newly modernizing militaries, along with expendable ranks of soldiers drawn from society's less valuable classes, was considered sufficient to handle societies and environments of the largely overseas colonial world. This ad hoc approach did not change rapidly even when better knowledge became possible to acquire and integrate into operations (Keegan 1978).

Often the colonial or larger power's resilience to surprise hinged on luck alone, especially before the telegraph was widely used. For example, in the First Sikh War, on December 22, 1845, in British northwest India, a large British Indian Army force was engaged in a bloody losing battle, having arrived the day before, poorly prepared as usual with insufficient water, food, and medical care. At the end of a grueling, hot, incredibly blood-filled day in which the British were clearly losing, a fresh, well-equipped Sikh enemy army arrived on the far edge of the battlefield. The next day would have certainly seen the massacre of the British forces, as recognized by both sides including the newly arrived Sikh general surveying the field. Suddenly, a battle-deranged British officer incomprehensively ordered the bulk of British cavalry and artillery units protecting critical flanks to wheel off down the road to another town. The sheer lunacy of this decision stunned the Sikh general. He then persuaded himself that this was an inconceivably fiendish trick to attack him from behind, and he suddenly withdrew from the entire battle back to his capital. As a result, the British forces were able to survive, later returning to attack and take the Sikh general's capital and country for British India (Farwell 1985).

If the same conditions had emerged only a few years later with the advent of field telegraph wires and the spread of railroads across India in particular, the same battle would likely have ended differently. The Sikhs were a wealthy, relatively modern military force and were likely to have made sure to have acquired a telegraph network once they saw its operational advantages. The Sikh senior commanders could have telegraphed down the road to find from their dispersed observers that there were no new British troops down the road. The British commander could have telegraphed to relieve the insane officer and recalled the troops. Unfortunately, they probably would have arrived in time to be slaughtered because of the poor resilience of most British forces in those days. The organization almost always fought poorly prepared for the environment's harshness and surprises.[27]

Two of four cases in this section, however, are British cases by dint of the disruption objectives of the operations. The two senior and successful officers involved demonstrated uncommon instincts by deliberately incorporating many of the elements of a security resilience strategy in their otherwise largely disruption operations. Each focused on accumulation and integration of knowledge in advance and during operations, as well as on the accommodation of surprise through redundancy and slack. Ironically the final two American cases in a much later, more communications-intensive era demonstrate how the lack of such an instinctive effort to honestly develop knowledge in accurate collective sense-making and to integrate it can result in a crippled operation or outcome. Having the communications network or even access to a global cyberspace does not deterministically channel the outcome if the strategic framework is incomplete.

In the first set of cases, a responding nation perceives a direct violent threat on its citizens going about their business and chooses to militarily disrupt the threatening actors. Conquest and annihilation are not part of the plan, just disrupting the threat with minimal forces. Writ large, this pattern is analogous to the international response to Barbary Pirates in the early 1800s and the periodic wars against piracy endemic in history since at least the Romans (Puchala 2005).[28] Two British campaigns offer disruption and resilience strategic lessons: Napier's 1867–68 War with Abyssinia, and Wolseley's 1873–74 War with the Ashanti. A few of the campaigns in the northwest in British India also come close to qualifying, but these two capture the lessons adequately from a limited population of examples. Each disrupted the threat, roughly mirroring the mix, and was resilient by deliberate design. They are discussed in the first half of this section.

The second set, found in a later era, the Cold War, involves the American

27. The story of the Sikhs, a monotheistic religion from the 1500s bracketed by Muslims and Hindus, is one of survival by being the toughest regime ever squeezed between hostile cultures. So warlike were the Sikhs and so admired by others that the British had enlisted whole battalions of Sikh soldiers into the British Indian Army within two years of the final defeat of their governing council, the Khalsa, in 1849 (Farwell 1985).

28. The U.S. actions in the Barbary Wars in the early 1800s would qualify as a disruption-heavy national strategy that occurred just before the modern period (Smith and Allison 2007).

military involved in disrupting organizations in other nations. These were viewed as strategic threats because of their adherence to ideas enabling non-democratic, oligarchic control of developing states of interest to the United States. In these cases, the U.S. national leaders felt the idea, communism, physically threatened their country. It was viewed as a mental infection that one could acquire by mere association with its adherents, especially if the already infected communists were able to organize. The two U.S. disruption operations studied here were part of a larger national "Cold War" to keep the United States free from the communism "virus" by directly stopping its spread in other nations. The two examples were operations in which short-term disruption occurs ("messing with the mix"), but the longer-term outcomes were undesirable. In the U.S. cases, each outcome tragically demonstrates the consequences of an imbalanced strategy, knowledge foregone due to arrogance, and a framework reinforcing a lack of interest in knowledge development. In these cases, the physical threat was indirect but honestly believed to be inevitably violent, real, and aimed at the homeland. Several Cold War–era small U.S. wars here qualify as responses against the presumed Soviet-directed communist global threat. Two of these cases — that of Guatemala and Vietnam — are discussed in the second half of this section.

Victorian Disruption of Perceived Abyssinian and Ashanti Threats

During the reign of Queen Victoria, hardly a year went by that the forces of the British Empire were not involved in armed conflict somewhere. Most were small, related to colonial expansion, reinforcement, or control, and far from posing any direct threat to the United Kingdom. The most exotic involved the British Navy showing up, scaring the rebellious into resubmission, and then sailing off again, not unlike the actions of the Athenian triremes. The most mundane and bloody involved the British (or for that matter, French, Russian, Japanese, German, and even American) Army marching in and sorting the rebellious into the dead, departed, or subdued. Not much information in advance was sought, nor was much strategic thinking involved in sending force on enemy military force or sometimes on the opponent's villages. Most of the conflicts were territorial, involving colonial, pseudocolonial, or continental disputes, and involved deliberate attempts at destruction of the enemy. These "little wars" for Britain especially are so numerous that it is not clear anyone knows how many there were. Most are ignored by even the most ardently British of historians (Reed 2001).

Few involved merely disruption, and even fewer some notions of resilience. Indeed, in the 1800s, the engine of colonialism was largely unintentional. Most western nations' leaders in the 1800s were at best "reluctant" colonialists (Farwell 1985, 190). Indeed, most of the early colonial wars were the product of rapacious adventurers, arrogant missionaries, and frustrated military men who simply claimed territories for their home nation. The unfettered actions of all three groups of wanderers then held unhappy civil servants at home politically hostage to public indignations or enthusiasms, should someone consider disavowing the wanderer's national claims. The profits of adventurers bought influence in homeland political circles, while missionaries had publicly advertised the souls to be forcibly saved. Any territory formally given to the state was hard, if not logistically impossible, to give back (Farwell 1985, 190). Usually the local social system had been destroyed in the process of the adventurers' or national forces' operations, and there was no one to take the territory back. Furthermore, the normal mismanagement of overseas lands usually generated massive problems with insurrections in the new imperial acquisitions, which had to be met with force for the sake of the home nations' murdered citizens as well as national pride (Strachan 1983).

The more forces that had to be sent forth to quell rebellions, the more the military men leading those forces discovered the drawbacks to punitive destructive raids without holding territories. Armies of the time were small cities on the move. If they moved forward, a long train of supplies trailed behind them. If they raided a good distance and then withdrew, angry locals would harass and ambush them the entire way. The object of punitive raids, the local princes, would instinctively withdraw deep into their territory, but chasing them meant repeating this cycle of penetrate, get harassed, win some conflicts, withdraw, get harassed, and then have to repeat it again in a few years. Thus many military men determined to always go forward and keep whatever territory they had fought for, often in spite of instructions to the contrary by headquarters. The more that territory was taken in the name of the home nation, the more people were needed to tend it. As more adventurers, missionaries, and shopkeepers arrived, the more military were sent to protect the expatriate citizens. The military men then decided to take more territory for security, and so the cycle went (Porch 2006b).

No major European nation was immune, irrespective of its preferences. For example, British cabinet ministers frequently tried to dump unprofitable West African colonies, and French civil servants were routinely instructing French military men to stay within existing borders, all to no avail. Like many of the imperial powers, Russia's political leaders were dragged into the logic of empire. In 1865, the Russian interior minister wrote plaintively in his diary, "General Chernyaev has taken Taskent, . . . and nobody knows why" (Geyer and Little 1987, 89). Once taken, Tashkent was certainly not going to be given back.

There are exceptions to be found in a few conflicts that induced disruption rather than destruction and colonial conquest cycle. The two cases described in this section by and large involved physical threats to major and otherwise legitimate economic outlets. Their characteristics enabled the larger nation feeling threatened, the United Kingdom, to act more like a city-state intending to disrupt a threat than as a rapacious conqueror.[29] In the first Abyssinian War of 1867–68 and the 1873 Ashanti War, critical elements of a disruption strategy were clearly present. The mission was clearly stated as being limited, essential knowledge was acquired in advance, and the forces moved in, disrupted the threat proportionately, and withdrew successfully (Farwell 1985, 166, 182, 332). The strategy pursued most closely approximated the modern notion of a war of disruption that successfully mirrors the mix of violence drivers on the part of the threat. Both commanding officers, like Pericles, also demonstrated an instinctive understanding for resilience, of their own forces at least.

The first case was the threat posed to British citizens by Emperor Theodore II of Abyssinia (1818–68), who ruled what is now Eritrea, a mountainous part of southwestern Ethiopia. His land was an inaccessible highland surrounded by deserts and not of much interest to external powers save Egyptian aristocracy. Within eight years of his coronation in 1855, he wrote a letter to the Queen of England as a fellow peer concerned with the oppression of Abyssinian Christians by his ever-warring Muslim neighbors and proposed an alliance.[30] When the letter went unanswered (having been sent by boat to

29. Over time and in frustration, the attacked responders might decide to go all out and simply conquer the territory harboring the violent threats. Wholesale land grabs, however, were not the original reason for either the presence of this economic outlet or the usually military response to attacks.

30. In fairness, Abyssinia was the continuous object of intrigue or attack by Egypt, which was intent upon adding some real estate and Islamicizing the Christian population (Dunn 2005).

London and then to India for a year), he imprisoned and tortured the British consul to the Abyssinian court, Captain Charles Cameron. When the plight of Cameron was known in Britain, along with that of some European missionaries, a reply was finally sent in late 1864 by the Foreign Office on behalf of the queen.

Unfortunately, it was not delivered until 1866, and the messenger, a Turkish Assyriologist, was then also imprisoned by the irate emperor. When another letter from Abyssinia arrived asking for workmen, machinery, and a munitions manufacturing expert, the British government actually recruited an engineer and six artisans. The seven individuals were sent halfway there before the British government realized it was just possible the emperor was not in possession of all his faculties. In August 1867, the cabinet decided the only way to get the consul and some other Europeans back was to disrupt the emperor using coercive force (Rodgers 1984).

The chosen commander, Lieutenant General Sir Robert Cornelius Napier, then commander-in-chief of the Bombay Army, convinced his London superiors to fund his supplies sufficiently for a long march.[31] Having grown up among the British India Army officers, he would have preferred to have some elephants on which to rely for the long transport from the port to the emperor's capital. Having done his homework, he had no intention of using humans or pack animals to carry across four hundred miles of desert all the supplies he had cajoled out of London (Jackson 2007). So Napier innovated. He imported about thirteen thousand veteran troops from India to do the fighting and ended up with about fourteen thousand more camp followers, construction, and support personnel (Ashcroft 2001). On the march as he moved slowly inland, he built a railroad.

Assembling his forces on the coast of Zula and benefiting from good staff work and planning, Napier arrived at about twelve miles from the perched mountaintop fortress of Magdala, the capital of Abyssinia, on April 8, 1868. "It was an operation of extraordinary complexity with formidable logistical prob-

31. This bit of persuasion was much easier because London was not footing most of the bill. Rather, about six hundred thousand pounds were foisted on the growing public debt of India. The India Council loaned the British India officers and soldiers whose pay and support were charged against their home offices in India (Dutt 2001). This transfer of burden was a common way that colonial powers extracted resources otherwise not easily obtained from their colonies. It had a side benefit in that native soldiers tended to die less from disease than the British regular soldiers would in those climates (Beckett 2001).

lems. Magdala lay in the centre of a range of mountains, the peaks of which reached 11,000 feet. Between the mountains and the coast was a barren plateau cut with precipitous fissures and rocky crevasses. It was a land of extremes. In the dry season, between autumn and spring, the temperature rose to over 50°C and fell to below freezing at night. In the wet season the plateau became an impassable morass of mud while the valleys became torrents" (Ashcroft 2001, 80).

Although Emperor Theodore's forces commanded the heights of the three mountain ranges surrounding Magdala, they did not have the equipment to match the British. Theodore had painstakingly developed artillery by virtually indenturing Egyptian artillerymen to cast the cannon. While these weapons were numerous and inspired fear in other princes, they were not effective against the British forces arranging themselves for an assault below his cliff-top fortress (Caulk 1972). The Abyssinian warriors were handicapped by using muskets against rifles, and to get within killing range they had to come down close to give battle. On April 9 they lost the first major battle (Bates 1979). Napier had mistakenly allowed his baggage trains to drift underneath the guns of the assembled Abyssinians. Emboldened by the apparent weakness, the Abyssinians swarmed out to take advantage of the opening. Napier recovered in time. He wheeled the well-trained Punjab Pioneers in place to intercept the oncoming infantry while the Naval Brigade fired its rockets at the attackers. The disparity in deaths was astounding, with about seven hundred dead Abyssinian warriors and only two British dead (Farwell 1985, 172).

Despite the emperor's efforts to open negotiations belatedly in the conflict, Napier's responding demands were always too high for the emperor, including releasing all the European prisoners and unconditional surrender of Magdala and himself. The emperor first threatened to kill all the prisoners in a rage, and then he released all forty-nine of them to see if Napier would withdraw. Napier, however, continued his advance as soon as the former prisoners were sent safely to the rear. The fortress was on a ledge three hundred feet above a plateau surrounded on three sides by impassible cliffs. The fourth face, however, was a steeply graduated set of rising terraces and conical mud houses. On April 13, 1868, Napier's forces began the tough slog up the slope toward a narrow passage to the main fortress gate, while unarmed Abyssinian women, children, and unarmed men ran down the terrace around them (Farwell 1985, 173).

In this operation, the only possibly major oversight in Napier's plan for disruption and resilience occurred at the gate itself. The British sappers had fought their way up through the passage but had forgotten their powder charges and scaling ladders in the melee further down the cliff. If the mass of Theodore's followers had stood by him, the narrow opening to the gate of the fortress would have been nearly impossible to take without crushing losses at least. But the emperor was abandoned by all but a few hundred warriors. He had spent his final night brutally killing hundreds of Abyssinian prisoners, some thrown over the precipice in chains. A few intrepid British soldiers tossed a small drummer boy up to the top of the gate and gave covering fire as he opened the gate from the inside. The emperor shot himself, and his followers melted away (Farwell 1985, 173; Woolbert 1935).

The next day, as a warning to others who might consider harming British citizens, at least in that region, Magdala was burned to the ground, while Theodore's cannon and the walls of the fortress were blown up. Napier then left without any territorial claims and started the two-month march back to the coast. Theodore's only son was taken to London for an education kindly subsidized by Queen Victoria. He would have been returned to his inheritance, presumably as a friend of Britain, but died soon after his arrival at age nineteen (Woolbert 1935). Magdala was never rebuilt, and Abyssinia passed back into chaotic struggles among warlords with neglectful Egyptian suzerainty. No other emperor arose to challenge British Crown representatives from the area (Farwell 1985, 175). The operation was labeled flawless, even by the war correspondents newly developed in the British press. The same community also noted how rarely this level of preparation, execution, and return was seen in other British operations elsewhere (Harcourt 1980).

A few years later, however, the British press had another example of disruption and resilience in British operations. The environment was British West Africa, and by the 1800s, it was not a profitable set of colonies. Its once chief export, slaves from the interior, was no longer an acceptable commodity. As usual, Britain's leaders could not politically give up the territories despite the abysmal harbors, vicious diseases, rotten climate, and dense dangerous jungle lurking just along the coast. As long as they lived, given the diseases, British officers did handle most threats using the coast tribes of former slave-selling middlemen as soldiers, although regarding them as cowards.

The Ashanti were the major exception to the largely pacified coastal clans who widely feared the inland Ashanti kingdom. In the early 1800s, just as the slave trade was being banned, both the British and the Ashanti were attempting to expand their territorial control. In 1823, the British governor at Cape Coast Castle, Sir Charles Macarthy, attempted an expedition inland with a West Indian Regiment and local coastal allies to challenge the Ashanti king's control of the nearby jungle. While the British band played "God Save the King" and the governor stood to attention, the Ashanti army cut him and his forces to pieces using their well-practiced military skill. The Ashanti army were experts at using the horseshoe formation, combining individual courage, jungle cover for surprise, and timing to envelop an enemy from the sides. For the next half century, the governor's skull was displayed in the Ashanti capital of Kumasi at the annual Yam Festival. For a while, the British left the troublesome Ashanti alone, and to keep them away, the British even routinely returned Ashanti runaway slaves to their owners in the jungle (Farwell 1985, 164).[32]

As the century wore on, the missionary zeal to civilize affected British governors in Africa as much as others. In 1862, Governor Richard Pine decided to defend the "laws of civilization" by refusing to return two Ashanti runaway slaves, a young boy and an old man. Rebuffed despite his reasonable (for the era) negotiations to get them back, the Ashanti king then sent troops across Pra River denoting the border between the British and Ashanti lands, pillaging and burning more than two dozen coastal tribal villages. London refused to send Governor Pine some regular trained British forces for a coercive disruptive expedition, so the governor sent six companies of West Indian troops to build a bridge across the Pra in preparation for an eventual expedition. Mysteriously the troops built a stockade and a bridge and then came home without weapons, ammunition, or stores. The Ashanti king, having lost face in the loss of the two slaves, presumably had redeemed it in the new slaves and booty from pillaging the villages. He did not need to further his stature and start a major war with the British, but he had made his point by returning the soldiers with no valuable equipment (Farwell 1985, 165).

No shot was fired, and nothing else happened for ten more years. In many

---

32. Among all the colonial wars that British historians tend to ignore, this expedition is not even counted as one of the wars against the Ashanti. It has all the same characteristics — extremely irritating Ashanti arrogance, firm determination to thrash the fellow once and for all, a fine expedition led by a brave British officer, and undoubtedly inspiring martial spirits among the men. Nonetheless one cannot help suspect the exceptional loss of the war and his head made Sir Charles's expedition entirely and desirably forgettable. It is also interesting how long it took the British to get around to avenging Sir Charles. Forty years is a long time to ignore a whole empire just inside the coast.

respects, it was the Ashanti who implemented a disruption strategy better than Governor Pine in this instance. Although he kept the boy and old man, Pine had no further resources to use against the king. Unwittingly, Pine had given the king what he needed, legitimacy among his warriors, as had the previous governor — although Pine did keep his skull (Farwell 1985, 166).

In 1873, an army of twelve thousand Ashantis crossed the Pra River and pillaged their way down to Elmina, a coastal fort recently given to the British by the Dutch. It is not clear what insult, theft, or threat precisely motivated the Ashanti at that moment to have moved beyond their bloody but small raids. However, the defeat of the Europeans and their coast allies appears to have been the objective (Farwell 1985, 190). This time the Ashanti could not be ignored in London. Besides, there was a new optimism after the modern conduct of the Abyssinian Campaign and its success. Unlike the previous Ashanti war in 1863–64, Napier's expedition had proved an enormous and highly publicized success. Not only was it lauded and Napier given a peerage, but it set the tone for the next Ashanti expedition in 1873 (Harcourt 1980, 103). The next campaign was expected to be an equally extensive show of imperial ability to constrain what it viewed as actions that attacked British interests.

To deal with the Ashanti violence, the British government picked the youngest and probably one of the brightest generals in its inventory, the recently promoted General Sir Garnet Wolseley. Wolseley had just distinguished himself in Canada as Colonel Wolseley, the quartermaster-general of Canada. In 1870 he had led a handpicked group of young, very bright officers to capture or dispel a group of Métis (of French and aboriginal descent) who had revolted against the Hudson Bay Company selling its land and their homes to English Canada. Their leader, a man named Louis Riel, had won cultural autonomy concessions from the Canadian government, but nonetheless there was controversy when his provisional government executed a British Canadian surveyor. Outrage prompted a British military response (Manning 2007). Like Napier in Abyssinia, Wolseley had planned what was called the 1870 Red River Campaign with a level of care exceptionally unusual for officers of his time. He handpicked his subordinate officers and led the expedition through very tough territory. He timed the expedition with weather and transport contingencies in mind. He made officers work out to acclimate and develop personal fitness as they would personally carry their boats and supplies at several points in the expedition. He issued standing orders for the collection of intelligence that would be credible today. Every officer was expected to constantly seek and record every item of possible interest, to include the time of day they encountered weather, bugs, or local natives (Manning 2007). He even allocated mosquito veils and oils to protect the soldiers from the black flies, mosquitoes, and sand flies endemic to the region in the summer. The long tough trip was so well prepared that their clothes suffered more than the troops when they finally arrived at the rebel Winnipeg village. Although Riel had been warned and fled to the United States, Wolseley's command and the enthusiastic response of his subordinate officers advanced his stature (Farwell 1985, 190).

For the Ashanti problem, Wolseley was ordered to take officers to the Gold Coast, gather native soldiers, and disrupt the Ashanti ability to cause violent problems on the coast. In preparation for what was seen as a tough battle ahead in awful conditions, Wolseley gathered his handpicked set of subordinate officers, many from the successful Red River Campaign. He arrived at the Gold Coast in October 1873, having anticipated that his native soldiers would not fight the Ashanti. When they had refused to fight by January 1874, he had requested and received three battalions of regular British troops of about four thousand men. He set off quickly to complete the disruption mission during the dry and healthier season of January to March. By using supply and bivouac assembly areas carefully prepared in advance by a particularly reliable officer, Wolseley quickly marched to the Ashanti border and into the king's lands (Farwell 1985, 191–92).

Responding to the king's last-minute conciliatory messages with impossible demands as Napier had done with the Abyssinian emperor, Wolseley deliberately forced the king to meet him in battle. Near an outlying village from the capital Kumasi, British native scouts were ambushed on January 31, 1874, formally initiating the conflict. The Ashanti were waiting in the dense foliage in their traditional horseshoe pattern, which normally worked well. The British troops, however, did not pause in confusion at the sudden appearance of enemies to their side because Wolseley had prepared his forces for the Ashanti horseshoe formation. The British formed a large square the Ashanti could not defeat despite the somewhat chaotic battle and pushed through the center of the horseshoe. The first village was taken, and the Ashanti broke into small harassing bands after the first battle was lost. Wolseley then kept moving through the jungle, arriving at the Ashanti capital of Kumasi by February 4, only three and a half weeks after starting out and well before the deadly disease-causing wet season would begin. The king and golden stool were gone. To send information both to the king and his wider empire of subordinate lords, Wolseley blew up the palace and burned the town. The king's legitimacy was profoundly undermined along with his confidence. Ashanti did not even raid the coast again for some time. While they remained a violent threat to British expatriate claims until the beginning of the 1900s, the Ashantis never again challenged the British at the level of major armed units (Farwell 1985, 193–199).

In both the case of the emperor of Abyssinia and the king of the Ashanti, it is difficult to ascribe motivations retrospectively with so little information about each man personally. Nonetheless, background and actions in power of Emperor Theodore II of Abyssinia (1818–68) suggest confidence in his ability to achieve against large odds was the primary motivator of violent actions, followed later by legitimacy in the form of a presumption of entitlement as an emperor and then followed by capital needs. Despite his later mental imbalance, Theodore began his adult life as a very successful, politically clever scribe of lower nobility origins who steadily accrued wealth and status. He used his advancing position to evolve into a rather capable hillside bandit and later assassin of opposing leaders. With ever-accumulating resources and legitimacy, he slowly defeated the other major warlords, eventually crowning himself emperor in 1855. Only after the death of his beloved wife a few years after his coronation did he become increasingly erratic and brutal. By the 1860s, he seems to have become deranged, not only considering himself the equivalent to the British queen but also ascribing a wide array of intolerable slights to the lack of rapid responses to his letters.

Other than the physical harm by torture and possible death of British citizens, the emperor had no ability to harm the British homeland. Nonetheless, he could hurt the reputation of the British government at home and abroad if nothing was done to rescue citizens clearly likely to be harmed by a barbaric actor. However insane the emperor may have become, his confidence and arrogance seemed present right up the end of the battle with Napier in his negotiation efforts and brutality to prisoners (Woolbert 1935).

For the Ashanti king, much the same can be said about his likely motivations. The Ashanti monarch, the "king on a golden stool," had a multicentury history of success in conflict and good reasons to be confident in any efforts to impose violence. His realm was as organized a monarchy as the coastal clans were not. The proud jungle Ashanti had little use for the arrogance of the lackluster coastal clans that once simply operated as obsequious merchants selling Ashanti war captives to the white man. The king used the Ashanti army to keep firm control of the territory and clans in the jungles neighboring the coast.

Evidence for legitimacy as a strong secondary motivation is found both in the raids on villages in retribution for the loss of the slaves and in the return of the otherwise disdained coastal soldiers to Governor Pine without their weapons, ammunition, or stores. The king could have killed the soldiers, but instead he indicated a decision not to be violent as long as the trade — coastal village pillaging for the loss of two slaves — was accepted by the British. Furthermore, for whatever reason that he attacked in largescale after the Dutch gave Britain their territories, he did not stay outside his territories. Rather, he went home, apparently confident that the British would not follow despite the attacks, or that his army could defeat any British armed force in the jungle as the Ashanti kings had done in the past.

In both cases, while the British Empire generally did not demonstrate a consistent command of the strategic elements of disruption and resilience, especially for its deployed forces, both commanding officers of these disruption-led strategies did. The disruption strategies were remarkably well tuned to the motivations of the threat actors and to the resilience needs of the circumstances. During the mad rush to build colonial empires, both the distance and the organization of far-flung armies dictated the kinds of strategies used to obtain the outcome. British colonies were expected to pay for themselves if possible, and British commanding officers were expected to improvise a response to threats as needed. For example, holding the British Indian and Asian colonies in particular to this requirement made the lucrative opium trade through Burma to China especially critical for the finances of those colonies. Ensuring that the Chinese emperor did not intervene in this trade did not necessarily require coercive action. If the innovative local British official could produce the outcome desired by an argument or bribery rather than force, that choice was fine with the Home Office. While a local British official might request support involving coercive British forces, the commanding military officer on the ground chose the actual force employed and thus its implications for effective disruption (Beckett 2003).

In the British Army, therefore, the personality of the local commander dictated nearly completely the choices in any processes of information collection and refinement, not to mention application or any form of surprise accommodation. The result was a highly fragmented and often incomplete flow of knowledge across a hodge-podge hierarchy linking the various elements of the far-flung military units. If a brash, old, or staff-bred commander was more arrogant or blustery than careful, then an enemy ambush would often succeed. If a more careful or experienced officer (especially one from British India Army service) was chosen, all things being equal, the ambush would be avoided. Each would have the same tools of preparation — which amounted to what each commander individually would have decided in advance to request and bring along. Thinking ahead about resilience was, in particular, not encouraged in the training of officers or operational processes of the British colonial army. As Farwell noted dryly about the British response to the First Sikh War in 1844, "The British were not fully prepared — they rarely were" (Farwell 1985, 39). Farwell also noted that the British Army finally was formally prepared to fight the Crimean War — only at its end. Unfortunately and typically enough, however, its senior officers were unable to see any future need for the effective ground-sea logistics system they had built during the war. After the Crimean War peace treaty, they promptly dismantled it (Farwell 1985, 39).[33]

In this environment, senior officers chose their strategies more often as a function of their own unique set of on-the-job training experiences than of the current mission's circumstances. Wolseley's famous obsession with being prepared for nature's ugly surprises in terrain and weather, for example, was again and again attributed to the seminal experiences of preparing a force to trek into the Canadian north on the Red River Campaign of 1870 (Spiers 2007). But he was unusual, as was Sir Charles Napier. For the most part, rarely did officers concern themselves in advance with details that might have dictated a different response to a threat. Emphasis on education outside of service was at best basic for gentlemen, especially for those not destined for the church, business, or academia. Even in 1912, with only 12 percent of the population in

33. Farwell stated: "The creaking army administrative departments had been oiled and kicked into some reasonable degree of efficiency; a transport department, non-existent at the beginning of the war, was now mobilized and 28,000 animals had been collected; replacements were at last arriving and reserves were stationed in Malta" (Farwell 1985, 79). "Even so, with the signing of the Crimean War peace treaty in Paris, the Army demobilized itself and abandoned its organizational progress. It did not show a semblance of having absorbed any of the lessons until the Caldwell reforms of 1868–1871. Even then, the reforms were bitterly opposed by the senior officers. Only a cabal of younger officers with the support of Prime Minister Gladstone was able to finally overturn the commission purchase system, and thus reorganize the infantry regiments and command structure more sensibly. The county names for regiments, territory-based recruiting system, and rotation of one of the regiment's two battalions along with shorter service for soldiers (12 years instead of 21) all began at this time. It well served the Army morale and training into WWI" (Farwell 1985, 188).

agriculture in the United Kingdom, fully 65 percent of senior officers came from rural farm backgrounds (Strachan 1983, 70).

Through most of the 1800s, British officers learned how to do their jobs after they were in their regiments. Often their commissions were purchased for them before puberty. Many started so young that their true strategic and tactical training occurred in wars up to forty years before they were in charge of a battle.[34] In fact, most officers destined to conduct the bulk of the conflicts over the second half of the 1800s were honed as lads in bloody battles of British India or the disasters of the Crimean War of 1854–55. Napier began his career in India as a junior officer with the Bengal Engineers in 1828 and participated in the First and Second Sikh Wars plus a number of other British Indian engagements. Wolseley was a product of Burma and, especially, the Crimean War; he also later served in India during the Sepoy Mutiny years in the late 1850s.[35]

34. Commissions in particular units were purchased for boys, some at the time of their birth. When officers moved up, they sold their old rank at an official price, thus constituting their only pension fund. The famous inane Charge of the Light Brigade in the Crimean War was led by Lord Cardigan, who bought his whole regiment. To take control of its officers, the British government had to "buy" back all these commissions in the 1870s (Farwell 1985, 187). The presumption that officers were gentlemen of independent means from landed gentry lasted for at least another half century after the 1871 Caldwell Reforms. Most of continental Europe had already dispensed with purchased commissions in the decades after Napoleon in the early 1800s (Strachan 1983, 70).

35. The literature on the Crimean War is enormous, especially the bits focused on the noble gallantry and unbelievable incompetence of the British participants. The most succinct summing up of the war, however, remains that provided by Farwell. Readers are warned that the following summary will not enable them to pass a history exam, but it suits the level of detail of this book quite well. "On 27 March 1854 Britain declared war on Russia because she did not want Russia to extend her power and influence over Turkey. With France, Turkey and Sardinia as allies, the British landed an army in the Crimea. After the French and British had fought and won the Battle of the Alma, they marched to the great Russian fortress of Sevastopol where they sat down for a long winter siege. In October came the Battle of Balaclava and in November the Battle of Inkerman. The siege itself followed the pattern of all sieges: there were trenches, redoubts, masked batteries, attacks, counterattacks, and a considerable amount of boredom, sickness and uncomfortable living. Before the winter was over, a great many soldiers froze to death or died of neglect, being given neither sufficient food nor adequate clothing. In September 1855, after the French had succeeded in capturing a key position, the Russians blew up the fortress and retired; the allies decided that they, too, had had enough and went home. This was the Crimean War" (Far-

In his formative years, Napier experienced a military paying for itself, little controlled by London, with good and awful senior officers, and a great deal of mismanagement leading to death. Wolseley had received an intense dose of the same in the Crimea. That war was the "worst managed war of the century: logistics, tactics and strategy were all badly handled. . . . there was no connection whatever between the Army and the Navy. . . . There was not even a single unified British army . . . it is doubtful if the Army of the East (sent to the Crimea) could have won the Battle of Waterloo . . . the brave stupid charge of the Light Brigade was the result of a mangled order: the entire brigade — half of the British cavalry in the Crimea — charged in the wrong direction . . . even when orders were clearly given (rare), their recipients often had not an idea as to how they should be carried out" (Farwell 1972, 69).

For Napier and Wolseley, then, there were no exact rules of how to get the British consul back from the Abyssinian emperor, stop the Irish-American anti-Canadian marauders, or deter the Ashanti to stay on their side of the Pra River. Both men chose strategies consistent with their personalities. At the end of the day, both Napier and Wolseley did their research. While legitimacy was the initial motivator for Emperor Theodore II, confidence was the strongest motivator for him, as it was for the Ashanti. Both officers chose measured force and prepared carefully. Napier had been trained as an engineer. Wolseley, experienced from the Crimea and the Red River disruption campaign of 1870 in Canada, was a battle-experienced quartermaster officer with enormous concern for having good intelligence before and during an operation (Manning 2007). Both had British India experience that made them more likely to pay attention to logistics before the battle, especially water, disease, and supply train protection.[36]

---

well 1985, 68). Ultimately, the war did not stop the Russians from subsequently exercising considerable control over weak, corrupt Turkey, despite all the lives lost to forestall this very outcome.

36. Leaving aside the poorly organized British Army in the Crimea, a parsimonious alternative explanation for the disastrous performance is also the social disdain that British line officers serving in European-only units had for the British officers serving in India. Since the colonies had to pay their own way, including their portion of the British Army, the British East India Company had for decades developed its own army and paid British officers to command native regiments. Sometimes, if the fight needed more resources, the Home Office would send all European regiments to fight with the British-led Indian units,

That experience also led both of them to engage in consultation, never a hallmark of British Army senior officers. Commanders went off to small wars consulting with nearly no one other than their accompanying officers, although they did send dispatches. Napier's decision to build a railroad, and even to fight for it bureaucratically in advance, suggested he did consult with and listen to other officers with different experiences. Wolseley was particular about the mix of officers serving with him and cared about how prepared they were intellectually to think through the surprises of the coming fight. Starting with the officers from the Red River Campaign who were all selected for their intelligence and bravery, Wolseley constructed a cohort of thirty-five of the brightest officers in the British Army to deal with the Ashanti. All were indeed considered exceptionally literate as well as personally brave. Later four would receive the rarely given medals for bravery, eleven would become general officers, and many of those who died also would have advanced far, had they lived (Farwell 1985, 191).

Wolseley insisted on collegial and honest consultations on the impending campaign beginning with the sea voyage on the way to the Gold Coast. Officers were required to read constantly and to meet every day to exchange everything they knew on West Africa — weather, terrain, customs, military techniques, disease, and survival. The new addition to a campaign — the war correspondents that Wolseley hated — noted the young officers constantly discussing collegially the West African theater rather than debating about cards or racing as young officers typically did (Farwell 1985, 193–95).

In stark contrast to the habits of British officers of the era, both Napier and Wolseley insisted upon comprehensive data collection well in advance and during the entire operation. Napier's intelligence gathering in preparation for the Abyssinian War was remarkably thorough. The telegraph played a role from the outset when the secretary of state for India, located in London, telegraphed the governor of Bombay in July 1867 to ask how long it would take to assemble forces for a campaign in Abyssinia. Unlike previous eras, the world

---

but the officers of the former disdained the social status of the officers of the latter. The war in the Crimea was seen as a major conflict, and the senior British commander, Lord Raglan, was contemptuous of the British Indian Army officers. Few were allowed to serve under him. The British in any case sent fewer forces to the war than had the French or the Turks, providing relatively fewer officer positions. The result was that the cadre of officers most able to fight in third-world conditions were left out of the battles for which they were the best trained (Farwell 1985, 69).

of the "mad dash" expedition had arrived, at least in the minds of the Home Office. The old fellows of the Horse Guards had, of course, no idea of the topography of the area around Abyssinia, but at least they now knew how long it might take to get over there (Farwell 1985, 167).

Fortunately Napier's carefulness extended to actually studying the terrain in advance, unlike most of his contemporaries in uniform. He advised London that rescuing the British consul would be expensive due to the ruggedness of the terrain. Based on his advance research, he argued that quickly dashing in to grab the prisoners from the emperor as envisioned by his London-based superiors was not physically possible. Instead, Napier took the time to make sensible plans for moving his army into the Abyssinian homeland and anticipated the provisioning needs of staying there for some time. At the end of the day, the expedition involved 13,000 British and Indian troops, 14,000 followers, 291 ships of all sizes, and about 30,000 camels, horses, elephants, and donkeys (Porch 2006a, 114). Convinced by a junior officer who was later to build railroads all over India, Napier chose to build a railroad across the trackless expanses en route to Abyssinia although the construction would slow his advance. Napier intended to use mainly Indian troops and had wanted to use elephants for transport, but they could not be acquired in Africa. Instead, he planned to import his own railroad track, engines, and cars and to order water purifiers from the United States (Porch 2006a, 116).

Wolseley, like Napier, stood out among his peers for his attention to intelligence collected in advance. Wolseley's ability to think of everything beforehand earned him the sobriquet of "All Sir Garnet," which meant everything was in good order (Campbell 2002). As Wolseley was always reading everything he could on the terrain, peoples, customs, weather, and economies of lands to which he was sent, so did the "Wolseley Gang" of handpicked officers. He was known for keeping a list of able officers and favored those formally educated in the Staff College over those who more or less bought their commissions with little other education than in the ranks (Campbell 2002).

Wolseley constantly educated himself on fighting obstacles ranging from weather to water to insects to disease. He orchestrated his campaign around the mosquito-free period of the year, noting that only during the dry season did Europeans have a prayer of surviving the disease-ridden Gold Coast. He timed the assembling of his officers and planned the campaign around the dry season months of December, January, and February. With so little time available, he decided on the mad dash expedition. He also knew that his current mission was to use local coastal tribes known for fearing the Ashanti and giving way suddenly. Not only would he have to arrange for London to send European soldiers, but something would have to make them approve that request quickly. Everything that could be done in advance to keep the European soldiers healthy enough to fight while racing inland had to be done in advance of London's approval (Beckett 2003).

Preparing for European soldiers began immediately on arrival. One senior and reliable officer was sent to construct and provision a series of assembly and bivouac points on the way to Ashanti lands, each complete with everything needed, including daily quinine doses for every soldier. As Wolseley anticipated, most of the officers and men who had come with him were sick upon arrival or shortly afterward. Nonetheless, he marched quickly off to attack villages that had refused to support his call for troops to fight the Ashanti. By proving in dispatches how hopeless it would be for him to succeed without European troops, within a month of arriving he received approval for three battalions of European troops to arrive in early January 1874. When they arrived, as in the Red River Campaign, Wolseley and his officers had already fully mapped the route, complete with the overnight supply points and even respirators, mosquito belts, and quinine (Farwell 1985, 194).

Collaborative and actionable knowledge development was clearly present with Wolseley, but Napier also collected and explicitly updated his analysis as the campaign progressed. Both officers showed the ability to adapt to new information. Napier responded quickly and precisely to the surprise attack of the Abyssinians on his momentary lapse of good attention while on the march to the route of his supply trains. Wolseley consistently demonstrated his ability to incorporate information before the operations began and then to update with new information. For example, during the Red River Campaign of 1870, Wolseley sent a trusted junior officer — added just for this mission — to the rebel-held Winnipeg to scout around. The officer even interviewed Riel, the leader of the provisional government, presumably under some cover story. This officer then met Wolseley's forces on the way in and reported on how well organized the enemy encampment had appeared (Campbell 2002). During the Ashanti War, after the initial victory the Ashanti warriors retreated in good order, indicating they were not conceding defeat. Accordingly, the warriors kept trying to harass Wolseley's flanks as his forces moved forward. The supply bearers from the coastal clans became terrified when they realized the Ashanti were not quite beaten, and they refused to carry any more supplies. Wolseley was able to suddenly put his soldiers on short rations and still press on to the capital. Wolseley's operational success was driven by the season. He knew he had only a few weeks of good weather and had provisioned well enough in advance for such surprises in the supply chain (Farwell 1985, 198).

Wolseley's interest in having a modern professionalized military included having a larger staff than any of his contemporaries and, in particular, in placing great stock in his intelligence officer. This focus on the development of timely knowledge led to Wolseley expressing critical remarks about one of his own handpicked officers if the officer failed in the intelligence aspect of war. For example, one of his consistently brave and enduring officers, Buller, who even abandoned a new bride and a command school course to serve under Wolseley, was sent to find the Ashanti concentrations using scouts, spies, local informants, and prisoners. But he conducted his own reconnaissance personally, losing a good deal of time (Manning 2007). Wolseley was extremely annoyed because he considered a single person's scouting too narrow a view, even if it was the intelligence officer's eyes (Farwell 1985, 260). Wolseley had his staff intelligence officer do more than find good water along the route. In addition to using the normal scouts and interrogation of natives for real-time information, the officer was also expected to set up a local native spy ring to keep information flowing during the expedition (Manning 2007).[37]

So attuned to developing new data patterns was Wolseley that he assumed the enemy could do that as well and incorporated this use of knowledge into his plan. Using information from his small intelligence staff, Wolseley prepared a deception plan to both obtain information and to spread false data to counter the spies the Ashanti king was known to have. His was one of the earliest campaigns to have news reporters along, and he not only routinely deceived them but even counseled such behavior to junior officers. He feared they would publish something about his plans that let the enemy know where his smaller forces would be marching. In this case, Wolseley let it be known among the coastal natives that he was preparing to attack inland along an-

---

37. One ironic obstacle that the intelligence officer had to overcome was the enormous fear the coastal natives had for the Ashanti. This fear inevitably made them kill any Ashanti prisoner they took before any information could be acquired (Manning 2007). Buller did overcome this cultural barrier eventually.

other route using a strongpoint held by a detachment under a certain Captain Glover. To make the story believable, he then sent off a gunboat with 90 men and no effort at secrecy. He elevated them to a diversionary column attracting the Ashanti spies into monitoring Glover's men while Wolseley dashed in along another route. It worked (Manning 2007).

At the end of the campaign, Wolseley suffered only 18 men killed in action to disease and 185 wounded. He spent less than a million pounds as opposed to the nearly nine million pounds spent in the Abyssinian War only six years earlier. His officers vied to serve with him at every occasion, leaving him usually in the situation of being able to choose among the best for his staff (Farwell 1985, 198). The British press disliked Wolseley and his tendency to deliberately mislead them as much as he disliked the press. Nonetheless they had to report a flawless small war of both disruption and resilience despite the escape of the king and his golden throne.

American Disruption of Perceived Threats in Guatemala and Vietnam

Security threats are so fundamental to the human fight or flight instinct that some do not have to objectively threaten and yet may invoke the same response as those threats that are physically real. It is an open question whether any of the "threats" in America's history of small wars ever truly threatened U.S. interests at a serious level.[38] None of them technically approached the kind

38. As fascinating as the early small wars of the United States are for military or economic history in general, raw imperial expansion following a threat to commercial interests is not the same as a threat of mass casualty violence by enemies who could actually touch the home society. Prior to the Cold War, it is reasonable to see most U.S. small wars as manufactured threats built on the disinclination of other interests in relinquishing often quite lucrative monopoly advantages in those backwater states. With the advent of the Cold War, a more credible threat emerged, that of what might happen with nuclear war if Russian confidence exceeded its caution as a function of encircling Western states with communist proxy states. That goal may never have been physically achievable, but it was cognitively powerful in the USSR as well as the United States (Burnham 1947). Even before the USSR had a nuclear device, American leaders believed encirclement could defeat the United States, while the fear of an American sudden surprise attack was used in the former Soviet Union to cover up Stalin's policy mistakes. In both nations, a surreal paranoia about who was responsible for any failure in the wider communist or Western community emerged rather rapidly and often politically conveniently (Mastny 1996).

of violence threats seen in the premodern city-state wars, and certainly none were likely to be as surprising as the chronic violent gray threats possible in a deeply connected cybered globe. However, in the "starkly clear world . . . of good and evil" of the Cold War, the global aims and machinations of the USSR were considered by senior American defense officials to be directly and imminently physically threatening (Wittkopf and McCormick 1990, 628). In the view of key American leaders such as Allen Dulles and his brother John Foster Dulles, communism as promoted by the Soviet Union was the hidden cancer that would destroy the United States (Whitfield 1996).

Confirming evidence of their worst fears about the nearness of this threat was not only the Russian nuclear bomb development in 1949 but also a string of late 1940s covert takeovers of whole countries by proxies of the USSR in the form of local communist parties. One by one, Eastern European post–World War II democracies fell. In 1947, even Italy looked to be tottering on the electoral successes of Italian Communists (Appy 2000, 56). If one added in the close association of Maoist China with Russia, the world was readily viewed as on the edge of being gobbled up around the westernized states, especially the United States (Bowen 1983, 99).

The U.S. cases of small wars of disruption are drawn from the post–World War II period. They demonstrate a U.S. strategic desire to disrupt the spread of communism globally promoted by the nuclear-armed Soviet Union. The threat was perceived to be physical and ultimately violent even when posed by proxy actors in otherwise minor states. American leaders did not want to conquer or occupy the USSR, but they did perceive an Eastern European–like coup by electoral manipulation to be a violent threat with long-term negative consequences for westernized states. Soviet proxy states could emerge if bad actors came from the Soviet Union originally and were able to embed themselves in otherwise noncommunist states. Or the proxy could be one or more of a seemingly growing circle of states whose leaders were bad actors.

The two American case studies demonstrate stark lessons about failures in knowledge collection and development in disruption strategies. One is the U.S. operation aimed at disrupting President Arbenz and his land reform plans in Guatemala in 1950–54, and the second is the period of early involvement in Vietnam prior to the massive introduction of U.S. ground troops from 1954 to 1965. Irrespective of the commercial interests in Central America or colonial affiliations in Asia, both share a striking commonality in the effects of abysmally poor institutional knowledge prior to and during the operation, leading to truly unfortunate long-term results (Marks 1990).[39] In Guatemala, the United States succeeded only in messing with the mix of motivations, even had Arbenz been a threat. Rather, the American efforts disrupted a progressive, democratic government profoundly but did not create an ally with a stable economy. Its longer-term interests in cultivating "pro-American attitudes" in the population morphed into a focus on solely political and then military leaders (Hove 2007). The U.S. campaign left a country more feudal than before and riven with brutal conflict for the next four decades (Fraser 2005). Furthermore, communism became more, not less, popular in the wider region. The abbreviated invasion of Guatemala by dissident exile Colonel Castillo Armas, funded by the Central Intelligence Agency (CIA) on June 18, 1954, started a ripple effect of fear throughout the younger and more idealistic of Latin America. This spreading concern about their own self-determination prompted a number of intellectuals to move closer to revolutionary positions, including the famous revolutionary Che Guevara (Hove 2007, 623; Immerman 1980).

In Vietnam from 1954 to 1964, the United States did not even succeed in disruption other than to pour resources into a delaying action that, for a time, masked the clear indications of its failure to understand the motivation profile of the opposition (Anderson 2006). In many respects, the 1965 reassurance speech of U.S. president Lyndon Johnson, entitled "Peace without Conquest," captured the position of the larger city-state feeling the need to respond to a threat it could not simply kill. The speech's rhetoric was meant to counter the growing domestic concern over an escalation of larger military forces sent to a distant battlefield and even included the promise of a one-billion-dollar Mekong River development project. The strategy emphasized coercion and offered the capital investment as a secondary emphasis, both designed with limited information behind these strategic choices (Yuravlivker 2006). In neither case did notions of resilience play a role, save perhaps in the normal logistics concerns of military expeditionary forces in Vietnam. Ironically enough, the political blowback later in the losing war was an early indicator of the reputa-

---

39. It is important to report that much of the literature on the CIA during the Cold War was only seriously challenged after the release of formerly highly classified papers in 1995. The revelations included new and confirming details on the overthrow of the elected government in Guatemala (Doyle 1997).

tional problem a city-state choosing destruction would have in an electronically connected global news environment. Along with other surprise events, this downside of embedded reporting from free-fire zones was not anticipated (Mack 1975).

The lack of accurate analysis begins with surprising successes in covert communist takeovers of Eastern European fledgling democracies at the outset of the Cold War. Within five years of the end of World War II, U.S. security institutions were exceptionally sensitive to any actions by political leaders of any non–Western European nations that could be interpreted as growing support for a covert Soviet expansion toward communist global domination. Opposing the striking symbol of anticommunism — capitalist corporations — was readily viewed in the Western nations' defense communities as a statement about one's ideological position in general (Fraser 2005, 490). The American actions over the Cold War era are marked by inability to develop sufficiently correct knowledge to accurately assess the violence motivations of any actors who happened to be perceived as communists. The presumption that powerful possible threats could operate secretly and indirectly through some otherwise innocent-looking proxy actor became a blinding and automatic knowledge filter for the U.S. strategic decision makers.

From the top to the bottom of the U.S. security institutions and, by extension or persuasion, its top political leaders, any actor labeled a "communist" was a threat anywhere. Any political idea viewed as supported by communists was also likely to be tainted and threatening. Since the communists were known to operate covertly, any opposition to Western European or American preferences could be interpreted as evidence of hidden antidemocratic sympathies by the security analysts of the United States. For example, the logic was that communism opposes capitalism, and capitalism was viewed as an essential environment for democracy. Any local progressive political steps, say to relieve poverty through minor land redistribution, could be seen as attacks on the property rights tenet of capitalism. Accordingly, land reform was therefore an idea both communist and antidemocratic.[40] Any related reform

40. Adler demonstrates a remarkably easy conversion of hatred of Nazi Germany to the communist Soviet Union that occurred among Americans in the 1940s and 1950s. It built easily upon the antisocialism and anti-unionism efforts of conservatives of the 1920s and 1930s as well, but that would not have been sufficient without prominent speakers equating communism with fascism in the broad term "totalitarianism" (Adler and Paterson 1970).

declarations or efforts were automatically perceived by U.S. security analysts as prima facie evidence of otherwise covert communist inclinations and likely control by the Russians (Kinzer 2006). So strong was this presumption that it became an axiom throughout the strategic planning and security elements of the American government. Contrary evidence was not sought or, if stumbled upon, was reinterpreted to support the axiom. The accurate, knowledge-based assessment necessary to understand the violence drivers of the threat actors was simply missing for at least forty years.

Both Jacopo Arbenz, the elected president of Guatemala, and Ho Chi Minh, prime minister and president of North Vietnam, had the bad luck to be interested in land reform and self-determination of their countries in the early years of the Cold War. Few Americans know that Ho Chi Minh in the 1940s had a great fondness for the United States. He expected American understanding of his self-determination struggle and even used words from the U.S. Declaration of Independence in his independence speech in 1945 after fighting the Japanese (Kinzer 2006, 150). In 1945, as the Chinese occupied Hanoi to cement the Japanese surrender, Ho Chi Minh told the head of the U.S. liaison team to the Chinese that Ho looked to the United States for support as a "savior of all small nations" (Spector 1983, 61). Fewer still even remember President Arbenz, whose short four years in office began with a plan to put uncultivated land into peasant hands against the objections of local landowners and foreign companies (Kinzer 2006, 135). The axiom of the Cold War — opposition to U.S. business is ipso facto evidence of being a communist — ensured that the true dominant motivation of both leaders — need — was never sought nor understood by the Americans when the actual fighting began. For the next forty years, Latin America would particularly feel the brunt of this reinterpreted anticommunism prism.

In Guatemala from 1945 to 1954, the misdiagnosis by ill-informed U.S. policymakers resulted in the destruction of a fledgling democracy rather than its salvation from communism. During the 1900s prior to the 1950s, the United

---

It is an old adage of uncertain origin that to make people believe something, one has to give it a name, and that certainly seems to have been the case here. The effect, generally called "the Cold War consensus" by security studies scholars, was so ubiquitous and deeply reinforced that even in the early 1990s a level of distrust of the former Soviet Union close to that of the 1950s was still present in American public opinion surveys (Wittkopf and McCormick 1990).

States generally neglected Central America beyond assuring the U.S. control of the essential Panama Canal.[41] The U.S. disinterest in most of what was happening to the isthmus connecting the north and south American continents was profound. Even thirty years later at the outset of the Reagan presidency in 1981, the number of analysts in the Central America section of the U.S. Defense Intelligence Agency was less than half a dozen, according to a personal comment from a DIA officer serving at the time. With so little sought or known by U.S. intelligence, it was not hard for politicians and public presses to believe misinterpretations of events, even some completely fabricated stories (Kinzer 2006, 135). By the onset of the Korean War, generally more objective knowledge was neither sought nor welcome.

At the end of World War II, while communists existed throughout Latin America, the closer proximity of Central America to the United States made the possibility of covert communist takeovers in Central America more threatening.[42] The rigid anticommunist fixation of CIA deputy director Allen Dulles, brother of Secretary of State John Foster Dulles, intensified this growing, if poorly informed, fear (Hove 2007, 629). In Guatemala, on the basis of unbelievably limited data, the United States via the CIA, with active endorsement

41. It is important to note that Europe and then Asia occupied most of the U.S. national security attention for most of the U.S. history. Issues of concern from Latin America were dealt with one by one, usually as one-off crises.

42. Sources for this section are weighted heavily toward those written after 1995 when formerly highly secret CIA documents from the 1950s were declassified. Prior to these revelations, the consensus in scholarly explanations for U.S. involvement in coups in Central America emphasized commercial political interests over the anticommunist rationale. The documents, however, reveal a much greater level of CIA interventions in the form of machination and money that were legitimated by internal concerns for the spread of communism. For example, the fortunes of United Fruit Company in Guatemala had already begun to decline long before the Truman administration became interested in the possible intrusion of communism in Central America (Fraser 2005). This is not to say that works prior to 1995 were inaccurate. Rather, it is merely to say the weight of the full evidence changes the dominant explanation with the advent of the Cold War. It is reasonable to argue that before the advent of the Cold War, small U.S. wars had little to do with violent threats to the United States and are well explained by ability of commercial interests to manipulate the resources of an otherwise uninterested hegemon, with ideology a secondary player if at all. After the advent of the Cold War and the transfer of anger and fear from Nazi Germany to Soviet Russia and its plan for a communist world, however, U.S. interventions in Latin American are better explained by the ways that evidence was interpreted to fit Cold War fears of covert communist subversions of struggling nations (Kinzer 2006; Doyle 1997).

by the State Department, went about disrupting what was viewed as a violent threat from an emerging Soviet communist foothold in Central America. The country was and is a tiny nation on the other side of Mexico, but it was viewed as only a long walk away from the United States. After a long-ruling dictator was overthrown in 1944, charismatic professor Juan Jose Arevalo was elected to run the nascent democracy. While he was careful to protect property rights, he walked a populist edge in his socialist rhetoric, which made those in Washington watch him carefully. Already dealing with more than two dozen coup attempts against him by various factions in the elite landowning class, Arevalo did not attempt any serious land reform (Fraser 2005, 487).

At the end of Arevalo's uninterrupted and thereby unprecedented single six-year term for a democratically elected president in 1950, two army officers vied as main candidates for the position. Francisco Arana was a serving army colonel, and Jacobo Arbenz Guzman was a former army captain. Both had played major roles in the revolution six years earlier and had also participated in recruiting the professor to come back from exile to run as the first president. Each had received a major role in the new administration, the more liberal Arbenz as defense minister and the more conservative and prickly Arana as chief of the armed forces. Even before the election, however, relations between the candidates and the sitting president had deteriorated. Arbenz was pushing Arevalo to be more ambitious in his socialist reforms while Arana was increasingly at odds with Arbenz over military matters and with Arevalo over the liberal bent of his cabinet. Furthermore, one of Arana's most talented officers, Colonel Carlos Castillo Armas, was newly in jail after having participated in one of the many conservative coups attempted against Arevalo. By the time of the election, Arana was so estranged that he was threatening to lead a coup himself against Arevalo.[43]

The electioneering process was bitter and the outcome unclear until Arana was ambushed and killed by gunmen in 1950. Arbenz was then elected easily, but his assumption of office was tainted by his association with some of the gunmen, as well as his subsequent land reform preferences. He tried to assuage the military in particular. Many of them, however, were from landowning families now even angrier about land issues than they had been with Arevalo's more careful steps (Fraser 2005, 488).

---

43. It is worth noting that in this world of universal suffrage, only educated males were allowed to vote in this election (Gleijeses 1991).

During the Cold War, to be seen as a threat by the CIA, it was not necessary to actually have a motivation to threaten the United States with violence — it was sufficient to be tagged with key indicators of a hidden association with the Soviet communist cause. Unfortunately Arbenz was known to consult occasionally with the very small Guatemalan communist party on the topic of land reform. This association, however limited, would have triggered CIA suspicion in any case, no matter how far Arbenz's motivations were objectively from the armed imperialist intentions attached to the Soviet plan for world domination. As a result, CIA and State Department observers early on interpreted Arbenz's actions and language to further land reform as support for communism. From a 1952 State Department analytical document comes the dire observation: "Communists already exercise, in Guatemala, a political influence far out of proportion to their small numerical strength. This influence will probably continue to grow. The political situation in Guatemala adversely affects U.S. interests and constitutes a potential threat to U.S. security" (Fraser 2005, 491).

On the basis of this entirely inferred characterization and extraordinarily weak evidence, the agency went to Central America to find someone to disrupt Arbenz, preferably in a coup. In 1952 in Mexico, they found Jose Castillo Armas, the angry conservative jail-escapee and exiled former colonel. The CIA representatives offered to fund him and some forces in an invasion to displace Arbenz. Popular in some circles for his resignation after Arana's assassination, Armas had supporters in Guatemala and seemed a reasonable alternative strongman (Marks 1990). He agreed for the funds and the opportunity for revenge (Fraser 2005, 488).

The coup was not quickly arranged due to poor communications and the need for secrecy in a third-world environment of cronyism. But the delay also came from the lack of management ability of the angry colonel. An aborted dry run in the fall of 1952 fizzled miserably, and then the State Department withdrew essential support when the cover was blown. One of the neighboring dictators informed of — and in favor of — the operation had nonetheless let it slip publicly that a coup was likely. The idea had not been popular with the Truman administration in any case, and its public exposure was enough to close down the formal U.S. plan (Fraser 2005, 491). To make things worse for the agency's disruption plan, in March 1953 some exiled Guatemalan agents in the loose network of opposition to Arbenz encouraged by the CIA attempted an invasion on their own. They failed miserably and were jailed or exiled. President Arbenz not only captured many of the actors who would have been in the CIA's coup, but he also rolled up many of the CIA's other assets in an increasingly hard-line stance. The disruption operation was put on hold, perhaps forever (Doyle 1997).

The new American administration under the more conservative Eisenhower and his even more fervently anticommunist advisers, however, resuscitated the operation. Eisenhower brought into the American government his own concern about Soviet-sponsored revolutions and a desire to avoid expensive conventional operations, especially during the Korean War's final years (Fraser 2005, 492). In February 1953 a new strategy to disrupt the communist threat perceived in Arbenz of Guatemala was devised with no new information confirming Arbenz's communist tendencies. Nonetheless, the new operation won the support of the State Department, especially the new, more conservative U.S. ambassador to Guatemala. The plan consisted of a grand feint using someone to lead a small physical invasion that the agency would bolster with pamphlets and false radio announcements to create a false but widely held, frightening image of a massive successful invasion. The goal was to induce the Guatemalan Army to save the nation from the invaders while also deposing what would widely appear to be a helpless elected leader, Arbenz (Fraser 2005, 492).

This plan was not, in fact, all that unusual for the region. The strategy of "strike from the neighboring nation" was used by Ponce to take over Guatemala briefly after the 1944 coup. To depose Ponce, Arana and Arbenz did the same thing from El Salvador (Marks 1990). The difference here was the CIA's true intent was not that the invasion should succeed, but that the army should think it was succeeding. The plan was, in effect, a giant scam whose main theme was to project the image of a huge, unbeatable invasion force to destroy the confidence of the army in the president's ability to lead and defend the country. Implicit in this picture was the consequence of the struggle for the civilian population, towns, and economy as the military forces rampaged against one another.

When the actual incursion occurred in the summer of 1954, the invasion force comprised a few hundred mercenaries and former soldiers relatively well equipped by U.S. resources: rockets, rifles, mortars, and even heavy artillery. The soldiers had been on retainer in training camps for up to two years prior to the incursion in 1954, and about a hundred were considered well enough trained. Inspired by the Armas imminent invasion, guerrilla bands were already causing difficulties in the countryside by hijacking trains and destroying bridges, railbeds, and telephone or telegraph wires (Marks 1990, 69). The image of its ferocious inexorable victory was greatly exaggerated via airdropped pamphlets and radio announcements. Furthermore, as the artificial sense of victory grew, the forces swelled by temporary volunteers from the countryside including angry ranchers, peasants, or merely anti-Arbenz sympathizers. The expectation was that shortly after the invasion, panic among the population would explode, stimulating the army to act (Marks 1990, 69).

Unfortunately so many errors borne of U.S. ignorance were in play that the plan as envisioned was destined from the outset to failure. The invasion began, and the forces went only a half-dozen miles into Guatemala and then slowed to a crawl. In part this was due to the poor management of Colonel Armas in conducting his forces, but it was also due to the inability of the CIA to provide him resources as rapidly as he demanded. The CIA psychological warfare program also failed to take effect.[44] Over the months, the success looked less and less likely, with no army coup and no presidential resignation in sight.

Against the Guatemalan Army of five thousand or more soldiers, this tiny force would have been doomed. The Guatemalan Army, however, sat on its hands, doing absolutely nothing to overthrow Arbenz or to stop the invaders. Even the agency's effort to directly persuade army officers to implement a coup was so ill informed and clumsy that the officers grew suspicious and did nothing. Despite the fine equipment, so poorly prepared were the invaders that, on one occasion, a Guatemalan Army unit of 30 men thrashed 120 invading soldiers. To make matters worse, the CIA planners did not realize that the radio station taken over for use by the rebels did not even reach much of the country. So poorly secured were the details that many plans were sold from the Argentine embassy staff to Arbenz himself during the slow progress of the plan (Fraser 2005, 492).

In a bit of luck only for the CIA, Arbenz had the ability to think longi-

---

44. Oddly enough, it is difficult to find detailed discussions by military historians concerning any actual battles conducted by Armas. While Marks (1990) provides battle data, his research predates the release of the internal CIA documents. Furthermore, the details are heavily drawn from nearly forty-year-old recollections by locals who, as most people do, are likely to overstate the reality in such a long retrospect. Nonetheless, the divergence in characterizations of the actual progress of the Armas invasion is unusual. In terms of this work, if there were real battles, then the coercive nature of the U.S. strategy is substantiated. If not, then the evidence that Arbenz believed there were or soon would be is still sufficient for the argument here.

tudinally about what would happen eventually if he waited for the pathetic invasion to inch into the capital. The Guatemalan Army was not moving to depose him, but neither were its officers doing much to stop the invasion, however big it truly was. The population in the capital was equal parts fearful and angry that the president could not get the army to stop the invaders. When at last Arbenz resigned, he did so for the same reason that other reformers in Central America have also sadly stepped into exile—loyalty to the poorer classes.[45] His land reforms had upset the elite landowning families of many of the military officers who then harbored resentments. When the time came to defend Guatemala from the angry exiled colonel and his army of marauders, the army shot only if shot at. The resentful officers would have allowed the invaders to rampage their way into the capital, if that is what it took to force Arbenz out. He then resigned at this realization. In the words of one author, he was "psyched out" (Marks 1990, 68). It was certainly not an internal army coup and definitely not as the CIA had envisioned or even desired, now having seen what a poor manager and leader their hired proxy, the angry colonel, had proved himself to be (Fraser 2005, 504).

Arbenz's land reform certainly was disrupted, but rather than killing emerg-

45. An even more tragic, well-meaning, bright, liberal figure for his nation was Jose Santos Zelaya, president of Nicaragua. As he tried to modernize his nation, he interfered in the extraordinary profits of rapacious Americans and simply angered men with short tempers and few scruples. These men used a soon-to-be-common strategy of a personalized, highly misleading vilification campaign in the U.S. press coupled with behind the scenes personal influences enabling senior U.S. leaders to approve use of U.S. military or other assets to remove Zelaya in 1909 and replace him with a dictator. Nearly free land and cheap labor were the profit-generating attractions of Central America throughout the first half of the 1900s, and the wealthy Americans benefiting from this no-rules capitalism routinely struck back if incoming leaders objected to their use of the land, including simply sitting on it, or abuse of the local population, including modern forms of serfdom. The abuse of agreements was so bold that in some cases whole large projects promised in treaties with the government, such as a railroad across the nation, were simply ignored as the profits were repatriated home. In response to any objection, the local leader was personally attacked hysterically in the U.S. press as a despot, and ultimately the manufactured rebellions were widely characterized as a revolt to save the people of the nation from this evil character, never mind that the reality on the ground was much otherwise. In this, as other occasions, it was always the young democracies and the interest in a fair wage and living conditions for the local population that the U.S. government was suckered into helping overthrow. In every case up to World War II, what U.S. leaders actually knew about the situation was uniformly minimal or deliberately inaccurate (Kinzer 2006).

ing communist sympathies, the crass coercive nature of the plan and subsequent strongmen wrenching power from each other assured forty-plus years of chaotic and violent social conflicts for Guatemala. After Arbenz's resignation, the angry Colonel Armas was sworn in and ruled so harshly that he was assassinated within several years, only to be followed by another round of autocratic military rule. Arbenz died in exile in Mexico forty years later, all but forgotten save as a tragic figure of U.S. imperialism.

For the United States, rather than nipping a communist incursion in the bud, the overthrow of charismatic and decidedly fairly elected Arbenz appalled the educated upper and middle classes across Latin America. Young people especially turned to the voices of rebellion in anger. The Arbenz story lived far beyond his short four years in office as a parable about having the North American capitalists deliberately crush the promise of a better life in any fledgling democracy in Latin America. In keeping with the times, young people began to fight back, inducing even greater barbarity from the various regimes.[46] The CIA and its analysts declared a victory for this kind of "fake, shake, and remake" method of eliminating threats by churning political systems. In the Cold War, the agency and its senior administration supporters would transfer the plan as a lesson learned from Guatemala to other theaters with equally limited knowledge. It would take forty years and more to recognize the lack of accuracy and knowledge development on the part of the Americans.

In Vietnam, the lesson about U.S. inability to know enough and act appropriately was clear by the mid-1970s, but it was not so clear when the United States became deeply engaged in the mid-1950s. Even today, Vietnam's struggle for independence is still raw in the minds of many Americans. That the American decisions seem to have been mistaken is not in question. Rather, the unsettled pain stays alive because there is little consensus about where the blame belongs — on the president, on one or the other political party, on the press, on the Vietcong, the North Vietnamese, and China, on naïveté, or poor conduct within the military hierarchy.[47] Whether any or all of these played a serious

46. Che Guevara was a doctor in Guatemala during the Arbenz years and dated his conversion to revolution to this overthrow. He told this story widely and often (Fraser 2005).

47. The range of culprits is demonstrated by a vast literature by literally hundreds of scholars. A Google Scholar search in December 2007 using the key words "Vietnam conflict U.S. policy" produced no less than 187,000 citations, putatively with no duplicates according to the Google preference list.

role, in the environment of the time it was not considered necessary to know more than that communists were somehow involved, and thereby the mental infection could spread far beyond Vietnam. The rigid, knowledge-stifling Cold War institutional axiom needed only some evidence of nationalist revolutionary excesses for confirmation of a violent communist threat to the Western world, specifically the United States.[48]

Vietnam and Guatemala are linked sequentially as well as conceptually. The U.S. disruption of the threat of communism in Guatemala in the form of the CIA "PBSUCCESS" plan was seen as a model for future efforts to disrupt a proxy-led expansion threat from the Soviet Union. Despite the appalling lack of accurate knowledge and foresight in the operation, the perception in Washington of success in Guatemala persuaded Eisenhower that clandestine operations could successfully substitute for armed forces on the ground (Doyle 1997). By the time that the 1954 Geneva Convention temporarily recognized the sovereignty of North Vietnam north of the seventeenth parallel, Ho Chi Minh was a communist leader openly garnering Soviet support to eject France from the south. In response, the ardent anticommunist secretary of state John Foster Dulles was determined that any spread of the communist infection into South Vietnam had to be stopped before more of the world was lost to the totalitarian threat (Anderson 2006).

From the outset, so little was known about Vietnam's history that baseless stereotypes were presumed to be true without question. With accurate and timely knowledge refinement highly unlikely, Vietnam was not seen as the ultimate test of containment, but more like another hole to be plugged in John Foster Dulles's dike (Krepinevich 2004). The rampant misunderstanding of the situation on the ground led inexorably to armed coercion as the means best known institutionally to disrupt enemies. The story of the Vietnam con-

---

48. As a junior Reserve Army officer associated with analysts at DIA in the mid-1980s Reagan era, I had several conversations with full-time Latin American analysts concerning colleagues who were ardent believers in the existence of a Soviet master plan. Even in the 1980s, only among some friends and quietly could one make jokes about the colleague who was known for interpreting everything as part of the Soviet master plan, including a bus falling off a mountain road in Chile. Twenty years later under another hard-line president, the communism threat was replaced by the terrorism global threat. Saddam Hussein of Iraq was firmly believed to be secretly in the grip of a worldwide terrorist cabal. Honest skepticism after 9/11 and before and during the early years of the U.S. invasion of Iraq was viewed with an equally automatic suspicion.

flict in its broad strokes is rather straightforward compared to many small wars in history. Over the first ten years, 1955–65, the United States slowly expanded its efforts to disrupt what it saw as the rising communist threat via an armed insurgency in South Vietnam (Karnow 1997). The American effort began with the early Truman decision to help fund the French struggle with the North's Viet Minh national liberation forces in the early 1950s. The decision was not casually taken, but it was certainly not seen as extraordinary at the time. In the contemporary view of existential threats of the era, support to France representing the democratic West against communist insurgents was a natural expression of the broader policy of stemming communism globally.

By 1954, U.S. aid to the French forces in Vietnam was nearly three-quarters of the financial burden of the large French force itself (B. Palmer 1984, 5). By then the French were well on the defensive militarily in their efforts to retain their colonial control of Vietnam. From 1950 on, the Viet Minh under Ho Chi Minh built a relatively powerful force supplied and trained by Chinese forces. They engaged the French at Dien Ben Phu in 1954 as would any conventional military. That siege and military defeat for the French set a tone for the war in which the United States would find itself roughly ten years later. In 1956, the French recognized that they were militarily defeated and abruptly left the problem to the United States.

Over the course of the next ten years, U.S. knowledge of Vietnam and, especially, the motivations of key enemy actors and organizations continued to be blinkered by anticommunist stereotypes. Like the French, the Americans expected eventually to be able to bring overwhelming military force, preferably South Vietnamese forces, to decisively defeat the North Vietnamese and thus disrupt the spread of communism. Much like the North Koreans had done, the North Vietnamese were expected eventually to have to commit to a massive military invasion for which the U.S. allies would be prepared (Boot 2002). Without any strong understanding of the motivations of the Northern enemies or of the members of the Southern insurgency, the Americans never properly weighted the motivations especially of the Vietcong agents embedded in the society.[49] Seeing them as merely tools by the North to soften the battle-

---

49. The term *Vietcong* is actually a short and derogatory term developed by the anticommunist Western force to designate the Vietnamese communists in the south controlled by the North Vietnamese communists. The Vietnamese term for a Vietnamese communist was *Cong San Viet Nam*. The organizational connection of the Vietcong to the North was often

field, from 1956 to 1965 Eisenhower, Kennedy, and other senior U.S. defense leaders focused on building a powerful patriotic South Vietnamese military force in preparation for the anticipated final battle with the North (B. Palmer 1984, 6–7).

In 1965, at the end of this disruption case study period, the U.S. president Lyndon Johnson approved a plan to massively increase American military forces in South Vietnam. The decision clearly shifted the strategy toward destruction of insurgent forces away from the indirect efforts to guide failing South Vietnamese military forces toward disruption. Even then, after ten years as advisers to the South Vietnamese Army, the U.S. Army as lead agency for the conflict had only a few people in South Vietnam who even spoke the language, let alone a process of honest, consensual, and tested knowledge development. That such a basic knowledge deficiency could exist after so many years engaged in the struggle is an exemplary indicator of the lack of necessary knowledge about Vietnam and the motivations of its good or bad actors. This poor preparation proved an exceptional and unappreciated harbinger of the final outcome of the small war of disruption.

In these two conflicts, the motivations of either Arbenz in Guatemala or Ho Chi Minh in Vietnam were never appreciated by U.S. analysts. Arbenz's motivations for action, although by no means violent, were a strong sense of need for land to develop a strong middle class in Guatemala. In terms of a theory of action, the evidence suggests the close second motivator was legitimacy, to wit, a strong if naive presumption that such reform was the right thing to do. The new charismatic but much more idealistic president, Jacobo Arbenz, did not believe the United States would object to something so noble for the little guy as fairness in land distribution, especially if the land was not being used. Thus he did not walk the populist line as carefully as had his apparently better-informed predecessor. He also had the bad luck to take office just as the United States was learning how the Soviet Union took nations from the inside, via Communist Party activists and semilegal coups. He ambitiously

---

confusing to outside observers because the forces in the South were conducted as a guerilla arm separate in both recruiting and operations from the more conventional North Vietnamese Army. The structure was a modification of the Maoist Chinese three-stage people's war (withdraw to build support, guerilla preparation of battlefield, well-timed final confrontation) created and conducted by North Vietnamese General Vo Nguyen Giap (Tanham 2006; Vo 1970).

endorsed the nationalization of a small portion of the mass land holdings of foreign companies and elites. To reduce the likelihood of an elite revolt, Arbenz focused his land reform on massive properties generally held by foreign firms and then only on a small percentage of land that was not being used for any productive purpose (Fraser 2005, 488). For Arbenz, need for national economic support was a second motivator, especially in his cautious steps in the extent of land reform, while confidence was a distant third. He had no support among the military, although he did not expect their active opposition, given his own background.

For the North Vietnamese, the motivations for violence in the South were dominated by a bitter sense of the illegitimacy of the continuing French colonial rule after the defeat of the Japanese, the French denial of a plebiscite election by 1956 despite earlier promises, and then growing foreign (U.S.) support for a dictator, Diem, in the still-occupied South. Throughout the rhetoric known at the time and published after the war, in Vietnamese and in translations, there is a strong indignant legitimacy objection to foreigner rule over — and division of — Vietnam. Almost immediately, rationales for fighting back were also explicitly tied to need for resources taken by arrogant elites such as the Mandarin-like local Vietnamese elite, the French colonial masters, Frenchified collaborating local elites, or finally the Americans and any associated elites (Vo 1970; Spector 1983). As for the third motivator, confidence, the Vietnamese have a long and impressive history of eight centuries fighting down to the wire to keep local control of territory despite sometimes extraordinary odds.[50]

Legitimacy and need motivators were strong enough to keep the Vietnamese fighting through the occupation by the Japanese, the repressive return of the French, and finally the twenty-five-year war with the United States. Confidence in victory was the third motivator because the people's war was a late arrival, and constant reinforcement was necessary to keep guerillas in place and on their mission. Mao certainly provided the blueprint for the "people's war," using both conventional and guerrilla means to wear down a central

---

50. It is a consistent and embarrassing reality that most westerners, even military historians, are remarkably ignorant of the fighting experiences of third-world nations. This neglect and, bluntly put, arrogance has its costs, as the United States learned in Vietnam. For an excellent introduction to what most do not know now and did not know in the early years of Vietnam see Spector (1983).

government and the best timing of an overwhelming general counteroffensive to eliminate the government forces. However, no one could say exactly how long, over decades or generations, might be required to achieve victory. There were never guarantees in a people's war, only the certainty of the long-term bloody slog (Vo 1970, 156). One might be tempted to shorten this discussion by noting that the Vietnamese motivation was the legitimate right to their own land free and clear 24/7/365, and that sense of injustice, so like our own two hundred years earlier, simply was not recognized or honored by the French or the Americans.

With nearly no effort made to understand accurately the motivations of Arbenz or Ho Chi Minh, the United States did not weight its strategic choices. It chose coercion in both cases. The form of coercion wandered in the strategy, especially in Vietnam, but it was uniformly lacking in critical development of contrasting knowledge for strategic use. In Guatemala, the goal was to disrupt the spread of communism using local putatively pro-democracy strongmen like Armas as soon as Arbenz was considered a communist. In Vietnam, over the ten years of the case study period, the Americans treated Ho Chi Minh and all armed insurgents as communists. Any other information on their motivations was irrelevant once they were so classed.

The strategy was instead to try to remake the incompetent South Vietnamese Army into a version of the American military, including structures, by embedding U.S. advisers in the major local units. In a clear example of misunderstanding local motivations, the United States attempted to stop the recruitment into the insurgency by doing what was sure to help the communists' resentment arguments. In particular, it supported the futile and widely hated Strategic Hamlet Program of forced relocation intended to deny communists their sea of people in which to hide. As the first ten years ended, the reality of losing ground to more increasingly embedded guerillas induced American escalation in forces. The military strategy in the country moved from mobile search-and-destroy raids to bolster otherwise still-failing South Vietnamese forces to bombing North Vietnam and supply routes in Laos and Cambodia and to a growing tendency to declare whole swathes of land as pacified areas or free-fire zones (Sheehan 1988, 540).

All the variations of coercion as the major component of the U.S. disruption strategy failed completely in Vietnam and did not ensure democracy in Guatemala. That the strategy in Vietnam was failing was apparent at the ten-year mark (1965) when the escalation began, had the appropriate data and knowledge refinement been pursued.[51] The U.S. had stepped into the shoes of the arrogant French colonial overseers and then emphasized the wrong response tool of coercion against exceptionally strongly felt legitimacy and need motivations of the North and then increasingly of the South Vietnamese.

In any case, for U.S. analysts, weighting the motivations and varying the response would have been contemporaneously seen to be a waste of time since a communist was a lost cause. Because the Soviets were viewed as using communism more like a contagion, the U.S. response to the threat was usually targeted at the elimination of any infected individual, even if it was a duly elected president of a fledgling democracy or a set of illiterate peasants clinging to their huts.[52] To be fair, the communists had clearly shown in Eastern Europe how elections could be stolen, and only one stolen election was needed to take national control in postwar, chaotic Eastern Europe. Thus, having had an election in a Central American nation did not, in the minds of the U.S. strategic planners, inoculate any society from this Soviet-dictated communist subversive threat before, during, or after the next election (Adler and Paterson 1970).

Over a short period of time, even populists would be condemned by American strategists for uttering policy preferences sympathetic to the rampantly exploited rural populations of the world. They often used a language that bore similarities to the communist statements about world revolution. Furthermore, while the threat was recognized as an idea at its base, communism was seen as being enforced by the strong, hidden antidemocratic arm of the Soviet Union, which would cause local political leaders to suddenly and brutally assume control of the population at Russia's command. A regrettable twist of logic by the U.S. security agencies thus equated any populist expression of prefer-

---

51. A good review of the variety of explanations from historians for why the United States lingered in defeat for so long is found in Anderson (2006).

52. Note that the disease metaphor was common. Communism always "spread" while democracy was always "embraced." The reader is invited to read some of the language of the time to note the strange leap from communism as an idea to its projection as an immutable corrosive force finding the bribable, the weak-minded, and the pure evil among us to pervert. Nowhere does it seem strategically acceptable to simply discuss why someone might want land reform and yet not be a communist. Simply supporting the fair distribution of a nation's wealth in order to pull the country out of absolute poverty was evidence of having been infected. Ironically, being against monopolies and having a fair wage were exactly the sorts of social realities for which America and these patriotic Americans prided themselves at home.

ences for fair land distribution as equivalent in eventual outcome to the often brutal historical record of totalitarian Nazi Germany and to Stalin's Russia and its world domination declarations (Adler and Paterson 1970). No effort was made to ascertain motivations if the equivalence could be argued on even the most limited set of facts. In both cases, the disruption options considered were rarely the output of a theory of action or of surprise accommodation or based on a large body of well-substantiated facts once the lead agency and its preferred mode of operation was chosen. Since it was widely presumed among American security professionals that communist sympathizers would not yield to negotiation, nothing but the elimination of the subversive human element was entertained generally by either the CIA or the military planners in either case.

In the case of Guatemala, there is no evidence that a weighted framework comparing evidence across motivations was even considered once Arbenz was characterized as a communist sympathizer. Having had an election in a Central American nation did not mean communists were not secretly about to launch a surprising coup. Once the CIA was selected as the lead agency in Guatemala, its bias toward covert, outsourced operations dominated. The agency automatically sought to use proxies where possible, with the State Department providing the political legitimacy and covert access needed for an operation (Fraser 2005, 491).

In Guatemala, therefore, the young agency sought actors to overthrow the suspected communist president of Guatemala. Both the CIA and the State Department (not to mention both Truman and Eisenhower) would have preferred a coup by the Guatemalan Army with no obvious involvement of the United States. No one in the U.S. hierarchy, however, had paid enough attention to Guatemala beforehand to have the kind of trusted access necessary to make such a bald suggestion to the senior army officers. Hence the backup plan was to induce the army to rise up in some fashion. In 1952 CIA representatives found in the regional Guatemalan exiles feuding factions too small to succeed without U.S. assistance and too bitterly divided to work together. The documents released in 1995 showed the president receiving only the strategic elimination options for Guatemala perceived as necessary by Dulles as deputy director of the CIA (Fraser 2005, 491). In October 1952, the State Department withdrew support for the plan but not because of new information or a flexible reconsideration of whether the use of force, even if simulated, was the right strategy. Rather, the loose lips of strongman Somoza of Nicaragua ruined the cover for the U.S. government, which did not want it to be seen to be deposing democratically elected leaders.

That no other approach was considered is further demonstrated by the internal fixation on this particular plan of disruption by coup. When other opposition forces did stage a pathetic invasion in March 1953 and the State Department dropped its support of the plan, the CIA did not conclude that another approach needed to be considered or discussed. Rather, the key decision was that an invasion plan needed to be sold better to the Guatemalan Army, with much more attention to reliably creating the illusion of unstoppable success across the nation. Thus, when the new, more amenable President Eisenhower came along, the original plan was resuscitated in toto but renamed PBSUCCESS. It was adjusted only by greater direct CIA support to the psychological operations needed to convince the Guatemalan Army of the likelihood of success (Fraser 2005, 493).

In the case of Vietnam, throughout the period 1954–64 right up to the massive expansion of U.S. forces, key American leaders only explored variations of coercive alternatives once the Department of Defense, specifically the U.S. Army, was chosen as the lead agency, although the early preference was for local nationals to do the fighting. Not only was Vietnam viewed through rigid anticommunist filters, but the initial approach to Vietnam was heavily influenced by the highly biased information from the French. Later a variety of overly rosy assessments of the benefits of local fighting strategies would dominate strategic disruption background presumptions (Anderson 2006, 3). After the United States took the lead in Vietnam from the French in 1956 and began sending military advisers to bolster local fighting units, knowledge on the ground continued to be filtered through Cold War presumptions. As a result, the American leadership never wavered from the concept of a "fight" against communism and never considered emphasizing other strategic disruption tools more heavily than coercion (D. R. Palmer 1978).

Eisenhower and Kennedy had two things in common in their strategic view: neither wanted involvement of U.S. ground forces in Asian jungles. Hence while the stern dedication to coercion to save the Western world from communism was embraced by both of them, the actual strategic implementation wandered through variations along with advisers and arguments. From "fight guerillas with guerillas" to "use technology as our overwhelming strength," it took the arrival of the prickly, combative nature of Lyndon Baines Johnson stepping into Kennedy's shoes to change the strategic focus in 1965 to attrition

(D. R. Palmer 1978, 141, 215). Weigley argues that using the raw economic and population size of the United States to wear down the enemy has become the U.S. preferred method of warfare (Weigley 1973). Thus, it is not surprising that after the first ten years of failure, the United States would ultimately settle on trying to bleed the North Vietnamese to submission through the deep commitment of U.S. forces, however miscalculated that choice.

Honest consultation did not happen in either case, in part due to the anticommunist blinders, but also due to the lesson from World War II that operations by U.S. institutions as lone wolf endeavors were not effective. However, the answer was to choose a lead agency whose approach drove the nature of any cross-institutional consultation for each specific mission. This narrowing of consultation was more often a reflection of a functional approach to national security. In World War II, more than in any prior war for the United States, operations were significant and complex enough to require lead agencies to direct and coordinate activities across many other players. The choice of the lead agency was driven by the nature of the action envisioned. For example, something requiring an amphibious landing would be given to the navy while occupation of some territory for any length of time was given to the army (Fraser 2005, 491). The lead agencies were largely able to control both the agenda for options considered and the information included in the considerations.

In the case of Guatemala, the more the threat involved communism in places relatively ignored, obscure, or considered insignificant, the more the issue was shoved off to internal CIA notions of honest consultation. As the rank of the players at the strategy table became lower, fewer people outside the agency were permitted to introduce information or disagreement into the considerations. Although the ultimate enemy was a conventional hard power state such as the Soviet Union, the feared long-range tool was this infectious viral communism ideology that operated in shadowy ways. This characterization dictated that the CIA be given the lead in non-NATO operations outside the United States if covert communist activities were suspected.

The CIA itself, however, was a new player in Washington and needed larger institutional allies for political legitimacy, not to mention support in other nations. For the presumed final showdown (since communists were always expected to attempt a final physical takeover), even the CIA would have to use U.S. or other conventional warriors. Thus, the agency sought coalition partners as necessary. This need did not mean a wide array of consultations; it usually meant a targeted group of useful institutional friends and close attention to the presumptions and perceptions of the president.

In Central or South America, no major CIA operation in the early Cold War era received much close scrutiny across a wide variety of actors, but usually the agency needed at least nominal support by the State Department. Embassies and consulates offer essential in-place overt intelligence collectors and useful pathways for both overt and covert access. In the Guatemalan case, consultation with the State Department was consistent throughout the Arbenz operation, and both agreed that clearly communists were covertly influencing Arbenz. The agency recognized its dependence on the State Department. The CIA even shut down the early operation when the State Department withdrew its support, although it kept Armas and others on a retainer pending a future renewal of the coup attempt. The support of the large dominant department was particularly necessary because other players had been at best lukewarm for the operation, including Truman himself, who stressed multilateralism (Fraser 2005, 491).

At the field level in the final PBSUCCESS operation, there was little honest joint consultation even between CIA subordinate sections. On several occasions, agents were suddenly removed from locations or found themselves shut off as misunderstandings grew between operatives in the field and the operational headquarters, oddly located in Lincoln, Nebraska. Field operatives were accused of poor judgment and recalled with a surprising frequency. One was even accused of leaving classified material with her housekeeper. This climate of internal distrust and administrative disconnects dampened honest sharing of critical information of which, in this case, the CIA already had precious little (Fraser 2005, 499).

In Vietnam just a few years after the Guatemalan disruption, the U.S. military was given the lead due to the armed nature of the Viet Minh insurgents. Consultation across key players did grow with the extent of the American engagement, involving by the ten-year mark of 1964 a good deal of the American strategic community. However, the multiple layers of people looking at Vietnam through the blinders of the unchallenged anticommunist presumptions did not mean the consultation was honest in its search for — or consideration of — contrary information throughout the period. For example, a U.S. military adviser with extensive experience on the ground in Vietnam and prior combat experience in Korea, Lieutenant Colonel John Paul Vann, wrote an assessment of the ground situation in 1963 that highlighted the U.S. failure to accommodate the legitimacy concerns of the local Vietnamese as a cause for lack of operational success in the country.[53] The report was buried by the commander of the Military Assistance Command Vietnam (MACV), Brigadier General Paul Harkins (B. Palmer 1984, 22). Consultation often consisted of sharing irrelevant, misleading, or overly optimistic but always incomplete data filtered through presumptions.

There is no evidence in either case study of comprehensive data being collected in sufficient variation, quantity, or quality to adequately challenge the inaccurate presumptions underpinning the American disruption strategies. The case of Guatemala was particularly egregious in the extent to which the decision to depose Arbenz was based on insufficient data collection. Not only were key decision makers disinclined to question the characterization of Arbenz as a communist, but it is not clear the CIA had created the mechanisms to even confirm the reasonableness of its plans for the overthrow. Based on the documents declassified in 1995, the CIA operations suffered from "chronic lapses in security, the failure to plan beyond the operation's first stages, the Agency's poor understanding of the intentions of the [Guatemalan] Army, the PGT [the Guatemalan Labor Party, e.g., the Communist Party], and the government, the hopeless weakness of [invasion leader Carlos] Castillo Armas' troops, and the failure to make provisions for the possibility of defeat" (Cullather 1999).

Ironically the paucity of information was known to some analysts, but their objections were muted and ignored. In a late 1953 report, internal evaluations emphasized what the United States did not know about the capabilities of the Guatemalan government. The CIA had no informants among key players in Guatemala's political parties, its army, the small Communist Party, or any other significant agency of the Arbenz administration. In fact, the analysts counseled a worst case presumption that a well-established intelligence

53. Two years later in 1965, after resigning from the U.S. Army in protest of the failing strategy in Vietnam, Lieutenant Colonel John Paul Vann finished a final draft of a disruption strategy emphasizing social change benefiting the Vietnamese population. He argued that the attrition strategy emerging by 1966 was inimical to the local population and long-term U.S. interests, both handing the population over to the communists and unnecessarily shedding U.S. blood (Sheehan 1988, 536–50). In a tragic irony, when Vann returned as a senior AID adviser to supervise the implementation of this strategy in 1968–72, it was already too late to turn the tide. At that point, the successes he demonstrated in small region by small region merely delayed the inevitable (Sheehan 1988, 726–751).

network served President Arbenz. This conclusion was common at the time. Since Arbenz and other supposed communist sympathizers would by now have already had ten years of Soviet assistance, the argument would state, it was therefore logical to assume the Soviets must have already and secretly provided such a network. There was, of course, no evidence of either the ten years of Soviet assistance or the network. Presumptions served as compensation for a lack of data collection, an approach not considered unusual in the Cold War (Fraser 2005, 495).

In fact, the evidence available at the time, if viewed without the filters, suggested exactly no Soviet assistance. Prior to establishment of the CIA, the FBI under J. Edgar Hoover had the foreign intelligence brief for Latin America and did an extensive investigation of the first postrevolution president, Arevalo, along with other Guatemalan political and especially labor leaders. The State Department was particularly concerned about the possible rise of communism, but State field representatives did not share their concern about Arevalo (Immerman 1980, 635). Edward Reed, chargé d'affaires of the United States embassy in Guatemala, wrote the State Department that the new president "desired a moderately liberal and constitutionally stable form of government." From the U.S. embassy in Argentina, and "responding for this embassy," John F. Griffiths wrote: "As far as we are concerned about the suspicions that might be had about Arevalo, it is my considered opinion that anyone even reasonably well informed about his teachings, writings and general activities would be inclined to pass over such suspicions as being so utterly without foundation as to call for no response" (Immerman 1980, 635).

Evidence for Arbenz's supposed communist ties grew from innuendo to conviction within a short space of time. In 1950, the U.S. ambassador to Guatemala, Richard C. Patterson, explained that one could detect communists by the "duck test." If a bird with no label as a duck swam, quacked, and looked like a duck, it probably was a duck whether or not it was so labeled. Similarly, he argued one could observe someone and determine their relative communist tendencies. In 1954, Patterson's successor as U.S. ambassador to Guatemala, John Peurifoy, testified before the House of Representatives that he had "spent six hours with him (Arbenz) one evening, and he talked like a Communist, and if he is not one, Mr. Chairman, he will do until one comes along. He had all the earmarks" (Immerman 1980, 637). In documents declassified in the early 1980s, Ambassador Peurifoy admits the meeting with Arbenz was tense from the outset, and that he, the ambassador, had cut off conversations about the United Fruit Company's abuse of Guatemalan law to turn to a discussion of the nascent Communist Party in Guatemala to "put first things first" (Bowen 1983).

After the Arbenz land reform declarations in 1951, with no new credible evidence of communist tendencies by Arbenz, the U.S. policy nonetheless hardened rapidly. Intelligence analysis became unsubstantiated confirmation of nonvalidated assertions. Putative observations by individuals not even in Guatemala were accepted as more evidence of Arbenz's communist activities. Any relaxation of anti-unionization laws or organizing activities was seen as evidence of communist subversion. Early reports of the impotence of the tiny Guatemalan Workers' Party (PGT) were construed as evidence of the eventual ascendancy of communism if a full-fledged electoral process was permitted and the PGT was allowed to run (Bowen 1983, 91). It did not help that in response to the rigid political pressure by landowners and the more conservative and older elements of the army, Arbenz began to adopt the language later to be seen as typical of wars of liberation. That rhetorical lack of care compounded the misunderstanding and was used by analysts to confirm his covert conversion to communism. During the actual operation, the intelligence data sought and acquired by analysts was simply done ad hoc and constructed as crises arose. What did arrive did not suggest success, but it was characterized that way later on in justification for operations in Vietnam.

In the case of Vietnam, verified knowledge on the ground was not collected systematically to evaluate and weight varying strategic choices. At the outset, critical data underpinning strategic choices were heavily influenced by highly biased information from the French. It is difficult to overstate the lamentable lack of accurate information held by U.S. policymakers at the outset and during this conflict. The data collected by the United States on the North Vietnamese threat as well as that known about the South Vietnamese was unconscionably poor throughout the war.

For example, by 1965, well into the U.S. participation in Vietnam and at the end of this case study period of ten years, the army's assistant chief of staff for intelligence in Vietnam characterized the military intelligence held by the main U.S. player, the U.S. Army, as less than that held by the enemy (McChristian 1974). In 1965 the newly arrived head of army intelligence in Vietnam, Colonel Joseph McChristian, was a veteran of the Greek counterinsurgency war and knew it took a very long time to develop the collection means to identify insurgents. He would observe later in his book that the "existing [intelligence collection and analysis] organization was not designed to support our new mission, especially this type of war" and that "few responsible people were familiar with area intelligence and how to use it" (McChristian 1974, 13, 107). After ten years in the country, the army intelligence staff on the ground was only about a hundred people (18). Other support was characterized as "limited." To wit, "Intelligence reports were received from the advisory system, limited bilateral operations with the Vietnamese clandestine collection organization, the 5th U.S. Special Forces Group, unilateral U.S. military collection resources which included special intelligence activities such as airborne radio direction finding, photo and visual reconnaissance, and infrared and side-looking airborne radar reconnaissance. These resources were provided on a very austere basis" (13).

For a war putatively against the secretive threat of global communism, the physical resources on the ground to collect information were close to laughable. Indeed some of the Vietnamese local intelligence cells providing information existed solely on paper (McChristian 1974, 70). While this intelligence shortcoming may not have been known widely, it was clear to the officers on the ground even in 1965. As McChristian received his incoming brief in 1965, "Colonel William H. Crosson, the chief of intelligence production, told me that he could not write a valid estimate of enemy capabilities and vulnerabilities because available intelligence was neither timely nor adequate and we were unable to evaluate much of it for accuracy" (4).

Despite clearly recognizing the nation-building aspect of the overall mission, McChristian nonetheless reorganized the U.S. Army's intelligence collection to focus on hard numbers related to traditional military data.[54] The

54. Joseph A. McChristian comments: "That mission was clear: we were to help the South Vietnamese fight a war to defend themselves and at the same time help them to build a nation. In order for the MACV commander to have adequate intelligence to conduct a defense of South Vietnam we had to consider a geographical area of intelligence interest much larger than that country itself. Not only must we concern ourselves with intelligence on the military, paramilitary, logistical, and political organizations of the enemy within South Vietnam, but we also had to concern ourselves with the location of enemy forces, logistical supplies, base areas, sanctuaries, trails, roads, and rivers located within Cambodia and Laos as well as throughout North Vietnam. We had to concern ourselves with the air space extending miles beyond the borders of South Vietnam in order to prevent surprise air attack. We were concerned with patrolling the South China Sea bordering South Vietnam and the extensive waterways within the Mekong Delta which were avenues of approach for

result was that his organization took pride in now having to monitor only about 20 percent of the country (McChristian 1974, 3). The reports his reorganized intelligence structure produced covered the following:

> Ambush tactics; Attack on fixed installations; Antiairborne and antiairmobile operations; Antiheliborne and antiairmobile operations; Antiaircraft defense by ground troops; Viet Cong and North Vietnamese Army night operations; Employment of snipers; Command and control of field units; Employment of guerrillas with local forces and main forces units; Night operations; Defense against armor; Reconnaissance tactics; River mine warfare; Crossing water obstacles; Command and control; Supply and resupply in combat; Employment of supporting weapons in attack and defense; Employment of guerrillas with local forces and main forces units; Viet Cong and North Vietnamese Army fire discipline; Enemy antiaircraft techniques, tactics, and employment; Viet Cong withdrawal tactics; Viet Cong evacuation of battlefield casualties; Viet Cong retrieval of weapons from battlefields; Viet Cong tactical use of inland waterways in South Vietnam; (and) Viet Cong structures and field fortifications (133–34)

Neither his list of factors to be thoroughly collected and analyzed nor the reports being produced for commanders in the field by 1967 included essential cultural and social factors to disrupt a people's war. What was missing was data on the following: recruitment and retention methods of the Vietnamese communists; population displacement and refugee effects on social cohesion; critical local cultural approaches to communications, technologies, and conflicts over such things a land ownership; third-world economic systems and corruption effects; or legacy effects of eight centuries of Vietnamese military experience.

Ironically, this very skilled intelligence officer seemed to understand the data collection shortcomings at first, but like others in the heyday of the Cold

---

logistical support and reinforcements for the enemy. Our future organization and requests for resources had to take into consideration our need to collect, evaluate, and produce intelligence on all of those areas. We needed to know the quantity and quality of war materials being supplied by China and the Soviet Union and her satellites. We needed to be kept informed of any changes of Chinese military forces which could influence the war in South Vietnam. Above all, we needed to know the quantity and quality of manpower the enemy could send to South Vietnam and the will of North Vietnamese leaders and soldiers to persist" (McChristian 1974, 5–6).

War he could not overcome a core disdain for the legitimacy concerns of the enemy. In noting an effort was indeed made to break Vietcong loyalties, Mc-Christian then disparaged these efforts by saying that most programs only dislodged very low-level guerrillas. His program focused on attracting higher-level Vietcong cadre if possible, but he also quickly noted that he did not have much hope for success. Note the comment about what happens when money is involved: "At best, we expected such programs to achieve only moderate success, and we would have been satisfied with merely reducing the morale and efficiency of a unit. Offering amnesty, for example, could cause the leaders to become distrustful of subordinates who did not devoutly follow the party line. We also used a rewards program whereby suppliers of information leading to the capture of high-ranking Communist officials were paid generously. These efforts did provide a commendable number of new sources for further exploitation; and regardless of reasons, returnee rates increased after the reward offers were made" (McChristian 1974, 108).

Written nine years after 1965 but before the final debacle in Vietnam, these comments from an insider echo the external critiques of a gross lack of adequate information and poor knowledge refinement on the part of the United States. Both before and during the conflict, the national policy was built on and sustained with a remarkably minimal collection of relevant data and subsequent understanding of the region.

Finally, despite the presence of formal mechanisms to discuss and presumably develop knowledge, in neither case did such knowledge reveal an accurate development of knowledge about threat actor motivations before or during the U.S. operations. The U.S. disruption operation was distorted by a grossly insufficient prior understanding of motivations, especially in the rural populations of both Guatemala and Vietnam (Fraser 2005, 505). For example, the fact that Guatemala's "revolutionaries" wanted a capitalist mode of production, free and fair elections, and a modernization of the social system was ignored or misinterpreted. Rather than seeing those objectives as similar to the aspirations of Americans as well, once the speakers were characterized as communists, the language was taken as mere cover for darker true intentions (Immerman 1980, 630).

Even with such logic, contrary information that was not consistent was often simply ignored rather than reinterpreted or used to question unexpected outcomes. For example, the CIA analysts did not integrate contrary facts such as that the members of Guatemala's Communist Party in Arbenz's government were very few, only 4 of 56 members in the legislature and none in the cabinet. The members were also small in number in the bureaucracy and restricted to education or agrarian positions; even in the latter, at their greatest representation, they were only 26 of 350 in the agrarian department. None of these indicators of a minor role were taken into account as possible evidence of limited communist influence. Rather, the analysts focused on Arbenz's tendency to consult occasionally with the tiny Communist Party specifically on land reform proposals, never incorporating the other known data (Fraser 2005, 489).

The U.S. government documents released in 1995 demonstrate that the analysts never asked counterfactual questions standard for analysis today. For example, why would members of the Communist Party, not a close favorite of military officers including reformers like Arbenz, have been appointed to several very particular official positions involving skills scarce in the Guatemalan society? That Arbenz might have simply needed their agrarian expertise is never developed as a possible explanation for all the evidence (Fraser 2005, 493).[55] Rather, one released document summed up the interpretation of the party members and their positions by saying: "In Guatemala communism has come from abroad, and been imposed from above. Even though their numerical strength is relatively low, they have secured key posts for themselves and have come to dominate the administration" (493).

Furthermore, in the analysis developed in the U.S. government, on the basis of remarkably little hard evidence, no one asked how it was that Arbenz's motivations — indeed his whole character — could have changed so dramatically in four years. In early 1950, neither the CIA nor the FBI was particularly concerned about Arbenz. One analysis cast Arbenz as someone "with no pronounced political convictions [who] plan[s] to eliminate the [leftist] extremists in due course," while another stated he was a realistic in his approach to U.S. companies in the country (Bowen 1983, 90). Only a few years later analysts would neither note nor refer to the data from the earlier analyses save to cherry-pick some ambiguous information. The supposed metamorphosis

---

55. Using the uniquely skilled members of a defeated enemy in a new structure, *faux de mieux*, is not unusual. After Germany's defeat in World War II, General Patton was criticized for using former Nazi bureaucrats to run aspects of postwar German public administration. His response was that there were no other people available with those skills, and the new administration could not function without the skills (Patton 1947).

of Arbenz into a committed, hidden communist was never challenged by any discernible process of fact-checking or hypothesis testing.

Similarly, after the Arbenz resignation, the agency apparently viewed the affair as a success foretold. Postoperation documents suggest no lessons were learned about how close the operation came to failure, given its internal shortcomings and unreliable partners. Nor did anyone remark in reports afterward on how lucky for the CIA that the military did not support their former fellow officer Arbenz, since there was no reason in advance to expect the army not to support him at least minimally. In fact, in an ironic example of institutional cognitive dissonance, the same project was suggested for Cuba by Allen Dulles and accepted by Kennedy based on the putative success of the Guatemalan operation (Fraser 2005, 505).

In Vietnam, known information was perniciously misinterpreted and not subjected to collaborative testing of alternative explanations or scenarios. Data that was collected and presented was consistently viewed through both anticommunist and quintessentially American military lenses. Any military or political organizational shortcomings were seen as correctable failings with the proper incentives, more demonstrations of proper behavior by advisers, refresher training, and better strategies, much as one would reorganize a U.S. division or administrative department. For example, it was known that the South Vietnamese Army, a critical and pivotal actor in the American coercion strategy, was beset by difficulties of professional military inferiority, rampant corruption, and lack of political legitimacy (Record and Terrill 2004, 24–27). In Vietnam, critical missions were left to units led by Vietnamese officers usually chosen for their family ties or allegiance rather than skills and widely known to be arrogant and elitist (Boot 2002, 289; Vo 1970). Unlike the other coercive operations waged by the United States in the Americas, the U.S. military in Vietnam did not use this knowledge to argue for American command of local soldiers in order to enforce critically missing professionalism.

For another example, a vibrant literature on the rationality of peasants during the 1950s and early 1960s was reinterpreted by U.S. intelligence analysts in an ominous self-confirming logic when applied to Vietnam. If peasant actions could be taken as a fully informed rational choice, then logically a rational peasant would not choose to stay in a place where bombs would shortly be falling in great numbers. Accordingly, the rural populations were warned of impending carpet bombing and given time to depart to government-supplied alternative land often far from their traditional homes. If any of these "rational" peasants did not leave as instructed, that choice was taken to have revealed their true communist sympathies, irrespective of how much time in advance they were given or what they had heard and knew about the life in the relocation villages. Therefore, as ipso facto sympathizers of the enemy, they were no longer innocents and could be bombed as desired, even children. Whole sections of Vietnam were declared free-fire zones once the warnings had been given, and no other explanation was developed or debated as to why peasants might "irrationally" choose to stay in the targeted areas (Sheehan 1988).

The poor development of accurate knowledge meant that the risks of such indirect leadership and large cultural bias were not weighted objectively across the evidence on the motivations of the enemy, challenging the rosy analyses given to stateside defense leaders by senior American officers (Boot 2002, 12). By early 1963, the Vietcong controlled at least 20 percent of South Vietnam, and the South Vietnamese Army was unwilling to put up much of a fight (Kinzer 2006, 157). Yet the U.S. analyses did not reflect this data or, for that matter, any other lurking cultural motivations that would eventually lead to failure. For example, in 1961–63, a series of war games on Vietnam held for senior U.S. military and civilian leaders included nearly no experts on Asia. In the games, both the U.S. (friendly) and opposing (communist) sides were conducted by Americans instinctively reflecting their biases in the outcomes (B. Palmer 1984, 29).

Compounding the problem was the use of misleading surrogate measures that had particularly pernicious effects on the comprehensiveness of analyses (Bird 2007). Vietnam occurred just as largescale computing moved from the world of nuclear targeting to a new, burgeoning academic field of systems analysis. Secretary of Defense Robert McNamara used the tools of cumulative analysis to browbeat the turf-ridden and secretive military services to more openly reveal their internal finances. It was only logical that the numerical measures of success being shoved down the throats of unwilling senior generals would find their way into battlefield analyses as well. This transfer was all the more inevitable because the American ethos has long considered any technological advance as an automatic improvement (Lebow 2006). Counting bodies or trails of blood as bodies was only the surface of the transfer of reality into quantitative measures. Pacification of a region was characterized in terms of percentages. Chances of success were listed as numerical odds. Vietcong strength was listed in absolute numbers.

In 1963, for example, the rosy analyses of the senior U.S. military commander in Vietnam always showed a decline in thousands of the number of Vietcong guerillas remaining in the country. By 1967, the multicolored charts had migrated to a computerized system of evaluating hamlets based on filling in computer forms monthly by the thousands. This Hamlet Evaluation System (HES) showed graphically who controlled each hamlet, showing quite precisely that the Vietcong controlled only 17 percent of the population, with another 16 percent open to being won back by the anticommunist forces. By subtraction, the figures meant that 67 percent of the population was controlled by the government in Saigon. Since this was exactly the same figure given by senior U.S. military leaders in 1963, either the war was at least not getting worse, or the 16 percent "swing" population could be cast as an improvement. In either case, neither the method nor the use of the figures reflected a collaborative capture of the true drivers of violence on the ground (Sheehan 1988, 697).

In the development of these misleading cumulative statistics, analysis was not challenged or forced to accommodate facts on the ground. For example, not included were the effects of mass population displacements where perhaps as much as a quarter of the population had run from the U.S. military's bombing runs in free-fire zones to the economic attractions of American military bases. Urban and national government services were completely inadequate to handle up to a fourfold increase in population migrating from the rural areas, especially when the infrastructure had not been able to provide services well enough even before the massive influx. A basic level of social observation was routinely missing from these analyses.

Also missing was the development of likely consequences from an overreliance on the exceptionally unreliable South Vietnamese Army (ARVN). On the ground, it was well known how profoundly inept and unwilling these forces were to fight for and keep secure the largely rural population. If not actively supervised by U.S. forces or advisers, the ARVN tended to vanish into strongholds and wait for further instruction (Krepinevich 1986). The two-thirds of the population routinely assessed by the Americans as putatively under Saigon's control lived by day in social chaos from displacement and lack of services and at night in fear with little protection from the pressures and persuasions of guerrilla cadres. Left out of the analyses reaching the senior strategists were integrative discussions of the blowback effects from leaving the population's security to the incompetent South Vietnamese Army.

From early on in the war, no analysis recognized and developed the consequences of the almost casual destruction of traditional Vietnamese social order and economic vitality by both pro- and anticommunist forces. It would not take many years for the local population to decide neither master was preferred and to opt for helping the one likely to hang around at night, certainly not the foreigners and the ARVN. On and off again, senior American officials would seem to recognize that the population was being lost, not just land. Yet, even then the analysis did not lead to strategies addressing the legitimacy and need concerns. Rather populations were treated like simplistic children to be herded one way or the other by arrogant, rapacious, and incompetent overlords in order that the children could escape the evil communist child predator. Local officials played both sides. As the United States counted and paid for rich militia rosters and did summary analysis on that data, the names on the rosters might be five or six times the actual male bodies in the area. And that number would include shopkeepers and old men (Sheehan 1988, 713).

Even the ardent optimist John Paul Vann noted that once a village had conceded to the Vietcong and been under their organized control for some years, it took extraordinary effort for the anticommunist forces, namely himself and a chosen few, to make progress in converting that village back to the side of the Americans, if it could be done at all. Often over time the locals absorbed the North Vietnamese tendency to transfer hatred for the French into hatred for the Americans. Vann would leave a village quickly when he noted the steely cold stares even from children (Sheehan 1988, 686). The U.S. processes of knowledge refinement in the first ten years of their disruption of communism in Vietnam did not integrate the already emerging indicators that this dynamic of lost villages and massive social churn was well underway.

LESSONS FOR DISRUPTION IN A SECURITY RESILIENCE STRATEGY

Each successful disruption indicated careful collection of data that was well tested for enemy motivations and systemic surprise accommodation before it was needed. Of the six cases considered, Pericles, Napier, and Wolseley did not depend on luck or presumptions. They prepared both for what they knew could happen and what they expected to have to learn during the disruption. Unlike the Florentines and the Americans, Napier, Wolseley, and Pericles demonstrated what needs to be known to both disrupt and to be resilient to a threat.

If the devastating plague had not taken off Pericles and his family along with up to one-third of the Athenian population at the beginning of the war, it is possible that a steady continuation of the Periclean disruption and resilience strategy would have forced Sparta back into its barracks again. However, the Periclean strategy would have only messed with the mix of Spartan motivations to attack over the long term. Pericles did not successfully dampen Sparta's major motivator, honor. Neither did his successors, except once by accident in the capture of the 120 elite Spartan warriors. This event, however, was not collectively assessed for its lessons about Sparta and future surprises. Once the captured Spartans were returned, Sparta returned immediately to its old annual attacks on Athens. Its fixation on its own importance in the world was never driven well below the violence threshold, and Sparta was able to keep its resource base sufficient for recurring attacks. Finally, Spartan use of Persian intrigue and resources bolstered Spartan confidence as well, and that aspect did not seem to be known to Pericles' young replacements.

Furthermore, it was the postplague Athenians in 425 BCE who taught the military of Sparta the value of an outpost for harrying, ravaging, and generally decreasing the resilience of an enemy's farming for more than one war season. While never key to the war itself, the Pylos outpost on the coast of the Spartan headlands was always a thorn, attracting freed slaves and runaways from Spartan and allied holdings. In the resurgence of the war after 413 BCE, it was also an Athenian, the traitor and exiled Athenian general Alcibiades, who showed the Spartans how and where to put their own much more influential Spartan outpost, the reinforced garrison at Decelea, only thirteen miles from Athens. With that garrison, which the Athenians were unable and unwilling to besiege and eliminate, the Spartans were able to disrupt Athenian farmlands and make the city's survival more costly well into the final days of this long dispute in 404 BCE.

Failing to disrupt the Spartans properly over the long term meant Athens merely messed with the Spartan mix of violence drivers after Pericles died. Pericles' successors on all sides made indeed a royal hash of Greek greatness and squandered its wealth by the next midcentury. Sparta did succeed in helping the Athenians to end their Athenian Empire and, with it, their Golden Age. At the end of the Second Peloponnesian War, the entire Greek community had moved to a brutal, destructive form of internecine warfare fought by irregulars. Especially after 421 BCE and the rise of the irregular forces to replace missing and increasingly irrelevant hoplites, the old ways of moderation and standard expectations disappeared. By that time, the old rules of warfare were gone, as was the relative moderation of hoplite fighting, in favor of peltast or irregular, brutal, no-quarter warfare (Forde 1989). As cities fell, now their males were murdered and females enslaved, while the city's slaves were freed. The freed slaves then added to the ranks of mercenary irregulars, with no socialized expectation of constraints in action or mercy in conquest. The rules of war and stable Greek society declined along with the quality of the soldiers as Greek society became more turbulent and unstable (V. D. Hanson 2005). Over time, this weakened the Greek city-states' own cumulative ability to resist rising semibarbaric princes from the north in Macedonia, ending seventy years after this period with the defeat of the Greeks by Philip of Macedonia (Cartledge 2003). Had Pericles' instinctive understanding of Sparta survived him, it is possible Philip of Macedonia could not have had such an easy time.

Florence survived by luck and, later on, by the machinations and wealth of the Medici banking family, not by its ability to either disrupt or be resilient to a serious threat such as the Duke of Milan. Although remarkable in so many civic achievements, Florence during this period of being attacked did not develop the kinds of institutions that would have enabled it to flexibly weight motivations and strategic emphases in responses and honestly consult on, comprehensively collect data for, and jointly collaborate in successful disruption, let alone resilience, operations. Although the city surged forward in its development of a modern state by incorporating public displays of consultation, yet the reinforcing, exceptionally strong, underlying traditional elements in its political system stalled the republic's ability to collect and develop essential data about violent threats. Designed precisely for the opposite purpose, the intricate processes of Florentine administration by the multiple lottery votes put a premium on the control of the names allowed in the sorting bags rather than on experience, knowledge, or innovative ideas. These names were controlled by powerful families and guilds. As a result the selection process seemed random, but the truth behind the sorting bonded political players ever more tightly to their family's ability to influence the roster of names (Kent 2004). Because the process appeared fair, it could not be questioned. Because it was not in truth fair, it could not be reformed by any means deemed legitimate.

The lesson for modern policymakers is that the information was there for the Florentines to infer correctly the proper mix of strategic tools in their response to the chronic violent threats and to prepare the form of attacks, if not the frequency. Such knowledge, however, was not sought or employed in time. The Florentine tendency to use capital, if used at the outset before the threat was secure financially, could have averted or at least delayed the later attacks by driving the attacker's violence equation below the threshold for longer intervals. Acquiring and developing accurate information throughout the period could also have shown the Florentines when capital would no longer serve to disrupt threatening ambitions by Milan or Naples and coercion was required. Then Florence could have prepared militarily before the last minute and with better trained troops.

In any case, the pay-first strategy was expensive. Unlike more muscular Venice, Florence sweetened treaties so often with its coffers of money that enemies planned on using the internal dissension to both weaken Florence and take it, or at least obtain funds from the city (Fratianni and Spinelli 2006; McLean 2005, 640 n15). If the lesson of security resilience had been embraced, Florence would not have had to rely on luck to survive.

The examples of the United States in Guatemala and Vietnam bear a remarkable resemblance to the difficulties of the Florentines in which good oratory installed blinding biases. Even if Arbenz and Ho Chi Minh were to be accepted as violent threats to the United States, at best the United States merely messed with the mix in both Guatemala and Vietnam by misunderstanding the motivators in both cases. Unlike the other cases, only the somewhat hysterical oratory could make these cases into threats to U.S. survival. In neither case did the disruption accomplish the putative overarching goals of stability and setting the stage for the development of democracy. In the strategic choices, ignorance made the outcome worse. Unfortunately there is little evidence that either the CIA or the U.S. Army learned that lesson until after the fall of the Berlin Wall in 1989 and the rise of nationalism, terrorism, and surprise in the 1990s forced both of them to embrace better knowledge development.[56]

The larger lesson for the cybered world, however, is how the ambiguity of the U.S. definition of the Soviet communist threat permitted the inadequate U.S. knowledge collection and refinement processes to be hijacked into a rigid axiomatic set of beliefs. While the physical threat of the Soviet Union

56. For the U.S. Army as an organization, the failure in Vietnam was a hard turning point, unsettling in the extreme for a service having been victorious in World War II. Soon after the loss in Vietnam, however, the consensus position of the army became aversion rather than a lesson learned about knowledge consensus, collection, and challenged development. Army doctrine was for years that nonwar counterinsurgency was not the mission of credible armies and was at all costs to be avoided (Buzzanco 1986; Bird 2007).

objectively existed, objective data on its true extent outside of Europe was not sought and tested accurately, consistently, and continuously by the institutional structures and cultures of the post–World War II U.S. security organizations. Rather, the axiomatic belief was reinforced by the evidence that could be interpreted as support of that belief, while contrary evidence was not sought or developed in analyses. Institutions have preferred logics embedded in their cultures just as individual actors do. Changing these systems is not impossible, but it is harder the more coherently socialized the institutions are and the less new information is sought to challenge current cause-effect presumptions. Conversely if the organization rewards and funds a wide knowledge search and a collaborative willingness to consider alternatives, then the organizational belief system is more likely to support a dynamic resilient institutional culture such as that needed for a successful disruption strategy (Selznick 1984; Thompson 1967; La Porte 1996).[57]

In both of these U.S. disruption cases, the lack of established, knowledge-refinement institutions socialized and encouraged to be counterfactual made it easier to interpret missing data as likely to support a preferred interpretation. For example, it was true that Stalin and his Soviets would have happily taken over everything they could, with or without guns. However, as George Kennan's original containment article pointed out in 1947, it was also true that the Soviet communists could not take over or even subvert everything they would have liked (Hyland 2006). Yet this latter, clear-eyed assessment did not guide the kind of coercive focus that would emerge in the U.S. containment strategy in the 1950s and 1960s.

Soon after World War II, containing the Soviet Union began to mean showing U.S. resolve and commitment in armed terms even in places where there was no clear strategic interest for the United States. Rather, the Soviet threat was translated into imperial terms with few internal U.S. analytical challenges.

---

57. In the study of high-reliability organizations, publications by La Porte and Consolini and by Rochlin have shown on various occasions that the no-fail situations tend to induce three levels of hierarchy: the normal hierarchy, a competence-based reshuffling in which the one seen as having the most knowledge assumes charge, and then a rigid preplanned response hierarchy for the ultimate surprise crisis where no one seems to have any better notion. That is, a lack of knowledge that might allow a less rigid response must somehow already be in hand for actors to avoid the predetermined response. Stunting knowledge collection therefore tends to produce this more rigid reinforcement of presumptions if organizations feel they cannot fail (La Porte and Consolini 1991; Rochlin 1997).

The Soviet empire was presumed to always be seeking advantage over the United States, and therefore the United States would always have to respond wherever the gauntlet was laid, even when the costs became exceptionally high, as in Vietnam (Boyle 2003). In these terms, the Russians were seen to be stealthily stealing the U.S. world around it while using the bomb to make it impossible for America to stop them permanently. Secretary of State Dean Rusk commented in 1965 that it was not a Soviet march into Europe that threatened so much as all the "wars of liberation" popping up all over (Boyle 2003, 45).

Security resilience involves learning to simply live with the ebb and flow of a long-term threat using something other than direct action. During the Cold War this approach would have been difficult to present as a demonstrated command of the situation to a fractious and often disinterested Congress in any case. Without the compelling framework, knowledge consensus, collection, and responsive development, this strategy was impossible to do as well as to persuade the Congress. Furthermore, it is easier for a national strategy to be captured by the particular interests of a lead agency if the knowledge is not developed in an honest consensus. As a lead agency, the CIA was an especially new actor at the security table in Washington and had a strong desire to rationalize its existence. It lacked internal traditions of deliberation, encouraging wide knowledge aggregation, and unfettered analysis. Without a contrary explanation or data, the CIA could, and did, strongly promote the notion that the Soviet Union's grand plan for world domination must be stopped dead by the United States everywhere. Since the CIA was given the lead outside the United States where coercive force and diplomacy were not involved, this global mission served well as a convenient justification for the CIA's existence and as a handy explanation for funding CIA interests anywhere the agency requested.

Ironically the British cases demonstrate the best examples of successful disruption-led strategies that also included resilience considerations (with all due respect to Pericles). In both case studies, successful disruption needed extensive knowledge development and preparation for surprise, whether inflicted or received. Both Napier and Wolseley prepared by studying and planning in advance. These habits are normal for expeditionary militaries today, but they were extraordinary for the times and their colleagues. Not only were the normal needs of officers and men considered in tricky environments, but both men sought to use all they knew from other areas not normally considered by British officers as well. Culture, disease, and transport were novel areas of concern for this class. Napier brought water purifiers with him; Wolseley brought mosquito oil and quinine. Napier built a railroad and Wolseley built a bridge to move troops in and out of a particularly vulnerable area and season quickly. Linking disruption with resilience, especially of domestic societal systems, is equally novel for the modern military officers focused on battle preparations, not that of whole societies.

Wolseley took it one step further, however, by emphasizing intelligence and personal trust in a cooperative, literate cohort, a key characteristic of an effective strategy for response to surprise. While quartermaster general of Canada, he kept and studied a list of promising, intelligent officers that he put to good use when given his own independent command mission. He then invited this group to reconvene as the core of the Ashanti cadre. Not only did they volunteer to serve again, but they willingly studied and collaboratively developed trust and knowledge on the ship en route to the theater of war. It is indeed not only what you know, but also who knows it with you and when.[58]

Ultimately, despite their era, the British officers demonstrated, unusually enough for their own institution, the kind of a careful selection process, comprehensive knowledge development, and intensive operational collaboration that are all critical elements for the institutionally successful disruption and resilience strategy. Sadly, these elements were rarely present in any subsequent British colonial campaigns, despite the lessons to be learned. They had not been institutionalized beyond these officers in a new strategic framework.

The sample cases described in this chapter include three cases of failure, one of likely success interrupted by plague, and two of well-designed disruption and resilience strategic implementation. These case studies offer lessons in how carefully structured must be the institutions or deliberate actions

---

58. As if to underscore this point, Wolseley would be given two more typical colonial empire missions, but he would no longer be allowed to completely control the officers he was given or the timing of the mission. As a result of these restrictions, he was unable to use intelligence and careful planning to succeed. The first was the two-month war in Egypt in 1882. Wolseley's response to not being able to control his staff and thus the intelligence they provided was to deceive not only the war correspondents but also the officers foisted on him against his preferences. His planning paid off but clearly only because he discarded officers who could fail him. In his next and final command, his innovative planning certainly would have produced results, but he was not allowed to pick either his staff or the timing of his plan. His portion of the plan worked, but the plans of the officers not under his control did not, and the result was the death of Gordon a mere forty-eight hours before the relief column arrived (Farwell 1985, 182).

meant to collect, refine, and disseminate the knowledge essential for strategic variety in responses to violent threats. Structuring institutions to develop knowledge in complex environments is much more than choosing flat organizations over tall hierarchies or just encouraging information sharing among institutional members. Rather, success in implementing a strategic resilience strategy imposes a systemic requirement for trial and error, for endorsement of long-run, slow, steady results, and for the ability to innovate through the ebbs and flows of smaller successes and even some nasty surprises.

CHAPTER THREE

Challenges in a New Strategy for Cybered Threats

Cybered conflict is a uniquely modern form of competition due to the globally open and easily accessible cyberspace. Modern city-states have much in common with their predecessors in Athens, Florence, and even the reluctant colonialists in London in terms of threats, save that today's threatening bad neighbors, nonstate raiders, and large aggressive states will inevitably use cybered means to attack. The lessons of previous city-states are applicable in that they reinforce the need for knowledge development well in advance. Florence did not have such knowledge and was constantly paying exorbitant funds to escape the consequences of its inaccurate and incomplete knowledge and its tendency to be swayed by biased oratory. The American anticommunist voraciously collected data but with considerable blinders on its interpretation, rarely challenged even as experience suggested other explanations. But time to consult and recover was on the side of the pre-cybered world. Pericles, Florence, London, and even Washington had time to discuss their disruption plans when indicators such as the war season or gatherings of armed invaders suggested an emerging problem.

Cybered conflict today, however, has significantly shortened the time horizon and the role played by strategic buffers. Distance, weather, seasons, and the lack of knowledge no longer buffer the defenders as they did the earlier city-states. All of the possible bad actors and many others can act through cyberspace as if they lived next door both inside and outside of the defending state. As a result, military forces and big walls are not sufficient, even with good long-range anticipation. In their past small wars of disruption, the UK and the U.S. officers needed to concern themselves with the resilience of only their deployed forces. Athens and Florence needed to consider resilience for the whole society, but only if the enemy looked like it would make it through to the gates of the city. City-states now need to consider disruption and resilience 24/7 even if they are not at war, in the war season, deployed in a battle, or facing a credible long-range nuclear or conventional missile-based state-level threat.

Modern city-states have to consider the whole world with cybered access to be potential enemies at currently unknown homeland gates or possibly already inside. Furthermore, a single cyberspace surprise attack devastating a major node and crippling a whole society is less likely than long waves of cumulatively cascading effects of a myriad of smaller attacks from possibly unrelated bad actors. The digital "Pearl Harbor" is more likely to be a slowly draining, long-lived, chronic digital "nuclear winter" particularly difficult to defend against if each wave of attacks is itself relatively small. Pericles built a wall to the port, Napier built a railroad, and Wolseley built a bridge to reduce the effects of small harassing attacks cumulating in catastrophe. But when physical attacks are critically dependent on virtual enablers, the strategic response has to be equally virtually enabled, and that is difficult when one cannot see or touch cyberspace.

This chapter discusses the challenges in and for modern democracies in instituting a security resilience strategic response. Left aside are the normal obstacles to institutional change such as public agency resistance to change, commercial interests' objection to security expenditures, and the ambiguities of the laws of war to the covert nature of cybered conflict. Those will be discussed in future works. Already discussed are the theoretical issues in international relations and the institutional issues in getting the knowledge development properly through consensus, comprehensive collection, and continuous development. Furthermore, the additional challenges in implementing domestic resilience strategies are also not discussed because another volume, *Designing Resilience: Preparing for Extreme Events*, presents concepts and solutions (Comfort, Boin, and Demchak 2010). Here, therefore, are discussed specific challenges often overlooked in the previous discussions. These include home state political acceptance of the seriousness of the cybered threat, technological design obstacles based on historical development timing and beliefs, mass societal turbulence and grievances on a global scale, the availability of bad behavior information and protection of privacy, and practical constraints in the implementation of disruption tools in particular.

POLITICAL ACCEPTANCE OF CYBERED THREAT
IN DEMOCRATIC CITY-STATES

Cyberspace as a concept emerged in the 1990s with a very positive image, especially in the United States. As it has progressed from something entertaining or generally useful into something critical for most major societal systems, its foundation story of a brave new positive and inclusive world has persisted. The reason in large part is due to the exceptional marketing by the computer industry, but also by the ease of use, growing ubiquity of multiple functions provided simultaneously, including entertainment, and the black box, nearly magical nature of its inner workings for most users. As a result, political acceptance of an urgent cybered threat is difficult to achieve, especially if the solution could involve a loss of convenience for the users of the globe's communications networks. Five particular acceptance challenges inhibit a broader political consensus on a need to confront cybered threats.

First, citizens share a deeply held *disbelief* that cybered attackers or attacks are serious enough to have long-term harmful effects. Because cyberspace is entirely human-made to provide positive goods, the dark side is especially difficult to accept given the obvious economic and social benefits of cyberspace so far. Many individuals from policymakers to scholars to teenagers find it difficult to conceive of the potential for systemic vulnerability in having so many nations depending critically on interwoven multitudes of open digital connections across continents and social systems (Morozov 2008). Very positive early notions of computer networks are now deeply imprinted in the popular consciousness of modern westernized populations. From the outset in the 1990s, computer networks were viewed as akin to telephone systems with automatic notepad attached; later the notepad became a television and an answering machine. These technologies could be used possibly to spread a bad story, but it would still have to be person by person, a slow process limiting the number of strangers who could view or change the information. Other than destroying the telephone system itself, it was hard to conceive of a possible widespread national threat that could be critically effective using a telephone network. The rising concern in Western nation security agencies has even been characterized as "cyber-hyperbole" and the need for new strategies disparaged (Morozov 2008).

Second, orchestrating a national security response to cybered threats is hard because cyberspace is *hard to see physically* in any case, but especially so now as it is deeply embedded in normal societal functions. Unlike most social and technical systems known to human history, cyberspace systems are exceptionally rapid and buried in large streams of data. Uses cannot be easily observed from the outside and therefore cannot be easily monitored for threats as global connectivity expands. Unless one "enters" cyberspace, one cannot "see" into it physically. A powerful, intrusive phenomenon, it has grown to much more than a communication device between people. Cyberspace penetrates far into the organizations sustaining modern westernized nations, and its open portals and standardized applications have become unique command conduits for critical, increasingly automated key societal functions (Curran, Concannon, and McKeever 2007). Western security agencies leaped to use the benefits of information exchange, but they along with the citizens were late to recognize the societal implications of an opaque global network reaching into everyone's lives simultaneously.

In another example of just how invisibly embedded cyberspace can be, Israeli agents are said to have inserted malware in a Syrian official's laptop left in a hotel room one year before the Israeli raid on a mysterious, putatively illegal nuclear site in Syria. The raid was flawless, and the Syrian air defenses did not work properly, allegedly due to the malware inserted at least a year in advance that gave Israeli cyber warriors access to hack Syrian computerized controls (Zetter 2009). Whether true in its public details or not, this story is one more reason given by Iran and Syria to justify their own aggressive efforts to control all internet access in their nations in order to curtail the unexpected and largely unseen connections between systems.

Third, orchestrating popular concern with cybered security at the national level is harder because of its *unexpected connections* between previously uncoupled activities, people, and tools in attacks. After 2003 Iraq experienced an unprecedented explosion in cell phone towers and cell phones in use all over the nation. The goal was to jumpstart commercial activities, but every family fearing a bomb or a kidnapping bought a cell phone and plan for every member. The result was a massive and immediate rise in cell phones for social as well as commercial use. It also enabled something unexpected, the widespread use of cell phones to remotely detonate roadside bombs when U.S. mobile forces passed by the disguised bomb. In 2007 then U.S. president Bush authorized the U.S. main electronic security agency, the National Security Agency (NSA) to help the U.S. military disable or deceive the computer- and cell phone–enabled operations of insurgents in Iraq. To respond to the uncertainties and deadly surprises of insurgents coordinating ambushes and detonating explosives with their new cellular or internet access, after 2004 U.S. military leaders developed a strategy with striking similarities to a security resilience strategy. Innovated on the spot was a combination of aggressively seeking out and disrupting bomb-planting teams using extensive knowledge collection and development, to include loitering electronic surveillance, but also ensuring resilience of units on the move by protectively using airborne systems to dampen commercial cell phone traffic as the units pass. The conclusion of American military officials was that only with cyber tools was the surge in Iraq in 2007–8 able to save American and Iraqi lives. While the massive increase in U.S. troops is credited publicly for calming the Iraqi violence, privately and anonymously U.S. defense officials say it was the ability to disrupt those highly mobile small insurgent cell phone–coordinated operations that laid the foundation for success (S. Harris 2009).

Nonstate actors are particularly likely to use these electronic, long-distance access ways to reach into unexpected areas to score political messages. But they are as unlikely as citizens of democracies to appreciate the possible coupling whose ripple effects can blow back on their own societies if they inflict devastation on key westernized states. The tools of attack are cheap, easy to use, and available even in developing country urban areas, but the knowledge about how all the various sections of the world's networks are connected is not easy to grasp. For the most part, Utopian hackers along with religious messianic groups tend to gloss over the possibility of system destruction if their attacks fully achieve their objectives. This blind spot was captured even by Hollywood in a recent movie about a terrorist mastermind fooling young, utopian, counterculture hackers into contributing destructive codes for his assault on the United States. Shocked by the devastation, the surviving young hacker tells the movie's cop hero that he had idolized his hacking in machine terms: as simply pushing the reset button on a corrupt, unclean, callous world to start over. In the movie script, the young man says he never thought the ripple effects would be so horrific (*Live Free* 2008). There are plenty of jihadi attackers who want the effects to be so horrific in the United States, but few if any perceive the unexpected connections producing cascading negative effects likely in their own societies if they succeed in disabling major westernized nations.

Fourth, tools, functions, and even knowledge itself easily have a *dual or triple use* in cyberspace. Connecting to a website means both opening a door out into the networked world occupied by the rest of global population and a window into one's own private part of it. For security services, cyberspace is a two-edged sword that is particularly challenging. Like trading city-states, one cannot close the borders and still receive any of its benefits, a characteristic of cyberspace that is both freeing and threatening for the structures of society. Often the same tool, site, application, group, or process can be used to kill or heal. Today would-be terrorists can learn online how to attack without formal training arrangements. They can build on everything hackers have developed and criminal gangs use for profit. They can use websites to market these capabilities to would-be terrorists or the curious. They can use today's personalization techniques to track those who return to their sites frequently and can intensify the lures and information as recruiting tools. They can inspire independent action that the website visitor may not have thought was moral or possible at first. And they can disclaim any responsibility while making violent attacks seem noble and laudable. The dual-use nature of the increasingly ubiquitous global communications networks is what makes this topic so difficult to sort out.

So possibly pernicious are the destructive access options opening up to a broad set of global actors that even the relatively conservative Chinese Army has labeled cyberspace the emerging fourth field of battle after land, air (space), and sea (Kyodo News 2008; Elegant 2007).[1] Russian leaders have been concerned about their relative lack of capability in cyberspace since at least 1999.[2] It should not be surprising that successful methods of cyber attacks are sought by those who see themselves as fighting a "war" but who lack the ability to actually strike their enemy in conventional ways. Seeking an advantage exploiting vulnerabilities of the opponent is called *asymmetrical warfare*. Using some information technology to level the relative difference in capabilities is

1. Space itself is internationally not "militarized," and so adding it as a fifth would be quite provocative in the international community, not to mention likely to spark a space arms race with the United States that at the moment the Chinese could not possibly keep going competitively.

2. Even the resurgent Russian political leadership has become concerned. Around 2000, Russia proposed to the United States an international treaty against cyber warfare much like the international treaty against the use of chemical weapons. It was rejected by the West as a mere ploy to keep Russia from falling behind technologically. The idea mutated over a decade of ad hoc discussions across the westernized nations into, for example, a recently signed agreement among some nations including the United States and Russia to share scientific data on cyber criminality.

no longer unusual; it is increasingly an explicit strategic goal of state and non-state actors alike.[3] U.S. forces in Afghanistan in 2001 found a letter from Osama Bin Laden to followers in the late 1990s in which he declares that 90 percent of the expansion of the jihad would be through the media, not the old-fashioned person-to-person spread of a social movement (bin Laden 1998–2001). This observation has been widely used by young would-be jihadists unable to go fight as a call to use the internet to continue the war of a thousand probes and strikes against what they see as a West trying to harm Islam.

Fifth, instituting a new cybered national security strategy is also tough when what makes otherwise distracted populations pay attention to security has not yet happened. We have seen a national government disabled and another nation attacked during a war, but it remains easy to doubt the seriousness of cyber-enabled threats with *no mass casualty attacks as of yet*. That we have not yet seen the full potential for human harm occur so clearly is a reflection of our current position at the mere beginning of the ubiquitously digital age. Up to now, the globalizing world community has been protected by an accidentally and historically developed set of digital disconnects in global and domestic networks. These have provided what has been called "security by obscurity" (Hoepman and Jacobs 2007, 82). Critical stand-alone computers and applications—the controlling computer brains of many of our essential service networks—were designed a long while ago for a pre-internet world. They often must be physically visited individually to determine exactly what kind of hardware and software is in place. Since attackers cannot physically visit all that they could if the systems were digitally controlled remotely, those older systems are inadvertently more secure although slower than other newer, internetted systems.

For an interesting example of cinema making this point about lucky discon-

---

3. As John Serabian, the CIA's information operations issue manager, stated in testimony before the Joint Economic Committee of Congress on March 4, 2000: "Information Warfare is becoming a strategic alternative for countries that realize that, in conventional military confrontation with the United States, they will not prevail. These countries perceive that cyber attacks launched within or outside of the U.S. represent the kind of asymmetric option they will need to level the playing field during an armed crisis against the U.S. The very same means that the cyber vandals used a few weeks ago could also be used on a much more massive scale at the nation-state level to generate truly damaging interruptions to the national economy and infrastructure" (Janczewski and Colarik 2008, 229).

nects, the 2008 movie *Live Free or Die Hard* showed a terrorist mastermind who orchestrated cyber attacks on critical infrastructure. Using extraordinary connectivity and expertise, some unwitting, the terrorists were ahead of the heroes at every step of the movie until their digital tools could no longer provide both knowledge and control as needed. Rather, the terrorists had to shorten the proximity dramatically to achieve their goals. They needed to physically occupy a critical electrical facility. Only when the terrorists were concentrated physically in a way the heroes recognized were the heroes able to respond physically (Sciretta 2007).

Having older, unwebbed equipment still widely in use across the United States and Europe is another reason the attacks have yet to succeed lethally. Not only is there limited knowledge available about what to hit, but much of what one might like to attack is still offline permanently, is only networked in a small closed group, or only touches the internet very infrequently. If the machine and applications are old enough, younger attackers simply do not have the background knowledge or expertise to break in even if they have the access. Often found in local infrastructure systems, including electrical grids, these systems require far more time, skill, and money for distant outsiders to reach and harm. They are distributed, tend to be in overlooked or obscure functions, and run privately. Even if one could find all of them, making all the physical visits to do attack reconnaissance would take time, and such an operation is likely to arouse suspicions on the part of the local operators. While they are old and inefficient, these systems provide inadvertent and unorganized dampeners to the rapid transmission of threats through cyberspace.

But this era of disjointed digitization of critical services is quickly passing. Those older computers are less reliable, less capable, and more expensive to maintain. Ten years ago a survey of fifty U.S. water facilities revealed that 60 percent of their control systems (supervisory control and data acquisition, or SCADA) could be reached by an unsecured modem. The internet access applications were backfilled on the top of much older technology not designed for Net-based security (Lemos 2002). As this perennially poor industry modernizes, however, these systems are being replaced with more efficient, less manually operated, fully integrated "enterprise-wide" systems with all the security benefits and vulnerabilities of any other modern networked system (Lewis 2002). In the coming decade or so, as the city-state democratic societies become more intricately digitized, the largely physical protections of having

obscure, offline, and critical central computer systems will decline dramatically. The access options using digital means at long distance have been expanding for those dedicated to such attacks as a life project. The disgruntled
unemployed worker who in 2000 released one million liters of raw sewage into
the local water supply of Maroochy Shire, Australia, required forty-six tries to
hack successfully into the electronic control systems (Lemos 2002). These attacks are not easy, but clearly the dedicated are willing to spend the time in
order to get lucky once (Smith 2001).

In this emerging era, a strategy combining both disruption and resilience
is necessary precisely because the future, mass-casualty, violent threats to
westernized states do not need to come solely from the usual set of state
suspects. David Copeland in 1999 built bombs using the infamous "Terrorist's Handbook" that he downloaded from the internet; as a result 2 people
died and 139 were maimed in London (Forest 2005). Just as cyberspace is the
progenitor of both the reach and influence of globalization, it also spawned a
growing set of chronic, violent capabilities available worldwide. If a bad actor
living abroad can make a critical system, such as the water filtering system
of New York City serving ten million people, fail suddenly and dramatically,
then the successful digital attack is no longer bloodless. People will sicken;
some will die; costs will be staggering, and societies will be harmed. In 2009
a disgruntled U.S. Transportation Safety Agency (TSA) officer went back into
work after dark to insert malicious code into the TSA computers managing the
nation's no-fly list. He had a pregnant wife and one child at home to support
and had just been told he would be soon laid off. The code was set to initiate
in several months and would have erased the key data used by TSA officers to
ensure that known or suspected terrorists are not allowed to board airplanes
in the United States (Constantin 2011). In this case terrorists could have opportunistically been lucky enough to get on board a flight during the period
the malware was active. It is more likely they would have learned they could
bribe or blackmail someone to do something similar and gain access. This
particular saboteur could have been more vindictive and enterprising. He
might have used his passes to sabotage other systems to which his status as a
security officer might have given him access, at least once. Had the attacker
been less bitter and more dedicated, the malware could have been targeted
for more instantaneous effects having to do perhaps with aircraft in the air or
refueling or scheduling. He, like the man who released sewage in Australia,

could have sold the knowledge to others to use in producing more sophisticated, longer-term attacks.[4]

Waiting for the mass casualty attack that could not occur without its cybered component is dangerous; if such an attack begins, there are no reasons to assume any restraint on the part of the attackers. Societal bounds on violent and destructive behavior are unlikely to operate any better at two a.m. on the internet than they do in dark streets of turbulent major cities at two a.m. For the open democratic society and its reliance on laws, citizen socialization, and courts, a critical challenge is produced by these largely unseen vulnerabilities developing innocuously through the emerging virtual world's hardware, applications, pathways, and social uses. A security resilience strategy and all its institutional bulwarks are necessary because the threats are expanding with the technology's global access.

TECHNICAL DESIGN FOR CYBERED CONFLICT

The origins and volume of technological design innovations today challenge security strategies of modern nations in ways unseen over most of history. The "information age" is really just beginning, and yet the puzzling threats are rising exponentially. Now web-based attacks are already growing in sophistication to include deception of the humans whose likely responses to being misled are included in the attack, even making the duped user into the attacker's proxy (Rowe and Custy 2006). Attackers wanting to attack again, or just testing their

---

4. Mark Leipnik quotes from a 2003 EPA report that states: "As part of the agency's mandate to regulate drinking water quality under the auspices of the Safe Drinking Water Act, the EPA placed on a website using interactive web-based maps showing the location of roads, hydrographic features, and the fairly exact location of the intakes for upwards of 25,000 domestic water supply systems in the United States. Many of these sites were not huge water treatment plants processing millions of gallons per day with appropriate fences, security, or procedures in place to protect the water system intake from unauthorized attack. Instead, many were simply an open pipe and grating at the end of an obscure county road with hardly a fence separating visitors from the intake (and generally no protection on the reservoir or stream side of the intake). The EPA promptly removed this material from the internet following 9/11." Leipnik also indicates that the Nuclear Regulatory Commission belatedly removed engineering drawings of commercial nuclear power plants from its websites after 9/11 (Leipnik 2007, 295).

skills in small attacks, will sometimes make essential systems fail for seemingly inexplicable reasons. Not only must society deal with the rippling physical effects of successful cybered attacks, but that remediation is itself likely to be delayed as experts puzzle their way through the maze. This complexity inside and outside the elements of the World Wide Web is, to some extent, a function of how it was viewed when it was first emerging.

Trust and Ease versus Security in Early Years

Vulnerability to remote bad actors depends on when the system was initially designed as much as which system it is and who is doing the hacking. Distance, network complexity, and the embedded flexibility of commands in such systems would make it hard to absolutely secure any web-based communications in any case.[5] However, today many critical infrastructure systems are especially vulnerable as a function of the utopian zeitgeist of the era in which they modernized.

High-volume, critical, and widely extended normal processes are usually built for speed and efficiency—funds are not expended to ensure a graceful degrade of the system when it is disrupted. Early computers, for example, used to simply stop with the so-called blue screen of death (Voas 2003). Many of the older systems do not even have limited backup functions precisely because they did not normally need them for their functions. They operated simple communal tasks in linked cascades of decisions essential for the whole process. If the right ones in the cascades simply stopped, with them a myriad of services essential for the larger system also ceased operating. Even today small continuous backups tucked in secure corners of the machine are often viewed

5. After the loss of the World Trade Center Towers from the 9/11 attack, major firms actively sought to harden their communications and move critical connections outside of Manhattan, only to discover it was not possible in many instances. Staying connected meant physically dispersed locations would all fall anyway to a cyber major strike on the firm. Furthermore, much communication was dependent on intensely concentrated phone hubs in the hands of large phone companies that had inherited or built these hubs so fast that they themselves had difficulty remotely locating and analyzing vulnerabilities (Junnarkar 2002). If these major firms moved critical connections far from their Manhatten operations, they would not be able to avoid or change the vulnerabilities buried in the existing phone company hubs.

as costing too much in speed and memory space during routine operations (Myers, Ng, and Zhang 2004).

Furthermore, managers of early information systems often conveniently concentrated servers and applications for reasons of efficiency and reliability with no thought to the security of these systems beyond maintenance. Passwords written on paper were taped to screens or sent unencrypted across similarly unprotected email systems. Security was not a dynamic function of the computer, the human, the tasks, and the network as it is today. Rather the focus was on easing the burden on humans and integrating whole systems at once for better managerial oversight. The security was left to locked doors on offices and stacks of computer logs that administrators would slog through to see if the machines were making errors or the employees were engaged in fraud (Kemmerer and Vigna 2002).

The social construction of the world held by both the early software and hardware creators and their eager business clients did not include the possibility that bored teenagers in, say, Romania could spend weeks just to gain remote access, break into a computer system across thousands of miles, and then, on a whim, destroy some files. It was inconceivable that anyone would even be interested in disrupting the underlying connections of technically confusing electronic systems. In the early 1990s, the only major threat to the westernized world, the Soviet Union, was gone, and by then many in a brave new shiny technological near-utopia awaited merely better computer speed, storage, and lower costs. Even democracies would move online and function more freely, openly, and communally (Rheingold 1993).

This rather utopian zeitgeist affected early computer designers who deeply embedded this free-from-fear character well into their basic structures. They built systems with most internal elements openly sharing data in unmonitored ways and each dependent on critical central processes. Once a bad actor could get inside the machine, the structures were open to anything that bad actor's skill would allow. The phenomenal rise of the Microsoft computer operating system provides a major example of this belated realization of the security threat. For the early Microsoft systems, the firm considered the major technical challenges to be solely memory, speed, and costs. The major external threat was simply the early market lead of the more secretive, monopolistic Apple system. So Microsoft took a different business and technology design path than the closed nature of the Apple design. The Microsoft designers opened up their internal code to a large extent in order to induce independent programmers, frustrated with Apple's closed doors, to develop applications for the Microsoft Windows system. It worked exceptionally well as a business model spreading usage of Windows. However, nowhere was there particular attention to the malicious, self-rationalizing side of human behavior that could pose threats as well as benefits.

Microsoft's relative openness about the internal workings of its systems decimated the market for the more secretive and controlling Apple, but this very key difference spread across millions of computers also allowed opportunities to intrude on the lives of strangers in ways that in the 1990s were not even illegal. As Microsoft began to control the bulk of the computer-using community with this technology-first focus, it was so very easy to keep expanding the things one could now do in half or a fraction of the time it used to require by networking. Bleak predictions were widely ignored. Over time, as Microsoft and its applications writers pushed out largely insecure and rapidly developed software and plug-and-play hardware, their rush and naïveté ensured unseen errors or "bugs" in the millions of lines of code that often existed in even a single program. Those bugs became the unexpected vulnerabilities that hackers could discover and try to exploit once the stand-alone machine connected openly to other computers on the web (Lindner 2006).

Disrupting highly intrusive bad actors has been made both harder and easier by the way in which the central systems of the infrastructure have emerged. The growth of the industry was marked by this driving interaction between Pollyanna-esque optimism, the fungibility of the technical innards, and the lack of clear boundaries set by laws with associated negative sanctions. The rapid, open spread of internet dependence (considered by many to be wonderful for global advancement) also built open doors for the widespread transfer of many human sociopathic tendencies directly onto the relatively cost-free global playground of the internet. Microsoft's systems are so likely to be hackable precisely because of their lineage; indeed, their basic cognitive structure is based on hope. Without scrapping the system and starting over, MS systems designers inevitably must act as if not every security hole will be found, and that it will cost more for the firm to close the unlikely hole than the discovery of the hole by black hats will cost the firm later (Model 2000).[6]

---

6. Early on, finding the Microsoft "Easter eggs" was considered a cute game. They were small, otherwise hidden applications embedded by MS software engineers in applications like Excel. One had to figure out the sequence and combination of keyboard keys that

The history of the Apple Mac systems illustrates the power of openness to change future paths. More secretive Apple created its systems protectively, deliberately refusing to share its inner systems characteristics widely. As a result, desktop Apple computers faced a slowly dwindling market for all-purpose home computers from its dominance in the early 1980s to under 10 percent of the operating system market until the creation of the iPad (Lane 2006). Due to Apple's secretiveness, the basic Apple operating system has not grown much of a market of spontaneous outside creators of applications, and Apple has become a minor player in the huge revenue niche of computer systems—the advanced independent game designers. Secrecy meant security but at the cost of a fantastic loss in market share to Microsoft. In recent years, to compete with the overwhelming ownership of the computer market held by Microsoft, Apple has had to break down its own walls and open up the details of its internal systems a great deal more. As a result, hacks on Apple systems are on the rise, spurred by two exquisitely foreseeable trends. First, it has become more profitable to hack Apple systems. As more nervous users move to Macs to avoid the constant insecurity of MS systems, the number of potential victims makes this market more interesting to hackers, especially as Macs are more likely to be owned by more affluent individuals. Second, opening up the Mac innards in order to entice more applications and compatibility with programs designed for Microsoft systems also invites more knowledge about where the unpatched holes in Mac systems might be. The cycle of networked discovery, attempts, and intrusions has begun again, this time for Apple systems (Munro 2006).

A third major operating system in global use, Linux, is founded more on hope than even Microsoft was initially, but its explicit openness was networked from the outset. Based on the even older UNIX network operating system, Linux uses internal designs that are fully open to anyone—"open source." Its designers presume that the world is webbed and populated by people sharing the profoundly Nordic belief in the power of collective wisdom and proactive civic volunteerism. Developed from an idealized concept espoused by

---

would initiate them, and then one could see something funny, usually an object spinning in a graphic. It was indulgently viewed as a community-wide joke. No one seemed to foresee the similarity between innocent cute eggs and the possibility of developing hidden, not so cute applications lying dormant until the programmed date, internet signal, or keystrokes stimulate it to wake up and reformat the hard drive or surf it for passwords (Jones and Jorgenson 2000).

like-minded computer hobbyists/hackers and academics, Linux is labeled a FOSS, or a free and open source system. Since all the code is available to everyone based on the old Unix systems of IBM, both good ("white hat") and bad ("black hat") actors can, in principle, equally understand any holes in the system (Cross 2006). Linux's security rests on the rapidity of response from the largely volunteer white hat hackers who test for these holes out of a sense of collective responsibility. They then construct and freely distribute patches before or after the black hats have scored a successful attack or someone has announced a newly discovered vulnerability.

For open source, the fixes are communally beneficial, but the operational and security cost lies in whatever harm is incurred during the lag in volunteer response and the skill or comprehensiveness of the fixes. Unpaid security watchers are not always on the job, nor do they necessarily have the time to fix everything. The black hats do have time, however. They are often the chronically underemployed, under-occupied students, bored middle-aged computer industry loners, or even full-time crackers (hackers who steal credit cards) paid by the Russian mafia or paying themselves with the returns from their exploits (Wales 2002).[7] Furthermore, without vetting one's entitlement to be a white hat, any black hat can be "gray," that is, pose as a white hat—to the extent of even having professional-looking websites and testimonials and offering a security application that is putatively intended to help the user but that is actually a destructive application for anyone who uses it (malware).

Cybercrime's Contributions to Cybered Conflict's Threats

The inattention to bad actions in the early computer industry laid the basic systems that today enable a large portion of the threats to the operating systems of about 90 percent of the world's computers (Keizer 2008). If one uses the battle analogy, the Microsoft-based systems are part of a massive, aging, sieved empire poorly designed for a resurgence of a multitude of surrounding ambitious, rapacious, and frequently malicious small warlords. Apple is a long-term, high mountain valley kingdom just now expanding outward, only now interacting with Microsoft and becoming a target for those same turbulent warlords.

---

7. The enormous and ruthless Russian mafia is widely conducting cybercrime at sophisticated levels against the West (Broadhurst 2006).

Linux is the very small, young, growing, nomadic society with ambitions, very few resources, and lots of promises for support from dispersed but busy allies. As of today, the empire and its holes offer the black hats plenty of targets and chances, and that is unlikely to change in the near to midterm.[8]

Beyond enabling access for attacks through software bugs or human inattention, and the sheer long reach for long-distance control of data or systems, cyberspace also offers cheap, 24/7, anonymous communities of practice for bad actors to upgrade their game. Like all people, hackers want to save time, get the concrete rewards at the least cost to themselves, avoid personal risk, and, if possible, get social recognition for achievements. The internet's spread offered exactly what the utopians saw as so very positive—chat rooms to create and deepen like-minded communities. In this case, attackers also now have a myriad of virtual social venues to share with and learn from others whom they would never have historically encountered.

From these usually free online environments, hacking has become a social movement with its own rationalizations. To survive and spread, social movements must have relatively easy, consistent transport of ideas. Ideas can be transmitted across closed borders without human transportation, but until the internet, just doing so reliably and over much distance was an expensive undertaking normally only done by governments. A good example of a movement spreading globally precisely because of low-cost communication is the rise of the global neo-Nazi movement. Without cyberspace, given the average income levels of members, it is highly improbable that this movement could have had the resources to develop the breadth of global support it has today (Adams and Roscigno 2005). In a similar fashion, radical jihadism only began

---

8. In principle, Linux should prove the more resilient system over time, having been incessantly tested, conflicted, resolved, and rechallenged openly by a wide variety of minds. But this reliance on a volunteer global white hat community as well as their collective Linux stakeholder enthusiasm is unlikely to be enough, even if Linux were the dominant system. Given the ferocity and volume of attacks today on Microsoft systems that are not as open as Linux, westernized society may not be able to risk an exploit-enabling mass violence that spreads too rapidly for the volunteer firefighters to recognize, fix, and then distribute globally. The risk may already be too great for many users. A secondary market has emerged offering clearly commercially proprietary and definitely not open source Linux-based security applications for those who cannot handle the risk in having a Linux exploit unfixed by the white hat vigilantes (West 2005).

to emerge in any significant fashion in the former Soviet Union states after the Cold War ended, borders for free communication opened, and access to radical ideas became possible.[9]

For the hacker social movement, breaking into a computer became rationalized collectively online as a morally acceptable way to show the lax or naive designers of systems how imperfect their work was. It was also seen as a way to punish the lazy or ignorant users of such systems for not adequately securing their data (Young 2007). It was cast as a civic virtue, and the movement spread to others who might not have considered hacking if the rationalization had not been promoted so widely as the internet spread.

Over time, this online social movement web has self-organized into a global and quite ecumenical virtual thieves' quarter. Used by the skilled loners, the mafia-paid workers, and the teenagers, entry requirements are today relatively low. Novice bad actors need relatively little and can anticipate at least a cost-free run on the malicious wild side. Personally remote from their victims and often the victim's security forces, most bad actors do not have to contend with two main deterrents to both terrorism and crime: getting enough information to make the hit on sight and getting out alive and free. It does not take much to become a "script kiddie," a minimally skilled user of the sophisticated intrusion tools helpfully shared by a faceless community of other bad actors proud of their creations. Beyond that, time and basic equipment are all that are necessary, neither particularly expensive in rapidly digitizing states. Most hackers do not themselves expect to risk much physically. Most of them expect considerable benefits in hacking, from increased status among their peers to illegal financial gains, face few if any informal constraints on any action, and calculate a very small to nil risk of any formal punishment (Young 2007).

In these virtual meeting places, hacking has become a career. Hackers can get hired as well, paid for one job by the cool program they are given, the

9. In fairness, cyberspace offers the opportunity to introduce individuals to new ideas or to deepen the notions of those already persuaded, but it has limits. It also matters how receptive the culture is to ideas that have few or no natural correlates already in place. Radical jihadist ideas spread in the post-Soviet states with Muslim majorities at different speeds. Often promoters from already radicalized communities were seen more as foreigners than co-religionists. They had to come personally and make the connections between local resentments and global jihadism recruit by recruit. In one culture in Uzbekistan, the recruiters of Hizb-ut-Tahrir found an antigovernment response helpful to their recruiting, whereas in Tajikistan recruiters are still few in number and not progressing well (Jonson 2005).

shortcut codes they are given, or some other desired benefit that would be hard or time consuming to obtain otherwise. The progression of types of access is similar to the expansion of the thieves' quarters of the medieval city. Before there was an underground sewer system, the thieves were bounded by the barriers of the various neighborhood watches. Once cities modernized to use and maintain large underground and widely networked sewer systems, however, thieves could pop up anywhere in any neighborhood connected to the sewer system. Similarly, cyberspace's ease of entry and the ability to feel empowered quickly by using the programs given in a chat room make the novice hackers vulnerable to manipulation by seasoned exploiters in the chat rooms. Far beyond merely hiding their identity, some hacker mentors in the meeting place can be agents of much larger organizations seeking to recruit proxy soldiers to make the true source of the attack even more difficult to determine (Kshetri 2005a). The recruits are usually young and susceptible to flattery or grievance development. As with most distance recruiting, they are not all that reliable, but for one-off attacks, just like teenage suicide bombers, they are expendable.[10]

So far it has sometimes been only luck that has prevailed against the bad actor because systems have not been as standardized as the attackers would prefer. Certainly the would-be attackers are helped by the perfect-storm convergence in the evolutionary timing of systems' digitization, the utopian social construction of their world held by the designers of a system, and the scope of the free-ranging, unseen but close-proximity contacts of the internet. Even more convenient is that most of the really vulnerable, critical systems (such as in the United States) are owned, operated, and secured by private firms. For these organizations, security is not a benefit; it is a large cost, to be minimized if possible. Across similar plants, companies, or regional production sites, each has its own legacy systems, those embedded and added-in security structures, and a vast range in the likelihood of vulnerabilities (Nakashima 2008).[11] The cyber playing field for the hacker is littered with unexpected digital rabbit

10. Naturally, older hackers know this, as they perhaps were burned once themselves. It does tend more to be the fame-driven young, not the game-driven elders, just as in the suicide bomber industry. See Leeson and Coyne (2005) and Cremonini and Nizovtsev (2006). For the suicide bomber equivalent, see Bloom (2005).

11. For a discussion of the economic effects of an information war spilling over into the society's well-being, see Knapp and Boulton (2006).

holes into which they fall by accident as they troll for open ports or receptive browsers.

On occasion, the luck is in the misinterpretation of the roles of the system a hacker serendipitously managed to crack. In such cases, the lucky find may be abandoned, misinterpreted as useless, and not exploited. For example, a politically motivated attack in 2001 by Chinese hackers mad at the U.S. winging of a Chinese fighter jet failed only because the nature of the hacked critical system was not understood. The hackers clearly worked for some time to try to enter and disrupt the California electrical grid system. They were foiled only by the fact that the server through which they managed to wander was not at that moment engaged in running massive electricity transfers. It was an administrative server that connected with the larger electricity management system only once every twenty-four hours for a limited time to upload and download data. The hackers got in during its off time, found nothing, and left. The hack itself was not noticed in the administrative logs for weeks. Had the hackers known the schedule or by luck gotten access during its active daily minutes, the outcome could easily have been massively different in the resulting violence foisted on a multitude of critical electrically operated services (Sterlicchi 2001).

Beyond the convenient designs, rationalizing social movement, payoffs, and luck, a major enabler of the hacker is the human who can chose to open that email or not, even to unplug the network or not. Networks only work well in technical or social terms if they have the ability to invoke some measure of trust in exchanges despite distance and a lack of a direct personal relationship.[12] The web exists only as long as nodes are *willing* to exchange something,

12. This is more than the "agent" problem of agency theory because, in this case, the agents are also unknown to the user and, in some cases, unknowable without exceptional effort. There is a massive literature on agent theory, but it has mostly developed in domains where the quality of performance can be measured, as in profits or sales. In those circumstances, the check on agent independence is post hoc but undeniable. These situations do not helpfully translate to public goods like security. Hence, agency theory is less well determined or universally considered credible. In nonprofits or public agencies, many normative presumptions underlie much of what passes for theory, making a good deal of it case based and difficult to generalize. Furthermore, there is a semantic problem with the term *agent*. Agent or agency theory is about ensuring that the agent is more of an avatar acting only within the bounds of what was intended by the employer (Pasman and Lindenberg 2006). Agent-based modeling (ABM) is widely used as a way to make agents with free will (Foster, Jennings, and Kesselman 2004; Ishida 2004). Furthermore, so much of the literature is deeply specific to the neutral-speaking, individualistic, participative,

whether by design or individual choice. This trust is essential for the vitality and exchange of experiences needed for innovation and survival, but it also carries a dark side. Very open, widely trading, and wealthy Athens fell devastatingly prey to an unknown awful plague brought in on the network of the very ships responsible for also bringing in the trade that made the city so wealthy. The plague never came to isolated, nontrading, relatively poor Sparta, living off the labor of indentured peoples who also did not trade (Platias 2002). Networks have value precisely because their nodes take chances on opening up to other nodes.

Today westernized states are increasingly online, presuming that this 24/7 convenience will both please their citizens but also save personnel expenditures. Those furthest along in embracing widespread technical networks pose especially attractive targets to both hackers and leaders of peer states who want the ability to conduct a strike but deny any involvement. In the spring of 2007, newspaper headlines screamed that hackers had taken down a nation, Estonia. This small country is a particularly attractive web target: its government, banks, and even elections are all conducted online. The three weeks of massive attacks took down agencies ranging from the Parliament, the prime minister's office, and defense ministries to a host of smaller units. Indeed, massive spam attacks that overwhelmed a multitude of Estonian government servers did seem to emanate from Russia, at least at the outset. Instructions for the attacks were circulating on Russian websites earlier than on any other. The grievance used to justify the massive attack was an Estonian government decision to move a memorial to fallen World War II Russian soldiers to a more obscure, less prominent location in the capital of Tallinn. The Russian government condemned the decision, and many in Russia were incensed, allegedly including senior officials in the Russian government. The Russian government denied any involvement in the attacks (BBC 2007b).

An interesting aspect of this cyberspace attack is its use of methods that take advantage of the often ephemeral nature of the record of the actions

---

and achievement-oriented American culture that an enormous deal of caution is recommended in using the results as a general guide. Some useful anecdotes are found in the international management literature. See, for example, Hodgetts and Luthans (2006). In the future, many of these problems may be solved by the emergence of "virtual world-making" and the field of experimental politics using agents (in the free will digital sense) to spontaneously create outcomes for research. See Borders, Bryan, and Mauve (2001) for an early discussion of this possibility.

producing harm. For Estonia, determining the source definitively was not possible given their systems' design. The evidence of patterns and signatures that forensic computer analysis produces is reported to indirectly support some official Russian involvement—at least to the extent of limiting the damage. The attacks were solely on senior government agencies, and however devastated those agencies and services were for weeks, that rather limited target set alone suggests some official control over which targets were chosen. The attacks simply stopped service across web portals without, as could have been the case, destroying any data or critical system functioning. No subways were taken down while trains hurtled along filled with people. The electricity grid continued to function.

This kind of attack signals displeasure more than an intent to do longlasting violent harm. It is easier to use such proxies, whether witting or unwitting, when the medium encourages anonymity. If the proxy actors would happily do on their own what the sponsoring state would like to have done, even if they are paid, facilitated, or simply tricked by intermediaries, an attack with deniability for the sponsoring state occurs. Bitterly angry would-be cyberspace attackers are, by most accounts, unlikely to have shown such concern for wider destruction or international condemnation. Nothing in the hacker culture imposes these kinds of limits—especially not on those working in Russia, often for the brutal Russian mafia (Kshetri 2005a). The challenge, of course, is controlling the proxy without revealing one's hand.

The ubiquity and ease of access in cyberspace also means less control over actions that may involve state interests. If the Russian government truly was not involved, then as a state it found itself dragged by unknown actors into an international incident that could have caused deaths in Estonia. In fact, overeager citizens have already dragged a westernized nation into a virtual conflict unilaterally. What may be seen as the first true cyber war with international players was actually started by teenagers and ended up involving governments all over the Middle East along with the United States. "In September 2000, Israeli teenage hackers (in the U.S.) . . . launched a sustained denial of service attack that effectively jammed six websites of the Hezbollah and Hamas organizations in Lebanon and the Palestinian National Authority. This seemingly minor website attack sparked a cyber war that quickly escalated into an international incident. Palestinian and other supporting Islamic organizations called for a cyber Holy War, also called a cyber-jihad or e-jihad. Soon after, hackers struck three high-profile Israeli sites belonging to the Israeli Parliament (the Knesset), the Ministry of Foreign Affairs, and an Israeli Defense Force information site. Later the Israeli Prime Minister's Office, the Bank of Israel, and the Tel Aviv Stock Exchange were also hit" (Allen and Demchak 2003). The restraint shown later in Estonia was not present in this conflict.

As the war dragged on, the wider hacker community became involved. The ease with which cyberspace enables long-distance access also makes organizing multiparty alliances and coalitions for attacks more likely. It also means uninvolved actors can spontaneously join in the conflict. In this cyber war, third parties joined the fray over time, sometimes on both sides. Brazilian hackers, for example, attacked both Israeli and Middle Eastern nation sites and, for good measure, some rather innocent, unprotected, tiny American nonprofit sites. It was a wakeup for the Israelis as international hackers walked down massive lists of websites whose URL ended in ".il," moving gradually from only military and government sites to completely unprotected minor sites. For their part, those hacking back from inside the Middle East were not Palestinians in the territories, as their telecommunications system was entirely Israeli from the outset. Everybody ran out of websites to attack, and eventually the war simply spluttered to a halt, leaving the Israeli society the net winner. Not only was Israel more sensitive to cyber security, but its websites across the range of societal importance were also simply much harder to attack successfully.[13]

Today, everything secular hackers, overeager citizens, and greedy Russian mafia organizations can do through global networks to attack other societies, Jihadi terrorists can do as well. They have learned to use cyberspace for its access, training, and community development. One of the longer-lasting effects of the Israeli-Palestinian hacker war of 2000–2001 is the spread of the term *jihad,* directly linking the jihadist struggle to hacking and destructive behavior enabled by access to the internet (Boni 2001). Given the messianic nature of the global jihad rationalizations of destructive actions, it is simply unlikely that any cyberspace-enabled terrorists will show the restraint in the societal functions they destroy that the past cyber conflicts have shown.

13. In this Middle Eastern conflict, everybody ran out of appropriate targets. The list of vulnerable Israeli sites for the tools at the time declined precipitously as Israeli sites became hardened. There never were many Palestinian sites, and the teenagers expanded to less enthusiastically attack some unremarkable ministries (agriculture) in neighbors such as Syria. Aside from the Brazilians, few efforts were made to expand the war to Israeli-associated sites in the United States, perhaps because of the number or because of the unknown response of the Americans (Allen and Demchak 2003).

Terrorist use of cyberspace so far can be ranked in the following list from most- to least-known activity: propaganda (directed at three distinct audiences), training (in operations and general skills,) and direct action (hacking). The websites are the main propaganda venue. The material emphasizes two main issues: resentment against having their freedom of speech curtailed and the sufferings of compatriots held by governments. Both topics are designed to elicit sympathy from all three of their intended audiences: their followers, the international public at large, and enemy publics such as the United States that value freedom of expression. Violence is not exalted but rather presented in three rhetorical masks. First, violence is cast as the only alternative of the weak. Second, government actions are presented as being brutal and barbaric, and thus illegitimate. Demonizing the authorities is used to rationalize the choice of violence as one forced on otherwise peaceful and noble freedom fighters of the terrorist group. Third, the language normally associated with nonviolence and peace groups is extensively employed to convey the impression of being a victim forced to use violence by the enemy. The goal is to persuade, but if that is not possible, to at least keep many westernized publics uncertain about how much of a threat is posed (Weimann 2004).

Training and gathering intelligence via cyberspace are growing activities among jihadi terrorists. As Gabriel Weimann noted in a 2004 report:

> The website operated by the Muslim Hackers Club (a group that U.S. security agencies believe aims to develop software tools with which to launch cyberattacks) has featured links to U.S. sites that purport to disclose sensitive information such as code names and radio frequencies used by the U.S. Secret Service. The same website offers tutorials in creating and spreading viruses, devising hacking stratagems, sabotaging networks, and developing codes; it also provides links to other militant Islamic and terrorist web addresses. Specific targets that al Qaeda–related websites have discussed include the Centers for Disease Control and Prevention in Atlanta; FedWire, the money-movement clearing system maintained by the Federal Reserve Board; and facilities controlling the flow of information over the Internet. Like many other Internet users, terrorists have access not only to maps and diagrams of potential targets but also to imaging data on those same facilities and networks that may reveal counterterrorist activities at a target site. One captured al Qaeda computer contained engineering and structural features of a dam, which had been downloaded from the Internet and which would

enable al Qaeda engineers and planners to simulate catastrophic failures. In other captured computers, U.S. investigators found evidence that al Qaeda operators spent time on sites that offer software and programming instructions for the digital switches that run power, water, transportation, and communications grids. (Weimann 2004, 7)

In 2008, a senior CIA cyberspace intelligence official announced without details that citywide infrastructure had already been attacked in several cities overseas (SANS 2008). Jihadi and other terrorists have also hijacked major oil tankers for days, putatively learning how to drive, but not dock, the intensely technological and satellite-linked ship filled with volatile material (Bateman, Ho, and Mathai 2007). If true (and there is confusion about the hijackers' intentions), then the similarities are striking to the 9/11 attackers who took flying, but not landing, lessons.

Making these attacks more likely is the destructive public fear effect that can be induced even if an attempt does not succeed. As long as the failure is publicized with sufficient discussions of how close it came to succeeding or that its failure is only one of scale rather than outcome, a physical as well as virtual rush to safety by the population can in itself be the final steps in an attack. A well-known internet security expert has noted that populations as a whole overestimate nonroutine risks, especially spectacular and rare ones. They ignore routine risks but give great weight to personified risks and those in situations out of their control or actively being publicly debated (Schneier 2003). An attack plan that was a slow roll of nasty but not catastrophic surprises well aimed to cripple confidence in key infrastructure or processes, for example, could in the end cause more suffering and disabling through panic for the defending nation than a major assault directly on infrastructure or on high-value symbolic targets (Schneier 2006). In the 1990s, one of the U.S. National Labs, Sandia, modeled the disabling effects of a single large nuclear strike on the United States versus a series of more limited strikes spread over time. The attrition plan was much more costly to the attacked society over time and much less amenable to recovery (Robinson, Woodard, and Varnado 1998).

With sufficient resources, a well-skilled organization, and enough time to prepare, an attacker can use cyberspace to combine a big strike, public panic, and follow-up smaller strikes that disable response and recovery. The availability of the global networks can produce a widely destructive campaign that would be difficult to combat if it is allowed to begin or progress very far in digitized societies (Kane 2002). The strategic goal is achieving security resilience in the proper balance between the efforts at disruption and at resilience for national security. The continuous global technological advance of the world's connectivity has made it necessary not only to prepare through resilience but also to attempt to head off the attacker before the attack begins, lest the speed and breadth of the attack overwhelm the nation's preparations. Both have operational constraints in a cybered world, especially disruption as it is focused outside the nation's sovereign territory.

OPERATIONAL CONSTRAINTS ON
IMPLEMENTATION OF DISRUPTION

Beyond political acceptance and technological design/exploitation challenges, there are operational constraints specifically critical for the disruption component of a security resilience strategy. In many respects, having a knowledge-enabled strategy makes choices more available for decision makers in the national security of a nation. This section particularly acknowledges the advantages of having a strategic choice in national security, especially for militaries, beyond an emphasis on coercion, but it also notes the choice constraints of disruption including attribution and political blowback if innocents are harmed.

Once the mix of violence motivators for an attacker or group is accurately developed, responding governments can integrate this knowledge into a disruption strategy weighting emphasis across the three main strategic tools of coercion, capital, and information.[14] A significant challenge for deeply embedded presumptions of existing national security institutions like the military is that in this process coercion does not become the automatic first choice of defense strategy. Rather, it is one of three choices to be weighted against the main motivators of the attacking group.

Knowledge of bad actors alone is not sufficient. Strategic tools have con-

---

14. One useful analytical tool is the "SWOT" (strengths, weaknesses, opportunities, and threats) analysis. Developed originally by business professors in the 1950s and based on military analysis, it is a convenient technique by which to keep track of both enemy and friendly forces in competition. It offers a short checklist to keep track of the data that one has and that one still needs to acquire. It does not dictate the way the data is framed or formatted for integration into policies (Panagiotou 2003; Friesner 2009).

straints from the application of the chosen tool itself. These also need to be weighted accurately into the calculations and choices of emphasis in the strategy. Because the attack field lies solely within or is critically enabled by the globalized web, each of the three strategic tools has its own set of challenges and potential blowback effects.

Coercion

Coercive conflict in cyberspace is so new that it has the hallmarks of the unregulated warfare of the fourteenth century—anything goes until the others gang up on one, and what goes around tends to come back around in ways one would rather not have stimulated. Using coercion is never without its difficulties. For example, the globalized nature of the field of conflict is that publicly known coercive U.S. actions could inspire counterattacks more vicious than those originally attempted by others who originally had no stake in the conflict. Members of NATO have been unwilling to attach the NATO Article V mutual defense agreement to cybered attacks against a member nation in large measure because of the difficulty knowing who really attacked and what will happen if NATO is mobilized (Ballard 2010). However, the discussion has slowly moved to a reconsideration of collective responsibilities for coercive cybered strike-backs at attackers as NATO members individually have uncovered their own large vulnerability to disruption in the fiber optic cables that all of the westernized world needs for critical communications (Smith and Warren 2010). Unfortunately coercion as an emphasis is not only legally problematic; it is operationally and reputationally problematic as well.

One major constraint is that the use of cybered coercion invites wider attacks on softer targets than the heavily defended military or government agencies. For the United States, a major complication in applying a coercive strike-back policy is that the federal government controls little of the critical infrastructure or the cyberspace talent in the country (Kshetri 2005b). While many parts of the American cyberspace infrastructure have been hardening for years, much remains poorly protected. Not only are these private assets only now becoming a target normally, but they could also reap the increased ire of attackers unable to get to U.S. government servers. For example, the U.S. government is a massively attractive target in all its websites. Those government sites dealing with security such as military servers endure thousands of probing efforts each day (Crovitz 2008). Actual attacks doubled from 2006 to 2007 (up to thirteen thousand) against Pentagon computers alone, and presumably the Pentagon is commensurately establishing defensive walls and procedures (*Wall Street Journal* 2009). But an attacker subject to a coercive strike-back by the United States but not without second strike capabilities would find many other sensitive U.S. targets if the proverbial gloves were taken off.

Another major constraint is that across nations the legal barriers to the use of coercion are unclear. Policy turbulence continues not only within nations but also across the varied modern digitized city-states. In fall 2008, in large part as a response to this critical infrastructure vulnerability, the Bush administration issued a highly classified U.S. policy of striking back at cybered attackers that was leaked to the public in late 2008 (Clarke and Knake 2010). The consensus on using coercion had been growing inside the U.S. senior security leadership since February 2007 when an orchestrated distributed denial of service (DDOS) attack nearly succeeded in taking down at least six of the thirteen root servers that manage all the domain names on the internet. Without these servers, no internet domain would be recognized as existing, thus disemboweling cyberspace as it stands today, at least for as long as the servers were down. The interpretation of this attack by the U.S. cyberspace defense community was that a purely defensive, hardening strategy would be insufficient, especially if it was largely voluntary outside of the government.

Before this attack and its potential catastrophic consequences, those responsible for government computer security operated on the policy that if the hackers were not on U.S. territory, they could not be touched. Thus only defenses on U.S. soil were legally allowed (Rogin 2007a). The near catastrophic attack suggested that as the U.S. government made itself less easy to attack, its success was redirecting the attacks at the rest of the population.[15] After the attack, a consensus emerged inside the government for a more offensive strike-back policy to level the playing field.

Unless changed in the future, as of now the United States has the domestic authority to strike back in cyberspace. The otherwise secret coercive policy

---

15. A DDOS attack literally barrages into paralysis the applications in the computer that are trying to receive all the requests for entry. As for the small number of absolutely critical root servers, in a strange continuation of the constraints of the early computer design of the internet, the original 512-byte limit hard-programmed in the UDP (User Data Program) could only hold thirteen server addresses. So far, everything has been built off of this constraint (J. Johnson 2007; Mueller 2002).

was joined in another fall 2008 policy change aimed at closing doors electroni-cally to regain control of the nation's strategic buffer that was being eroded by mass attacks. In an oddly uncharacteristically low-key unannounced fashion, the outgoing U.S. administration issued the Comprehensive National Cyber Security Initiative allowing the NSA, the CIA, and the FBI's Cyber Division to "deploy technologies for preventing attacks" rather than waiting for an attack and deflecting it (Nakashima 2008). The implementation details are highly classified, but the language used is extraordinary in its potential for permitting a covert coercive strategy to strike back. To wit, "The Pentagon can (now) plan attacks on adversaries' networks if, for example, the NSA determines that a par-ticular server in a foreign country needs to be taken down to disrupt an attack on an information system critical to the U.S. government. That could include responding to an attack against a private-sector network, such as the telecom industries, sources said" (Nakashima 2008).

If there is a way to strike back accurately and legally, the U.S. government clearly intends to find it. In a sign that this change may be permanent, and coercive action through cyberspace a viable strategic tool, President Obama used one of his earliest strategic comments to "'declare the cyber infrastruc-ture a strategic asset'" (*Wall Street Journal* 2009). Such language in the U.S. political system tends to support a harsher stance against anyone threatening the asset. Many of the national defense policies supporting nuclear defense began with declarations of what were the strategic assets to be protected (Sagan and Waltz 1995).

The policy is not unrealistic in principle. The web is purely a human crea-tion, with no natural pathways not maintained by organizations and no power source not provided through human intervention. The impotence of govern-ments against the magic of cyberspace is a myth much beloved by the under-ground hacker community; it helps spread the sense of power associated and rationalized in cyberspace-enabled attacks (Young 2007). The strategic tools to find bad actors and coercively strike back at them already exist across the access points, energy sources, and technologies sustaining the networks of the westernized world. Not only is the means to attack back the same as those used in initial attacks, but the very fabric underpinning cyberspace is under the control of governments more than the largely anarchistic hackers in open societies believe (Young 2007). The web's design comes from a previous and more utopian era, but it and the anonymity assumed in its processes are arti-facts of human consensus.

When governments decide their part of the World Wide Web will not be anonymous, it is not. China today has a small army of internet controllers who curtail internal web use with automated tools, rows of reviewing uniformed inspectors, and even enthusiastic pro-government citizen-snitches (Goldsmith and Wu 2006). In principle, with enough resources and efforts, any exchange involving networked nodes can technically be tracked with the proper institutions, policies, access, and equipment in place.

Another major constraint is the anonymity offered by the globally complex and easily accessed internet. Coercive actions could easily strike innocent intervening computers whose owners were unaware of the bad actors' intents or identities. Today governmental and nongovernmental efforts to identify the bad actors are increasingly and inevitably leading to digital and globally implemented tracing operations, whether or not privacy is protected for citizens. Much can be done in cyberspace when the current physical location, established and most-likely patterns of behavior, and clear identification of a bad actor are simultaneously recognized. Using the same tools, direct action can be applied remotely, from the ultimate destruction of flying controlled drones overhead with missiles to hacking back into the attackers' computers and perhaps scrambling their hard drives to reporting them to arresting authorities. That governments have not done all this is not because they do not know how.

The international community slowly is enacting rules of engagement in cyberspace that are likely to make coercion more difficult as a first choice against cyberspace-enabled attacks over time. In 2001 the Council of Europe Convention on Cybercrime was first published, and in November 2007 the United States was the latest of sixteen countries to ratify it formally. The treaty has been criticized for not taking human rights adequately into account, and its main theme does not address any constraints to a national response for attacks by perpetrators causing physical harm in particular (Settings 2006). Nonetheless if human rights as a restraint are added to the already clearly established privacy concerns in westernized states, it is possible that the resulting international definitions will preclude, say, destroying the servers of attackers as violation of the attackers' rights to their own property. The more likely future path is that unintended blowback of a mistakenly directed coercion-first disruption operation being used by the signatories—say, the United States—will be used as a reason for explicit constraints.

With no current international constraints, however, governments hesitate because of political, social, and economic contingencies. Using coercion—that is, "hacking back" or tricking the enemy—engages the complexities of cyberspace as a global and interconnected socioeconomic infrastructure. The legal, societal, and even international contingencies make coercion technically possible but politically challenging. The automatic use of a responding coercive strike could easily be costly and counterproductive. Global cyberspace is emerging as a sensitive competitive playing field between potentially warring states. Embedded actors use the same servers and networks as millions of innocent civilians. Any hack-back at a server by a democratic government faces exceptional requirements for accuracy to limit disruptive damage proportionately to the threat. The bad actor may be embedded in the home or other westernized democracies, in relatively open developing nations, or in relatively controlled nondemocratic systems. Each population or political system in which the coercive action target is hidden poses considerable challenges in acquiring and refining knowledge for an accurate and effective disruptive strike.

If an attacking group has hidden itself using the openness of a westernized democracy, coercively striking that group is complicated by variations of the democratic cultures, laws, systems, and threat definitions that are involved. To gather the information necessary to make sure an internet-enabled strike is accurate, privacy concerns in particular have to be accommodated in any democracies whose internet space is involved. Privacy laws are stronger in Europe and have been so since at least the 1990s. The European Union's extension of these laws to citizens' use of the internet has widened the gap between the United States and its democratic peer states. For example, the United States had a great deal of difficulty persuading the European democracies of the jihadi terrorist threat in general, even after 2001, let alone persuading them of the internet jihadi threat.

More recently, however, the attacks in Madrid and London in 2005 and 2007 have brought home the possibility of embedded and violent threats inside otherwise quite open EU societies. Many European nations are finding that their formerly relatively homogeneous societies have become fractionated with many more places for bad actors to hide and indeed to develop mass casualty attack plans. Some European nations are moving toward the U.S. position in seeking to monitor citizens, if not exactly internet communications, with the intent of identifying bad actors. Great Britain, for example, has succeeded in passing legislation early after the attacks of 9/11 that extended the government's ability to surveil telecommunications of any kind if considered warrantable legally and to retain that data for future use. The Anti-Terrorism Crime and Security Act of 2001 expanded the powers of the government while still tying those actions to the kind of evidentiary laws typical of a criminal case (Whitley and Hosein 2005).

More dramatic policy changes moving toward the U.S. position emerged in 2008 from a surprising quarter—Sweden, home of some of the earliest personal data protection legislation. After years of strenuous debate, the Swedish Parliament on the morning of June 18, 2008, voted to surveil all internet communications via its national electronic security agency, the National Defense Radio Establishment (FRA). The afternoon of the same day, the Parliament rescinded the vote pending its rewriting with more privacy protections (Haikola and Jonsson 2007). That evening, however, the Parliament voted the act back into effect with more privacy protection and with the intention of it taking effect in January 2009 (Thelenius-Wanler 2008). "The government cited the changing nature of security threats, terrorism, international crime and the specter of cyber warfare to push through the law which hands intelligence agencies far-ranging powers to snoop on citizens' personal data . . . [enabling] the military National Defense Radio Establishment (FRA) to monitor Swedes' internet usage as well as content from e-mails, phone calls and text messages" (*Deutsche-Welle* 2008).

If Sweden as the original home of policies about privacy and electronic data protection was willing to consider this policy, there is quite a sea change in the perspectives of Europe concerning what needs to be done via the internet for security. Solving the privacy issue in a democracy not only sets the stage for better behavior data collection but also helps to present strike-back policies as less likely to damage the democracies they are intended to protect. Such a policy by the United States is likely to be less difficult to sell to European allies.

Beyond Western democracies, coercively striking attackers hidden in or through cyberspace operating in a country with a weak government is less complicated by laws and privacy expectations than by the turbulent infrastructure and large nondigital society surrounding the attackers. With the only digital aspect of their lives being the internet—and that often in an internet café—the cyber terrorist could set up anywhere where internet cafés are found and remain anonymous (Gertz 2010). The challenges to Western security forces

trying to disable these attackers are the social conditions. A developing country with a weak government oversees a population more interested in daily
survival than in abstract curiosity about strangers. The governing structure is
impotent and thus provides some measure of looking away from curious activities for the right payments to officials with pathetic and inadequate salaries.
Furthermore there is a tendency to view such attacks as not posing a threat
to the local and nondigitized government. There is little to no effort made to
provide security and surveillance in and over the internet networks in many
of these societies.

In these nations, there are too few resources to control internet users, even
if well-intentioned officials promise just that to the international community.
Most of them do not understand computer networks in any technical sense.
Furthermore they assume institutions in a weak, developing country are not
attractive targets. If money just might be forthcoming if attacking a westernized country succeeds, most officials simply turn a blind eye even if they know
or disapprove of such behaviors (Curran, Concannon, and McKeever 2007).
All this is even more pronounced if the cyber attackers have a narrative that
portrays their efforts as the underdog striking the exploiting, and sometimes
infidel, rich, Western states in the name of the poor. This narrative is not only
rampant in the westernized community of hackers but has also transferred easily and rapidly to those in the developing world.

Attacking back through this societal maze is also problematic simply because of the fragile infrastructure. Attackers may want to take down a dam in
the United States, but the response cannot be taking down the one functioning dam built expensively by good-hearted Europeans in the target nation shel-
tering the attackers. Hence a cyber strike-back in these nations has a precision
requirement not unlike that needed to reach through European networks, but
for moral reasons. If the accuracy of the strike-back is poor and infrastructure
for necessary services is profoundly interrupted, the public outcry could make
degrading the confidence of attackers more difficult. For example, a young
activist cousin with several like-minded friends could be using his uncle's
computer for the attacks. He is the only westernized doctor in a surrounding
region with the ability to use telemedicine and possibly is a part-time public
official. His resources were not involved, nor those of the wider clan, until the
coercive attack destroyed the only access he had to the internet to continue
his medical work. In anger, he could easily orchestrate contributions into the

cyberspace conflict that worsen the hand of a westernized country alleged to have inaccurately struck back.[16]

There are, however, advantages in having attackers hiding in these cultures precisely because of their lack of resources. Finding the internet cafés is not as difficult as it might be if they are located in other westernized nations with strong privacy laws. There will be many fewer of them per capita, and they will be in urban areas. Satellite uplinks or cell phone minutes as a way to avoid internet cafés is very expensive. Generally these attackers are using cyberspace precisely because they have few concrete resources. Having the wealth to pay for such access is unlikely to be common as well. In addition, electricity is problematic in these nations. Often the electrical system only functions a limited number of hours during the day for the wider population without the funds to buy generators and the gas for them. Even then, the system can work intermittently, depending on the losses on the line before it even reaches the computer at which a group of attackers sit. Thus, the pattern of an attack suggests where the attacker might be found, when, and the likely access to resources, if an attacker can be traced to a nation with these infrastructure issues. These issues make it harder for the attacker, but when linked to other information about cyberspace and skills in the nation, it potentially makes accurate targeting easier.

Across the nondemocratic states of the world, political control now means internet control, at least in terms of the servers reaching to the outside world. It also often means controlling the kinds of equipment permitted for imports into the nations. In these kinds of nations, such as China and Iran, lone rogue hackers and their community simply cannot get access to skills, equipment, and web gateways if they are not seen as trustworthy by the government. They may be left in peace to attack foreign servers, for example, but this freedom is always contingent on government will. In recent years, a number of attacks have been traced to China, for example, but the Chinese government has denied any involvement (Kyodo 2008). In most cases of sophisticated attacks, the attackers from China are unlikely to independently have the equipment

16. This scenario has happened a number of times outside of cyberspace where the young clan member's death awakens a search for revenge on the part of uncles and cousins with more resources and organizational connections (Lance 2003; Speckhard and Ahkmedova 2006).

in their homes or offices that is not untraceable by the government. Like the developing but ungoverned nation, the complication is making sure whose system or files were destroyed in a coercive response.

The world of cyber proxy wars in general is in its infancy. However, there are good reasons to think many people are making their careers in China hacking U.S. agencies (Elegant 2007). The targets range widely from "technology theft, intelligence gathering, exfiltration, research on DOD [Department of Defense] operations and the creation of dormant presences in DOD networks for future action" (Rogin 2007b). The attacks have grown beyond hacking for business intelligence, theft, and military spying (Elegant 2007). Normal human behavior in large, secretive bureaucracies does not vanish just because the tools are virtual. One can speculate with good reason that there are bureaucratic advancement incentives to at least doing something in cyberspace against the United States. It is known that some Soviet spies would order by mail the otherwise free U.S. government documents, smudge them, and then use them to build their reputation inside the Soviet Union's spy agencies. Similarly, successful attack operations in cyberspace with few tracks back to the host government can be very enhancing to one's internal reputation. A coup here does not have to be publicly announced to benefit the insiders' rising stars.

Today the Chinese People's Liberation Army (PLA) routinely runs competitions with big cash prizes to attract and encourage the best hackers in the country; the targets are not specified (Elegant 2007). But the Chinese government control of its internet is extraordinarily strong right now, and it is difficult to create a scenario of fully independent Chinese hackers doing anything, let alone orchestrating mass attacks, without government approval, if only by officials looking away. The internet gateways and content are massively surveilled and managed by huge internet control staffs, censors, and authorities with exceptionally sophisticated tools. Thus, even if no formal government involvement is detectable, Chinese hack attacks putatively emanating from the China mainland are usually considered proxy operations (U.S. Office 2007).

Responding by coercively disrupting a server abroad will have international repercussions if the attackers are acting as proxies and the strike-back is revealed publicly. A mistake in targeting the coercive second strike could be minor unless the operation inadvertently takes down something so obvious or so enraging that it would force public Chinese denouncement.[17] At the very least, the prickly Chinese state would be forced to at least rattle a saber, intimating questions of sovereignty and war. A new flood of attacks from "eager" citizens would most certainly come as a riposte, this time possibly with more destructive effects, though still denied by the government. Even if the proxy cover were blown conclusively, from the Chinese authorities' view, acting to defend themselves proactively in cyberspace is legitimate in the competition for resources with the West, especially the United States. To have the United States strike back at what turns out to be a Chinese government internet facility pretending to be an unknown hacker could easily make a strategy emphasizing coercion particularly Pyrrhic in its effects. Furthermore, a coercive strike-back attack might just be more difficult because the Chinese internet is newer and has designed into it more secure sets of protocols to control what commands are allowed to pass in or through its links. It is easier, in principle, for Chinese to hack into the United States than for the United States to hack back into China (Crovitz 2008).

Autocratic states are, paradoxically, increasing the difficulty of disrupting distant attackers by moving rapidly to try to control their internet along the Chinese model, by owning the central gateways in and out of the nation. Originally it was thought the internet was uncontrollable and could be a great stimulus to the development of democracy in nonwesternized states. Indeed, many leaders of weakly democratic states opened up to cyberspace to help advance their economies through computerization and the associated education of young people. It did not take long to realize how quickly an international network for playing games, stealing music, and sending email can morph into a support system for dissenters. For example, to be sure the offline repression of reformist parties is not undermined by mobile and internet communications, the Iranian government now idiosyncratically closes sites, access, and even whole ISPs (internet service providers) within their territories to suppress dissent, alternative narratives, facts differing from the government description, or contacts outside the country (Berkeley 2006).

The irony of this political control lies in the advantages it offers for at least

17. For example, if the U.S. security agencies were put on the spot publicly and chose not to lie about their actions to the American public, the Chinese would feel compelled to act back forcefully.

tracing the origins of an attack. Autocratic leaders have reduced the possibility of attackers unaffiliated with the government being able to operate from their territory and inadvertently and conveniently concentrated the control mechanisms for sophisticated and preferably nearly invisible intrusion efforts. If sufficient skill is engaged in the strike-back effort by the defending westernized nation, it could inflict violence that is not traceable, which is exactly as often intended by the very attackers one seeks to disrupt.

Keeping the focus on disruption, repeatedly and nonobviously over time, is essential if proxies are involved. As all governments get involved in protecting their societies in cyberspace, these activities are becoming part of a competitive arena between states, and also between governments and their people. So far, a "war" in which states use cyber means to harm each other as they would use their military forces has yet to occur. However, operations dangerously close to that level of explicit coercive use of cyberspace are not so unlikely. The Cold War demonstrated the vigorous efforts employed by large states to cause trouble for peer competitors in third-state areas considered resource rich. The tools were often chosen so that sponsor states could deny what they were doing, especially by using proxy actors. Cyberspace offers this ability to cause trouble as well while remaining hidden. Striking back at the actual attackers requires sufficient accuracy to know when they are acting alone or acting as proxies for a sponsoring government. It also requires a high-level policy decision about how much damage is acceptable if the sponsoring government is a well-armed peer competitor.

Since the goal of coercion is to directly degrade the confidence of the attacker, when proxies of major peer competitors are the target, subtlety will always be essential. Too anonymous a coercive strike back, however, runs the risk of being misunderstood as random or bad luck, rather than as a confidence deflator when attacking a westernized nation. Therefore, the cautionary note focuses on the proxy host. If the proxies are the target but not in the pay of a major peer competitor, a well-noted, repeatable second strike known to the attackers as such may be necessary to disrupt attacker confidence as profoundly as desired. Such distinctions will critically depend on the knowledge acquired and the weighted mix of action motivators attached to each set of attackers.

Coercion always has its limits, even in the currently free-wheeling world of cyberspace. Conversely, the other two strategic tools, capital and information, have more clear correlates in other human activities not associated with any kind of attack scenario. They may take longer and work more indirectly than taking down a host of cyber cafés, but they may also be better long-run disruption options.

Capital

Capital is more subtle than coercion as a main strategic emphasis against an attacking organization using cyberspace. Once the information on the attacker and organization are collected and developed into a theory-of-action profile, a capital-focused disruption strategy chooses from an array of options to degrade the needs perceived to be met by attacking westernized societies. These range from more traditional means of applying capital such as direct contact and bribery of key attackers to broader, less direct community resource support. The latter can, for example, create alternative employment for attackers or negate resource-defined grievances. As the attackers are using cyberspace, the strategy can also operate digitally, providing websites offering bounties, running false-flag counteroperations involving snitches and payoffs, or even cyberspace "honeypot" operations. In the latter, a fake server offers information or pseudo-access that lures attackers to keep checking back to obtain false or misleading information. Each time attackers return, the operators of the server acquire more and more clues as to their life circumstances, current whereabouts, skill levels, and targets (Romney et al. 2005). The game continues until enough information about attacker patterns can be acquired to then enable using capital most effectively. The United States already conducts operations with capital as a tool for finding information, often to support larger, more coercive operations. For example, offering a reward has been successful in Pakistan in U.S. government operations to capture particular terrorists after 9/11 (Michael 2007). So common is this procedure that terrorist organizations put a bounty on killing U.S. soldiers at $25,000, or about one-tenth the U.S. bounty (Petrusic 2006).

If capital is deemed the best emphasis in a disruption strategy, the important question of format will particularly matter in using virtual means to communicate. A desire to offer resources in exchange for stopping undesirable behavior is not as straightforward in other cultures as it is in the United States. Much needs to be known in the initial development of the violence profile of attackers in order to anticipate how capital inducements and the logistics of payoff will be viewed by the target and their supporters.[18] For example, in World War II, what worked for Nazis hunting Jews in parts of Europe—cash offers—did not work in Algeria and Morocco. Even when the bribe was modified to simply allowing any snitch to keep the property of the Jews who were reported, everyone knew it was a bribe. Respected elders from imams to royalty condemned the policy, and the population refused (Satloff 2007). It has been argued that U.S. bounties on terrorists after 9/11 advertised in Pakistan were misdirected. While they did produce a few terrorists on the most wanted list, the bigger effect was the interpretation of the bounty by pro-Islamic Pakistani intelligence service (Inter-Services Intelligence, or ISI). The agency used the bounty to justify imprisoning or killing moderate political opponents under the guise of catching terrorists (Gregory 2007).

Rather than direct bribes or bounties, developing the knowledge of how to effectively insert other resources into a community can reveal ways to disrupt cyber-enabled attacks. Counterinsurgency doctrine being refined by the U.S. Army after years in Iraq emphasizes services that get local leaders to keep the level of overall grievance down and reduce the connection between violence and need (Berman, Shapiro, and Felter 2008). The young men in the Middle East most likely to join radical causes are those with education, no jobs, lots of free time, and a great deal of resentment. The latter is especially likely because they cannot possibly afford the enormous costs of a wedding, which Islamic culture in that region requires of them (Rashad et al. 2005).

Advantages of a capital-heavy disruption strategy derive from the breadth and variety of the globalizing world financial infrastructure and the strong correlation between resentful, unemployed youth and a surge of radicalism in either westernized minority communities or developing nations. The wide variety of delivery mechanisms enabled by global financial flows means, with sufficient specificity about a payee or investment outlet, nearly any targeted group can be given resources. Applying resources can be accomplished in

18. Bounty hunters are an exception. Every culture has them, and their profession is focused on taking money. They are a possible target of a capital campaign, though misleading clients for money is a large reliability hazard. An interesting mix of bounty hunters and geographical information occurred in 2001. In the hunt for bin Laden, a U.S. geographer with deep knowledge of Afghanistan used details from long-range videos, bounty hunter pictures of hills and vegetation, and prior knowledge of the country to deduce where bin Laden's house was located (Shroder 2005).

creative and deniable ways for states wishing to disrupt violence but not spark resentment among those who were not able to get paid. Knowing the target audience in depth allows for tailoring a capital-emphasis strategy. For example, if the more skilled among Muslim moderates form the pool of new recruits for jihadi violence, capital is likely to be an effective tool. Muslim moderates list economic circumstances as their main concern (Esposito and Mogahed 2007).

For example, decoupling need from a choice of violence with virtual delivery mechanisms could focus on those addicted to internet cafés. An alternative is to offer highly discrete marriage "loans" at very liberal repayment terms. The vetting, negotiations, and payment would be conducted virtually and extremely confidentially. As the only guarantor useful in a distant but shame-based society, the deal might include a personal oath to keep the deal secret and the information that it is a Western non-Islamic source, perhaps no more specific than that. As evidence, a video of the oath, much like the death videos of suicide bombers, could be made. All these more ritualistic reliability aspects would not work well in another, more modernized culture. However, in these affective, shame-based cultures these aspects could nonetheless obligate the person to the lender, who could also require that they swear not to participate in attacks involving any form of violence.[19] The capital then meets a major need driving a violence profile, and the odds that this strategy will be successful go up as well.

Constraints on capital-heavy disruption strategies, however, rest in the vulnerability to deception and extortion, especially if undertaken remotely and virtually with no trusted actors able to physically verify the recipients, the transfers, and the results. Making sure one is reaching the real attacker or a subgroup that might really know who the attacker is, was, or will be critically demands knowledge. Humans routinely are more cruel, dismissive, suspicious, and violent toward strangers. In economic exchanges across cultures, cities, or even clans, people learn quickly how to systematically extort resources from those viewed as strangers. A poorly designed and informed capital emphasis

19. If lendees later radicalize, they can declare they were coerced or in other ways repudiate the video. However, they will know the powerful reality of imagery broadcast. They will be viewed as weak for taking the money in their culture, no matter what they say, and thus it is less likely they will take the final steps. In any case, if the funds work as well as intended to drive down the need motivator, the radicalization is also less likely.

strategy could be expending large sums while the recipients do not actually abide by the required agreement to desist in violent behaviors. Since capital, unlike coercion, is not intended to disable the ability to attack but reduce the need to do so, it is particularly dependent on the extensive development of an array of background information and specific indicators to reduce the chances of successful deceptions and extortions.

Meeting these drawbacks of trust and greed requires creative implementations in which checks are embedded nonobviously in all exchanges, feedback is continuously assessed, and new knowledge is constantly sought to refine the operation. None of these requirements are unusual in the world of finance generally, but cyberspace both allows more reach and more moral hazard. Overall, however, capital is no more or less difficult to apply than coercion but generally breaks fewer things when it lands on a target.

Legitimacy

A disruption strategy emphasizing legitimacy focuses primarily on the attacker's sense of the moral or peer-approved nature of using violence. It then attempts to directly relate any hesitation to the use of cyberspace. Its implementation rests in some form of persuasive information to the attacker or organization, and possibly the surrounding supporting community. The message has to be accepted as trustworthy, it must be interpreted to mean what is intended, and the message delivery method also must be also considered reliable and acceptable. The first two are well-known challenges to any cross-group communication, but the third is a particular challenge of cyberspace's distance and interface characteristics (Kreijns, Kirschner, and Jochems 2003). Not only the content but also the delivery need to be designed with considerable knowledge of how trust in peers, information, and technology is constructed in the target group.

Designing persuasive content in a disruptive strategy against violence is helped by the fact that no culture in the world approves of murder (O'Connell 1989). An important objective, then, is to construct the message that correlates violent attacks as murder, even if accomplished remotely and indirectly. Cialdini (2001) offers six laws of persuasion that operate in some fashion across most cultures. This list offers a guide to emphasizing information to challenge effectively the legitimacy of cyber-enabled attacks or violence. The law of reciprocity (1) states that humans like to repay gifts. The law of commitment and consistency (2) states that humans like to appear consistent and will often cling to a prior decision to do so. The law of liking (3) states that humans want to please those they like or do something that demonstrates they are "just like those they like." The law of scarcity (4) states that humans are more likely to buy if the product appears to be the last one and will shortly be scarce. The law of authority (5) states that if it is good enough for esteemed person "X," it must be good enough for oneself. Finally the law of social proof (6) states that if normally respected others are doing something, it must be considered OK to do (Cialdini 2001). These six rules of persuasion suggest that a message effectively delegitimizing violence should invoke these elements. Perhaps the act of cyber-enabled violence is culturally portrayed as poorly repaying someone in inconsistent ways that denigrate the preferences of a well-respected elder while also seeming very common and not worthy of the esteem of those one likes. For example, U.S. commanders in Iraq have been advised to try to see military operations in Muslim terms, including employing the local terminology, in order to further cooperation from the local elders (Edwards 2005). This approach is more likely to get elder support. To the extent that these elders are still liked and esteemed by violence-prone young men, the message of restraint is also more likely to be accepted and spread among peer groups.

Leaving aside the need for the knowledge necessary to design the message content, the second major requirement—the effective delivery medium—poses an intricate challenge. Any message must be adjusted for the physical distances between senders and receivers, how it is experienced in the bad actor's peer group and culture, and the raw logistics of delivery and feedback. Across cultures, the virtual world is pushing the limits of trust extension between humans using the internet for any reason. Because humans are more willing to be callous about harm to those at a physical distance, cyberspace attacks are more likely to be treated as less morally constrained than direct physical assaults. Murder by attacking an electrical system has more unreality in both magnitude and moral rules than blowing up the power plant directly. Hence, to delegitimize attacks via cyberspace requires a deep and enhanced understanding of social trust, peer group reinforcements, communications intricacy and social sensors, and even the taken-for-granted messages in imagery in the attacker's referent community. These are discussed below.

A major challenge for the use of legitimacy to disrupt bad actors rests in the variations of social trust across cultures, especially in the amount of time critical to developing trust in clan-based societies. Time must be spent if the persuasive message and medium of delivery are to be believed when the bad actors are located in or originate in strongly kin-based cultures such as those in the developing world. Normally, after the initial personal contact is made, time must be spent to create and seal a friendship. For virtual connections to be strong enough to sustain long-term relations, this time must have been spent watching each other's face for subtle clues. Then messages are interpreted correctly in an online setting. Investigations of internet trust development in China and Japan concluded that the prior associations in Japan and the Chinese culture's wide use of *guanxi*—obligations to each other—both strongly affected the levels of trust members of each society exhibited on the Net (Takahashi et al. 2008).

For all the same reasons, social distance or how close individuals feel to each other (in-group–out-group) markedly constrains the boundaries of trust among people in "affective" cultures more than it does in "neutral" cultures (Buchan and Croson 2004). Affective speakers dominate the developing world while the likely westernized security forces attempting to disrupt attacks are from the smaller group of neutral-speaking societies. Globally, 80 percent of the population are affective speakers; only about 20 percent are neutral speakers. In work and nonwork settings, affective cultures pay more attention to the indirect, often visual cues that are missed by most neutral speakers. They are also not generally found in online communications unless personal videos are present (Sanchez-Burks et al. 2003). Neutral speakers focus on the content of the message, and much less on its delivery medium or the effect it has on the listener.

For a westernized security force to disrupt a developing world bad actor requires considerable development of advance knowledge. Neutral speakers will instinctively overlook subtle indicators clearly visible to, or expected by, affective speakers in the same culture. Neutral speakers often experience affective speakers as devious and indirect, while affective speakers experience neutral speakers as tactless and naive. Consider this operational conundrum that undoubtedly frustrates Western interrogators in Iraq. In neutral societies, one can ask three independent sources the same question. All will try to ingratiate by giving some portions of the truth while leaving out others. The culture makes it unlikely all three will fabricate completely ingratiating stories. Thus one can "triangulate" on what they say, and extract at least some indication of where common objective truths may be located. But in interrogating three affective speakers, all three will instinctively say what is least likely to offend the questioner to the extent of literally saying no when they mean yes. Giving parts of the truth might reveal the alteration of the other bits, and so there is a tendency to read body cues and keep elaborating on the pleasing rather than accurate story. It is very possible none of the stories correspond in any particular way to any other, leaving the interrogator with literally nothing accurate to go on (Kersten and Sidky 2005).[20] Without considerable attention to this distinction, messages designed by neutral speakers in the Western states—whether or not they are digitally delivered—are likely to be received by their affective speaker audience as ham-handed and ineffective. It has already happened several times since 2001 for the United States in its global marketing of the war on terror to Muslim populations (Sepp 2007).

Aside from direct camera views across computer nodes, cyberspace-enabled communications are still hampered in substituting for human relations.[21] This is especially true for the broad-spectrum trust that facilitates confidence that carries over into new situations. Narrow-spectrum trust is the kind of trust tied to domains or services. One trusts one's mail carrier to deliver all the mail without stealing but not to paint one's house. Even aside from the distance in cyberspace, cultures differ widely in the extent to which broad-spectrum trust is universally transferable, obtainable, renewable, or constructed. Non-clan-based neutral cultures are more likely to extend trust broadly than clan-based or affective cultures. However, even in the prototypical neutral culture of the United States, long-term trust in working relations tends to require an initial

20. It is perhaps sadly instructive that leaders in many of these non-Western autocratic and affective societies routinely up the ante in interrogation or social controls, creating some fear greater than the fear of causing offense by the message. Often this is torture or the threat of harming the individual's entire family, from parents to children to uncles, aunts, and cousins. So endemic is this method of getting some level of accurate transmission that, for example, swearing an oath of loyalty to Saddam Hussein of Iraq usually meant agreeing to forfeit one's own life *and* the lives of three generations of one's family as a guarantee of loyalty. See U.S. Institute for Defense Analysis (2007:37).

21. Holographic communications that stream into one's room, for example, may be possible in the future. That is, one could be in one's office working next to the seemingly sitting holographic coworker. One might turn to this coworker for a casual comment just as one would do normally. The difference would be, of course, that the interaction ends and probably cannot extend to the bar down the street after work or the local coffee house at lunch. At the moment, the computing power and need are not on the horizon to develop this technology widely.

physical contact to provide the basis for longer-term trust. Only then can communication by the internet keep the connection alive.[22]

Hackers attacking westernized societies for money have paved the way for terrorist attackers by developing a variety of sophisticated operations to get around the trust hurdle. In particular, they use the level of casual trust available in a more neutral, likely westernized society in order to trick their human target to give up information that would otherwise be hidden. Since broad-spectrum trust is the hardest to create or use, attackers try to mimic the attributes of narrow-spectrum trust—that is, they pretend to be support sites to get necessary information. In this field the use of such trickery to obtain information otherwise much harder to get is called *social engineering*. It is a method of access often preferred by many cybercriminals because getting victims to divulge their passwords freely saves a great deal of time (Bhagyavati 2007).[23]

Terrorists have taken advantage of the pioneering efforts of hackers. They also use social engineering, false-flag appeals, and other variations of the kinds of cybercriminal tools developed and refined by the hacker and cracker communities. For example, online charity appeals for, say, widows and orphans by both criminal and violent jihadi organizations are not all that unusual in both the developed and developing world. These charities were particularly effective in the Muslim world, where one of the five obligations for a Muslim is charity. Usually, because donors are related to the Muslim communities for which the money was putatively collected, some portion of the funds is spent as advertised. But other portions on these completely unregulated sites are given to the more militant wings of the charitable organization (Winer

22. Note that all these observations are based on a world in which the web-based communication is still largely based on text, static imagery, or audio. The world of avatars with our movements and faces overlaid on them is still ahead of us. VVTCs, or video virtual teleconferences, are still the minority of communications. Businesspeople still fly to conferences. For a host of reasons ranging from environmental to fuel to time costs, such gadding about is inefficient, but it is still considered unavoidable today. For an example of how one might conduct completely virtual conferences today, see, for example, the joint real-life and virtual conference on Nanoscale Science and Technology that occurred in October 2007 (http://www.ibiblio.org/oahost/nst/). Note again that this is still clumsy and a poor replication of the actual conference experience.

23. Michael Aiello quotes a March 15, 2005, U.S. Treasury report in which "it was shown that out of 100 employees auditors were 'able to convince 35 managers and employees to provide their username and to change their password.' This figure is 'about a 50 percent improvement over the previous test conducted in 2001'" (Aiello 2007, 192).

2008).[24] Terrorists also use tools of corporate online tracking and targeting of a market segment. Just visiting a Muslim site more frequently can result in being tracked as a likely recruit or potential donor by the owners of the site, with personalized messages sent thereafter (Awan 2007).

Social engineering works both ways, of course, and a modified form of social engineering incorporated into the disruption strategy can be a viable option even at a distance. The goal would be to persuade others in a process called *social construction* to see the act of copying a violent action differently and to view it as a culturally disdained act in order to disrupt attacks (Pech 2003).[25] To use the information tool at a distance requires at least a rough idea of the attacking group or its origins. Humans tend to be more casually cruel at a distance, and finding out the groups with which the attackers have little knowledge or no common empathy reveals much about the personal preferences of the targeted group. For example, neutral and more individualistic cultures are more likely to produce braggart hackers eager to try new exploits on the spot for the thrill, possibly for the money. They are less constrained by a concern for community or clan as a whole. Information can be used to encourage excess responses online on the part of the bragging bad actor and thereby force inadvertent revelations of identifying data. Subsequently messages, or any other disruptive action can be tailored for the apparent audience. Affective and more communal cultures consistently produce more modest students of hacking. The latter's motivating narrative includes self-congratulatory tales of successes that, however personally defined, can be interpreted to have improved enormously the wider community as a whole. For the latter, a disruption message would emphasize a link between the digital jihad and a lack of nobility in the crass pursuit of thrill or money. For right-wing or anarchist neutral society hackers, destroying a "corrupt" society is the goal, so the mes-

24. The extent of this raising of charity funds for militant purposes has been disputed (Rosen 2008).

25. This approach of changing the information perceived is similar to having spray-paint-resistant city walls while also designating specific walls for select graffiti artists to use. The taggers who simply need an expressive outlet go for the walls; those simply interested in rebellious protests will still wander around trying to find the now fewer walls without the resistant paint. At the end of the day, using this approach has lowered the success and confidence of the simply destructive taggers while meeting the main need of those who simply wanted to speak publicly.

sage must link the attack to weakness or to something with which they would abhor being connected (Euben 2002).

Challenging the emphasis of legitimacy in a cybered disruption strategy is the delivery format that strongly influences likely acceptance and interpretation of the content of any message. Considerable knowledge development in advance is required in order to avoid using an ineffective delivery medium. In some cases, the only way to disrupt attacks will be to reach into the community enveloping the attackers and deliver the de-legitimizing message through the peer group. The goal could be to develop a broader spectrum of trust on the part of the bad actor's peer group such that attacks are disdained as low-class antics (Pech and Slade 2005). This approach especially requires knowing how the culture interprets messages differently across varying media. For example, communicating in one's own culturally persuasive manner sometimes results not in the message being rejected but in it being reinterpreted with highly undesirable effects in another culture.

Many violent conflicts have started for reasons of a message-medium disconnect in the audience. One of these is the 1991 Gulf War I. Saddam Hussein by all accounts misunderstood the message given by Ambassador April Glaspie to mean the United States would not respond to an attack on Kuwait precisely because it came from the ambassador. The ambassador said something quite clear to a neutral American speaker, in text as well as by phone. As an affective speaker, however, Hussein inferred hidden signals in what was seen as a much too bald statement delivered by a person in her particular role. In Hussein's clan-based, affective culture normally riven with high-level intrigue, no one accepts blunt statements as meaning what they say. In this case, Hussein knew the United States could not afford to lose their preferred balancing ally to a resurgent Iran (Mearsheimer and Walt 2003). He not only heard what he wanted to hear, but from the perspective of how senior political figures spoke with each other in his context, it was the correct interpretation that the United States would not oppose an invasion of Kuwait.

Another example of the wrong message being heard due to the medium occurred before the fall of the shah of Iran. When the shah visited President Carter in 1977, American laws on free speech required that President Carter allow anti-shah protesters to gather, and television cameras broadcast the small group's vigorous rally. Unfortunately Carter was also mildly pressing the shah on human rights issues in his country. The combination of allowing the protest and mentioning human rights was interpreted by the opposition and the shah's own intelligence leaders in Iran as evidence that the Americans were going to abandon the shah. While this message was quite a far stretch from what President Carter intended, the religious and secular opposition was emboldened at the prospect of the United States abandoning support for the shah. His security forces read the message similarly and were disheartened. Thinking themselves to be shortly on their own, the shah's security leaders tightened the social controls, and the rippling resentments contributed majorly to the overthrow (D. Harris 2004).

The medium-message disconnect affects even many corporate ventures where one would presume a common set of goals and values would be present. International corporate teams often implode on the difficulty of transcending cultures and medium simultaneously to change communications patterns so that all players are comfortable with each other (Hodgetts and Luthans 2006). For example, while the social group most likely to need large amounts of trust is the cross-domain, geographically dispersed team in the corporate world, it is one of the most difficult social groups for the transnational corporation to establish and maintain without the comfort, cohesion, and expense of the traditional face-to-face settings. The result is a great deal of misunderstanding and the need for many rounds of clarification, not to mention the distrust that is endemic over time (Powell, Piccoli, and Ives 2004).

To deliver a message in cyberspace that keeps the intent and likely interpretation the same, the medium must deal with variability not only in societal trust, language, and history but also in the ways graphical choices alter patterns of response to any message (Lee, Yang, and Graham 2006). It matters if a message is purely text based or spoken. For neutral speakers in general, text messages such as email are nearly as powerful as spoken communications. The affective speakers comprising 80 percent of the world need to see the listener for visual cues about the effect the message is having on the listener. They are uncomfortable solely with text, tending to supplement the lack of visual cues by relying heavily on prior social developments of trust. For that reason in part, the text-based web took off more quickly in westernized states, even if one controls for the level of digital advancement. However, once graphics indicating emotions or human faces were possible, the rest of the world exploded onto the Net. In keeping with its cultural preferences, images of people dominate the preferred communications avenues of affective speakers. While text-based SMS (Short Message Service) still dominates the neutral speakers' regions, Asian markets innovated camera phones and other ways to see the other person as one talks, making graphical MMS (Multimedia Messaging Service) exceptionally widespread. If one can see the other person, one is more able to discern the effects of the communication (Wang and Fulop 2007).

The result is profound in the likely effectiveness of a violence-delegitimizing disruption operation. In neutral societies, technology rather than cultural trust disparities will strongly influence the trust given a message and its medium. Particularly if the targets are of the same culture as the security forces trying to stop the attacks, there is more likely to be an adequate knowledge base in the forces to correctly match the message with trust needs and the technology in delivery. If the attackers' narrative hinges on bettering the world rather than destroying people, this key belief becomes a possible persuasive hook. It is more disruptive to in-group rationales if they or their trusted peer groups are consistently exposed to a large body of information about how such attacks by others as well as themselves make matters worse. For example, during the Vietnam War, the United States had a violent antiwar terrorist group called the Weather Underground. Like the later generations of hackers who cast themselves as doing good by revealing security flaws, this group rationalized its attacks on banks, for example, as a service to the public. Harming their audience was not the goal. The group broke up when, in close succession, they inadvertently blew up a homeless man, and their own bomb-making squad blew themselves up. These events were widely publicized with video images. Because the television image is so accepted in U.S. society, the stories were believed widely, including by the terrorist group members themselves. Unlike a wide variety of Holocaust deniers who see photos and dismiss them, the photos were immediately believed, and the latent support for the Weather Underground vanished (Isserman 2007).

Using social engineering in the chat rooms and other virtual venues could provide opportunities to reduce underlying grievance narratives legitimizing violent acts. The messenger would focus on assuaging some rather universal human needs and redirecting anger or resentment. In that case, a combination of a honeypot operation to offer some capital with an offline human contact to undermine the legitimacy of violence could provide the most disruptive effect. In this regard, the virtual world has great graphics where individuals are represented by customized "avatars" (characters that represent the humans moving them around). This blend of a honeypot and offline contact could be more tightly connected when one person "sees" the other moving the avatar around. Avatars can also show emotion and make decisions just as the human operating them would. For neutral speakers, trusting complete strangers is not common but is more likely when tied to performance. The virtual world does work to have players in it see the world differently (Gee 2005). In addition, even if indirect persuasion is not likely, technology, especially via a myriad of communications pathways, can be used to pinpoint key figures in the groups in order to tailor and deliver the message directly.

It is important to note that "massively multiplayer online role-playing games" (MMORPGs) online today offer opportunities for both bad actors and effective disruptive strategies. On the one hand, such games used to offer what were uncontrolled or supervised chat rooms that bad actors could use to make plans at a distance while appearing to play a game. On the other hand, these games are strongly attractive to young people for the intensity of the experience. In avatar-based games, trust is largely narrow and strongly based on pure performance. That is, players want to group with fellow players of an online game only after they have shown an ability to perform adequately. Even if the individual claiming to be an attorney plays the game reliably, supportively, and well, other players will not rely on that player's self-proclaimed legal ability. This means players have to broaden the trust considerably, perhaps checking the credentials of the alleged attorney and even seeing the person F2F (face-to-face) to use age-old human visual sensors in judging reliability (Feng, Lazar, and Preece 2004).[26] Nonetheless, the fact that the venue is engaging and attractive could provide opportunities for a delegitimizing disruption strategy to use the virtual to make sure the message and medium match. A cricket game online would not be the place, for example, to launch a message about bombs, but a very violent online game might be appropriate if properly researched and employed.

Several caveats must be noted. All applications of a disruption strategy are based on comprehensively derived, consensual, developed knowledge constantly reevaluated and validated through experience. There have been successes. While detailed information is not publicly available, in the past few years members of al Qaeda in Iraq were found and targeted by a U.S. cyber attack that altered key data in their computer databases. The result—called

26. This hesitation may be overcome by the increasing realism in the online virtual worlds and their intrusion into the rest of society—for example, in shopping. Over time, the experiences of shopping virtually, seeing the goods in dynamic ways and then obtaining the goods physically, may overcome the trust disparity. Research on that topic is ongoing.

the indirect effect—was for them to believe the data and blindly enter a trap that, in this case, was deadly for them (Sanger 2009).

In sum, taken alone without resilience, disruption is a rather high-risk strategy encouraging blowback, costs, disdain, and disabled critical systems. The new strategy requires the nation's institutions to deliberately recognize the new dimension of "virtuality" (a combination of virtual worlds created by computer systems and reality) as an operational tool for knowing enough to disrupt threats as they emerge and to be resilient to attacks as they happen. The learning curve is steep, and all of us, the responders and the attackers, are at the lower rungs. Each is making missteps and recalculating for the next round. Without a guiding strategy that includes the motivations of the at-tackers and deliberate surprise accommodation, merely battening down the hatches or battering attackers in one area only leaves many other vulnerabili-ties unaddressed. The challenges and constraints underscore how deeply tied are disruption as a strategy and resilience. They also underscore how both are intimately knowledge dependent. The next chapter discusses in greater detail the institutional adaptations necessary to provide the right knowledge at the right time for the modern digitized democratic city-state open in cyberspace to the wider uncivil turbulent and also digitizing world.

CHAPTER FOUR

Institutional Design for Cybered Power and National Security

Any book on international security in a time of cybered conflict needs to deal directly with the asymmetric knowledge challenges that enable offense advantages — scale, proximity, and precision. Cybered conflict requires a uniquely modern, highly informed, rapid way of fighting that accommodates the topology for the international system. Success in the face of surprise in large, dispersed, complex systems is crucially based on knowledge at the right moment, in the right form, and used in the most accurate and timely way. In particular, international security is no longer purely external, and any successful strategy must necessarily explain its prerequisites in domestic knowledge development as well as its external implications. It is not sufficient to simply have a strategy of disruption. Without resilience, the surprises of the cybered world will achieve what the attackers seek at some point simply due to the complexity of the environment. Therefore the strategy requires three particularly knowledge-enhancing institutional adaptations beyond just incorporating the theory of action and of surprise accommodation as a framework in national thinking.

The knowledge development process begins with identifying what must be known and then collectively sharing those insights for implementation with three major elements: nurtured interstate and interagency institutionalization of collaboration, masked but searchable broad collection of international and domestic behavior data, and the innovative, even virtual refinement of patterns into collectively wise strategic foreign policy and domestic security options. First, the theory of action is detailed more closely as a way to organize and identify what must be known to implement a successful strategy. This theory builds directly on the main ground truths about human motivation to commit violence embedded respectively in the three major schools of international relations.

Second, easy and useful knowledge sharing is essential to distill collective perspectives on weighting the drivers of an emerging threat, but nothing happens without a process, place, and incentives. This need to collectively consult routinely is already recognized in most westernized nations, although its implementation varies widely in its formality, breadth of purview, and apparent effectiveness. The failures of the U.S. Department of Homeland Security in providing effective joint consultation across security agencies are widely recognized. This section presents the concept of a *knowledge nexus* intended to support the collective social and technical consultations needs of all national-level security communities playing a role in devising and implementing any wars-of-disruption strategy. These include the normally insular domains of intelligence, police, and military agencies.

Effective strategies require more, however, than a mere well-intentioned effort to share. Without sufficiently broad inputs of usable information on potentially violent threats and also the ability to creatively refine the data into guidance, the intention will fail to produce effective strategies. But both are hard to do. Democracies are especially difficult places to collect mass amounts of data if the citizens feel the collection itself is threatening for either abuse or disabling error. The concept of "behavior-based privacy" addresses the paradox of needing data on the behavior of all citizens in order to filter for emerging bad actor violence and yet being unable today to protect those individuals from abuse or seemingly irremediable error. Both national and domestic security agencies struggle with the structural openness of Western nations to bad actors in gray activities. Their ability to blend in means that *all* residents need to be surveilled for suspicious action patterns while bother and damage to truly innocent civilians must be minimized.

Furthermore, data needs to be traceable but controllable in an optimum use of scarce security resources. Built into the behavior-based privacy framework (Behavior-Identity-Knowledge, or BIK model) are institutionalized and enforced validation and appeal (V&A) processes for citizens and noncitizens. There is no reason for local city parking and traffic agencies to be able to access international travel, complete credit, and health histories of any citizen. Yet patterns of behavior odd for a nearly indigent small family firm selling imported ethnic goods — sudden long trips to Pakistan and Sudan — and noted only when cars are towed may need to be shared in an identity-protecting fashion with both domestic and national, even international, security centers. This privacy-protective sharing of behavior data needs to be relatively seamless with existing forms of international and domestic exchange, fortunately enabled easily by the mass digital smart card pathways handily built and maintained by international credit card consortia.

Even with this data, however, successful diminution of a security threat depends on the full picture being wisely interpreted. If one has broad streams of behavior data to interpret and integrate into actionable strategic elements, the final essential element is the collaborative social structure itself. For this need, the Atrium model of an organization capable of social and virtual integration of tacit knowledge with operations is discussed in the next section. It has the good fortune of being adaptable to both scale and the number of organizations involved. The Atrium is needed to massage the mass of data that needs to be interchanged throughout the various systems and agencies responsible for security. This socio-technical structure builds on existing institutional forms but specifically incorporates social and digital capabilities matching those enabling the surprising rise of violent threats threatening to cascade inside traditional borders from external and internal bad actors. It is, in short, designed for meeting surprising chronic threats and is an essential component underlying the effective development of a national-level wars-of-disruption overarching strategy. Furthermore, the Atrium can be constructed within an organization or between them in the associated knowledge nexus.

Taken together these elements sustain strategy by providing the raw materials for successful long-term and routine iterative disruption of complex chronic violent and gray threats. The nation's implementation of a security resilience strategy needs a deliberate institutionalization of processes of cross-actor consensus, comprehensive systemic information sources, and continuous knowledge development. Put in other words, national security needs to be better at using cybered means to outwit the surprisers. That goal requires better ways of conducting nurtured interstate and interagency institutionalization of cooperation; of routinely acquiring a masked but searchable broad collection of international and domestic behavior data; and unflagging support for the innovative, even virtual collaborative refinement of patterns into collectively wise strategic foreign policy and domestic security options. Failure to disrupt over the long or short term or to adequately accommodate nasty surprises can, naturally, come from the many unpredictable convergences of dynamic, complex, social systems, the infamous "sheer damn bad luck," or, on a lesser scale, the friction of operating in complex turbulent environments. Not doing one's homework, however, virtually assures the responding actor a tougher time in figuring out the threat's violence equation and then preparing a response.

What organizations know about their enemies determines the emphases placed in their national strategic choices. In cybered conflict, as in war, each side is trying to reduce its own internal uncertainty, while imposing as much uncertainty as possible on the other via surprise. First, organizations try to expand in the direction of their greatest contingency in order to control it (Thompson 1967). To protect themselves, military organizations traditionally try to gather as much knowledge as they can in advance or acquire such forces and weapons that nearly all surprises thrown at them are unlikely to succeed. The ancient phalanx, with its close step and overlapping overhead shields, is a method of restricting the possible outcomes in battle. While moving forward, the uniform strict phalanx rules made the unit nearly impossible to break unless the shields could be made to drop by the sheer weight of the opposing phalanx or its long spears leveled straight in through the shield barriers. Thus the phalanx was a way to control the possibility of soldiers dropping their shields and running.

The second organizational constant is that organizations will constantly try to weaken or work around their constraints after having moved against the contingencies (Thompson 1967). A well-trained enemy phalanx becomes a constraint for the opposition, one best weakened by besieging the camp, surprising through trickery or betrayal in the night, or attacking on the march. Knowing that, capable Roman officers in particular always had a wide array of scouts and spies moving ahead of and parallel to the main columns of forces (Russell 1999).

What the organization knows from study or experience normally drives how it prepares for surprise. Each organization has an underlying guiding theory — an internalized image and the "deep institutions" guiding the members' presumptions — about what is important to know to protect one's institution (G. Morgan 2006; Fountain 2001). If that understanding is too narrow, limited, or biased, then bad outcomes that could have been known in advance can nonetheless travel along the otherwise ignored information channels to become catastrophic surprises (Steinbruner 2002). For example, if one thinks that only the deliberate use of long-range weapons, nuclear arsenals, or deployed mechanized armies can hurt the nation in important ways, then one does not collect information on or prepare strategies for dealing with accidents, biological threats, massive currency fraud, or even hostile social movements with air travel access into the nation (Sagan 2004).

A security resilience strategy rests on institutionalized and long-term comprehensive and consistent knowledge development. The need to collectively consult routinely is already recognized in most westernized nations, although its implementation varies widely in its formality, breadth of purview, and apparent effectiveness. Required is some institutionalized form of a *knowledge nexus* to support the collective social and technical consultation requirements of all national-level security communities playing a role in devising and implementing any national-level strategy. In the modern state, the key communities across the levels of society include the normally insular domains of intelligence, police, and military agencies. To date, a number of nations are nominally encouraging such interagency consultations, but the results so far have had limited successes, especially in incorporating all three domains of police, military, and intelligence (Demchak and Werner 2007a).

Effective security resilience strategy requires more, however, than a mere well-intentioned effort to share. Without sufficiently broad inputs of usable information on potentially violent threats and also the ability to creatively refine the data into guidance, the intention will fail to produce effective strategies. But both are hard to do. Democracies are especially difficult places to collect mass amounts of data if the citizens feel the collection itself is threatening. The next section on *behavior-based privacy* discusses the conflict for complex connected democratic societies of requiring comprehensive timely data on all possible activities for security agencies to detect and disrupt the bad actors' harmful efforts while also needing to preserve the privacy of their citizens. The institutional adaptations offered in this section are intended to provide a middle ground by which the security services can legally sort through comprehensive but anonymous behavior data in order to see emergent threats without having all the personally identifiable data of all citizens. This proposed institutional adaptation is only possible in a highly digitized society where key elements of personal data can be filtered out behind anonymizing techniques, and behavior patterns can be assessed digitally and rapidly before any disruptive actions are requested and legal warrants issued. Finally, the proposal emphasizes the validation and appeal (V&A) processes that must accompany the processes of citizen traceable anonymity for privacy and behavior transparency for security.

Save for the need to ensure special judicial reviews for the V&A processes, the institutional changes suggested build largely on what exists today. Adopting a behavior-based privacy system could be institutionally seamless using digital anonymizing smart cards and a trusted third party (TTP) system that could be built on the existing credit card bureau institutions or their nonprofit equivalent. The applicable technologies are being built for related purposes already; as this work notes, the institutions are needed to adapt and adopt these mechanisms and solve the privacy-security conundrum of an advanced, digitally tightly connected society.

Finally, a third institutional adaptation is ensuring a full picture wisely interpreted and continuously updated and tested. Even with this data, however, successful diminution of a security threat depends on knowledge development processes structured into and across security institutions. If one has broad streams of behavior data to interpret and integrate into actionable strategic elements, the final essential element is the collaborative social structure itself. For this need, the Atrium model of social and virtual integrated tacit knowledge development is discussed. It has the good fortune of being adaptable to both the scale and the number of organizations involved. The Atrium is needed to massage the mass of data that needs to be interchanged throughout the various systems and agencies responsible for security. This socio-technical structure builds on existing institutional forms but specifically incorporates social and digital capabilities matching those enabling the surprising rise of violent threats threatening to cascade inside traditional borders from external and internal bad actors. It is, in short, designed for meeting surprising chronic threats and is an essential component underlying the effective development of an overarching national-level disruption strategy. Furthermore, the Atrium can be constructed either within an organization or between them in the associated knowledge nexus.

For today, the critical societal systems of westernized states are at exceptional risk without agreement, data, and corrected interpretations in national security strategies, decision making, and action organizations. Cybered surprises are simply more likely to be successful and brutally disabling with the further intensity of globalization. The theory of action has already been presented. This chapter provides details on the three institutional adaptations that provide the knowledge needed for the surprises of a cybered world, and it is not an unreasonable list of requirements.

HONEST JOINT CONSULTATION—KNOWLEDGE NEXUS

Strategy is more than recognition of likely axioms and the tools to be employed somehow. Daily practices determine much of what truly constitutes a strategy.[1] Success in a national war of disruption is built on mutual recognition of value among actors involved in the response strategy. The larger the nation's administrative structure, the more likely the players, in Weberian fashion, operate relatively independently and are acculturated to sovereignty in their processes. Historically many of these communities simply did not need each other, except occasionally. As a result, even when the need to operate jointly emerges, it is slow to be recognized inside these usually large organizations. Furthermore, since these organizations are competitors for national resources, there is little incentive for an agency to recognize or desire help, guidance, or interference from other agencies that may be peers or merely functional supports. The oft-seen bureaucratic response to a threat is for one or more agencies to declare themselves the logically best organization to be empowered with mission and resources to take care of the problem. For example, the 1990s NATO role in the Bosnia conflict was initially a U.S. Air Force–led response in large part because of the persuasiveness of that service in claiming sole ability to solve the violent threat (Byman and Waxman 2000).

In their search for certainty and survival, organizations conduct wars and end up building the infrastructure to create societies (Finer 1999). Militaries historically create organizations to control their soldiers as the chief weapon of the force. At the same time, armies often build roads, dig wells and establish oases or resupply towns, and then leave structures behind to be reoccupied again if needed. These expensive efforts come solely out of a desire to control the uncertainties of collective behavior while employing its advantages. The more advanced militaries historically demonstrated considerable skill in developing processes to control highly uncertain behaviors of soldiers, ani-

1. The literature defining and studying strategy is enormous. However, strategy is often understood as merely the statement of intent—or lack thereof—rather than a process beginning with the statement or presumptions and then the actions that follow. "Strategy as practice" is one way in which this combinatorial reality is portrayed (Jarzabkowski 2004). There are, however, a multitude of other formulations of the same idea stretching as far back as Sun Tzu's Art of War to the oft-quoted and misquoted Clausewitz (Heuser 2002) to examinations of more modern strategists (such as Paret, Craig, and Gilbert 1986) to the more practical works (such as Benjamin and Simon 2006).

mals, terrain, and other leaders. The Roman Army, for example, would take weeks to prepare to deploy, on foot, to the distant borders of the empire. In the preparations, units would construct and demolish an entire fortification up to three times a day for week. The goal was to have a secure campsite every night despite being on the move (Goldsworthy 1998). It would take over a thousand years for warring nations of Europe to replicate the kind of intense drill and professionalism developed by the Roman Army in its determination never to be surprised.

The more that newly organized social groups develop unique identities and interests in collective survival, the more they tend to reach out for knowledge in order to control internal and external uncertainties. Membership lists, for example, are used to control the uncertainty of who may and may not be called upon to perform some task. The more successful they are in hoarding their information and influence, the more organizations are able to insulate themselves from outside intervention by building strongly held domain and resource boundaries (Weber 1991). They add internal capabilities to meet contingencies of importance, in the process expanding in the direction of emerging threats (Thompson 1967). As a result, the larger the state's recognized political problems, the larger its agencies become over time, and the more rigidly defended is the societal topology of turf and entitlements (Allison 1999).

For example, an unclassified RAND study of the U.S. top-level leaders and their plan for the Iraq War II was kept from public release by the U.S. Army in 2007. The report concluded that many of the postwar failures were due to the lack of honest collaboration across agencies. In the structure of the U.S. decision making under the secretive second Bush presidency, Bush, Deputy Chief of Staff Karl Rove, and Vice President Dick Cheney made no efforts to mediate among key competing agencies (Gordon 2008). With no institutionalized way of honest collaboration across domains or even a way to develop that discourse among players, knowledge development critical for whatever success path was possible simply did not happen across agency barriers for the war or the putative global war on terror (Croft 2006).

A knowledge nexus exists where these organizational walls are breached in order for the institutions to share conversations and needs in ways seen to be of mutual benefit. The definition of knowledge here is broad; it encompasses anything that reduces the unknowns associated with a contingency and helps the recipient counter an uncertainty. Knowledge can be found in a spare part, a supplemental external training course, access to new databases, or seconded experts (Demchak 1991). Unless organizations perceive a need to seek knowledge by developing external knowledge delivery ties, the nexus remains essentially unclaimed domain space among otherwise allocated social responsibilities. No meetings are held or cross-institutional-boundaries overtures are made unless both sides agree to a need, and that need usually must be exceptionally powerful. In principle, a nexus should only begin to take shape when an identifiable largescale problem emerges and is widely recognized to have knowledge demands beyond the internal capabilities of any one institution.[2] To meet their individual obligations, then, each institution will have to recognize the need to reach beyond its own strongly maintained boundaries and link with the other organizations in some process of knowledge exchange. Figure 7 models this process of institutional development.

Knowledge, Power, and Ownership

The classic massive divide in national security for modern democratic states is that existing between military services and police services, followed closely by the strong classification and ego walls between intelligence services and everybody else (Zegart 1999). The result normally is a massive empty virtual and cognitive space between agencies. Unless a war or catastrophe calls for different actions, the nexus space between otherwise insular communities like police, intelligence, and the military forces is generally crossed only by heavily filtered internet data streams, occasional conferences and task force meetings, and enforced joint reports, if any. It is, however, surrounded by much handwringing over intelligence failures and misinterpretations and a wide

---

2. Information technologies by their very name imply the use of information, writ large, in structured ways. However, thinking about these systems more organically by incorporating them as human appendages is difficult for many to envision. That is necessary to fully appreciate the role they play in determining the new security threats and tools of the digitized globe. For example, internet pirates and the threat they pose are well known. One early attempt to create an international legal consensus to control internet hackers was to try to relate them to cross-border pirates. The argument was that whereas pirates took goods, hackers used credulousness in the tools of social engineering and then society's instruments of credibility to provide goods. That argument has not succeeded, and the international effort has had slow success at best because not all nations see any threat to themselves (Goth 2007). That leaders do not understand the new technologies greatly reduces the urgency to discuss it or come to some common consensus.

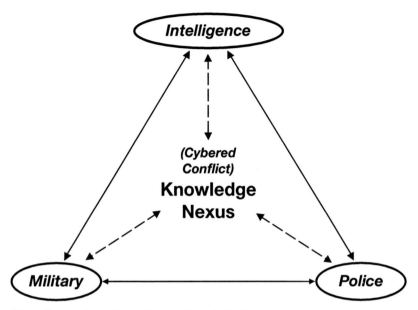

Figure 7. Inter-Institutional Domain Knowledge Nexus

literature of dispassionate and self-interested observers seeking to improve the situation.

City-states interpenetrated by cybered bad actors need the knowledge that all three distinct domains — intelligence, military, and police — can jointly bring to bear on emerging complex surprises. In Madrid after the train yard bombings of 2004, unclassified after-action analyses suggested that the bombers had not only been known but were being loosely observed by police authorities worried more about drugs than religious terrorism. Data about the bombers' activities was thus not shared with intelligence units looking for terrorists (Benjamin and Simon 2006).

Tracking a sense of urgency that motivates an unusual reaching across borders is challenging. In general, such powerful but inchoate motivators are not quantifiable. A good example is the prestige-related desire to be seen as part of a professional referent group. After 9/11 in the United States, counterterrorism served as a motivator for cross-agency cooperation even where it was not much experienced. For example, since 2001 and aided by events of 2004 and 2005, there was plenty of international discourse — some quite emotional — about the imminent threat of foreign-based terrorism. The discourse alone had extraordinary framing effects across agencies and later national borders to include Sweden, which had no experience in external terrorism (Croft 2006). The year 2001 is really only a watershed for the United States, and yet the American framing of the "global war on terrorism" has seemingly imprinted security discourses far beyond the experience of many nations. This process of emulation of other professional developments ("mimetic isomorphism") is historically not common in most public service domains, especially across national borders, because most public agencies do not look at their colleagues in other nations or even other provinces and states for guidance on how to structure or operate themselves (DiMaggio and Powell 1983).

Such copying, however, is more common in militaries, which often seek to mirror each other in hopes of averting surprise technological or operational advantages (McNeill 1982). To the extent that the perception of life-threatening possibilities from cybered attacks is accepted in nonmilitary organizations, institutionalization across organizational borders is more likely. The knowledge nexus, as it emerges, becomes in effect an indirect test of the motivating power of the risk to move actors beyond their normal comfort zones (Castells 1998).

Institutional Change Requires Great and Enduring National Threats

For any nation to implement a disruption strategy involving cybered conflict, the problem must be presented, or "framed," in a way that encourages members to view honest joint consultation positively. The long-term effect of such activities in a normally empty policy space depends on how formal the interactions become — that is, in Selznick's terms, how "institutionalized" is the process. In the digitizing world, this formalization can proceed along technical or social paths initially. Eventually, however, the consensus will have to involve advances in both technical and social means to meet the short time horizons of cybered attacks on major interlinked systems. Moving along the social axis — say, having monthly meetings — does not require or force any exchanges of data along the technical axis. That is, one may show a paper copy of information to colleagues without giving them a way to further exploit that data in their own analytical systems. Conversely, sharing massive databases does not mean there will be any social response for consultation. The database may or may not be accessed by the individuals across organizational boundaries, even if given permission. Outside of one's own organization, the usefulness of one's data may not be perceived, or the learning curve to figure out how to use it may be considered too high. For full and enduring institutionalization of a cybered conflict-ready knowledge nexus, movement far along both social and technical axes is required.

A comparison of relative institutionalizations of a counterterrorism knowledge nexus in natural experiments across the United States, UK, India, and Sweden shows that such consultative deliberation needs a strong overarching purpose to keep the processes alive (Burch 2007). Normally absent in modern stovepiped and smaller-scale bureaucratic organizations are the processes to stimulate and nurture cooperative behavior and its extension in both social and technical terms beyond daily task requirements. A spontaneously institutionalizing knowledge nexus indicates organizations reaching out proactively beyond their borders to perhaps unwittingly create the conditions favoring successful disruption as well as resilience strategies. Cybered conflict, especially the violent possibilities of inadequate knowledge, need to be taken as serious enough threats to spark useful institutionalization. The threat needs to be both surprising and personal, and the responses not hastily organized as the United States did with the U.S. Department of Homeland Security (DHS) after 9/11. The lengthy but steady European tendency toward institutional development could in the end produce a more enduring and welcome knowledge structure than, in particular, the American solution.

Counterterrorism over time sparked the perception of a great and enduring national threat, prompting efforts, however effective, in creating a knowledge nexus. Distinctly different levels and formation paths of institutionalization occurred across nations concerned with being surprised by terrorists. Figure 8 shows the relative position of the United States and India with regard to their relative social and technological institutionalization of a knowledge nexus for counterterrorism. As shown in this figure, the more technologically advanced state, the United States in its Department of Homeland Security (DHS), and the developing state, India in its twenty-eight-state government Anti-Terrorism Squads (ATS), both first moved further along (if at all) the social axis of institutional development. In many respects, this is not surprising because databases in a computer network even in the more technically advanced nations are not able to mobilize human interest in understanding their potential as another human could in a social network. Even in the most technical example, the DHS, the use of technical means to advance the knowledge nexus has not produced widespread understanding or demonstrably effective use. The lag in technological institutionalization is due, in part, to the greater knowledge required to correct an early design flaw in a massive database than in persuading

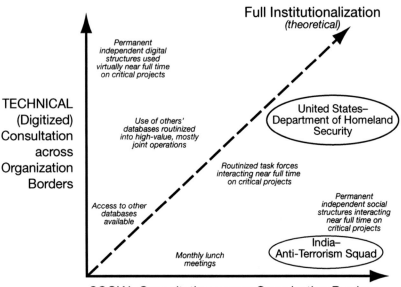

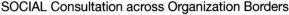

Figure 8. Relative Institutionalization

another person to change his or her presumptions for a strategy or operation. A lack of clearly institutionalizing use also occurs if the data is insufficient to be usefully shared across actors or if the access experiences do not develop the knowledge in the varying formats needed by the different actors and agencies in a nexus.

While it is possible to be slow to institutionalize technologically in counter-terrorism efforts, in a cybered world the nexus cannot effectively stay primarily social. A cybersecurity institutionalization of a knowledge nexus will inevitably begin more heavily technical and social due to the medium. However, humans in organizations will have to decide to willingly share their experiences with attacks, effective resistance or resilience measures, and hypotheses about future mitigation or innovation needs. Beyond the willingness of partners in a knowledge nexus to collaborate with whatever data, expertise, and experiences each agency has, the security resilience strategy will also need to provide them with comprehensive streams of digital evidence and a workable design of organizational mechanisms to effectively develop that massed data into usable knowledge (Demchak and Werner 2007a). The next section on behavior-based privacy addresses acquiring enough data in a privacy constrained democracy;

the subsequent section on the Atrium organizational model addresses tacit knowledge development across security services in a surprise-ridden cybered world.[3]

COMPREHENSIVE DATA—PRIVACY IN BEHAVIOR-BASED ADAPTATIONS

Today, successfully defending a society requires an extraordinary amount of knowledge (before, during, and after the attack attempt) about the defending side and the vulnerabilities presented by its citizens, their actions, and their systems. However this massive amount of information is gathered, the process and institutions need to systemically take care to sustain the privacy expected by individuals and the confidentiality required by businesses across western-ized democratic states.

The key to disruption and resilience is the acquisition of data on a scale commensurate with the exponential rise in global population, complex inter-dependence, and the surprises that could follow. What the responding nation knows, and continuously refreshes and refines, determines in large measure how effectively tailored the disruption and resilience strategy can be. The emphasis in an effectively tailored disruption strategy for each set of linked attackers and on the coordination of societal resilience will differ according to what information is sought, refined, and then taken into account by national security institutions as the strategy is implemented.[4] Knowledge is needed not

3. The discussion of the knowledge nexus draws from Demchak and Werner (2007a, 2007b). The subsequent discussion of behavior-based privacy draws from Fenstermacher and Demchak (2004) and Demchak and Fenstermacher (2009); discussion of the Atrium model relies on several explorations of the model, most recently in Demchak (2010).

4. One computer forensics expert aiming at this kind of intensely analytical detection of a cyberspace attacker suggests beginning with what the attack suggests are the goods sought by the terrorists, especially how they instrumentally view the tools of cyberspace. "[Experts need to know] how the terrorist group either uses or anticipates the use of information systems. . . . [Do they] use information systems to recruit . . . to seek greater legitimacy within their society . . . [to enhance] their opportunity to recruit more participants and members to their cause . . . to more efficiently market their message . . . [to] confuse many people who otherwise would remain in more established opposition to the terrorist group . . . to more surgically disrupt their targets through the use of information technologies . . . [or to] repeat attacks, which will have the cumulative effect of not only causing greater disruption and loss but also will induce greater psychological distress to those members of the society

only to find embedded or remote cybered bad actors but also to persuade existing agencies and even private owners of infrastructure to jointly and honestly
consult on a national security resilience strategy.

An extensive knowledge base enables the responding institutions to accept
new alternatives in their responses. National security is dominated by agencies
where coercion is the historically more automatic answer in part because it
is easier to consider and implement institutionally.[5] Even the language often
used in the U.S. defense community for operations involving the web suggests a largely physical and coercive character to actions. One intends to "take
down" websites or servers even if the goal is to merely get the host computer
server to close the public access to a web page. To choose other than a coercive emphasis requires particularly well-developed knowledge to convince
the responding state actors to operate disruptively without trying to use their
best-known tools.

The challenge is large. While the violent attacks of web-using threat actors
can be exceptionally dangerous, they and their motivations are difficult to
fully profile. Their identities are multiply masked (the computer term of art
is *spoofed*) as they inch their way past security walls into the westernized democracy's digital society. They can sit physically far away and operate unseen,
yet virtually they are very close to critical nodes. Often they do not personally
implement the violence. What their life's educational, social, religious, and
personal cognitive circumstances are can only be inferred by their patterns and
signatures in implementing attacks, not usually in any other directly linked

---

attacked[?] The more traditional terrorist attack modality, which results in bodily injury or
death, results in society focusing great consensus against the attacking terrorist organization.
On the other hand, the terrorist group that utilizes a more economically disruptive attack
focused more on the critical infrastructure of a society may not encounter such total societal
rejection. This permits a greater opportunity to mold public opinion toward their objectives. If combined with appealing arguments designed to market and sell their belief system,
such a terrorist group might require a totally different response on the part of authorities"
(T. A. Johnson 2005, 223).

5. Coercion can easily be encouraged in a population prone to be impatient or have
a short range view of the future, such as that of the United States. There is "an under-
appreciated and unstudied relationship between societal space-time orientations and those
adopted by military leaders and strategists, a relationship that sometimes biases both military
decision-makers and civilian leaders toward temporal chauvinism and offensive military
postures" (Cunningham and Tomes 2004, 123).

physical evidence.[6] Attacks using cyberspace for physical harm combine the technology, institutions, and culture issues in an exceptionally complex violence profile that needs to be fleshed out and refreshed carefully.

Furthermore, the information needs to be comprehensive because cyberspace has distinctive conflict-widening aspects due to global access. It is easy for more players than merely the attacking person or group and the responding nation to become involved. If the attackers are using a social movement as part of their legitimizing internal narrative, other adherents to the movement may pile on in an ongoing operation or simple attempt to replicate it, perhaps even badly. Because it is so easy for anyone to get on the internet and roam around, there is a tit-for-tat dynamic that changes the landscape relatively often. It can spiral out of all proportion to the original dispute. The process of refining information into disruption operations needs to be particularly sensitive to the fact that both attackers and responders can make things worse for themselves by accident if they are ignorant of critical data buried in the complexity of a globalizing system.

It may seem odd to scholars, practitioners, and students reading about international security to find a section on privacy of information in a democracy, but today national security rests on knowing enough even in a privacy-sensitive society. Not solving this conundrum of knowing enough about embedded bad actors or their actions via cyberspace while knowing only just enough about citizens means the security forces will forever be one step behind those who can hide among the citizens. This unprecedented information collection challenge, for the sake of national security, cannot be ignored, nor can it be satisfied safely with the systems of data collection, refinement, and application that are in place or emerging today. Ironically, much of this data is already being collected by nongovernmental organizations, but the difficulty is that it

6. The police community infers the profile of criminals by looking comparatively at the *modus operandi* (M.O.), which is quite similar to the computer industry's term for an attack's *manifestation* (Kemmerer and Vigna 2002). Especially in the electronic field, the equivalent phrase is *patterns and signatures*, to mean the distinctive and hence trackable ways an unknown actor does something. For example, radio operators were trained over and over not to develop particular ways of communicating (signatures) or consistent times of communication (patterns) in order to avoid being trackable by those spying on the communications. It is exactly these patterns and signatures in both open-air communications and logistical preparations for operations that revealed U.S. military plans to the observing Vietcong during the Vietnam War (J. W. Gibson 1988).

is not coalesced into the kinds of analytical deliberations needed for an effective, tailored, disruption strategy. If westernized democracies are to stay open and tolerant in the coming massively digitizing and globalizing years even though globally connected to turbulent dysfunctional regions, *behavior-based privacy* is one compromise that could help fill the widening knowledge gap. Its implementation in some form is one of the institutional adaptations required for a fully effective disruption strategy. Knowing enough about bad actors but not too much about citizens is what institutionalizing behavior-based privacy permits.

Impediments to Knowing Enough

Modern democracies trying to proactively find and disrupt such embedded bad actors as well as design resilience in their offense advantages inevitably must struggle with the privacy rights of their own citizens.[7] Citizens have often taken individual freedom to include some measures of personal obscurity from the authorities, which then extends to visitors among them. Often this assumption is borne of a bad experience, as the political and institutional difficulties with transnational jihadist terrorism have shown since 2001. In France, for example, one of the difficulties in determining the size of the immigrant or native-born Muslim population is the restriction against recording a religion of a citizen on public records, including the public census. This law arose from the horror of the Holocaust, to avoid the use of religion against a group, but it now hampers collecting the data for a good understanding of violent co-religious networks, the hallmark of terrorists in the West since 2001 (Mathieson 2007). Thus, figures for the ethnic group are always estimates based on names. French security services develop internal workarounds, but these are often ad hoc codes to note those religious connections without formally having collected that information widely or, importantly, very systematically.

So strong are the privacy traditions that it often takes a direct experience to force onto the public stage the usually bitter debate about how security agencies can obtain data on embedded threats. For example, the deliberate open tolerance of British society was adamantly supported by the British public even

---

7. For a much more detailed discussion of privacy rights see Demchak and Fenstermacher 2009.

after the events of 2001 in the United States. The public could not believe that certain ethnic communities were increasingly likely to harbor violent terrorists interested in mass casualty attacks. For reasons of crime rather than terrorism in an increasingly multiethnic London, closed-circuit street surveillance cameras (CCTV) began to pop up around main pedestrian arteries. They engendered some debate, but no great resolve for or against them. After the attacks on British soil in 2005, however, British public preference for civil liberties and privacy over security dramatically switched to support for relatively more intrusive data collection and even holding suspects without charge (C. Walker 2006).

Still, there are limits to the tolerance of a democratic Western public for public security agencies to have unfettered access to their data. When the public agencies seem to demand complete data on citizens without warning or reason, the debate grows bitter. Even worse is the situation when acquiring complete access is made much easier, as it is now in the increasingly digital world. Able to digitally fit on only two CDs, tax records for 40 percent of UK citizens went missing while being sent via unsecured carrier between national-level offices in November 2007. Everything needed for identity theft, not to mention blackmail, phishing, and other ways in which individuals are vulnerable when their personal data is given to strangers, was on those two CDs (British Broadcasting Corporation 2007a). Collection and mass processing of millions of citizens' personal information is now exponentially simpler for good or bad purposes. Ease of ordering goods online grows along with ease of stealing the same credit card numbers and the owner's identity to use for criminal gain. Still, identity theft does not occur uniformly, and often the widespread effects are obscured as the commercial firms respond by simply insuring themselves and reimbursing the victim for the cash stolen (although not for the time or hassle involved in straightening out the mess). Often the public does not see the steady loss of control over personal data as clearly threatening until a government entity formally declares a desire for the data. Then fears of abuse, revelations about tax evasion, and just a general sense of unease of having unseen eyes prying into one's closest environs push a vocal portion of the population to actively oppose public agency collections.

The response to the disastrously marketed Total Information Awareness (TIA) program proposed in the United States is a good example. In this political fiasco for the proponents, otherwise well-intentioned security forces decided to openly use all the available corporate stocks of personal information collected in a myriad of ways and compiled by middleman services for sale. The goal was to sift through this data on citizens and noncitizens alike for indications of terrorist activity, to link and validate suspects or activities with data from intelligence and police sources in order to find the bad guys. To the security forces in the throes of finding a good path to security after 9/11, this program seemed not only innocent enough but also completely appropriate given the technology and the masses of data already floating about unbeknownst to the wider public (Poindexter, Popp, and Sharkey 2003).

Announced with the usual defense industry hyperbole, the well-intentioned desire to know enough to catch hidden evil was overwhelmed by the mass negative response. Unaware of how much they individually give away and how much is floating in the commercial marketplace for sale, the American public was shocked that the government would casually expect to collect so much information so comprehensively on them. Activist and influence leaders in particular, mindful of the probability of false positives and simpler but devastating abuse, fought back publicly and loudly to keep personally identifiable information (PII) from the hands of authorities (Safire 2002). The TIA promoters in the defense community were astounded at the response and retreated ungracefully. The chief champion resigned (R. D. Hanson 2006). The goal of comprehensively pulling together all the piles of personal data receded dramatically as an explicit unified program. Meanwhile, all over the nation and the government, digital databases went on growing in regulated and unregulated ways (Madsen 2004).[8]

For a world of cybered conflict, the lack of a compromise in digitized vulnerable democracies on the legal and privacy-ensured collection of all the necessary security relevant data is particularly dangerous. Digitization is massively more ubiquitous, and the threat from chronic violent threats has no definable end in sight. The trust and openness of such societies are used by the violent,

---

8. Perez described the ease of obtaining personal information: In 2005, sales employees at Choicepoint, a customer data broker, were socially engineered into selling 145,000 customer records to attackers "posing as businesses seeking information on potential employees and customers. They paid fees of $100 to $200, and provided fake documentation, gaining access to a trove of personal data including addresses, phone numbers, and social security numbers" (Perez 2005).

the criminal, and the insurgent against the rest of the community. Finding the threats, then, involves collecting and inspecting data on innocent citizens in amounts, types, and frequency not traditionally considered necessary.

Today strangers stream into Western nations by the millions on airplanes, boats, and trains, as well as virtually on the internet, phone, radio, and mail. National borders are hard to filter for bad intentions.[9] Once the bad actors have slipped inside borders, it is difficult, if not inaccurate and just plain slow, to attempt to do *intelligence-led policing* (ILP), without using the mass data-processing abilities of modern technology (John and Maguire 2007).[10] In 2007, a report circulated that over four thousand fighters trained in Afghanistan terrorist camps had managed to infiltrate into Britain's large immigrant communities (Leapman 2007). Regardless of whether most of those returnees plan ill for the larger British society, having some way to discern the indications before the few succeed in another attack requires data across a wide swath of people in whom there is no security interest. The situation is increasingly the same across all westernized nations, leaving privacy advocates and security promoters at loggerheads, as well as damaging the governments' abilities to know enough for an effective disruption strategy.

Needed is a way to institutionally design a middle path that also fits relatively seamlessly into the modern patterns of data exchange. Behavior-based privacy offers this compromise by breaking privacy into two data streams, one stream that provides the information needed for security and the other stream that provides the obscurity needed for privacy. Information about any individual is divided into both behavior data devoid of personal identity, and more static personal identity data masked from behavioral connections. This channeling of mass amounts of data offers the security forces all the behavior data they want, but it is associated only with masked identities. Citizens allow their public actions to be more visible but closely hold information about their immutable basic identity, including biometrics. The identity information is not

9. Considerable efforts are made to try to detect bad actors engaged in deception in order to enter the United States. See the deception detection work of Judee Burgoon and Jay Nunamaker (2004).

10. The process of *intelligence-led policing* applies the technologies and techniques of national security intelligence to information management and processing in policing (Sheptycki and Innes 2004).

revealed save by regulated legal procedures and protected by required rapid validation and appeals processes.[11]

A strategy for disruption but also for resilience needs behavior data to discern the emerging evidence of a bad actor's plans and the normal activities of innocent citizens. Not until that pattern is observed and analyzed do the responders need more static and private information such as a name and home address. When determining whether individuals are potential bad actors, it is more relevant to know what they are doing (dynamic information) than who they are (static information). Behavior data is dynamic and personal — identity is static. In intercepting developing patterns of violent actors, behavior information is intrinsically more useful for rapidly responding to threats. Names in a globalizing, turbulent society, on the other hand, reveal too little for security, and too much for privacy in a digitized world.

Even in ancient Greece among the squabbling city-states, what the person did was considered more revealing than who they claimed to be. Greek generals in interrogating and evaluating sources for reports of the enemy wanted to know what the enemy was doing, not who was doing it — unless some singular person had some particular importance. Eyewitnesses were preferred and often kept in bonds until their reporting of the behavior of the enemies could be verified by at least two other sources (a process today called *triangulation*). In considering the information, the generals would ask others about the character, access, and motives of the source. The first two are clearly behavior data and the last is an interpretation of preferences usually drawn from the circumstances of life as well as demonstrated behavior (Russell 1999).

Even then a name was useful to suggest city origin and class, but only if the name was real and the story behind the name also real. The old military spy dictum still applies that spies need to defend both their status and current action if they are caught. To be believable, the spy claiming to be a pharmacist needs to prove that professional status and also explain why a pharmacist is in a frogman suit on a beach at three a.m. This behavior-identity divide is, as Gill (2006) argues, common to the definitions of surveillance offered by Christo-

---

11. The model was developed by a team of researchers at the University of Arizona, in both social science and computer science, to create a model of behavior-based privacy called the Behavior-Identity-Knowledge (BIK) framework and then validate it in a proof-of-concept virtual experiment completed initially in late 2007 (Demchak et al. 2007; Demchak and Fenstermacher 2004).

pher Dandeker, Anthony Giddens, and Michel Foucault. Each separates the collection of static data from the observation of behavior in discussions of governmental surveillance. The behavior-based privacy framework here takes the next step and separates the two digitally (Gill 2006).

The goal of the behavior-based policy solution is to be able to use behavior — something one publicly shares generally and increasingly without compunction — without needing identity to hone in on bad patterns of action that suggest "gray" threats. If one can reasonably pursue this approach in a digitizing world, then the rules and procedures now emerging in a vain effort to protect both names and behavior from the onslaught of clever technical tricks to gather them could be put to more targeted use. In a society under threat, westerners want to "know" everything about potential terrorists, but as citizens in democracies, they do not want others to fully "know" their personal lives.

Security cannot trump liberty indefinitely, even against embedded threats, without ultimately undermining the openness and vibrancy of westernized democratic systems. They have survived by a rough balance in governmental openness and rules that channel much of the citizens' life experiences and ultimately their trust in their political system (Wamsley 1990; J. Q. Wilson 1989). In the massively digitizing world, getting the data needed for effective disruption strategies will require some way to get the desired behavior data to the security forces but with the protections that make privacy still possible and maintain citizens' social trust. So rapidly has the widespread, subtle decline in personal privacy occurred since 2000 that it is not clear what or when something will push the tolerance of portions of the population too far without sufficient warning. Evolutions in social arrangements emerge and survive undeterred until they prove unacceptable to the subject populations. There is always this tension between security and liberty in democracies, but there is also a sudden tip-over point at which a widespread loss of public trust in digital exchange mechanisms could be exceptionally disruptive politically and economically (Stone 1997). The current rapid and massive digitization of all otherwise public exchanges has the potential to produce just such a sudden loss in public trust if no dampener is found to curb the casualness by which personal identity data is traded to strangers. With an increasing focus on names *and* behavior, plus the casual addition of unfettered biometric use, the unregulated pooling of data far beyond their owners presages future crises. Not only will security services not obtain systematic data they need, but it will become impossible to cleanse later the irrelevant data in all these privately accumulated databases.

A behavior-based approach to finding security data and preserving privacy is especially useful when there is no accepted theory of privacy to indicate when too much has been lost from the citizen.[12] If the crisis has no foreseeable end, then the data collection needs to be objectively oriented before the tools exceed the comprehension of their users. The ubiquitous spread of lives digitally and not obviously recorded ensures that as long as both behavior and identity are rolled up into one package, privacy rights will erode globally. Although protected by law, especially in Europe, the extent of truly personally controlled identity data is in both obvious and nonobvious technical and social retreat throughout the Western world. The possibility of unknown and uncontrollable actors beyond national boundaries changing the internal dynamics of our nation in millions of small decisions is hugely problematical in practical and theoretical terms. Whatever the solution undertaken comprises, it must directly deal with the ever-increasing ease of many-to-many simultaneous global interactions that information and communication technologies (ICT) provide, often keyed to names, birthdates, and addresses.

In particular, the speed at which data can be exchanged, stolen, accumulated, and mined is unprecedented, and the implications in capital, product, media, and even military flight are profound. The ability of the emerging global transport, commercial, and telecommunications systems to reach deep within communities and far beyond borders has raised the security-versus-liberty dilemma to new, but different, heights. While early public administration scholars and occasionally political scientists were declaring the new information technologies to be important but not determinative, networked technologies were being enthusiastically adopted within and across the lowest

---

12. Curiously enough, while U.S. scholars have developed theories of national security, criminal justice, and social order, no widely accepted theory of privacy informs the resolution of this dilemma. The literature that exists tends to predate the digital age (Laufer and Wolfe 1977) or be driven by economic considerations such as acceptable marketing mechanisms (Luo 2002). Palen and Dourish (2003) argue one needs to return to the precomputer era to find theorists of sufficient stature dealing with the difficulties of privacy theory in the modern world. In a large nation of immigrants such as the United States, privacy expectations become an afterthought and are taken for granted. Attributes of privacy expectations emerge over time as side effects of various legal rulings and local tolerance for intrusions.

levels of organizations, families, and public methods of interaction with the surrounding society (Heintze and Bretschneider 2000).

Not attempting to separate behavior from identity to meet both the security data needs and the privacy needs under the modern chronic threats sets up the democratic state not only for a strategic failure in detection but also for unintentional political trends that may be nonobvious until irreversible. Networked technologies have become embedded in modern Western organizations and public expectations such that they are beginning to alter what Fountain would call the "deep institutions" of the society (Fountain 2001). Unfortunately, all too likely radical, negative, catalyzing, and rippling events typical of complex systems are increasingly enabled by these ubiquitous networks carrying linked personal data and behavior. When the cascading events happen, they ripple through this complacency to make a widespread sense of surprise and dismay, and eagerness for something, anything, to return the social system to the previous state (La Porte 1975).

Thus, after the attacks of September 11, 2001, technological responses were highlighted, from the permission granted in the USA PATRIOT Act (Uniting and Strengthening America by Providing Appropriate Tools Required to Intercept and Obstruct Terrorism Act) to collect library book borrowing records to the Total Information Awareness proposal. Digital face screening in airports and the eventual, questionably legal, wireless eavesdropping on international phone calls all emerged as technical but not socially integrated solutions to a lack of knowledge about possible threats. Diving clubs were unceremoniously told to provide detail data on members; internet providers quietly handed reams of data to federal agents; even giant data warehouses such as LexisNexis admitted to working without announcement with federal authorities (Borland and Bowman 2002). The tolerance of the American public, traditionally fond of the technical solutions, endured a great while. As the revelations of federal overreach in the pursuit of pockets of personal data spread, suddenly the U.S. willingness to ignore the widespread collection of data about them plummeted for unexpected reasons. The public had grown exceptionally unhappy with the second Bush administration and its secrecy when revelations of a wireless eavesdropping program were revealed. It was championed by an unpopular president who was considered responsible for an increasingly unpopular, seemingly endless war, and the wiretapping program paid the political price in public unhappiness with it (Kreimer 2008). Whether it provided good behavioral data or not in order to catch bad actors, the fact that the program combined both personal identity and behavior made it seem extreme and intrusive to audiences outside of the security agencies (*Economist* 2008).

Without a way to keep both privacy and security, security will triumph more often than privacy until crises occur. But over time an enduring imbalance between security and privacy threatens the remarkable tolerance and community cohesion forged deliberately across a large immigrant nation. Buried in the language of the canceled TIA program, the USA PATRIOT Act, and other governmental actions are large transfers of power to the executive branch using new technologies. Not only can these new authorities tip the balance to favor security over privacy for the near future, but the associated language of endless war also suggests the intent to make the transfers permanent. Furthermore, the unregulated, interdependent, and wide-ranging aspects of a networked society mean the new governance and power regime emphasizing security over privacy can exist and even expand nearly unnoticed for the foreseeable future (Carey-Smith and May 2006).

Institutionalizing Behavior-Based Privacy for Security

The Behavior-Identity-Knowledge (BIK) framework implements a seamless behavior-based privacy process.[13] It uses largely existing institutions and recently emerging technologies to separate the security interest in behavior data with individuals' interest in protecting their identity data.

In the behavior-based privacy work, individuals store the five or six critical elements of their identity with independent and regulated trusted third parties (TTPs). Whether newly constructed nonprofits or adapted formerly for-profit credit bureaus, these TTPs use physical and technical means to maintain the true identities and pseudonyms of individuals conducting business as normal. For security, TTPs are likely to be multiple grid-based regional entities, no one of which has anyone's complete files, and at least two of which must agree to release a true identity to security forces (SF) including law-enforcement organizations — but only when provided with probable-cause warrants. With

---

13. While behavior-based privacy has been used sporadically in the computer science community in discussions of encryption for privacy purposes, this appears to be the first social and institutional model of how to implement this approach (Demchak and Fenstermacher 2004).

no routine access to masked private records, security agencies at all levels will be regulated in their retention of any records provided and must treat such records as evidence to be handled with documentation through existing laws. Commercial entities will not be given PII data except under strictly controlled circumstances, especially any biometrics. With the critical five or six elements of identity as well as confirming biometrics strongly encrypted and known normally only to the individual and the TTP, individuals then do all of their normal actions such as commercial transactions, communications, and movement under the guise of one or more these pseudonyms.

Over time, the mass databases formerly filled with a mix of personal identities and behaviors become solely filled with dissociated behaviors and meaningless pseudonyms. These pseudonyms frustrate identity theft as well (a dynamically encrypted thumbprint is much harder to fake). Used along with pseudonymized credit cards everywhere credit cards are used now, encrypted smart cards would send only behavior data and biometric confirmation, but never useable personal data, to credit processing bureaus or loyalty card marketing centers. Furthermore, if the system was designed for the use of dynamic or multiple pseudonyms (traceable only with legal warrant), that addition would make it exceptionally difficult to use any given set of pseudonyms as a unique identifier to the individual across multiple organizations.

For citizens, the process would be relatively simple, just as acquiring and using credit cards are today. The masked identities could be obtained at kiosks run by the TTPs located with motor vehicle registration points. The individual would provide the old card or a validation biometric such as a thumbprint and receive the anonymized smart cards with dynamically encrypted biometrics built into the chip on the card. These could be issued for all citizens in lieu of paper social security cards, and temporary cards could be issued to all visitors in lieu of visas. When the card is used, the masked data is collected at the point of each transaction, much like credit cards are charged today. A citizen using a masked credit card touches a thumb pad, which checks to see that the encrypted data is the same as that on the smart masked-ID card, but no merchant or processer collects the thumbprint data. It merely must match what is on the chip and what was put there when the citizen acquired the card at the TTP kiosk. The use of this credit card then sends a notice that the biometrics did or did not match and the desired purchases to the TTP servers. The TTP servers confirm the biometrics match and send along the desired cost to the credit card company processers to see if there is available credit. At that point, the system is the same as it is today. The credit card company confirms that the anonymized cardholder has sufficient credit and approves the transaction, sending a note of purchase approval to the TTP as well as to the merchant's cash register. The TTP's servers do not interfere in the near-instantaneous approval of the sale unless the biometrics do not match, and they collect the privacy-free behavior and context data of the purchase. The data is then added to massed volumes of data that can be used for data mining by business and security, the former looking for changing purchase patterns across large groups and locations, the latter looking for emerging patterns of likely harmful behavior. In neither case does the TTP provide any personal details unless a court order or legislative ruling requires this sharing.

The routine result will be to produce unprecedented volumes of data solely on behavior and masked to be free of privacy considerations and open to bad actor pattern analysis by security agencies at all levels and historically unprecedented in depth and breadth. But there will also be unequivocal protection for individuals who are the only other controllers of the access keys to their personal data. TTPs may offer data-sifting services, but it is more likely existing data analysis firms would perform those services under contract to security agencies at all levels or to merchants. Strong regulation would be emplaced in how security agencies at all levels can request a warrant for personal information, how long any true identity data may be maintained either singly or mixed, and what validation and appeal processes are automatically to be available to citizens whose identity has been shared.

This framework has the virtue of being seamless with the transaction patterns of today's Americans in particular, and in being compatible with current and emerging filtering technologies, to include dynamic encryption of biometric data on smart identity cards. Only the TTPs do not exist per se, but there are candidate agencies available for mission extension under strict legal regimes.

This distinction between behavior and identity fits well with modern sociotechnical, institutional, and legal developments, requiring some relatively seamless adaptations. However, a critical presumption of behavior-based privacy is that security forces can in fact technologically find bad actors when those security forces have only behavior data in massively greater quantities than they can acquire today. Ultimately actors and organizations in Western democracies are more likely to accept the collection of purely behavior data if their privacy concerns are resolved and they can be assured that the behavior data can actually identify bad actors in the process of creating largescale harm. For example, during nine months in 2006 the British government ordered more than 250,000 warrants for communications information (not phone taps) such as who phoned whom. Yet, of the 474 local authorities making requests for communications information, only 122 of them ever used the warrants to tap phones, and apparently not to catch violent bad actors. Most of the warrants were for real-time surveillance by those local authorities (totaling about 1,700 requests) of fully known likely miscreants listed as "rogue traders, fly tippers and housing benefit cheats" (Oates 2008).

If, at the end of the day, the only targets found by the counterterrorist local authorities in the UK were the financial fraud perpetrators not known for violence or wide systemic disruptions, then these security agencies did not get enough behavior-based data to be able to filter accurately for their targeted activities. Whether the bad actors being sought are terrorists, cybered attackers, or both, sufficiently comprehensive data and the ability to scan rapidly for verifiably suspicious patterns without violating privacy is essential to having some foreknowledge of likely patterns of attempted harm to the wider system. Across the business and computer science industries extremely fast largescale data mining, encryption, storage, and security applications are being developed that can be productively put to use in a behavior-based privacy system. What is required is providing the security services legally the breadth of behavior data they need to filter out the small but potentially devastating number of bad actor patterns from the mass of good citizen actions.

One often overlooked advantage of a focus on behavioral data for striking the balance between security and privacy is that even in a digitally complex cybered world, truly massive attacks require more than one person. And people use cyber means to organize, especially at a distance. The days of a lone teenager taking down the internet never existed and certainly do not now. Even the highly complex Stuxnet attack on Iranian nuclear fuel reprocessing plants in 2010 required at least ten to fifteen highly skilled programmers to create just the sophisticated payload part of the application (Falliere, Murchu, and Chien 2010). While no system with any personal privacy would catch the singleton bomber such as Timothy McVeigh, a behavior-based system would have alerted authorities to the 9/11 crew of terrorists. It would also alert authorities to multitudes of digital identity thieves and cohorts of abortion clinic bombers, while still maintaining essential and legally enforced personal privacy. Today none of these behaviors can readily be spotted for security purposes, yet our identity with or without behavior data *is* being collected by a myriad of uncontrolled actors without any assurance of increased security at home. Behavior-based privacy offers the data needed for national security without endangering the democratic presumptions of privacy that sustain the democracy.

COLLABORATIVE ACTIONABLE KNOWLEDGE— THE ATRIUM MODEL

Disrupting chronic, violent, and, especially, embedded threats located anywhere and using cybered means takes more than a theory, honest consultation, and even masses of privacy-ensured behavior data. The security strategy, as institutionalized, needs to continuously be able to make usable sense out of the flood of seemingly unrelated indicators swirling around in the wider, complexly connected cybered world. Collaboration is, in a sense, a golden prize in which the individual attentiveness, systemic joint thinking, and trustful action are effectively socialized and operationalized to produce a long-term, successful, institutional, strategically thoughtful entity. This corporate entity, whether a community of jointly operating first responders, a military, or another group routinely facing these threats, in particular must find ways to mine its own learning and then develop itself in response, to "leverage" what it has been experiencing without recognition (Stenmark 2000). Thus, the final piece in implementing a security resilience strategy has to be a consideration of the organizational structures to take all that knowledge, develop it, and then act on it. According to a report by the House Armed Services Committee, "To 'know with assurance' is the new dimension of warfare" (U.S. Congress 2008).

The Atrium model of "computer as colleague" deliberately structures as routine the tacit knowledge collaborative development across otherwise disparate communities needed to meet critical infrastructure crises.[14] The Atrium model was originally designed for use by militaries modernizing into network

---

14. An interesting alternative formulation to "computer as colleague" might be "companion computers" (Van Doren 1991). First developed for the modernization of the Israeli Defense Forces, the Atrium model embeds the notion of a computer as colleague into its structures and processes. The model has since been applied in analysis of several other militaries to include the U.S. Army, Taiwan, and several developing nations, and more recently to first responder communities (Demchak 1996, 2000, 2001a, 2001b, 2010).

warfare and needing to capture and develop tacit knowledge from many sub-ordinate organizations in order to meet surprises. It embodies the "collective mind" concept of "heedful interrelations" suggested by Weick and Roberts (1993). In the situations of crisis where the failure is associated with death, individuals tend to be more attentive to ways to reduce mistakes. "Actors in the system construct their actions (contributions), understanding that the system consists of connected actions by themselves and others (representation), and interrelate their actions within the system (subordination). Ongoing variation in the heed with which individual contributions, representations, and subor-dinations are interrelated influences comprehension of unfolding events and the incidence of errors. As heedful interrelating and mindful comprehension increase, organizational errors decrease" (Weick and Roberts 1993). Imagin-ing worst-case scenarios does more than help planning; it also helps deflate the tendency to magnify the loss potential when a surprise occurs. Using tacit knowledge to explore routine and worst-case scenarios thus helps the cognitive stress that reduces adaptive behavior (Billings, Milburn, and Schaalman 1980; Pan et al. 2007).

The Atrium model is specifically designed to capture tacit knowledge that enables this heedfulness across surprise. Intended to be an alternative socio-technical organizational design for technically advanced or modernizing secu-rity forces, the model is based loosely on Nonaka and Takeuchi's original and corporate hyperlinked model. In one of its distinctions from the model of the two Japanese scholars, the Atrium model incorporates the computer as a col-league, not as a library or controller, and specifically envisions a virtual world in which hypotheses are tested by members of the organization (Nonaka and Takeuchi 1997). Here the knowledge base of the organization explicitly pro-vides a familiar virtual space to get information and to acquire lessons learned while sharing and testing one's own experiences and hypotheses.

Recognizing Knowledge as a Social Product

The field of organizational or group tacit knowledge development rests on two presumptions directly relevant to resilience in organizations and societies. It is argued, first, that we do not routinely know what we all know collectively and, second, if we did, it would help us to accommodate the surprises and the knowledge burdens of the complex systems we share. The lessons in military history, complexity theory, largescale technical systems, and the emerging field of computational organization science support both assertions well.[15] Modern forms of organizational collaboration are, at their core, tools for resilience in a world of "fundamental socio-technical problems that are so complex and dynamic that they cannot be fully addressed by traditional techniques" (Carley 2002, 253). Tailored for the knowledge burden involved, the emerging, generally virtual collaborative means of productive sharing provide the arenas by which to gather and refine the ground truth in tacit knowledge and creative skills walking around in the heads and unrecorded conversations of the organization's experienced, creative, and observant members.

The tacit knowledge matters because, in the natural and orchestrated trials and errors of a system's life, it provides surprise's warning lights.[16] For many surprises, available warning knowledge about forms or frequencies of surprise was neglected in advance (Schulman and Roe 2007). Suddenness does not mean impossible to anticipate; suddenness is subjectively felt by humans, not objectively present in all cases that we would accept as surprising. Often the design of the system discourages a broad scanning of events for new knowledge, and the path-dependent culture of the organization reinforces inaccurate valuation of unusual sources of information (Schulman et al. 2004; Boin et al. 2005).

The design of a system meant to embrace and survive surprise needs to recognize the value of making resilience part of the routine and the processes routinely tested for resilience. In late 2007, RAND Corporation analysts looked at the risk modeling used by the U.S. Department of Homeland Security (DHS). Their major findings, posed as recommendations, were that DHS needed to develop what was known about terrorist planning processes and operations in order to create sensible scenarios based on risk. Furthermore DHS was explicitly told to create "tabletop exercises to test the scenarios and provide feedback" (Willis et al. 2007). The recommendations are never made for an activity currently being pursued well, and the report makes it quite clear that whatever DHS was doing to collate what it might already know, the sum was insufficient for the job.

What the RAND analysts were reiterating was that useful capture of tacit knowledge occurs in streams, not occasional collections, and then in the per-

15. See the accumulated works of Kathleen Carley for a broad introduction to the field of computational organization science. See, in particular, Carley (2002) for a useful overview.

16. For two particularly good discussions of this research's implication, see Roe (1998) and Rochlin (1997).

sistent application and validation in system actions. Equally critical within as well as external to organizations, processes blending the social and technical need to co-evolve over time (Haythornthwaite 2005). Unfortunately and quite frequently for efficiency purposes or from simple managerial ignorance, the knowledge needed for surprise is undervalued. It is expected to emerge from only occasional exercises of short duration across mass groups of people, especially if the means to go on communicating (email, a website, occasionally a blog) are provided. A recent trade journal article lauded a set of preparatory exercises for state-level personnel in preparation for disastrous disruptions in the state's water supply. Unfortunately these exercises were nonroutine, involved mass numbers of participants for a short period, and included a good deal of passive knowledge one-way transfers. The exercises did not attempt longer-term iterative knowledge development, and if it did happen across a few participants, that result would have been serendipitous (Whelton et al. 2006). It is commonly and mistakenly assumed that these collaborative learning processes need only a minor social stimulus and the proper technical tools to persist and succeed. The field research suggests otherwise (Kreijns, Kirschner, and Jochems 2003).

To succeed, collective problem solving must be made easy, useful, and routine. "Collaboration is the mutual engagement of participants in a coordinated effort to solve a problem together" (Mühlenbrock and Hoppe 1999, 398). In large organizations, routinized procedures matter greatly in their influence on crisis decisions.[17] Practicing collaboration as a procedure embedded in shared daily practices provides legitimacy, sound group cohesion development, opportunities to tailor the tools to local needs for knowledge, and a widened base of known actors whose trust attributes are experientially tested. Interestingly enough, one scholar found in a study of cross-cultural collaboration for problem solving that the participants who communicated most frequently were seen by both cultures as being more effective at knowledge transfer (Sarker 2005). Repetitious interactions are necessary to build the foundations for resilience by blending the social with the technical for collaborative knowledge development (Kreijins, Kirschner, and Jochems 2003).

This embedded collaboration is not easy even if great similarity in socializa-

---

17. An interesting example of this power of routine is found in the myriad of ways that procedures in the UN have strongly affected the policies adopted by the entire international body (Stiles 2006).

tion, motivations, context, and missions exist, as in the modern military across a number of westernized nations. The tacit knowledge and trust benefits of joint operations, often called "combined arms," have proven time and again extremely difficult to maintain between deployments, even when promotions are tied to demonstrating time spent in joint operations, as in the U.S. military (D. E. Johnson 2002). The continuing difficulty of militaries in collaboration, despite their historical interest in collective action, strongly underscores the need to socially construct a positive view of collaboration. The participants must be helped to see the value in providing missing and needed knowledge in any collaboration. For effective collective problem solving and action, the collaborators must already recognize the holistic aspects of this process in terms of social acceptance, endorsement, and return for effort (Dirckinck-Holmfeld and Sorensen 1999). Without this nurtured openness to mutually agreed-upon change, collective improvisation may be delayed for time-consuming negotiations that may doom effective responses to surprise. Innovation — the more permanent response to surprise — usually requires even more good will among actors and, hence, is even more hampered when collective knowledge development is not valued.

Organizing an Atrium Model to Develop Knowledge and Trust

The model has three main organizational elements: the *Atrium*, underlying technological system, the *core organization*, and the *task forces* enacting strategic decisions. Entering into and interacting with the Atrium is essentially interrelating with a major player in the institution in a heedful manner. Figure 9 shows the Atrium model notionally as the underlying space linking individual, sections, and units within organizations.

One "goes into" the Atrium as a consumer, contributor, or producer. Each individual in the allied organizations cycles through every role — no exceptions for leaders — in order to provide the stabilizing locus of institutional memory and opportunity for creativity. As individuals transfer into a new long-term position, they spend about ten days in each transition as "contributor" doing a tacit data dump — including frustrations about process, data, and ideas — into their organization's share of the Atrium files. They would also spend up to half of that time in virtual simulations with other members across organizations, creating or recreating problematic situations for collaborative solutions. Noncritical identifying tags may be masked to encourage honesty, and then

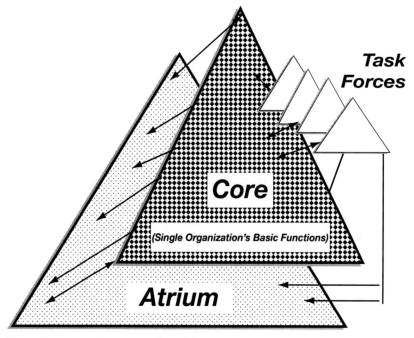

Figure 9. Atrium Organizational Model

the knowledge is added to the central pools. While everyone routinely cycles through the Atrium to download experiences, every so often — perhaps once every six months — each person also spends a week or so as a "producer." In this role, individuals set up questions and look at the data for the benefit of their organization and the entire community. As "consumers," all Atrium organization members can tap into what contributors have input and also the results of these simulations. Furthermore, they can apply simple language queries, data mining, or other applications to expanding pools of knowledge created by the producers in order to guide their future processes.

Entering the Atrium are the members of the organization who create the core or main stem of operations. Often functionally divided, especially in the usual largescale corporate divisional model, here are the finance, personnel, transportation, operations, logistics, and recruitment elements that keep main systems functioning.

Finally, there are the task forces. These are specialized units that have existed for years in preparation for specialized missions that may or may not ever emerge. In the Atrium model, a cadre of permanent support staff is left in task forces that are specialized. But the mission or the task force is time limited, and the bulk of the members rotate in and out on six- to twelve-month assignments, developing skills but also staying connected with the needs and problems of the main stem of operations.

Key to this model is the stabilizing locus of institutional memory and creativity in the human-Atrium networks. Everyone according to their career primary and secondary specialties rotates between the main set of organizations, task forces, and Atrium support activities. Often at the same desk, everyone from senior leaders on down cycles through all three roles in the Atrium. Each individual is a daily *consumer* of the Atrium's knowledge support as it organically expands and self-organizes. But each person periodically is also a *contributor*, making that support credible, accurate, and creative, and, less frequently, a *producer* gathering up the lessons from his or her experiences, other real experiences, and simulated trials and error.

Some of this data will be captured implicitly as contributors are encouraged to "act out" their concerns in the form of challenges or changes to game-based simulations played through by themselves or others in the system. Research suggests that relatively high-fidelity game-based interactions facilitate the kind of deep learning that asynchronous communications like email do not. During this period, employees will play out scenarios that they or others construct. They can construct them directly or ask to play a scenario described by someone else in their data dumps, expected to be in the form of complaints. In playing through the virtual world scenario jointly with others in similar roles or supporting roles, employees engage in a dialog about what should and should not happen. In playing out their own or another's hypotheses through scenarios, they inevitably engage with others' perceptions. It is the simultaneity, the fidelity, the flexibility, and, importantly, the legitimacy of this exchange that makes for deep learning (Kreijns, Kirschner, and Jochems 2003).

The choices made in the simulations constitute inputs to the knowledge of the Atrium as much as any set of numbers. System members elsewhere can then apply data mining or other applications on this expanding pool of knowledge elements to guide their future processes. Explicit and implicit comparative institutional knowledge thus becomes instinctively valued and actively retained and maintained for use in ongoing or future operations.

While everyone cycles through the Atrium routinely to download experiences, every so often, perhaps once every six months, each person also spends an additional week or so as a producer setting up questions and looking at the data for all the system's benefit. Compiling the tacit knowledge is thus not outsourced to those far from the day-to-day needs, experiences, and challenges of that Atrium's active community. Firefighters review the words or simulation behaviors of others like themselves and like others with whom they may have to work. In this they would try to define the kinds of questions they or people like them would like to have answered. They would also look at new data with an eye to what kinds of questions that data might answer. The goal is for them to understand what knowledge is out there beyond what they have asked so far and to see new patterns they had not thought of before. Technological support for this kind of cross-fertilization lies not only in the fields of visualization but also in conceptual mapping such as the emerging field of "co-term" network analysis (Jacobs 2002). The effect will be a broadening of understanding of other organizational dilemmas as well as of others' approaches to solutions. This commonality in experience permits easier cycling through collaborative task forces as well, discussed later in the Joint or Emergency-Atrium.

Surrounded by complex systems as well as being a complex system itself, the core and its Atrium denizens will face constantly emerging problems beyond their normal operations. Some of these will be physically dangerous and immediate. Some will be prospective, such as determining why certain neighboring political leaders have allocated budget amounts to shadowy organizations. Some will be long term, such as rechanneling the design goals of key data chunk allocations within the Atrium or retargeting some of its uses in the light of wider global trends. For these kinds of problems, a matrix organization is eminently preferred, and hence we come to the final element, the task forces.

The third element of an Atrium is the groups sent outward from the core to act on the knowledge developed. For militaries, these are deployed forces; for police forces, these are normally called task forces, while, for corporations, the term more often used is teams, usually problem-solving cross-function groups specifically created for particular purposes. Across all these labels and formats, however, these specialized formations are the pointy end of the organizational stick; they enact the decisions of the core facilitated by the Atrium systems and processes.

Extreme events, in particular, tend to produce these specialized formations if they deeply surprise organizational leaders and are seen to be likely to happen again. Organizations with the mission to be prepared for nasty surprises, like militaries or police, are particularly but not uniquely prone to forming these small, unique, and specialized task forces meant to forestall, mitigate, or at least provide warning of such extreme events in the future. Each of them develops a broad and deep array of implicit knowledge that is often lost as individuals retire or rotate around the organization. This model would be able to capture and put to good use this tacit knowledge for a single organization and even more productively for a joint organization with many organizations contributing task force members. In an extreme event with some prior knowledge of form or frequency, *and* with considerable interorganizational trust and consensus, a task force with many divergent units could be equipped to function jointly with a clearer definition of what is to be done if they have the ability to use an Atrium before, during, and after any significant activities. The key is frequent and easy interorganizational operations in advance under nonemergency situations. If the four stages of sense-making—shared goal definition; recognition and clarification of all participants' organizational practices and tacit assumptions; external influences identification; and the explicit creation of mutually useful knowledge (Gasson 2005)—are to occur rapidly in task forces when these responders are surprised, the preparatory process requires considerable social and technical practice.

The knowledge creation in the Atrium not only serves the needs of member institutions but also allows an empirical dataset to be accrued for use in online high-fidelity trial-and-error scenarios as well as speculative routine exercises for each organization. The more the Atrium is virtual, realistic, and flexibly and easily used, the more participants would instinctively incorporate what they know well. Thus, routine use of the Atrium would capture the implicit information currently lost or buried after each previous routine related event or emergency experience. As members are tagged to be on call as first responders, they rotate into online virtual simulations, experiment with choices in scenarios built by the experiences of others like them, and play out decisions jointly with others also online testing their decisions.

The developing research into online multiuser gaming suggests this kind of frequent exercise, in combination with real-time operations, is exceptionally valuable in developing both expertise and trust across partners (Jay, Glencross, and Hubbold 2007). As the emerging "augmented reality gaming" develops and is adapted into the Atrium environment, it will be possible for police officers in New York City to walk through graphically realistic, surprising, and demanding missions while seeing what kinds of help they can expect or can extract from state and federal individuals also online experiencing these situations (Liarokapis 2006). Periodic physical exercises will always be necessary to cement lessons learned or reintegrate some physical constraints as yet not incorporated into the virtual world.[18] Exercises held today in real time with individuals or organizations on call as first responders are expensive and rarely frequent. Through Atrium mechanisms, they can more easily be orchestrated by the coordinators across organizations and task forces in advance, can more readily be practiced prior to a physical test, and can more rapidly provide lessons to be learned for real circumstances of disastrous surprises. And, of course, after the real-world experiences — routine or not — individuals would then reflect their interpretations of what happened back into the Atrium for the use of their organization and the wider relevant community.

Joint Atrium Model for Combinatorial Innovative Solutions and Rapid Reaction Trust

An Atrium model works for either a single organization or a group of jointly operating agencies, but it is particularly useful across combined forces from several communities, agencies, regions, or nations. While it is rarely noted, most domestic emergency operations as well as UN interventions share this "combined arms" property of needing surprise resilience built through collective foreshadowing and trust. Thus an Atrium digital and social environment dedicated to those features has considerable appeal. Adding to the value of an Atrium is that deeper learning is associated with real-time dialogues over asynchronous communication.

The Atrium model is therefore adjustable for the jointly operating environment. The underlying Atrium is shared across organizations rather than internal sections of a single institution. A well-institutionalized knowledge nexus, for example, would constitute a core for the missions that are jointly

18. For example, today's *avatars* (or computerized representations of physical bodies) do not yet provide as much implicit body information that individuals in normal life collect instinctively in face-to-face encounters, although that fidelity is improving rapidly (Moore, Ducheneaut, and Nickell 2007). In recent tests of how well avatars can represent reality, scientists were able to design a library environment with neutral avatars, place nonclinically paranoid subjects in the library, and have a portion of these subjects develop paranoid thoughts about the avatars as though they and the avatars shared the same reality (Freeman et al. 2005).

and continuously engaged. With this new social construction of what one does with information, each organization in the joint Atrium system creates, stores, refines, connects, weights, shares, and nurtures its own knowledge, while common applications blend the tacit information into wider knowledge queries and lessons. Doing what is needed for their own organizations in capturing tacit knowledge and in searching for comparative lessons, individuals learn how to engage the Atrium as a trusted colleague. There will be plenty of tasks routinely done singly in organizations that can also be associated with the Atrium, not only in initial creation of applications, elements, processes, and uses but also in the coordination and integration of these evolutions. In a joint Atrium, the core exists between these organizations virtually, shepherded by the cadre element located wherever emergency management coordination would normally be housed. Individuals serving in the core will come to understand the Atrium as an intelligent world of knowledge and experimentation rather than a mindless amalgamation of individual databases. In short, the vibrancy of the Atrium in providing knowledge to accommodate surprise is due not to the professionalism of the small permanent core party but to the newness of perspective and, importantly, rising familiarity of both the active and part-time participants.

Driven by the need to act effectively together across domain or national borders, the joint Atrium can provide a model for an organic, immersive, and useful knowledge management system for both emergency management settings and deployed military settings.[19] Both types of missions involve being ready for surprise amid complex dynamic environments and then to resiliently improvise and innovate nonetheless. As such it incorporates the 1990s *knowledge management* emphasis on adjusting the human to technical applications by moving their work from localized relationship-based "controlled hoards" to web-based "trusted source" structures. This model is focused on the social and technical aspects in balance. It is designed for consistent, accessible, useful, and rewarded virtual workspaces necessary for the "support, openness, trust, mutual respect, and risk taking" necessary for effective innovation across remoted, culturally diverse, and yet reciprocally dependent organizations (C. B. Gibson and Gibbs 2006).

19. This application of the original Atrium model was designed for a book on resilience incorporating the views of both European and American scholars. In that piece, it is called the E2-Atrium for "Emergency Events-Atrium" (Comfort, Boin, and Demchak 2010).

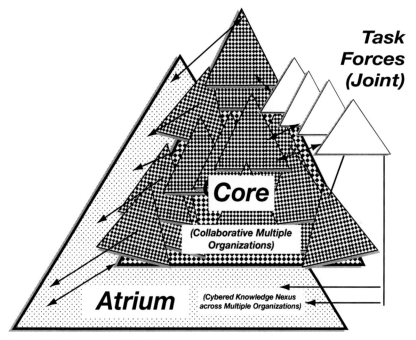

Task Forces (Joint)

Core

(Collaborative Multiple Organizations)

Atrium (Cybered Knowledge Nexus across Multiple Organizations)

Figure 10. Joint Atrium Model

Once the crisis response operation begins, each organization leaps into surprise-response activities that have been enhanced along with social trust, respect, cohesion, and credibility in virtual spaces. Through the Atrium, member organization decision makers are more aware of the roles and likely actions of other agencies in their grand alliance. They are also more likely to know many of their corresponding actors in other organizations through the simulations. The key here is that all members, including leaders, cycle through each section: the Atrium, core duties, and their joint duties in task forces as shown in figure 10.

The virtual scenarios that would be organically developed in an Atrium have two particular advantages. First, the knowledge inputted, manipulated, saved, and redeveloped comes from the members of the organization most likely to know what is not known, not yet noted, and is needed. Second, by having everyone rotate, from top leaders on down, everyone develops an understanding in the group of what they must do, might have to do, could rely on others to do, and will have to consider improvising on the spot. These virtual scenarios encourage innovation and ultimately resilience. In contrast, the vast majority of simulations, exercises, and models prepared and delivered to security agencies today look remarkably like the following description of a relatively recent model predicting terrorist risk developed for the DHS. "The RMS [Risk Management Solutions] model estimates the risks of macroterrorism, which RMS defines as attacks capable of causing (1) more than $1 billion in economic losses, (2) more than 100 fatalities or 500 injuries, or (3) massively symbolic damage. Starting with specific attack scenarios, the model assesses the threat of various types of attack on different targets, the vulnerability of those targets to those attacks, and the expected annual consequences of successful attacks in terms of casualties and property loss. The overall risk of any given attack scenario reflects all three of these factors" (Willis 2007). This model has a high level of abstraction far from the knowledge needed by the bulk of the members of DHS. The rest of its discussion and the sources suggested no experiential input from DHS to even alter what was considered attacks worthy of DHS consideration. Presumably some operational need would be affected by this analysis, but it is difficult to see from the document who other than senior leaders could use the results generated by running this model.

Explicit and implicit comparative institutional knowledge thus becomes instinctively valued and actively retained and maintained for use in ongoing or future operations. Frontline interrogators, for example, would try to define the kinds of questions they or people like them would like to have answered. They would also look at new data with an eye to what kinds of questions that data might answer. The goal is for them to understand what knowledge is out there beyond what they have asked so far and to see new patterns they had not thought of before. Visualization is exceptionally powerful in this process. The effect is a broader understanding of other organizational dilemmas and approaches to solutions.

This commonality in experience permits easier cycling through collaborative task forces as well, the kind of coordinated behaviors critical for crisis and deployed operations and so dependent on trust and inter-actor knowledge. For the members of a joint operations system, this cycling needs to be both routine and of value to their own work in their own organization. Hence, interrogators in Iraq as well as supply reservists in California would need to find something of use for them when they share their tacit experiences in the joint Atrium. Once operations begin, each organization leaps into surprise-response activities with greater knowledge of what other agencies can reasonably be expected to do and also with greater possibilities for trust since many of the corresponding actors will have become acquainted through the simulations.

The Atrium model is many times more collaborative and developing than the host of centers and task forces dotting the national-level security structures of most westernized nations. It is both hierarchically, technically, and socially constructed to make it easy to employ and accept, as well as be desirably useful to participants. This is a socio-technical format intended to provide the best possible knowledge stream possible from collective thinking in double-looped learning mechanisms sensitive to human motivations and feedback.

When decision makers just as mid- and low-level employees cycle through the Atrium in order to truly know their organization and the wider system's players, the shared experiences widen the chances of domain consensus, role acceptance, trust, shared contextual knowledge, and innovation across organizations, individuals, and environments. Even rogue outcomes may be less catastrophic when Atrium institutions respond due to the human ownership of systemic resilience. Tacit knowledge collection is organically built from common experiences through institutionally and cognitively sensitive virtuality aimed at trust across disparate actors as well as solutions.

The "socio" part of socio-technical systems cannot be overstated. The history of war is replete with examples of how personal trust across unexpected lines enabled survival of a set of units. When that trust was disrupted by the departure of some players, the units began to fail.[20] A joint Atrium provides the leaders with what they need in more holistic knowledge of their own organizations as well as other partners on whom their people will depend in anticipating and responding to an emergency. Since one uses or cycles "into" the Atrium at one's desk, the ubiquitous sharing is possible at smaller time increments, increasing the chances of an accurate picture of events emerging before memories are fuzzed and reconstructed rationally by other pressing needs.

20. There are many examples, but a good one is that of General von Balck, head of armor forces on the miserable Eastern Front in World War II. Although the Germany Army was never fully motorized and air support very limited, Balck's personal friendship with the Luftwaffe commander in his area meant operationally advantageous collegial coordination. His troops received the kind of air support they needed for success. When this friend was assigned elsewhere and a new air commander was assigned, that successful arrangement simply vanished (Balck 1979).

GATHERING WHAT EXISTS TODAY

Technologies and organizations that would support all three institutional adaptations — from the knowledge nexus to behavior-based privacy to an Atrium — exist today in nascent form. Missing is the national-level strategy that allows these varied experiments and innovations to be brought together and refined for the needs of modern digitized democracies individually and jointly.

For the knowledge nexus requirement, ten years of counterterrorism strategic collaboration offer some lessons in structures, tools, trial and error, and even cognitive rethinking. But for the United States as well as the UK and even Spain, the level of concern enabling the cross-agency consultations required a massive physical attack. Only slowly have westernized democracies begun to realize the cybered threat, and their interpretations of what agency actors need to sit at the table, or share digital databases, varies greatly. In the United States, in mid-2009 after a presidential statement elevating cyber security to a matter of national security, a cyber "solving" frenzy similar to that seen right after the attack of 2001 flooded the overarching policy, strategy, and even institutional debates in Washington, D.C.[21] With many of limited expertise declaring cyber power, cyber war, or cyber security to be either all new or all well known, and many others with great technical expertise, it is not clear that the lessons of joint honest consultations from ten years of counterterrorism have been adequately explored for what can and cannot work in cybered conflict. Cybered conflict mechanisms and threats coalesce all too easily and systemically with terrorism and even the short time horizons of nuclear threats. Many terrorists would eagerly use cybered means to obtain nuclear material for attacks. However, the ubiquity of the cybered access, the ability to make choices instantly about scale, proximity, and precision on limited budgets save that of time, marks the cybered threat as distinct from these others.

The distinctive characteristics of cybered threats in the current and emerging topology of the World Wide Web require dedicated efforts to create the urgency and the nexus space for cybered conflict on its own systemic terms.

---

21. A remarkable number of individuals with little to no background in technical or social networks of any kind are now "cyberizing" their résumés just as many "terrorized" theirs right after the attack of 2001. The goal is to exploit the federal monies being thrown massively and somewhat indiscriminately at the threat, which itself has not been well understood (author's bemused observation).

Scattered across a myriad of contracts, tools, agencies, and queries are inno-vations in data mining, presentation, and dissemination. Institutionalization of a security resilience strategy in a cybered world, however, demands a less fragmented way to reach a consensus on orchestrated disruption and resilience operations. One institution cannot be fully secured and vast swathes of the rest of the nation left on their own. If, at the end of the day, the attacker still has advantages in scale, proximity, and precision, needing only to change the target to get around the secured institution, then inevitably the secured institu-tion will also fall.

For a seamless institution of behavior-based privacy, the key elements ex-ist as well, scattered across the existing systems of commerce and communi-cation. Such a system can exist only in a digitized society, but the threats also can function only in this world. Therefore a second critical requirement also exists — that masses of data masked from identity can indeed be mined quickly to find groups of bad actors revealing themselves solely by their ac-tions. One important question is whether pure behavior data is sufficient to identify bad actors or patterns of bad actions. A recent work tested that ability by constructing an intellective model as a proof of concept (Pew and Mavor 1998). In 2007, using the NetLogo small world simulation application, the CyPRG team of the University of Arizona created a small world of actors going about daily lives whose essential identity is masked but behaviors are not. The mass behavior data unattached to personal identity was then analyzed using machine-learning techniques. The goal was to determine whether the hid-den terrorist living normally among a multitude of others could be identified through individual patterns of suspect behaviors.

This proof of concept virtual experiment produced accuracy levels exceed-ing 95 percent across a variety of learning algorithms (Demchak et al. 2007). This accuracy is certainly better than could be expected today without ex-tensive intrusion into personal privacy and the questionable use of profiling. Thus, on a small but replicable scale, it is possible to enhance current privacy standards while providing massively more behavior data to security forces both in quantity and validity. The results showed how a democracy awash in digital data could indeed parse the streams to achieve varying preferred privacy and security outcomes institutionally without damaging the economic or institu-tional underpinnings of its society.

Finally, neither the nexus nor the behavior data can support the security and resilience strategy unless the technologies making an Atrium possible are being developed across defense, intelligence, corporate management, and even online gaming fields. They are, and these Atrium-like game-based simulations are showing great promise in learning, economies, and new knowledge development. They capture the human need to test hypotheses in environments that feel real, and they meet the institutional need to record those tests to capture tacit knowledge. One of the more interesting examples has been developed in the University of Maryland's Intelligent Transportation System (ITS) research laboratory, called the Center for Advanced Transportation Technology Laboratory, or CATT Lab. These researchers have fully embraced remoted, highly interactive virtual worlds as teaching, learning, and research tools. One of their applications is intended solely for the training of emergency first responders. "CATT Lab's three-dimensional, multi-player computer gaming simulation technology . . . allows hundreds of remote participants to interact with one another online in various virtual disasters and accident scenarios" (Center for Advanced Transportation 2008).

In a recent and televised exercise, emergency personnel sat at computers around the country with microphoned headphones similar to what they would use in real life and played a scenario by moving their "avatars" (online characters portraying themselves) in smooth replications of what they would do if there really were a "four-vehicle tractor trailer incident with multiple, serious injuries" on their own local highway. In the televised video by the History Channel's *Modern Marvels* series, the participants were talking and acting in accordance with their own level of training. One observation made by the researchers was how quickly the disparate emergency personnel, especially police officers, realized their own mistakes in orchestrating traffic flow as a function of having been in the scenario. The statistics suggest that for every small increment of time that the highway is blocked by an accident, the chances of someone at the far end of the backed-up traffic will cause a second major accident increase enormously. Police officers participating in the scenarios reported that they had not realized how much their own actions, or inaction, tended to contribute to the second accident (Center for Advanced Transportation 2008).

Another advantage of such a large remoted scenario among professionals in the same occupation is the chance to discover not only standard operating procedures in conflict but also linguistic differences that will have disastrous consequences where clear communications are needed. For example, police units around Washington, D.C., are switching to plain language since their experiences in 9/11 and Katrina. Maryland sent officers to help with Katrina only to discover joint police teams could not understand each other. The famous 10X police codes used across the United States since the 1920s were developed when most radios had only one channel, and communicating in absolutely the least amount of air time was essential. The local and regional evolution of meaning, however, meant the code was no longer uniform. For example, the numbers 10–50 mean an auto accident in Virginia but that an officer has been hurt in Maryland (Associated Press 2006).

This experimental exercise occurred only once so far as the researchers develop more scenarios and even possible portable versions. The rudiments of an Atrium without the necessary organizational processes have been constructed. If each department were also to have a local Atrium to practice common language development with adjacent departments as well as organically generated scenarios, the learning would be continuous, affordable, and productive. The game-based (avatars with high-fidelity graphics) simulation explosion is emerging across a wide variety of professions, fields, and venues, ranging from NASA using simulations to train its astronauts in emergency repair to submarine drivers to boat builders to tourists. The difference between this transportation simulation and the Atrium is only partly in the technology. In the CATT Lab application, one plays the game as designed to learn or test embedded hypotheses. In an Atrium, the members design the game they will then play to test their hypotheses multiple times across many members rotating in with new experiences and ideas. From the community-built Second Life online simulation to a host of emerging experiments, all the technical pieces of an Atrium are in place in one way or another. Missing is the organization model to pull them all together institutionally and the strategic framework to justify and guide the knowledge implementation in strategic actions.

CHAPTER FIVE

Disruption and Resilience for National Security and Power in a Cybered World

History tells us much about human social tendencies, a good deal about prior experiments in social control and security, and only a little about today's circumstances of multiply netted, chronic, violent, and gray threats to westernized city-states from turbulent, densely populated, dysfunctional regions of the world. In recorded history, such serious security threats induced conquest, neglect, brutal internal suppression, or annihilation (the ultimate submission of one side).[1] Today westernized nations would neither seek nor accept these outcomes. Yet one cannot allow the offensive advantages of a global cybered world—scale, precision, and proximity—to disable critical functions of modern nations at whim, in revenge, or in concerted malicious campaigns.

This book argues for a knowledge-led strategy presuming that the global

---

1. A nod must be made to nomadic raiding warfare between roughly equal strong clans. Their records are not written or preserved, save by often exceptionally biased foreign and conquering observers or oral histories heavily distorted by decades of foreigner rule. On the surface, this kind of warfare seems somewhat akin to city-state warfare. Over time, there were rules to it such as the acceptable response to an insult or a death. But it bears only limited similarity to organized warfare of even early civilizations. It was also highly proximate; neighbors fought neighbors. Finally, whereas the rules held while there was rough symmetry in power between related tribes, they broke down quickly if one party grew much weaker or a foreign tribe considered outside the species of human was involved. See O'Connell for a discussion of the difference between predatory or intraspecies warfare (O'Connell 1989, 124). Today, even if Angola is harboring the entire mass of Muslim extremists, the United States will not invade Angola and kill everyone down to the children. It is simply not the same worldview.

society is linking critically in ways we have never seen save historically in small communities. Rather than having nationally critical integrated systems contained behind sovereign borders and protections, the digitizing nations of the world are creating remotely accessible globally connected socio-technical infrastructures (GSTIS) whose disruption could catastrophically disable critical functions within many nations individually or simultaneously. The financial system meltdown of 2008 was a foretaste of the kinds of cascades that are conceivable in the future as this process continues.

Scale and interconnection matter enormously in today's national security. In August 2010, for reasons unknown, the largest to date attack denying internet service to major integrated enterprises was launched against a backbone network whose servers are in the United States. The attack continued for eight hours, disrupting all services for one and a half hours. Surviving the waves of email from infected computers worldwide required the assistance of at least five other major communications networks across other nations, including Deutsche Telekom (Leyden 2010). The ability to link remote actors easily to the critical functions of globally open national systems means we must move to a new level of understanding of threats, complex systems we unknowingly share, and the surprises of a largescale worldwide system. This book offers a clear proposal about what this kind of strategy needs to look like and how to proceed today.

Complex systems do not offer answers easily, whether social or technical (Miller and Page 2007). Globalizing complex combined socio-technical systems can be even less helpful. Their answers are hard to find and are good for only a short time as a myriad of small decisions cumulate into evolving trends. Continuous knowledge collection, development, and retesting as well as dissemination are essential for security and must be built into institutions very deliberately. While some *rogue* outcomes will never be known in advance,[2] only well-collected and refined knowledge dispels the secrets of emerging bad actors. But its pursuit has to be built into the framework of strategic perception, design, implementation, and adaptation. In an ever more interdependent

---

2. Complexity theory is quite clear on this point: the more complex the situation, the more likely some nasty outcomes are not knowable in advance; nor are they open to inadvertent accommodation (Waldrop 1992; Horgan 1995; La Porte 1975; Perrow 1984; Jervis 1997; Sagan 2004; Rochlin 1997; Mayntz and Hughes 1988; Summerton 1994; Kaijser 2004; De Bruijne and Van Eeten 2007).

and complex world, the balance between secrets and mysteries will never be clearly defined, but it can be roughly outlined if the security agencies have a way to coordinate the search for knowledge.[3]

In this world, especially as globalization and population growth proceed, the rest of the world is refusing to operate by the rules of international conflict established by the three main schools of international relations. For example, realist and even liberal institutionalist logics (when applied individually) always have difficulty explaining why a weak state challenges a patently stronger enemy. Even more perplexing is when it is done publicly out of a sense of cultural superiority — a constructivist explanation (Fischerkeller 1998). China refused the British demands for concessions in the opium wars out of a sense of cultural disdain. By no stretch could Imperial China have truly resisted a moderately constructed British expeditionary force, and yet there was no question but that the Western "barbarians" needed to be challenged (Fay 1975). It was definitely a bad war for a country that had up to one-third of its population addicted to opium already by the early 1800s. The emperor was well aware of the economic destruction of this epidemic just as his population was beginning to soar. But he lacked sufficient knowledge himself. Like many others, he clearly would ignore his own quantitative shortcomings and come out fighting. In the process, he caused enormous turmoil, suffering, and ugly ripple effects that ranged far from the original conflict (Lodwick 1996). In mid-2003, a realist would be tempted to argue that Iraq was all over but for the rearguard actions of a few disgruntled types — "foreign fighters" they were called (Mearsheimer 2005). And yet, in Iraq and other developing nations, nonobjective notions of

3. Personal comment, 2003. A senior U.S. intelligence officer once remarked that the world was filled with secrets and mysteries. Secrets can be found out because someone was actually hiding them. Like the rogue outcomes of a complex system, however, mysteries simply must be endured. For him, the critical question was to determine what one was facing: secrets or mysteries. One collects widely and continuously on secrets, less so on mysteries. For the record, this officer (name and position withheld) considered that the then Iraqi leader, Saddam Hussein, was a man of secrets and that his putative weapons of mass destruction were a secret, not a mystery. This officer was not persuaded later that we would find any such weapons in Iraq. To quiet his persistent questions about the lack of evidence prior to the 2003 invasion, this officer was moved around several times by the Bush administration's intelligence aide to Secretary of Defense Donald Rumsfeld and effectively driven out of his home institution, the U.S. Defense Intelligence Agency. This personal comment was made in 2003 prior to the invasion and confirmation of his instincts.

cultural superiority and entitlement routinely roil what passes for government capacity and semistable societal functions.

Had either China or the British used a knowledge-enabled disruption strategy, the originating insult of the Opium Wars and the resulting destruction of the small social control the emperor retained would not have been necessary. At the least, any ensuring war would have been fought for what was really at stake — the emperor's opposition to opening even wider British access to the profitable Chinese addict market for the British East India Company's opium trade. Those revenues financed colonial rule of British India. In the case that everyone knew what was really being contested, it very likely would have been politically more difficult for the United States and others to justify their contributions, making the conflict more costly for Britain. The outcome might indeed have been at least a bit more favorable for China (Lodwick 1996). Without the framework and institutions of a security resilience strategy prior to 2003, President Bush and his advisers lacked open and honest consultation about Iraqi society, economy, and cultural predilections, and they did not thoroughly play through realistic scenarios involving regional blowback in their knowledge development prior to the invasion (Mearsheimer 2005).

MARKS OF THE NEW CYBERED AGE: SOVEREIGNTY, DISRUPTION, AND RESILIENCE

Resilience has become a fashionable term now because we are globally in a particularly obvious time of metamorphosis. New terms and frameworks emerge when the world as known becomes hard to understand, and even hegemons are puzzled or seem wavering and weakened.[4] As long as there is the desire to have globalized, affordable trade with relative security, the era of nations against nations in unfettered destruction is passing rapidly. Rather, the international and domestic spheres are increasingly reciprocal across borders, especially in each level's ability to inflict nasty surprises on the other through globalization and digitization pathways. In one way or another, a nation's strat-

---

4. Readers interested in other periods of exceptional change are encouraged to read Barbara Tuchman's (1978) discussion of the fourteenth century in her seminal book, *A Distant Mirror*. In so many ways, this discussion is placed so far from our normal reference points that it is exceptionally useful for seeing patterns in human behaviors that are or may be repeating themselves.

egy for cybered conflict and its power to act will have to effectively disrupt and be resilient to any globally located attackers' ease in scale of organization, proximity of attackers, and precision of attack. Without a graduated and institutionally supported strategy of disruption and resilience, shorter-term political crises spilling over from the world's dysfunctional and yet connected areas can suddenly morph into networked and long-term chronic violent threats. Not only can they come as a complete surprise, but every actor anywhere with web access, a few skills, time, and a grudge will pile on via cyberspace to make the nasty surprise worse for the defending nations. In combinatorial cascades of otherwise independent actions, the original parties to the crisis or dispute can find themselves assaulted across all fronts within minutes or hours. Knowledge and collaboration cost time and money in a complex, surprising world, but even more expensive will be the national costs of not having a resilient, systematic response to chronic, violent, gray, and inevitably cybered threats (Berkes, Colding, and Folke 2003).

The fall 2010 public disclosure of a very sophisticated, precisely targeted, and undoubtedly expensively produced worm called Stuxnet, spread only by infected USB thumb drives, demonstrates the new level in the security uncertainties of cybered conflict. Fingerprinting targets in close detail in order to effectively attack them is the stuff of good old-fashioned spying, but delivering the killing blow usually required some form of close proximity to the target in question. This attack on (apparently) specifically Iran's nuclear plants by scattering around the region infected thumb drives, one of which finally floated into the targeted plant, has changed the global perception of the scope and complexity of the national security challenge. Not only did the designers of this malware have the detailed information to create a highly sophisticated self-spreading application whose trigger was exquisitely precise to particular centrifuges, but they also were able to successfully deliver the sleeping saboteur through the ubiquity of digital, unwitting, easily subverted, and globally dispersed cutouts (Sanger 2010).

This new level of a cybered attack with a thumb drive delivery vehicle is only the beginning of state versus state, state versus opposing group, and interstate versus nonstate groups battling to "own" the other's critical systems. Malicious software can be the nonhuman equivalent of designer sleeper sabotage cells, floating around from machine to machine harmlessly until infecting the target whose fingerprints the program seeks. While this method of inflicting harm was always possible from the outset of the rise of pathology on the earlier new World Wide Web, it was usually viewed by hackers as too much trouble, given the existence of easier paths not involving such sophistication, inefficient delivery, and delay or even the potential for failure in delivery. Furthermore, in a world of wide standardization of applications and machines, if one did not have exceptionally precise information about the target's critical systems, one might even harm many similar machines unintentionally and miss the true target completely. The inability to be sure the malware would not do anything until triggered meant, for most early hackers and crackers, too much risk. A great deal of effort could be completely wasted if the wrongly targeted and harmed machine owners fired up a wide array of security responses that both revealed the exploit and nullified its effects before the desired target was reached (Young 2007; Nuwere and Chanoff 2002).

The precision of the Stuxnet worm suggests those early constraints have been overcome, producing a new level in national security uncertainties due to the easy global reach of cybered conflict. Now, if one knows enough very precisely about a cybered target halfway around the world, one can widely scatter a malware that does nothing to any target it rides through unless that target matches exceptionally closely the intended victim (Sanger 2010). With this development, country leaders now may face the possibly crushing weight of a global crowd of spies, criminals, vigilantes, military units, cuckcolded citizens, terrorists, and opportunistic attackers attempting to reach anywhere that cyberspace extends.

With the advent of such sophisticated, tailored malware across largely unfettered global networks, the web's anonymity and ability to inject pathologies inside any nation now threaten a wide range of key elements of modern economies and social contracts not historically at risk. In recent years, leaders of countries have increasingly grown nervous about the massive, rapid, and ubiquitous spread of the web for a variety of reasons. Some fear the influence on the thinking of their citizens, such as China, Burma (Myanmar), and Tunisia. Other leaders fear for the moral weakening of society by pornographers or the loss of political, cultural, or religious control, such as Saudi Arabia and Egypt. Some leaders express fear for everyone's identity and the loss of an individual's assets, or the illegal use of national benefits meant only for citizens, such as Germany and France. Others fear the harm of malware in distorting essential but automated financial systems, the theft of critical competitive business intelligence, and the theft of critical national information, such as the United Kingdom and Australia. Other states fear the active use of the web by hostile organized opponents to steal national security information, impose physical harm on critical infrastructure, and directly endanger the nation and its key functions, such as the United States and Israel.

Stuxnet is the marker noting the beginning of the new cybered conflict age. When it is widely accepted that critical systems can no longer be trusted if they are open to the web beyond the territory of their owning nation, then political leaders begin to demand a way to cut off the threats to their territory. Forcing slack at the interaction edges with other cultures or possible threats by enforcing a border is historically common. Being able to establish sovereign control is one of the hallmarks of a functioning state. This need is true whether the border is enforced in the form of passports for people, customs inspections for goods, or two-way filters for electronic bits. No frontier lasts forever. No freely occupied and used commons extends endlessly where human societies are involved. Sooner or later, good fences are erected to enforce good neighbors, and so it must be with cyberspace.

Today we are seeing the beginnings of the border-making process across the world's nations. From the Chinese intent to create their own, controlled internal internet through the increasingly controlled access to the internet in less democratic states to the rise of internet filters and rules in Western democracies, states are establishing the bounds of their sovereign control in the virtual world in the name of security and economic sustainability. The topology of the internet, like the prairie of the 1800s American Midwest, is about to be changed forever — rationally, conflictually, or collaterally — by the decisions of states individually trying to keep certainty high within their already defined territory.

These emerging state borders, while virtual, are possible technologically with the advances in ubiquitous, uniquely identifying surveillance and sanction technologies. They are arguably desirable for the cumulative zeitgeist and state-based structures of collaborative institutions of international civil global society. These disparate efforts are slowly morphing into the frameworks that will eventually define the international system's topology in the virtual world. As the process emerges from inklings to the self-evident, the implications of pulling cyberspace back into the known world of international relations are profound — an emerging age of cybered conflict in which power rests on two pillars: the ability to disrupt in advance and to be resilient to badlands threats coming in any form, including electronic.

INKLINGS OF THE FUTURE: THE RISE OF THE CYBER COMMAND

Militaries are the traditional keepers of the nation's security, and for those in modern digitizing democracies, the world of cybered conflict is particularly challenging. There is no conceivable "new world architecture" likely to emerge with a stable, prospering globe unless, at the very least, the remaining hegemon—the United States—is able to show relationally and structurally some success against surprising threats (Volgy and Imwalle 2000). The distinction between foreign and domestic is increasingly muddled, and the increasingly unrealistic separation in terms of national security can be used against modern democratic society in ways unanticipated by any theories or experiences. The narrow restriction of military organizational missions in modern states in order to maintain civilian control of military power is rapidly being trumped by the globally linked nature of cyberspace. Yet today no threat—whether jihadist, neo-Nazi, organized crime, rising power, or peer state—will conduct any cold or warm conflict without using cybered means to violate national borders long before and massively during any declared hostilities. Militaries, along with their colleagues in police and intelligence services, must prepare to serve best with a framework beyond the coercion missions that currently largely define their contributions. In institutionalized honest consensus such as the knowledge nexus, military, police, and intelligence services along with private owners of infrastructure need to confer on how to make it simply more costly, risky, or difficult to attack. They need to use comprehensive data sources that protect the privacy of citizens such as the behavior-based privacy scheme presented in chapter 4. Equally critically, they all need to jointly play through their collective data, ideas, capabilities, and cultural blinders in the coauthored game-based simulations integrated into the Atrium organizational model. In short, military forces in a cybered world have a critical role to play in resilience and nonwar disruption operations as society savers as much as they do in the destructive operations of declared conflicts as war fighters.

The adaptation processes of the world's militaries for this age are expressed in particular in the emergence of a new form of national security unit—the "cyber command." Although the unit was first formally established by the United States in 2009, the trend culminating in this institutional marker of the new age actually began decades ago with the popularity of having highly technically advanced armed force capabilities. The reorienting of the world's biggest militaries began arguably and most identifiably in the 1980s with the U.S. military's broad embrace of new, smaller, and electronically networked weapon and communications systems. As the computer expanded broadly into the wider society and the world in the 1990s, such terms as *information warfare* or *network centric warfare* pointed the military zeitgeist in the United States toward an active role in struggles found largely within electronic exchanges. As the rest of the world's nations followed or reacted, the idea of a highly advanced armed force protection for a nation, albeit within the context of physical struggles, became accepted and even desired (Adams 2001). Even tiny Botswana declared an intent to have an electronic military, with no conceivable congruent threat or realistic hope of achieving this aim (Demchak 2000).

With the public admission of vulnerability to Stuxnet and the hordes of attempts like it that are to follow, state leaders find overwhelming their inability to identify a specific actor for sanction and end up focusing on the ability to reach inside the nation with impunity. From the perspective of cultural concerns, the current global internet looks to state leaders like millions of cheap 24/7, unregulated, and ever-shifting pirate radio stations beaming directly into homes with no societal controls on accuracy, harm, predatory behavior, or norms. For those concerned with financial losses, the current web topology seems to encourage millions of muggers, burglars, and bank robbers with seconds-fast reach-in-and-snatch abilities and near instantaneous untraceable escape routes. For those with national security concerns, the wide-open internet seems a massive crowd of strange bedfellows including saboteurs, grudge fighters, spies, vengeful insurgents, opportunistic malicious joyriders, and hostile nation-state competitors. All of these bad actors can today use cyberspace to enter and maneuver relatively easily inside the physical nation to execute harm without ever having to risk a physical entry and exit.

Among national security experts, in official documents (Joint Forces Command 2010), and even on the pages of general interest magazines, it has become common to define the cyberspace as a "domain" of warfare as much as land, sea, and air (Murphy 2010). In the fall of 2010 the United States formally completed the establishment of its national cyber command begun in 2009. The new organization is a purely military joint institution able to employ the resources of subordinate cyber commands in each of its services (Lynn 2010). It is dual-hatted with the U.S. National Intelligence Agency but the first of its kind in that it is explicitly military and a major new institution with a mission to fight for the nation using cybered means. But other nations are already on this path under different names and less explicitly military intentions. Israel has had its unit 8088 for some time, a more secretive organization as much espionage as military, while Russia has its cyber military forces embedded in its radio-electronic (communications and jamming essential) unit (Gates 2009). China has been developing doctrine on "informationized" war for ten years and reputedly has a large number of civilian and military groups working on aspects of fighting in cyberspace (Gompert et al. 2007).

The club of nations iterating to control what cyberspace brings into their nations or what malicious software is passing through their nation is growing slowly formally but rapidly informally under nonmilitary structures. Some nations are instituting national filters of the internet as it passes across their nation, such as Estonia and Sweden. Others are establishing civilian national cyber security institutions with ever-broadening powers, iterating informally to include police and military, such as France and Germany. Others are moving to coalesce civilian and military explicitly at the national political level (the United Kingdom). Most have not yet formally established a cyber command, but the necessary precursors for social acceptance are being laid. Slowly it is becoming assumed that as a part of civil society and functioning political systems, government has a large role to play in protecting the citizens from terrorizing bad actors, nuclear weapons, epidemics, and destructive cybered attacks on them and their critical needs. With this understanding and the demonstration of a functioning cyber command or two, most states will regard having a national cyber command to be as necessary as a border police or an air force.

ADAPTING THE SOCIAL CONTRACT FOR CYBERED UNCERTAINTY

Resilience and disruption are concepts emerging in their own time of upheaval in frameworks and expectations concerning national security and power across an increasingly internetted world. In such periods, scholars and writers usually seek ways to explain the threats and improve the defenses.[5] The concept of a social contract emerged at just such a time — the period of massive change during the 1600–1700s with such thinkers as Hobbes,

---

5. At the time of this writing, *resilience* is the emerging term for the westernized response to globalization and the contagion of chaos from the badlands. The ever eager business community has begun to pick it up over the *warrior* metaphors of the previous decade (B. Walker and Salt 2006).

Rousseau, and Locke. The industrialization of the 1800s produced the concepts of free markets and liberalism with Adam Smith and John Stuart Mills. Post-industrialization has produced first the euphoria in concepts of digital worlds and cyberspace à la William Gibson and the third and fourth waves of Alvin and Heidi Toffler (W. Gibson 1986; Toffler and Toffler 1995). Globalization was early on associated with positive outcomes. Early environmentalism carried within it the concept of remediation and avoidance, all positive actions that would allow the global system to progress positively. It took a while for the dark side of intricate, inextricable globally tight coupling to emerge widely in the later 1990s, and we are still in the transition period. These concepts are still stabilizing as we collectively walk through the various iterations and paths of this emerging set of trends.

And walk through these processes of turbulence we must. The globalization process has made it much easier for formerly localized perceptions of threats to travel via the cyber communication channels and be elaborated and accepted by populations previously uninformed about the threat or the possibility of action. For example, the strategic response to existing notions of legitimate action is information. Globalizing notions of what is legitimate for governments and their citizens to do and to expect are tied up and affected in this worldwide cybered turbulence. Perhaps the exemplar case for the start of this age is the massive number of leaked U.S. government files put out on the internet by the WikiLeaks organization in 2010. The files did not change perceptions too dramatically in places where citizens assume governments lie to them, such as in the struggling states of the badlands. But that it was taken as true by the victim state, the United States, gave others the confidence to try using such releases to force political actions. Thus if the WikiLeaks revelations and their successors are believed to be true, they change what leaders must take into account in diplomacy or public state-citizens relations in a cybered age, accurate or not.

Some national leaders respond by declaring the revelations lies or distortions of real documents. For example, Palestine Liberation Organization (PLO) leaders say that the references to their dealings with Israel in the original WikiLeaks documents or the copycat site the "Palestinian Papers" put forth by Al Jazeera are lies or have been doctored into lies (British Broadcasting Corporation 2011). In principle, the U.S. government could also have chosen to challenge the accuracy of the released WikiLeaks files, but to do so would have meant lying to Americans. Legitimacy expectations matter and are often so embedded in the perceiving population that some responses are simply not acceptable. The government is not legally permitted to lie to the American public in general, although refusing to comment is a common response when one would prefer to lie. That the U.S. leaders refused to call the WikiLeaks material lies gave the released files prima facie validity, changing the global diplomatic and public perception environment for the United States immediately. Now, irrespective of how accurate or misleading the material from the leaked files is, the U.S. government has to have a response, lest the fragments of information coalesce in unexpected ways threatening U.S. security (Drezner 2010).[6]

Turbulence in the emerging cybered world will come from more than mass releases of actual or fabricated formerly secret government documents. Indeed, the rise of social media across the exceptionally large and economically draining "youth bulge" of the Middle East has enabled the flow of information to be used for coordination as much, if not more, than it was used in the mobilization of the uncommitted masses. That practical use is far from the anarchic and anti-organization vision of the web held by the WikiLeaks organization's founder and members. Rather, in the spark and spread of the uprisings ongoing as this is written, one can see the physical manifestation of how the final driver is met in individuals' own legitimacy-need-confidence equation, and then masses of independent individuals suddenly act in ways to disrupt existing socio-technical environments. The unemployed Arab youth's strongest driver to act is universally accepted to be the need for adequate employment. Legitimacy to act against the standing social system is a close second, especially in secular states where no religious authorities reinforce government actions with religious edicts. In this region, it is more legitimate to rise up against humans than the wishes of God. It is not by accident that the current uprisings have progressed furthest in the states with either a secular state, such as Egypt or Tunisia, or at least an elite that views itself as modern and secular, as in Bahrain.

But it has been the final driver of a decision to act, confidence, that has been so far particularly enabled in ways only a cybered age could provide — that is, the ability to use scale, proximity, and precision advantages across a variety of

---

6. Indeed, one could argue the most damaging effect of WikiLeaks will be the clampdown inside the U.S. government stifling critical knowledge sharing central to accommodating the coming surprises of the cybered age (Drezner 2010).

communication mechanisms. In Egypt, the microblog web service Twitter enabled the organization of thousands of protesters directed to one city square in Cairo and also enabled repetitious reiterations of an adherence to no violence, forcing any questions of legitimacy onto the nature of the security force actions. The same mechanisms allowed people in the square to communicate outside of Cairo and, by checking on events, also be able to calibrate their confidence in how well the protests were succeeding. Now, after the resignation of President Mubarak as demanded by the protesters, student organizers are sharing an equally critical information flow that sustained their confidence: members serving in the Egyptian military who assured the protesters using the same cyber means that the Egyptian Army had no orders or intentions to fire on the protesters (Levinson, Coker, and El-Ghobashy 2011).

With confidence as the final critical motivator necessary for the uprisings in Egypt and elsewhere in 2011, a ubiquitous near real-time news presence across cybered outlets from cell phones to internet cafés showed others how students could act to overthrow governments. Until the Egyptian students rose peacefully and used cybered organizing to keep the crowds coming and under control, others in other nations could see no way to act on their already strong legitimacy and need motivations to act against corrupt governments. The images of success elsewhere along with the clear indications of how it might be done does help push the sum of legitimacy, need, and confidence assessments over the threshold and motivate action.

Confidence can be dampened as well as energized if experience differs locally or via social media. The social media as confidence-building mechanisms in support of uprisings have operated less well in more strongly religious or blatantly brutally repressive nations such as Iran or Libya under Ghadafy. When religious leaders are a part of the repressive hierarchy, they are able to declare the students to be against the holy orders and turn both government agencies and more conservative parts of the population against those who act in uprisings (Sageman 2004). When the Libyan leader Ghadafy brutally repressed protesters in March 2011 in the Libyan capital of Tripoli, only those in outlying cities continued to come out into the streets. In 2011 Iranian young people also tried to emulate the success of peaceful protesters elsewhere in more secular, less brutal nations, but their religious leaders allied with the brutal elements of the government authorized the declaration of protest leaders as possible apostates who can be arrested and possibly killed (Wolin 2011).

At the end of the day, the effects of WikiLeaks-like transparency websites and the cascade of attempted peaceful societal uprisings instigated by cyber-savvy young Tunisians and the largely secular middle-class Egyptian students are the kinds of surprises soon to be seen as normal in a complex, cybered world. Buoyed on its cybered underpinning, globalization seeps about changing flows and outcomes both in the international system and in the homelands of nations. In the emerging intertwined globe, information flows are built, expanded, and built up some more on networks resting on mostly unmonitored long-distance undersea cables, creating a worldwide dynamic mesh, all maintained by thousands of organizations, redirected by thousands of others, and used to their own purposes by millions of actors. Masses of stolen files will be leaked, sold, or used to gain economic advance by displacing local research and development costs. Outbreaks of terrorist manipulations and operational coordination, widely fragmented mainstream and fringe activism, and a full range of cybered attack attempts at all skill levels will continue to emerge all over the globe, sometimes simultaneously. In this huge globally complex but critically connected socio-technical world system, how any nation frames, designs, and implements its national security resilience strategy will be critical to its likely success in disrupting attacks and enduring those surprises that inevitably will succeed in getting through anyway. Being effective at both is the hallmark of national cyber power in the emerging cybered conflict age.

Two large intensely competitive city-states emblematic of the new cybered conflict age, the United States and China, are today each engaged in a natural experiment revealing how being effective at both disruption and resilience underpins cyber power. Traditional nation-state power rests generally on economic robustness, societal dynamism and education, military capacities, and international recognition of those advantages. Today all of these elements are singularly influenced by cyberspace. Especially affected is the ability to influence national and international outcomes by acquiring scarce knowledge available overtly or covertly through cyberspace's myriad of connections. In this area, the responses of the United States and China to cybered knowledge-related threats differ markedly.

The United States is a geographically large city-state with a huge albeit increasingly stratified economy, a hands-off national planning tradition, an open dynamic internetted society, a globally powerful military, and one-third the population of its closest competitor. It has long assumed that its own free-wheeling educational institutions will develop innovations for its entrepreneurs to embed in profitable products faster than any competitor globally can match. Unfortunately all this innovation value creation is sustained with and shared across cyber networks that are little understood by most of its population. The American innovation engine is also the only form of industrial planning in the United States and has been brokered through national security investments into universities and large contract research programs since World War II. For some time, the engine of sustaining economic activity in the United States has been left vulnerable to dedicated knowledge theft from competitors able to use the nation's general openness. The nation's ad hoc myriad of educational systems and the basic computer system designs were never constructed with the reality of serious socio-technical knowledge competition in mind.

The United States as a city-state owes its economic status largely to lucky timing so far, a fact which is yet to be politically recognized as no longer a reliable advantage in a globally cybered world. Because it was first in developing largescale computer systems, the United States has benefited for twenty years as first mover even though its systems were poorly designed to protect the knowledge invested in their development and their use. Thus these systems are both easily reverse-engineered for low-cost export by companies not having to pay for the research and easily hacked by bad actors seeking the knowledge to make money or wreak havoc on the cheap (Rogin 2007). Furthermore, the United States has no nationally directed effort to educate a population able to innovate in socio-technical terms through the thefts or intrusions. Rather, the relative educational level of U.S. youth in terms of knowledge acquired is dropping dramatically in science and technology (Ramirez 2008). For a demographically inferior nation compared to its major competitor, these are systemic indicators of losing the knowledge acquisition and innovative use competition over the longer term. The United States' natural experiment in laissez faire responses to assuring sufficient national knowledge capital in a surprising cybered world is today more likely to result in a slow, obscured, and fundamental internal decline in cybered national capacity. Especially at risk is national resilience that requires extensive prior development of social and technical knowledge of systems in order to improvise and innovate when surprises happen (Comfort, Boin, and Demchak 2010).

The competitor, China, is a geographically smaller but demographically huge city-state with an enormously expanding economy now second to the United States globally. It is geographically smaller than the United States but must contend with the expectations of the poorer rural part of its population, which is equal in size to the entire U.S. population. As a centrally guided nation with a long-term and systemic planning tradition, China has a much less powerful military and yet increasingly globally large financial leverage. Most important to this discussion, recognizing the power of knowledge acquisition for international power, the Chinese leadership has spent the past ten years creating its own natural experiment. It has been building a semiclosed and manipulated Chinese section of the global internet for its society as well as the educational bases for a large population of individuals to become skilled in computerized socio-technical systems. In the late 1990s, Chinese leaders recognized what national comparative advantages could be obtained through the open doors of the global cyberspace substrate. In particular, the access to the knowledge banks of the more-advanced westernized world offered a way to mitigate the internal problems China would face if it did not rapidly advance its economy and to counter the military ability of the United States to hinder Chinese actions internationally (Thomas 2004). In this traditionally inwardly focused nation, the Chinese leaders unleashed the brighter portion of their already larger population to use cyberspace in every internationally legal or illegal manner that could advance Chinese modernization.

Over the past ten years, these activities from both government and semigovernmental groups have ranged widely. China has joined organizations to obtain critical information or to push the interests of an organization such as the ITU (International Telecommunication Union) away from international rules to stem the Chinese knowledge acquisition onslaught. The government has encouraged with financial, regulatory, and social supports the behaviors of its semiprivate business community in purchasing or subcontracting to produce products that are then reverse-engineered to save research and development costs. On massive scales unprecedented and largely unexpected in cyberspace, actors inside or closely associated with the government have further enabled Chinese technological leaps forward by simply widely stealing the R&D information right off the computers of the developing and owning enterprise or the networks of other nations' government agencies. Often former Chinese military firms that are relabeled as purely commercial enterprises, such as Huawei, use the reverse-engineered or stolen R&D knowledge to create products sold aggressively for half price to unaware buyers, undercutting every market for the original non-Chinese owner of that intellectual property who paid for the expensive research.

A good example of the Chinese approach to gaining knowledge advantage in a cybered world is the massive success of the Huawei firm in copying the globally dominant Cisco computer network router, which was then purchased by British Telecom. The Huawei router is now apparently located through about half the British Telecom system, making it difficult to remove.[7] Its widespread use by British and other clients, including enterprises, citizens, and government agencies, offers potentially a myriad of access points to other sources of desired knowledge. Either by embedding backdoors to computer systems in the manufacturing of the routers or by using the knowledge of their distribution and internal connection requirements, the Chinese designers of this copied router enable a wide variety of difficult-to-find new networked backdoors into user networks. These networks sought only to save money, but now they and the societal exchanges that depend on them are vulnerable in ways not likely with the original Cisco routers. And many more knowledge-based innovations in theft and then alteration of products are certainly in the offing as a large Chinese youth population educated in the cybered age comes into a world in which such activities are not only personally advantageous but are also encouraged as patriotic activities for the modernization of the state (U.S. Office of the Secretary of Defense 2010).

The future trends in cybered conflict rest on how each of these two major players in the international cybered world pursue their competition going forward. The indicators will be found in how and to what extent each emphasizes disruption and resilience. For this competition, the Chinese actions suggest that in cyberspace, the attack equation threshold has been well passed. Chinese-instigated cyber attacks are considered defensively legitimate, critical to counter economic imbalance in resources for the life of the nation, and clearly doable with proper socio-technical education as shown by experience. As of today, the United States has great difficulty disrupting the sheer volume of attacks. The closed internet of the Chinese system makes it difficult to use countervailing knowledge, "lateral leverage," as a strategic tool to dissuade the Chinese actors across a large, insular population widely convinced that such uses are legitimate. Disrupting attacks by offering capital is less useful because the United States cannot offer the Chinese attackers more capital than they are already obtaining today using these attacks. The Chinese economy is clearly advancing at the expense of the resource stream of the United States, given the unprecedented trade deficit.

7. Personal observation by senior British cybersecurity expert, spring 2010.

It is not surprising, then, that the United States pursues disruption by cybered coercion, using a small, very adept population focused on frustrating attack successes and operated through its new, legally mandated national CyberCommand. For the United States, however, disruption is harder than it might be for Chinese leaders able to use their more-limited digitization and strong control of three main internet gateways to control masses of attacks. The new U.S. agency is not mandated to defend the whole of the nation, just its military networks. The confidence of these attackers is built on aspects of the national cybered system that the U.S. government does not centrally influence as the Chinese leadership can — that is, the openness of the global internet as a physically easy set of pathways for knowledge extraction and misrepresentation of reality (Halliday 2010). The current situation leaves those attempting defense in cyberspace engaged in what is sometimes colloquially referred to as a "whack a mole" operation similar to the arcade game of hitting targets that pop up anywhere. With so many ways to enter the nation, if an attack is disrupted successfully along one exploit path, the attacker can easily regain confidence simply by switching targets or access points (Markoff, Sanger, and Shanker 2010). The current U.S. governmental response aims to disrupt, in advance if possible, any attacks on either military or government agencies but cannot easily address the surprises, vulnerabilities, or harm that affect the wider national cyberspace outside these official systems.

Resilience as the second half of a security resilience strategy is hampered in both nations, but to a lesser extent in China. The Chinese infrastructure is at an earlier stage in the integration of massively complex and often ad hoc cyber systems underpinning its society; fewer of its essential processes depend on the internet or computerized systems. To the extent possible its designs have had security embedded in their architectures from the outset for social control purposes but also to make U.S. incursions less easy. These efforts include redesigning basic computer operating systems not shared with the United States and so raising the difficulty of knowing enough to attack successfully from outside China (Krekel 2009). For the United States, resilience is not only a major physical challenge; it also poses cognitive, political, and legal challenges not shared by its centrally controlled peer competitor, China. The massive volume of connections to the United States' deeply interdependent critical societal and commercial systems, their poor security design, and the relative technical ignorance of the smaller U.S. population all hamper resilience when an accident or attack disables key systems (Mills 2010). Equally difficult, however, is the laissez-faire attitude to largescale architectures, including economic, business, and social networking systems. Linking them together as needed with limited to no central oversight or review is hallowed as a measure of the freedom of the society. Complex systems being linked and linked again are still commonly cognitively envisioned as something installed in isolation, equivalent to a lone farm on a prairie somewhere that can bring only benefit. In their designs and endless extensions, the wider societal effects are rarely considered; new systems are viewed as though they harm none if they operate as planned or even if they catastrophically fail (Brenner 2010). This normatively positive view of all technical mechanisms, especially those associated with cyberspace, has made designing or redesigning resilience into society as a matter of overriding national policy extraordinarily difficult for the United States in ways not faced by its chief competitor.

In terms of cyber power's disruption and resilience capacities, the asymmetries are not trending in favor of the United States over the medium and longer term. The United States and China are currently the most influential national-level players of the emerging cybered conflict age. How these two leading states, already possibly engaged in cybered conflict, reciprocally iterate in designing their strategic responses will largely influence the future trends of harmony or tension in cyberspace. If the United States remains fixed on its laissez-faire attitude toward nationally integrated systems, nearly random in its financial and political support for socio-technical skill education, systemically poor in catching up to and rapidly remediating or neutralizing the basic design flaws in security of the basic computers and their networks, and uncoordinated in its massively increasing dependence on insecure, widely spread networks, it will lose its cyber power capacity over time to do anything but raid Chinese targets occasionally in retaliation.

For the United States, disruption and resilience are critical capacities to vigorously develop for the emerging age, and the great challenges the nation faces. The national zeitgeist is individualistic and traditionally more comfortable focusing federally on military shortcomings in systems and leaving all other interconnected systems to the wishes of their owners and clients. When a major trend leader tries to maintain cyber power parity primarily based on military disruption skills, however well skilled its cyber command, it neglects the resilience part of cyber power. Furthermore, so many attacks will still succeed that such a choice strongly encourages tense relations between the two major states. Hostile cybered relations can rather easily move from contained networked spying wars to larger cybered conflicts if the military power held by one nation is perceived to be itself undermined through cyberspace activities of the other.

Furthermore, military capabilities in a widely connected cybered world rest as much on the ability of the wider society to withstand attacks as they do on that ability in the military itself. When applications can ferret through terabytes of data in very short time to obtain and use information destructive to a competitor business's or state's advantage, any open port that eventually leads to nationally critical systems becomes a resilience issue for the military as well. When "security by obscurity" no longer works as a way to avoid being found and attacked anywhere in the society, resilience becomes more critical to relative cyber power of the nation well beyond its military's disruption capacity. For the United States, it will be critically important to federally orchestrate the necessary resilience aspect of national cyber power because attackers will not observe the federal-state relationship, civil-military authorities, or foreign-domestic agency distinctions save to exploit jurisdictional weaknesses. The nation will need, at a minimum, to have cooperative and timely development, enforcement, and dynamic adaptation of national knowledge, mechanisms, and standards ensuring redundancy, slack, and trial-and-error learning across all aspects of economically and societally critical, largescale systems. The necessary knowledge, collective sense-making, and timely active action responses to surprise must be developed even if these critical systems are corporately owned and run. For the United States, avoiding a slow attrition of its cyber power will mean recognizing the need to face the scale, speed, and interconnectedness of the emerging world. It will mean realizing the country is no longer a loosely populated, largely autarkic collection of ruggedly self-sustaining frontier states able to leave largely to chance its own collective existence in splendid and exceptional isolation far from what happens in the rest of the world. The United States is now fully a deeply internally interconnected large complex socio-technical system embedded for its quality of life in an even larger, more complex, turbulent, and dynamically surprising global socio-technical system. National responses will need to be much beyond simply securing the borders and hoping to reach a technological breakthrough before the main competitor does. Rising worldwide complexity in security challenges requires a systemic strategy of security resilience to counter accidental or imposed surprise, and national power will rest on successfully pursuing such a strategy as the cybered conflict age unfolds.

To further the development of such a national strategy for cybered conflict and its surprises, this book makes varying contributions to interested and relevant communities. For international relations theorists, this work is intended to help them to use their otherwise well-founded insights in complementing each other's contributions; it is essential to match complex threats to the international system with resilient understandings and responses. For IR scholars in particular, this work is intended to show them how to reach into the domestic realms and draw from or apply their knowledge to these formerly lower-level, often more domestic forums, a task that is essential to make concrete contributions to security emerging complexly across and from all levels of the widely cybered international system. For resilience, human security, or global sustainability scholars, this book is designed to draw their already strong sense of the complexity of things into contemplation of the ugly realities faced by those who must occasionally choose destruction, but who are more likely to only have disruption as an option. Finally, for practitioners, it is a book of possibilities to be considered and of actionable ideas to be developed in a world where wars will involve disruption, not dominance, and security requires deep resilience when any actor connected to the globalized and cybered world could conceivably start a cascade of nasty surprises from inside or outside the nation.

In the words of a seminal thinker in the field of international security speaking on knowledge and the changing threats facing nations: "This shift has demanded a greater understanding of local history, culture, and socioeconomic conditions. . . . Academics have by and large adapted well in developing this new agenda. Their difficulty has been in convincing colleagues and government of its importance, given the absence of the overriding strategic imperatives of the Cold War" (Freedman 1998). While several seminal American scholars such as Robert Jervis and Joseph Nye understand the interconnectedness of the global system and its inherently surprising cognitive, strategic, and institutional challenges, the wider community of international relations scholars and their practitioner peers in the governments of the westernized world have proven slow to grasp the essential change in the world due to the rise of the web and the emergence of the cybered conflict age (Jervis 1997; Nye 2011). My goal for this book has been to make clear the interconnections of basic largescale human systems security in the emerging age while offering a method of achieving more adept resilience and long-term relative global civility, preferably both in good measure. Welcome to the cybered conflict age.

BIBLIOGRAPHY

Achen, C. H. 2005. "Let's Put Garbage-Can Regressions and Garbage-Can Probits Where They Belong." *Conflict Management and Peace Science* 22 (4): 327–39.

Adams, J. 1998. *The Next World War: Computers Are the Weapons and the Front Line Is Everywhere*. New York: Simon and Schuster.

——. 2001. "Virtual Defense." *Foreign Affairs* 80 (3): 98–112.

Adams, J., and V. J. Roscigno. 2005. "White Supremacists, Oppositional Culture and the World Wide Web." *Social Forces* 84:759.

Adcock, F. E. 1957. *The Greek and Macedonian Art of War*. Berkeley: University of California Press.

Adelman, J., and S. Aron. 1999. "From Borderlands to Borders: Empires, Nation-States, and the Peoples in between in North American History." *American Historical Review* 104 (3): 814–41.

Adler, L. K., and T. G. Paterson. 1970. "Red Fascism: The Merger of Nazi Germany and Soviet Russia in the American Image of Totalitarianism, 1930's–1950's." *American Historical Review* 75 (4): 1046–64.

Aiello, M. 2007. "Social Engineering." In *Cyber Warfare and Cyber Terrorism*, ed. L. J. Janczewski and A. M. Colarik. New York: IGI Global.

Allen, P. D. 2007. *Information Operations Planning*. Norwood, Mass.: Artech House.

Allen, P. D., and C. Demchak. 2003. "The Palestinian-Israeli Cyberwar." *Military Review* 83 (2): 52–59.

Allison, G. T. 1999. *Essence of Decision: Explaining the Cuban Missile Crisis*. New York: Longman.

Al-Rasheed, M. 2007. "Saudi Arabia Post 9/11: History, Religion and Security." *Middle Eastern Studies* 43 (1): 153–60.

Anderson, D. L. 2006. "SHAFR Presidential Address: One Vietnam War Should Be Enough and Other Reflections on Diplomatic History and the Making of Foreign Policy." *Diplomatic History* 30 (1): 1–21.

Appy, C. G. 2000. *Cold War Constructions: The Political Culture of United States Imperialism, 1945–1966*. Amherst: University of Massachusetts Press.

Armstrong, D. 1999. "Making Absences Present: The Contribution of WR Bion to Understanding Unconscious Social Phenomena." In *Group Relations, Management, and Organizations*, ed. R. French and R. Vince. Oxford: Oxford University Press.

Art, R. J. 1998–99. "Geopolitics Updated: The Strategy of Selective Engagement." *International Security* 23 (3): 79–113.

Ascher, W. 1986. "The Moralism of Attitudes Supporting Intergroup Violence." *Political Psychology* 7 (3): 403–25.

Ashcroft, A. C. 2001. "As Britain Returns to an Expeditionary Strategy, Do We Have Anything to Learn from the Victorians?" *Defence Studies* 1 (1): 75–98.

Associated Press Wire Service. 2006. "'10-4': Police Radio Codes 'Over and Out.'" *Newsmax* online, November 18. http://archive.newsmax.com/archives/articles/2006/11/18/84251.shtml?s=us.

———. 2007. "Europe Surveys Deadly Billion-Dollar Storm: 47 Died, More Than Two Million Lost Power; Germany's Losses Are Huge." msnbc.com., January 19. http://www.msnbc.msn.com/id/16687660/.

Avant, D. D. 2005. *The Market for Force: The Consequences of Privatizing Security.* Cambridge: Cambridge University Press.

Awan, A. N. 2007. "Radicalization on the Internet?" *RUSI Journal* 152 (3): 76–81.

Balck, H. 1979. "Translations of Taped Conversations with General Hermann Balck." In *Battelle Tactical Technology Center.* Columbus, Ohio: Battelle Battle Lab, U.S. Army.

Ballard, M. 2010. "UN Rejects International Cybercrime Treaty." *Computer Weekly,* April 20.

Barkan, S. E., and L. L. Snowden. 2008. *Collective Violence.* 2nd ed. Boston: Allyn and Bacon.

Barker, G. T. 2005. *Dying to Be Men: Youth, Masculinity and Social Exclusion.* London: Routledge.

Baron, H. 1953. "A Struggle for Liberty in the Renaissance: Florence, Venice, and Milan in the Early Quattrocento." *American Historical Review* 58 (3): 544–70.

Bar-Yam, Y. 2003. *Dynamics of Complex Systems.* Boulder, Colo.: Westview Press.

Bateman, S., J. Ho, and M. Mathai. 2007. "Shipping Patterns in the Malacca and Singapore Straits: An Assessment of the Risks to Different Types of Vessel." *Contemporary Southeast Asia* 29 (2): 309.

Bates, D. 1979. *The Abyssinian Difficulty: The Emperor Theodorus and the Magdala Campaign, 1867–68* Oxford: Oxford University Press.

Beauchamp, K. 2001. *History of Telegraphy.* London: Institution of Electrical Engineers.

Becker, M. B. 1976. "Changing Patterns of Violence and Justice in Fourteenth- and Fifteenth-Century Florence." *Comparative Studies in Society and History* 18 (3): 281–96.

Beckett, I. F. W. 2001. *Modern Insurgencies and Counter-Insurgencies: Guerrillas and Their Opponents since 1750.* London: Routledge.

———. 2003. *The Victorians at War.* London: Hambledon Continuum.

Benford, R. D. 1997. "An Insider's Critique of the Social Movement Framing Perspective: Social Movements." *Sociological Inquiry* 67 (4): 409–30.

Benjamin, D., and S. Simon. 2006. *The Next Attack: The Failure of the War on Terror and a Strategy for Getting It Right*. New York: Owl Books.

Bergen, P. L. 2001. *Holy War, Inc.: Inside the Secret World of Osama Bin Laden*. New York: Simon and Schuster.

Berger, J., C. L. Ridgeway, M. H. Fisek, and R. Z. Norman. 1998. "The Legitimation and Delegitimation of Power and Prestige Orders." *American Sociological Review* 63 (3): 379–405.

Berkeley, B. 2006. "Bloggers vs. Mullahs: How the Internet Roils Iran." *World Policy Journal* 23 (1): 71.

Berkes, F., J. Colding, and C. Folke, eds. 2003. *Navigating Social-Ecological Systems: Building Resilience for Complexity and Change*. Cambridge: Cambridge University Press.

Berkowitz, P. 2004. "Politicizing Reason." *Policy Review* no. 127 (October): 89–96.

Berman, E., J. N. Shapiro, and J. Felter. 2008. "Can Hearts and Minds Be Bought? The Economics of Counterinsurgency in Iraq." In *NBER Working Paper*. Carlisle, Pa.: U.S. Army War College.

Betts, R. K. 2007. "A Disciplined Defense: How to Regain Strategic Solvency." *Foreign Affairs* 86 (6): 67–75.

Bhagyavati, B. 2007. "Social Engineering." In *Cyber Warfare and Cyber Terrorism*, ed. L. J. Janczewski and A. M. Colarik. New York: Information Science Reference. 181–91.

Billings, R. S., T. W. Milburn, and M. L. Schaalman. 1980. "A Model of Crisis Perception: A Theoretical and Empirical Analysis." *Administrative Science Quarterly* 25 (2): 300–316.

Billon, P. L. 2005. "Corruption, Reconstruction and Oil Governance in Iraq." *Third World Quarterly* 26 (4): 685–703.

bin Laden, O. 1998–2001. "Captured Letter to Mullah Mohammed Omar from bin Laden (translated 2002)." In *CTC's Harmony Document Database*, ed. Combating Terrorism Center. West Point, N.Y.: United States Military Academy, U.S. Army.

Bird, N. E. 2007. "Vietnam: Lessons for Intelligence in Wartime." *International Journal of Intelligence and CounterIntelligence* 20 (2): 317–26.

Blatter, J., and T. Blume. 2008. "In Search of Co-variance, Causal Mechanisms or Congruence? Towards a Plural Understanding of Case Studies." *Swiss Political Science Review* 14 (2):315–56.

Bloom, M. 2005. *Dying To Kill: The Allure of Suicide Terror*. New York: Columbia University Press.

Boer, A. M., and V. M. Hudson. 2004. "The Security Threat of Asia's Sex Ratios." *SAIS Review* 24 (2): 27–43.

Boin, A., E. J. Stern, P. T. Hart, and B. Sundelius. 2005. *The Politics of Crisis Management: Public Leadership under Pressure*. Cambridge: Cambridge University Press.

Boni, B. 2001. "Cyber-terrorists and Counter Spies." *Network Security* 2001 (12): 17–18.

Boot, M. 2002. *The Savage Wars of Peace: Small Wars and the Rise of American Power*. New York: Basic Books.

Booth, K. 1991. "Security in Anarchy: Utopian Realism in Theory and Practice." *International Affairs (Royal Institute of International Affairs 1944–)* 67 (3): 527–45.

Borders, M., D. Bryan, and M. Mauve. 2001. "Experimental Politics: Ways of Virtual Worldmaking." In *Cognitive Technology: Instruments of Mind*, ed. M. Beynon, C. L. Nehaniv, and K. Dautenhahn. Proceedings of 4th international conference; lecture notes in artificial intelligence. Berlin: Springer-Verlag. 432–42.

Borland, J., and L. Bowman. 2002. "Politics: Weighing Security against Liberties (E-Terrorism Special Report)." CNET News.com, 26 August. http://news.cnet.com/2009-1001-954565.html.

Bowen, G. L. 1983. "U.S. Foreign Policy toward Radical Change: Covert Operations in Guatemala, 1950–1954." *Latin American Perspectives* 10 (1): 88–102.

Boyle, K. 2003. "The Price of Peace: Vietnam, the Pound, and the Crisis of the American Empire." *Diplomatic History* 27 (1): 37–72.

Brenner, J. F. 2010. "Why Isn't Cyberspace More Secure?" *Communications of the ACM* 53 (11): 33–35.

British Broadcasting Corporation. 2007a. "Brown Apologises for Records Loss." BBC News, November 27. http://news.bbc.co.uk/2/hi/7104945.stm.

———. 2007b. "Estonia Hit by 'Moscow Cyber War.'" BBC News, May 17. http://news.bbc.co.uk/2/hi/europe/6665145.stm.

———. 2011. "Palestinians Attack al-Jazeera 'Distorted' Talks Leaks." BBC News, January 24.

Broadhurst, R. 2006. "Developments in the Global Law Enforcement of Cyber-crime." *Policing: An International Journal of Police Strategies and Management* 29 (3): 408–33.

Brown, C. L., and P. D. Morgan. 2006. *Arming Slaves: From Classical Times to the Modern Age*. New Haven, Conn.: Yale University Press.

Browning, O. 2001. *The Age of the Condottieri: A Short History of Medieval Italy From 1409–1530*. New York: Adamant Media. (Orig. pub. 1895.)

Bruner, J. S., and C. C. Goodman. 1947. "Value and Need as Organizing Factors in Perception." *Journal of Abnormal Psychology* 42 (1): 33–44.

Buchan, N., and R. Croson. 2004. "The Boundaries of Trust: Own and Others' Actions in the U.S. and China." *Journal of Economic Behavior and Organization* 55 (4): 485–504.

Burch, J. 2007. "A Domestic Intelligence Agency for the United States? A Comparative Analysis of Domestic Intelligence Agencies and Their Implications for Homeland Security." *Homeland Security Affairs* 3 (2).

Burghardt, S. 1982. *The Other Side of Organizing: Resolving the Personal Dilemmas and Political Demands of Daily Practice*. Cambridge, Mass.: Schenkman.

Burgoon, J., and J. Nunamaker. 2004. "Toward Computer-Aided Support for the Detection of Deception." *Group Decision and Negotiation* 13 (1): 1–4.

Burnham, J. 1947. *The Struggle for the World*. London: J. Cape.

Buzan, B. 2001. "The English School: An Underexploited Resource in IR." *Review of International Studies* 27 (3): 471–88.

Buzzanco, B. 1986. "The American Military's Rationale against the Vietnam War." *Political Science Quarterly* 101 (4): 559–76.

Byman, D. L., and M. C. Waxman. 2000. "Kosovo and the Great Air Power Debate." *International Security* 24 (4): 5–38.

Caferro, W. 1996. "Italy and the Companies of Adventure in the Fourteenth Century." *Historian* 58 (4): 795–810.

Calhoun, C. 1989. "Classical Social Theory and the French Revolution of 1848." *Sociological Theory* 7 (2): 210–25.

Campbell, W. E. (Gary). 2002. "Getting There Was the Challenge! The Red River Expedition of 1870." *Canadian Army Doctrine and Training Bulletin* 5 (1): 58–64.

Carey-Smith, M., and L. May. 2006. "The Impact of Information Security Technologies upon Society." Paper presented at Social Change in the 21st Century Conference 2006, Carseldine, Brisbane, Australia, October 27, 2006.

Carley, K. M. 2002. "Computational Organizational Science and Organizational Engineering." *Simulation Modelling Practice and Theory* 10 (5–7): 253–69.

——. 2004. "Estimating Vulnerabilities in Large Covert Networks Using Multi-Level Data." Proceedings of the 2004 International Symposium on Command and Control Research and Technology.

Carragee, K. M. 2004. "The Neglect of Power in Recent Framing Research." *Journal of Communication* 54 (2): 214–33.

Cartledge, P. 2003. *The Spartans: The World of the Warrior-Heroes of Ancient Greece, from Utopia to Crisis and Collapse*. Woodstock, N.Y.: Overlook Press.

Castells, M. 1997. *The Power of Identity*. Information Age: Economy, Society and Culture, vol. 2. Cambridge, Mass.: Blackwell.

——. 1998. *The Rise of the Network Society*. Information Age: Economy, Society, and Culture, vol. 1. Cambridge, Mass.: Blackwell.

Casti, J. L. 1994. *Complexification: Explaining a Paradoxical World through the Science of Surprise*. New York: Abacus.

Caulk, R. A. 1972. "Firearms and Princely Power in Ethiopia in the Nineteenth Century." *Journal of African History* 13 (4): 609–30.

Center for Advanced Transportation Technology Laboratory. 2008. "CATT Lab's Three-Dimensional, Multi-Player Computer Gaming Simulation Technology." CATT Lab,

University of Maryland Intelligent Transportation System. http://www.cattlab.umd
.edu/.

Chambers, D. S. 2006. *Popes, Cardinals and War: The Military Church in Renaissance and Early Modern Europe*. London: I. B. Tauris.

Chandra, S., and A. W. Foster. 2005. "The Revolution of Rising Expectations," Relative Deprivation, and the Urban Social Disorders of the 1960s Evidence from State-Level Data." *Social Science History* 29 (2): 299–332.

Chen, H., F. Y. Wang, and D. Zeng. 2004. "Intelligence and Security Informatics for Homeland Security: Information, Communication, and Transportation." *IEEE Transactions on Intelligent Transportation Systems* 5 (4): 329–41.

Chua, B. H. 1997. *Communitarian Ideology and Democracy in Singapore*. London: Routledge.

Cialdini, R. B. 2001. "Harnessing the Science of Persuasion." *Harvard Business Review* 79 (9): 72–81.

Clarke, R. A., and R. Knake. 2010. *Cyber War: The Next Threat to National Security and What to Do about It*. New York: Ecco Books.

CNN Staff. 2010. "Sherrod: Andrew Breitbart Is 'a Liar.'" CNN online, July 22. http:// articles.cnn.com.

Cohen, C. 2007. *A Perilous Course: U.S. Strategy and Assistance to Pakistan*. Washington, D.C.: Center for Strategic and International Studies.

Cohen, E. A. 2004. "History and the Hyperpower." *Foreign Affairs* 83 (4): 49–63.

Cohen, E. E. 1992. *Athenian Economy and Society: A Banking Perspective*. Princeton, N.J.: Princeton University Press.

Cohn, S. K. 1999. *Creating the Florentine State: Peasants and Rebellion, 1348–1434*. Cambridge: Cambridge University Press.

Comfort, L., A. Boin, and C. Demchak, eds. 2010. *Designing Resilience: Preparing for Extreme Events*. Pittsburgh: University of Pittsburgh Press.

Connor, W. R. 1988. "Early Greek Land Warfare as Symbolic Expression." *Past and Present* (119): 3–29.

——. 1992. *The New Politicians of Fifth-Century Athens*. Indianapolis: Hackett.

Constantin, L. 2011. "Former TSA Worker Jailed for Attempted Computer Sabotage." *Softpedia Security News* online, January 12. http:// news.softpedia.com/.

Copeland, D. C. 2001. *The Origins of Major War*. Ithaca, N.Y.: Cornell University Press.

——. 2003. "A Realist Critique of the English School." *Review of International Studies* 29 (03): 427–41.

Correia, A. M. R., and M. de Castro Neto. 2002. "The Role of Eprint Archives in the Access to, and Dissemination of, Scientific Grey Literature: LIZA—A Case Study by the National Library of Portugal." *Journal of Information Science* 28 (3): 231.

Cremonini, M., and D. Nizovtsev. 2006. "Understanding and Influencing Attackers' Decisions: Implications for Security Investment Strategies." Topeka, Kan.:

Washburn University School of Business. http://weis2006.econinfosec.org/docs/ 3.pdf.

Croft, S. 2006. *Culture, Crisis and America's War on Terror*. Cambridge: Cambridge University Press.

Cronin, A. K. 2002. "Behind the Curve: Globalization and International Terrorism." *International Security* 27 (3): 30–58.

Cross, T. 2006. "Academic Freedom and the Hacker Ethic." *Communications of the ACM* 49 (6): 37–40.

Crovitz, G. 2008. "Internet Attacks Are a Real and Growing Problem." *Wall Street Journal* online, December 15. http://online.wsj.com/article/SB122930102219005425.html.

Cullather, N. 1999. *Secret History: The CIA's Classified Account of Its Operations in Guatemala, 1952–1954*. Stanford, Calif.: Stanford University Press.

Cunha, B. A. 2004. "The Cause of the Plague of Athens: Plague, Typhoid, Typhus, Smallpox, or Measles?" *Infectious Disease Clinics of North America* 18 (1): 29–43.

Cunningham, K., and R. R. Tomes. 2004. "Space-Time Orientations and Contemporary Political-Military Thought." *Armed Forces and Society* 31 (1): 119–40.

Curran, K., K. Concannon, and S. McKeever. 2007. "Cyber Terrorism Attacks." In *Cyber Warfare and Cyber Terrorism*, ed. L. Janczewski and A. M. Colarik. New York: Information Science Reference (IGI).

Curtin, D., and A. J. Meijer. 2006. "Does Transparency Strengthen Legitimacy?" *Information Polity* 11 (2): 109–22.

Dean, T. 1988. *Land and Power in Late Medieval Ferrara: The Rule of the Este, 1350–1450*. Cambridge: Cambridge University Press.

De Bruijne, M., and M. Van Eeten. 2007. "Systems That Should Have Failed: Critical Infrastructure Protection in an Institutionally Fragmented Environment." *Journal of Contingencies and Crisis Management* 15 (1): 18–29.

Demchak, C. C. 1991. *Military Organizations, Complex Machines: Modernization in the U.S. Armed Services*. Ithaca, N.Y.: Cornell University Press.

——. 1992. "Complexity, Rogue Outcomes and Weapon Systems." *Public Administration Review* 52 (4): 347–55.

——. 1994. "Colonies or Computers: Modernization Challenges to the Future British Army." *Defense Analysis* 10 (1): 3–32.

——. 1996. "Numbers or Networks: Social Constructions of Technology and Organizational Dilemmas in IDF Modernization." *Armed Forces and Society* 23 (2): 179.

——. 2000. "Revolution in Military Affairs in Developing States: Botswana, Chile, and Thailand Dilemmas of Image, Operations, and Democracy." *National Security Studies Quarterly* (6): 1–45.

——. 2003. "Wars of Disruption: International Competition and Information Technology–Driven Military Organizations." *Contemporary Security Policy* 24 (1): 75–112.

———. 2006. "A Theory of Action in Iraq: The Three State Partition and a "Mirror the Mix" Strategy." *Forum* 4 (23), article 12.

Demchak, C. C., and K. D. Fenstermacher. 2004. "Balancing Security and Privacy in the 21st Century." Paper read at Intelligence and Security Informatics: Second Symposium on Intelligence and Security Informatics, ISI 2004 Proceedings, June 10–11, at Tucson, Arizona.

———. 2009. "Institutionalizing Behavior-Based Privacy." *Administration and Society* 41 (November): 783–814.

———. 2010. "Lessons from the Military: Surprise, Resilience, and the Atrium Model." In *Designing Resilience: Preparing for Extreme Events*, ed. L. Comfort, A. Boin, and C. Demchak. Pittsburgh: University of Pittsburgh Press. 62–83.

Demchak, C. C., K. Fenstermacher, M. Ryckman, P. Tanimoto, and E. Skidmore. 2007. "Institutionalizing Privacy and Future Security: Testing the Value of Behavior-Based Privacy for Finding Bad Actors." Unpublished working paper. Tucson: University of Arizona, School of PA and Policy and Management Information Systems Department.

Demchak, C. C., and E. Werner. 2007a. "Exploring the Knowledge Nexus—Lessons from India in Terrorism-Driven Institutional Growth." In *Civil-Military Coordination in Multinational Missions*, ed. Witold M. Patoka. Conference Report of the Forum for Security Studies, Swedish National Defence College, Stockholm, January 18–19, 2007. http://www.scribd.com/doc/20606401/2007-ConferenceReportCiv Mi-Compresed.

———. 2007b. "Exploring the Knowledge Nexus: India's Path in Terrorism-Driven Institutional Growth." *Strategic Studies Quarterly* 1 (2): 58–97.

Denison, G. T. 1913. *A History of Cavalry from the Earliest Times: With Lessons for the Future.* London: Macmillan.

Dennen, J. M. G. van der. 1995. "Of Badges, Bonds and Boundaries: Ethnocentrism, Xenophobia, and War." *The Origin of War: The Evolution of a Male-Coalitional Reproductive Strategy.* Groningen, Netherlands: Origin Press.

DeSanctis, G., and M. S. Poole. 1994. "Capturing the Complexity in Advanced Technology Use: Adaptive Structuration Theory." *Organization Science* 5 (2): 121–47.

Deutsche Welle. 2008. "Swedish Government Clears Hurdles to Pass Surveillance Bill." *Deutsche Welle—World*, June 19. http://www.dw-world.de/dw/article/0,,3421627,00 .html.

DiMaggio, P. J., and W. W. Powell. 1983. "The Iron Cage Revisited: Institutional Isomorphism and Collective Rationality in Organizational Fields." *American Sociological Review* 48 (2): 147–60.

Dimitrova, D. V., and C. Connolly-Ahern. 2007. "A Tale of Two Wars: Framing Analysis of Online News Sites in Coalition Countries and the Arab World during the Iraq War." *Howard Journal of Communications* 18 (2): 153–68.

Dirckinck-Holmfeld, L., and E. K. Sorensen. 1999. "Distributed Computer Supported Collaborative Learning through Shared Practice and Social Participation." In *Proceedings of the Computer Support doe Collaborative Learning (CSCL) 1999 Conference*, ed. C. Hoadley and J. Roschelle. December 12–15, Stanford University, Palo Alto, Calif. Mahwah, N.J.: Lawrence Erlbaum.

Doumato, E. A., and M. P. Posusney. 2003. *Women and Globalization in the Arab Middle East: Gender, Economy, and Society*. Boulder, Colo.: Lynne Rienner.

Doyle, K. 1997. "The Art of the Coup: A Paper Trail of Covert Actions in Guatemala." *NACLA Report on the Americas* 31 (2): 34–39.

Drezner, D. W. 2010. "The Chronicle Review: Why WikiLeaks Is Bad for Scholars." *Chronicle of Higher Education*, December 5.

Dunn, J. P. 2005. *Khedive Ismail's Army*. Cass Military Studies. London: Routledge.

Dupuy, R. E., and T. N. Dupuy. 1970. *The Encyclopedia of Military History: From 3500 BC to the Present*. New York: Harper and Row.

Dutt, R. C. 2001. *The Economic History of India in the Victorian Age: From the Accession of Queen Victoria in 1837 to the Commencement of the Twentieth Century*. London: Routledge.

Economist. 2008. "Polls Show Americans Approve of . . . Some Stuff We Just Made Up." *Economist.com*, February 29. http://www.economist.com/blogs/democracyin america/2008/02/polls_show_americans_approve_0.

Edler, F. M. 1930. "The Silk Trade of Lucca during the Thirteenth and Fourteenth Centuries." PhD diss., University of Chicago, Department of History.

Edwards, J. 2005. "The Role of Islam in Winning Hearts and Minds in Iraq." Report available from Storming Media.

Elegant, S. 2007. "Enemies at the Firewall." *Time.com*, December 6. http://www.time .com/time/magazine/article/0,9171,1692063,00.html.

Ember, C. R., M. Ember, and B. Russett. 1992. "Peace between Participatory Polities: A Cross-Cultural Test of the 'Democracies Rarely Fight Each Other' Hypothesis." *World Politics* 44 (4): 573–99.

Englebert, P. 2000. "Pre-Colonial Institutions, Post-Colonial States, and Economic Development in Tropical Africa." *Political Research Quarterly* 53 (1): 7.

Esposito, J. L., and D. Mogahed. 2007. "Battle for Muslims' Hearts and Minds: The Road Not (Yet) Taken." *Middle East Policy* 14 (1): 27–41.

Euben, R. L. 2002. "Jihad and Political Violence." *Current History* 101 (638): 365–76.

EurActive Network. 2010. "EU Wins Concessions on U.S. Bank Data-Sharing Deal." *EurActiv* online, June 25. http://www.euractiv.com/en/justice/eu-wins-concessions-on-US-bank-data-sharing-deal-news-495585.

Everett, C., J. Chadwell, and J. C. McChesney. 2002. "Successful Programs for At-Risk Youths." *JOPERD—The Journal of Physical Education, Recreation and Dance* 73 (9): 38–44.

Falliere, N., L. O. Murchu, and E. Chien. 2010. "W32.Stuxnet Dossier: Version 1.3 (November 2010)." Symantec Security Response. http://www.symantec.com/content/en/us/enterprise/media/security_response/whitepapers/w32_stuxnet_dossier.pdf.

Farwell, B. 1985. *Queen Victoria's Little Wars*. New York: W. W. Norton.

Fay, P. W. 1975. *The Opium War, 1840–1842: Barbarians in the Celestial Empire in the Early Part of the Nineteenth Century and the War by Which They Forced Her Gates Ajar*. Chapel Hill: University of North Carolina Press.

Fein, H. 1993. "Revolutionary and Antirevolutionary Genocides: A Comparison of State Murders in Democratic Kampuchea, 1975 to 1979, and in Indonesia, 1965 to 1966." *Comparative Studies in Society and History* 35 (4): 796–823.

Feng, J., J. Lazar, and J. Preece. 2004. "Empathy and Online Interpersonal Trust: A Fragile Relationship." *Behaviour and Information Technology* 23 (2): 97–106.

Finer, S. E. 1999. *The History of Government from the Earliest Times*. Oxford: Oxford University Press.

Fischerkeller, M. P. 1998. "David versus Goliath Cultural Judgments in Asymmetric Wars." *Security Studies Journal* 7 (4): 1–43.

Ford, J. D., and L. W. Ford. 1995. "The Role of Conversations in Producing Intentional Change in Organizations." *Academy of Management Review* 20 (3): 541–70.

Forde, S. 1989. *The Ambition to Rule: Alcibiades and the Politics of Imperialism in Thucydides*. Ithaca, N.Y.: Cornell University Press.

Forest, J. 2005. The Making of a Terrorist: Recruitment, Training and Root Causes. Westport, Conn.: Praeger.

Forte, D., and R. Power. 2008. "Unanswered Questions, International Intrigue and the Unintended Consequences of Facile Thinking." *Computer Fraud and Security* 2008 (4):18–20.

Fortson, D. 2007. "Victoria Mortgage Becomes First UK Failure." *Independent*, September 11.

Foster, I., N. R. Jennings, and C. Kesselman. 2004. "Brain Meets Brawn: Why Grid and Agents Need Each Other." Paper read at AAMAS 2004, Proceedings of the Third International Joint Conference on Autonomous Agents and Multiagent Systems. New York, July 19–23.

Fountain, J. E. 2001. *Building the Virtual State: Information Technology and Institutional Change*. Washington, D.C.: Brookings Institution Press.

Foxhall, L. 1995. "Farming and Fighting in Ancient Greece." In *War and Society in the Greek World*, ed. J. Rich and G. Shipley. London: Routledge.

Fraser, A. 2005. "Architecture of a Broken Dream: The CIA and Guatemala, 1952–54." *Intelligence and National Security* 20 (3): 486–508.

Fratianni, M., and F. Spinelli. 2006. "Italian City-States and Financial Evolution." *European Review of Economic History* 10 (3): 257–78.

Freedman, L. 1998. "International Security: Changing Targets." *Foreign Policy*, no. 110 (Spring): 48–63.

Freeman, C. 2000. *The Greek Achievement*. New York: Penguin Books.

Freeman, D., P. A. Garety, P. Bebbington, M. Slater, E. Kuipers, D. Fowler, C. Green, J. Jordan, K. Ray, and G. Dunn. 2005. "The Psychology of Persecutory Ideation II: A Virtual Reality Experimental Study." *Journal of Nervous and Mental Disease* 193 (5): 309–15.

Friedman, D. 1999. "Why Not Hang Them All: The Virtues of Inefficient Punishment." *Journal of Political Economy* 107 (s6): 259–69.

Friedrichs, J. 2001. "The Meaning of New Medievalism." *European Journal of International Relations* 7 (4): 475.

Friesner, T. 2009. "History of SWOT Analysis." Marketing Teacher. http://www.marketingteacher.com/swot/history-of-swot.html.

Frisch, H. 2001. "Guns and Butter in the Egyptian Army." *Middle East Review of International Affairs* 5 (2). http://meria.idc.ac.il/journal/2001/issue2/jv5n2a1.html.

Frith, C. D., and U. Frith. 2006. "How We Predict What Other People Are Going to Do." *Brain Research* 1079 (1): 36–46.

Fuller, G. E. 2003. *The Youth Factor: The New Demographics of the Middle East and the Implications for U.S. Policy*. Washington, D.C.: Saban Center for Middle East Policy at the Brookings Institution.

Galbraith, J. R. 1977. *Organization Design*. Reading, Mass.: Addison-Wesley.

Gandy, M. 2006. "Planning, Anti-Planning and the Infrastructure Crisis Facing Metropolitan Lagos." *Urban Studies* 43 (2): 371.

Gasson, S. 2005. "The Dynamics of Sensemaking, Knowledge, and Expertise in Collaborative, Boundary-Spanning Design." *Journal of Computer-Mediated Communication* 10 (4).

Gates, R. M. 2009. "A Balanced Strategy." *Foreign Affairs* 88 (1):28–40.

Gee, J. P. 2005. "Video Games, Mind, and Learning." *Interactive Digital Media and Arts Association Journal* 2 (1): 37–42.

General Accounting Office. 1992. "Organizational Culture: Techniques Companies Use to Perpetuate or Change Beliefs and Values." Report to the Chairman, Committee on Government Affairs, U.S. Senate. Washington D.C.: U.S. Government Printing Office. http://archive.gao.gov/d31t10/146086.pdf.

Gertz, B. 2010. "Inside the Ring: Hacker Training." *Washington Post*, March 4.

Geyer, D., and B. Little. 1987. *Russian Imperialism: The Interaction of Domestic and Foreign Policy, 1860–1914*. New Haven, Conn.: Yale University Press.

Gibson, C. B., and J. L. Gibbs. 2006. "Unpacking the Concept of Virtuality: The Effects of Geographic Dispersion, Electronic Dependence." *Administrative Science Quarterly* 51:451–95.

Gibson, J. W. 1988. *The Perfect War: The War We Couldn't Lose and How We Did.* New York: Vintage Books.

Gibson, W. 1986. *Neuromancer.* London: Grafton.

Gill, P. 2006. "Not Just Joining the Dots but Crossing the Borders and Bridging the Voids: Constructing Security Networks after 11 September 2001." *Policing and Society* 16 (1): 27–49.

Ginzberg, L., and H. Szold. 1998. *The Legends of the Jews.* Baltimore: Johns Hopkins University Press.

Glaser, B. G. 2001. *The Grounded Theory Perspective: Conceptualization Contrasted with Description.* Mill Valley, Calif.: Sociology Press.

Gleick, J. 1988. *Chaos: The Making of a Science.* New York: Vintage Books.

———. 1997. *Chaos: The Amazing Science of the Unpredictable.* London: Minerva.

Gleijeses, P. 1991. *Shattered Hope: The Guatemalan Revolution and the United States, 1944–1954.* Princeton, N.J.: Princeton University Press.

Goldberg, R. A. 2004. "'Who Profited from the Crime?' Intelligence Failure, Conspiracy Theories and the Case of September 11." *Intelligence and National Security* 19 (2): 249–61.

Goldsmith, J. L., and T. Wu. 2006. *Who Controls the Internet? Illusions of a Borderless World.* New York: Oxford University Press.

Goldsworthy, A. K. 1998. *The Roman Army at War, 100 BC–AD 200.* Oxford: Oxford University Press.

Gomory, R. E. 1995. "An Essay on the Known, the Unknown and the Unknowable." *Scientific American* 272:120.

Gompert, D. C., T. M. Cheung, T. Lo, M. McDevitt, J. Mulvenon, D. Shlapak, M. Libicki, D. Long, and S. Johnson. 2007. *Coping with the Dragon: Essays on PLA Transformation and the U.S. Military.* Washington, D.C.: National Defense University, Center for Technology and National Security Policy.

Gordon, M. 2008. "Army Buried Study Faulting Iraq Planning." *New York Times,* February 11.

Gosman, M., A. A. MacDonald, and A. J. Vanderjagt, eds. 2005. *Princes and Princely Culture, 1450–1650.* Leiden, Netherlands: Brill.

Goth, G. 2007. "The Politics of DDoS Attacks." *IEEE-Distributed Systems* online 8 (8): 3. http://ieeexplore.ieee.org/xpls/abs_all.jsp?arnumber=4302636.

Gregory, S. 2007. "The ISI and the War on Terrorism." *Studies in Conflict and Terrorism* 30 (12): 1013–31.

Gurney, P. J. 2006. "'The Sublime of the Bazaar': A Moment in the Making of a Consumer Culture in Mid-Nineteenth Century England." *Journal of Social History* 40 (2): 385–405.

Hafner, K. 1999. *Where Wizards Stay Up Late: The Origins of the Internet.* New York: Simon and Schuster.

Haikola, S., and S. Jonsson. 2007. "State Surveillance on the Internet—The Swedish Debate and the Future Role of Libraries and LIS." *Libri-Copenhagen* 57 (4): 209.

Halliday, J. 2010. "US Report Claims Chinese Telecoms Company Had Access to 15% of Global Traffic, Including Military Emails, for 18 Minutes." *Guardian*, November 18.

Hanson, R. D. 2006. "Designing Real Terrorism Futures." *Public Choice* 128 (1): 257–74.

Hanson, V. D. 2001. *Carnage and Culture: Landmark Battles in the Rise of Western Power*. New York: Doubleday.

———. 2005. *A War Like No Other: How the Athenians and Spartans Fought the Peloponnesian War*. New York: Random House.

Harcourt, F. 1980. "Disraeli's Imperialism, 1866–1868: A Question of Timing." *Historical Journal* 23 (1): 87–109.

Harris, D. 2004. *The Crisis: The President, the Prophet, and the Shah—1979 and the Coming of Militant Islam*. New York: Little, Brown.

Harris, S. 2009. "The CyberWar Plan." *National Journal*, November 14.

Hasenclever, A., P. Mayer, and V. Rittberger. 1996. "Interests, Power, Knowledge: The Study of International Regimes." *Mershon International Studies Review* 40 (2): 177–228.

Hau, M. 2007. "Regulation of Male Traits by Testosterone: Implications for the Evolution of Vertebrate Life Histories." *BioEssays* 29: 133–44.

Haythornthwaite, C. 2005. "Introduction: Computer-Mediated Collaborative Practices." *Journal of Computer-Mediated Communication* 10 (4). http://jcmc.indiana.edu/vol10/issue4/.

Heintze, T., and S. Bretschneider. 2000. "Information Technology and Restructuring in Public Organizations: Does Adoption of Information Technology Affect Organizational Structures, Communications, and Decision Making?" *Journal of Public Administration Research and Theory* 10 (4). http://jpart.oxfordjournals.org/content/10/4/801.abstract.

Held, D. 1992. "Democracy: From City-States to a Cosmopolitan Order?" *Political Studies* 40 (5): 10–39.

Henderson, J. 1986. "Society and Religion in Renaissance Florence." *Historical Journal* 29 (1): 213–25.

Herlihy, D., and C. Klapisch-Zuber. 1985. *Tuscans and Their Families: A Study of the Florentine Catasto of 1427*. New Haven, Conn.: Yale University Press.

Hesketh, T., and Z. W. Xing. 2006. "Abnormal Sex Ratios in Human Populations: Causes and Consequences." *Proceedings of the National Academy of Sciences* 103 (36): 13271.

Heuser, B. 2002. *Reading Clausewitz*. London: Pimlico.

Hibbert, C. 1975. *The House of Medici: Its Rise and Fall*. New York: William Morrow.

Hilton, B. 2006. *A Mad, Bad, and Dangerous People? England, 1783–1846*. Oxford: Clarendon.

Hodgetts, R. M., and F. Luthans. 2006. *International Management: Culture, Strategy, and Behavior.* New York: McGraw-Hill.

Hoepman, J. H., and B. Jacobs. 2007. "Increased Security through Open Source." *Communications of the ACM* 50 (1): 79–83.

Hofstadter, D. R. 1999. *Godel, Escher, Bach: An Eternal Braid.* New York: Basic Books.

Hofstede, G. 1999. "Problems Remain, but Theories Will Change: The Universal and the Specific in 21st-Century Global Management." *Organizational Dynamics* 28 (1): 34–44.

Holmes, G., ed. 1988. *The Oxford History of Medieval Europe.* Oxford: Oxford University Press.

Home, G. H. Q. 2000. "Lionel Wigram, Battle Drill and the British Army in the Second World War." *War in History* 7 (4): 442–62.

Horgan, J. 1995. "From Complexity to Perplexity." *Scientific American* 272 (6): 104–9.

Houkes, A., and M. Janse. 2005. "Foreign Examples as Eye Openers and Justification: The Transfer of the Anti-Corn Law League and the Anti-Prostitution Movement to the Netherlands." *European Review of History—Revue européenne d'Histoire* 12 (2): 321–44.

Hove, M. T. 2007. "The Arbenz Factor: Salvador Allende, U.S.-Chilean Relations, and the 1954 U.S. Intervention in Guatemala." *Diplomatic History* 31 (4): 623–63.

Huth, P., and B. Russett. 1984. "What Makes Deterrence Work? Cases from 1900 to 1980." *World Politics* 36 (4): 496–526.

Hyland, W. G. 1987. "Containment: 40 Years Later: Introduction." *Foreign Affairs* 65 (4). http://www.foreignaffairs.com/issues/1987/65/4.

Immerman, R. H. 1980. "Guatemala as Cold War History." *Political Science Quarterly* 95 (4): 629–53.

Ishida, T. 2004. "Society-Centered Design for Socially Embedded Multiagent Systems." International Workshop on Cooperative Information Agents (CIA-04), Lecture Notes in Computer Science 3191:16–29.

Isserman, M. 2007. "How Old Is the New SDS?" *Chronicle of Higher Education* 53 (26): 1.

Jackson, A. 2007. "The Evolution of the Division in British Military History." *RUSI Journal* 152 (6): 76–81.

Jacobs, N. 2002. "Co-term Network Analysis as a Means of Describing the Information Landscapes of Knowledge Communities across Sectors." *Journal of Documentation* 58 (5): 548–62.

Jacoby, L. E. 2005. "Current and Projected National Security Threats to the United States." Presentation to the U.S. Senate Armed Services Committee Hearing on Future Threats to U.S. National Security, March 17.

Janczewski, L., and A. M. Colarik, eds. 2007. *Cyber Warfare and Cyber Terrorism.* New York: IGI Global.

Jarzabkowski, P. 2004. "Strategy as Practice: Recursiveness, Adaptation, and Practices-in-Use." *Organization Studies* 25 (4): 529.

Jay, C., M. Glencross, and R. Hubbold. 2007. "Modeling the Effects of Delayed Haptic and Visual Feedback in a Collaborative Virtual Environment." *ACM Transactions on Computer-Human Interaction* 14 (2). http://portal.acm.org/citation.cfm?doid=1275511.1275514.

Jeffery, K. G. 2000. "An Architecture for Grey Literature in a R&D Context." *International Journal on Grey Literature* 1 (2): 64–72.

Jervis, R. L. 1997. *System Effects: Complexity in Political and Social Life.* Princeton, N.J.: Princeton University Press.

———. 2003. "The Confrontation between Iraq and the U.S.: Implications for the Theory and Practice of Deterrence." *European Journal of International Relations* 9 (2): 315.

John, T., and M. Maguire. 2007. "Criminal Intelligence and the National Intelligence Model." In *Handbook of Criminal Investigation*, ed. T. Newburn, T. Williamson, and A. Wright. Cullompton, U.K.: Willan.

Johnson, D. E. 2002. "Preparing Potential Senior Army Leaders for the Future." Santa Monica, Calif.: RAND CORPORATION.

Johnson, J. 2009. "Hack Attack: Is the Whole Internet at Risk?" *Popular Mechanics*, June, 1. http://www.popularmechanics.com/technology/gadgets/news/4216293.

Johnson, T. A. 2005. "Cyber Terrorism." In *Forensic Computer Crime Investigation*, ed. T. A. Johnson. London: CRC Press.

Joint Forces Command JFC. 2010. "Joint Operating Environment (JOE) 2010." U.S. Department of Defense. Washington, D.C.: U.S. Government Printing Office.

Jolles, F., and S. Jolles. 2000. "Zulu Ritual Immunisation in Perspective." *Africa: Journal of the International African Institute* 70 (2): 229–48.

Jones, P., and M. B. Jorgenson. 2000. "Linux and Open-Source Applications." *Linux Journal*, issue 70 (February). http://www.linuxjournal.com/article/3683.

Jonson, L. 2005. "Russia and the Strategic Relationship with Tajikistan." In *The New Security Environment: The Impact on Russia, Central and Eastern Europe*, ed. R. E. Kanet. London: Ashgate.

Jönsson, C., and J. Tallberg. 2008. "Institutional Theory in International Relations." In *Debating Institutionalism*, ed. J. Pierre, G. Peters, and G. Stoker. Manchester: Manchester University Press.

Jowett, G. S., and V. O'Donnell. 2006. *Propaganda and Persuasion.* 4th ed. Thousand Oaks, Calif.: Sage.

Junnarkar, S. 2002. "Lessons: Keeping Networks Alive in New York." E-Terrorism Special Report. CNET News, August 28. http://news.cnet.com/2009-1001-954796.html.

Kahn, A. E. 1966. "The Tyranny of Small Decisions: Market Failures, Imperfections, and the Limits of Economics." *Kyklos* 19 (1): 23–47.

Kaijser, A. 2004. "The Dynamics of Infrasystems: Lessons from History." Paper read at 6th International Summer Academy on Technology Studies: "Urban Infrastructure in Transition: What Can We Learn from History?" Deutschlandsberg, Austria, July 11–17.

Kane, M. 2002. "U.S. Vulnerable to Data Sneak Attack." CNET News, August 13. http://news.cnet.com/2100-1017-949605.html.

Karnow, S. 1997. *Vietnam: A History*. New York: Penguin Books.

Keegan, J. 1978. *The Face of Battle*. New York: Penguin Books.

Keizer, G. 2008. "Windows Market Share Dives below 90% for First Time." *Computerworld* online, December 1, 1. http://www.computerworld.com/s/article/9121938/Windows_market_share_dives_below_90_for_first_time.

Kemmerer, R. A., and G. Vigna. 2002. "Intrusion Detection: A Brief History and Overview." *Computer* 35 (4): 27–30.

Kenny, C. 2007. "Internet Governance on a Dollar a Day." *Information Polity* 12 (1): 83–94.

Kent, D. 2004. "The Power of the Elites: Family, Patronage and the State." In *Italy in the Age of the Renaissance: 1300–1550*, ed. J. M. Najemy. Oxford: Oxford University Press.

Keohane, R. O., and J. S. Nye. 1972. *Transnational Relations and World Politics*. Cambridge, Mass.: Harvard University Press.

Kersten, A., and M. Sidky. 2005. "Re-aligning Rationality: Crisis Management and Prisoner Abuses in Iraq." *Public Relations Review* 31 (4): 471–78.

Kieve, J. L. 1973. *The Electric Telegraph: A Social and Economic History*. Newton Abbot, U.K.: David and Charles.

Kinzer, S. 2006. *Overthrow: America's Century of Regime Change from Hawaii to Iraq*. New York: Times Books/Henry Holt.

Knapp, K. J., and W. R. Boulton. 2006. "Cyber-Warfare Threatens Corporations: Expansion into Commercial Environments." *Information Systems Management* 23 (2): 76–87.

———. 2007. "Ten Information Warfare Trends." In *Cyber Warfare and Cyber Terrorism*, ed. L. Janczewski and A. M. Colarik. New York: (IGI) Global.

Knuesel, A. 2007. "British Diplomacy and the Telegraph in Nineteenth-Century China." *Diplomacy and Statecraft* 18 (3): 517–37.

Kohn, G. C. 1986. *Dictionary of Wars*. New York: Facts on File.

Kolodziej, E. 2005. "Flawed Governance of a Global Society." *International Studies Review* 7 (2): 298–300.

Kraidy, M. M. 2005. "Cultural Hybridity and International Communication." *Hybridity, or The Cultural Logic Of Globalization*. Philadelphia: Temple University Press.

Krasner, S. D. 1999. *Sovereignty: Organized Hypocrisy*. Princeton, N.J.: Princeton University Press.

———. 2004. "Sharing Sovereignty: New Institutions for Collapsed and Failing States." *International Security* 29 (2): 85–120.

Krebs, B. 2010. "'Mariposa' Botnet Authors May Avoid Jail Time." *Krebs on Security.* http://krebsonsecurity.com/2010/03/mariposa-botnet-authors-may-avoid-jail-time/.

Kreijns, K., P. A. Kirschner, and W. Jochems. 2003. "Identifying the Pitfalls for Social Interaction in Computer-Supported Collaborative Learning Environments: A Review of the Research." *Computers in Human Behavior* 19 (3): 335–53.

Kreimer, S. F. 2008. "The Freedom of Information Act and the Ecology of Transparency." *University of Pennsylvania Journal of Constitutional Law* 10 (5) 1011–80.

Krekel, B. 2009. *Capability of the People's Republic of China to Conduct Cyber Warfare and Computer Network Exploitation.* Report prepared for the US-China Economic and Security Review Commission by Northrup Grumman Corp. McLean, Va.: Northrup Grumman Corp.

Krepinevich, A. F. 1986. *The Army and Vietnam.* Baltimore: Johns Hopkins University Press.

———. 2004. "Iraq and Vietnam: Déjà Vu All Over Again?" Center for Strategic and Budgetary Assessments, July 8. http://www.csbaonline.org.

Kshetri, N. 2005a. "Information and Communications Technologies, Strategic Asymmetry and National Security." *Journal of International Management* 11 (4): 563–80.

———. 2005b. "Pattern of Global Cyber War and Crime: A Conceptual Framework." *Journal of International Management* 11 (4): 541–62.

Kyodo News International. 2008. "China Denies Involvement in Cyber Attacks." Kyodo News International online, March 4. http://www.macroworldinvestor.com/m/m.w?lp=GetStory&id=296389101.

Lance, P. 2003. *1000 Years for Revenge: International Terrorism and the FBI—the Untold Story.* New York: Regan Books.

Landau, M. 1969. "Redundancy, Rationality, and the Problem of Duplication and Overlap." *Public Administration Review* 29 (4): 346–58.

Lane, S. 2006. "Overall Mac OS Usage Market Share Declining?" AppleInsider.com, September 8. http://www.appleinsider.com/articles/06/09/18/overall_mac_os_usage_market_share_declining.html.

Lanir, Z., B. Fischhoff, and S. Johnson. 1988. "Military Risk-Taking: C3I and the Cognitive Functions of Boldness in War." *Journal of Strategic Studies* 11 (1): 96–114.

La Porte, T. R. 1975. *Organized Social Complexity: Challenge to Politics and Policy.* Princeton, N.J.: Princeton University Press.

———. 1996. "High Reliability Organizations: Unlikely, Demanding and at Risk." *Journal of Contingencies and Crisis Management* 4 (2): 60–71.

La Porte, T. R., and P. M. Consolini. 1991. "Working in Practice but Not in Theory: Theoretical Challenges of 'High-Reliability Organizations.'" *Journal of Public Administration Research and Theory: J-PART* 1 (1): 19–48.

Laufer, R. S., and M. Wolfe. 1977. "Privacy as a Concept and a Social Issue: A Multidimensional Developmental Theory." *Journal of Social Issues* 33 (3): 22–42.

Layne, C. 2006. *The Peace of Illusions: International Relations Theory and American Grand Strategy from 1940 to the Present.* Ithaca, N.Y.: Cornell University Press.

Leapman, B. 2007. "4,000 Trained at Afghan Terror Camps and Returned to UK." *Sunday Telegraph* (London), July 15.

Lebow, R. N. 2006. "Robert S. McNamara: Max Weber's Nightmare." *International Relations* 20 (2): 211.

Lebow, R. N., and R. Kelly. 2001. "Thucydides and Hegemony: Athens and the United States." *Review of International Studies* 27 (04): 593–609.

Lee, K.-H., G. Yang, and J. L. Graham. 2006. "Tension and Trust in International Business Negotiations: American Executives Negotiating with Chinese Executives." *Journal of International Business Studies* 37 (September): 623–41.

Leeson, P. T., and C. J. Coyne. 2005. "The Economics of Computer Hacking." *Journal of Law, Economics and Policy* 1 (2): 511–32.

Legro, J. W. 2005. *Rethinking the World: Great Power Strategies and International Order.* Ithaca, N.Y.: Cornell University Press.

Leipnik, Mark. 2007. "Use of Geographic Information Systems in Cyber Warfare and Cyber Counterterrorism." In *Cyber Warfare and Cyber Terrorism*, ed. L. Janczewski and A. M. Colarik. New York: Information Science Reference. 291–97.

Lemos, R. 2002. "Safety: Assessing the Infrastructure Risk." E-Terrorism Special Report. CNET New,, 26 August. http://news.cnet.com/2009-1001-954780.html.

Levinson, C., M. Coker, and T. El-Ghobashy. 2011. "Strikes Worry Egypt's Military, Youth." *Wall Street Journal*, February 15. http://www.eurasiareview.com/analysis/inside-the-egyptian-military-15022011/.

Lewis, J. A.. 2002. *Assessing the Risks of Cyber Terrorism, Cyber War and Other Cyber Threats.* Washington, D.C.: Center for Strategic and International Studies.

Leyden, J. 2010. "DNS Made Easy Rallies after Punishing DDoS Attack: 50Gbps of Botnet-Powered Badness." *Register* (London), August 9.

Liarokapis, F. 2006. "An Exploration from Virtual to Augmented Reality Gaming." *Simulation and Gaming* 37 (4): 507.

Lindner, F. 2006. "Software Security Is Software Reliability." *Communications of the ACM* 49 (6): 57–61.

Lipson, M. 2007. "Peacekeeping: Organized Hypocrisy?" *European Journal of International Relations* 13 (1): 5.

Live Free or Die Hard. 2008. Dir. Len Wiseman. Los Angeles: 20th Century Fox.

Lodwick, K. L. 1996. *Crusaders against Opium: Protestant Missionaries in China, 1874–1917.* Lexington: University Press of Kentucky.

Luo, X. 2002. "Trust Production and Privacy Concerns on the Internet: A Framework

Based on Relationship Marketing and Social Exchange Theory." *Industrial Marketing Management* 31 (2): 111–18.

Lutters, W. G., and C. B. Seaman. 2007. "Revealing Actual Documentation Usage in Software Maintenance through War Stories." *Information and Software Technology* 49 (6): 576–87.

Lynn, W. 2010. "Introducing U.S. Cyber Command." *Wall Street Journal*, June 3.

Machiavelli, N. 1906. *The Florentine History.* Trans. N. H. Thomson. Vol. 2. London: Archibald Constable.

Mack, A. 1975. "Why Big Nations Lose Small Wars: The Politics of Asymmetric Conflict." *World Politics* 27 (2): 175–200.

Madsen, W. 2004. "Total Information System Reborn in Other U.S. Agencies." *Computer Fraud and Security* 2004 (3): 2–3.

Mahoney, M. R. 2003. "The Zulu Kingdom as a Genocidal and Post-Genocidal Society, c. 1810 to the Present." *Journal of Genocide Research* 5 (2): 251–68.

Maikovich, A. K. 2005. "A New Understanding of Terrorism Using Cognitive Dissonance Principles." *Journal for the Theory of Social Behaviour* 35 (4): 373–97.

Maldonado, G., and S. Greenland. 2002. "Estimating Causal Effects." *International Journal of Epidemiology* 31 (2): 422–29.

Mallett, M. 1994. "Ambassadors and Their Audiences in Renaissance Italy." *Renaissance Studies* 8 (3): 229–43.

———. 2003. "Condottieri and Captains in Renaissance Italy." In *The Chivalric Ethos and the Development of Military Professionalism*, ed. D. J. B. Trim. Leiden, Netherlands: Brill.

Manicas, P. T. 1982. "War, Stasis, and Greek Political Thought." *Comparative Studies in Society and History* 24 (4): 673–88.

Manning, S. 2007. "Learning the Trade: Use and Misuse of Intelligence during the British Colonial Campaigns of the 1870s." *Intelligence and National Security* 22 (5): 644–60.

Markoff, J., D. E. Sanger, and T. Shanker. 2010. "Cyberwar: In Digital Combat, U.S. Finds No Easy Deterrent." *New York Times*, January 26.

Marks, F. W. 1990. "The CIA and Castillo Armas in Guatemala, 1954: New Clues to an Old Puzzle." *Diplomatic History* 14: 67–86.

Markwell, D. J. 1995. *John Maynard Keynes and International Relations: Idealism, Economic Paths to War and Peace, and Post-war Reconstruction.* Oxford: Oxford University Press.

Martin, T. R. 1996. *Ancient Greece: From Prehistoric to Hellenistic Times.* New Haven, Conn.: Yale University Press.

Martines, L. 1968. *Lawyers and Statecraft in Renaissance Florence.* Princeton, N.J.: Princeton University Press.

Mastanduno, M. 1998. "Economics and Security in Statecraft and Scholarship." *International Organization* 52 (4): 825–54.

Mastny, V. 1996. *The Cold War and Soviet Insecurity: The Stalin Years.* New York: Oxford University Press.

Mathieson, S. A. 2007. "Legislation at War." *Infosecurity* 4 (3): 26–28.

Mayntz, R., and T. Hughes, eds. 1988. *The Development of Large Technical Systems (LTS).* Boulder, Colo.: Westview Press.

McChristian, J. A. 1974. *Vietnam Studies: The Role of Military Intelligence, 1965–1967.* Washington D.C.: Department of the Army, U.S. Government Printing Office.

McDermott, P. 2003. "Withhold and Control: Information in the Bush Administration." *Kansas Journal of Law and Public Policy* 12:671.

McLean, P. D. 2005. "Patronage, Citizenship, and the Stalled Emergence of the Modern State in Renaissance Florence." *Comparative Studies in Society and History* 47 (03): 638–64.

McNeill, W. H. 1982. The Pursuit of Power: Technology, Armed Force, and Society since AD 1000: University of Chicago Press.

Mearsheimer, J. J. 1990. "Why We Will Soon Miss the Cold War." *Atlantic Monthly*, August: 35–50.

——. 1994. "The False Promise of International Institutions." *International Security* 19 (3): 5–49.

——. 2005. "Hans Morgenthau and the Iraq War: Realism versus Neo-conservatism." *Open Democracy: Free Thinking for the World*, May 18. http://www.opendemocracy .net/democracy-americanpower/morgenthau_2522.jsp.

Mearsheimer, J. J., and S. M. Walt. 2003. "An Unnecessary War." *Foreign Policy* (134): 50–59.

Meeuwesen, L., J. A. M. Harmsen, R. M. D. Bernsen, and M. A. Bruijnzeels. 2006. "Do Dutch Doctors Communicate Differently with Immigrant Patients Than with Dutch Patients?" *Social Science and Medicine* 63 (9): 2407–17.

Michael, G. 2007. "The Legend and Legacy of Abu Musab al-Zarqawi." *Defence Studies* 7 (3): 338–57.

Miller, J. H., and S. E. Page. 2007. *Complex Adaptive Systems.* Princeton, N.J.: Princeton University Press.

Mills, E. 2010. "Insecurity Complex: In Their Words: Experts Weigh In on Mac vs. PC security." CNET online, February 1. http://news.cnet.com/8301-27080_3-10444561-245 .html.

Milward, H. B., and J. Raab. 2002. "Dark Networks: The Structure, Operation, and Performance of International Drug, Terror, and Arms Trafficking Networks." International Conference on the Empirical Study of Governance, Management and Performance, Barcelona, May 4–5, Institut Internacional de Governabilitat de Catalunya.

Model, H. 2000. "Organizational Success and Failure." *European Management Journal* 18 (5): 488–98.

Montrose, L. 1944. *War through the Ages.* New York: Harper and Bros.

Moore, R. J., N. Ducheneaut, and E. Nickell. 2007. "Doing Virtually Nothing: Awareness and Accountability in Massively Multiplayer Online Worlds." *Computer Supported Cooperative Work (CSCW)* 16 (3): 265–305.

Morgan, D. 2007. *The Mongols.* London: Blackwell.

Morgan, G. 2006. *Images of Organization.* Rev. ed. Thousand Oaks, Calif.: Sage.

Morozov, E. 2008. "An Army of Ones and Zeroes: How I Became a Soldier in the Georgia-Russia Cyberwar." *Slate* online, August 14. http://www.slate.com/id/2197514/.

Mueller, C. W., and M. J. Landsman. 2004. "Legitimacy and Justice Perceptions." *Social Psychology Quarterly* 67 (2): 189–202.

Mueller, M. 2002. *Ruling the Root: Internet Governance and the Taming of Cyberspace.* Cambridge, Mass.: MIT Press.

Mühlenbrock, M., and U. Hoppe. 1999. "Computer Supported Interaction Analysis of Group Problem Solving." In *Proceedings of the Computer Support doe Collaborative Learning (CSCL) 1999 Conference,* ed. C. Hoadley and J. Roschelle. December 12–15, Stanford University, Palo Alto, Calif. Mahwah, N.J.: Lawrence Erlbaum. 398–405.

Mummendey, A., and S. Otten. 2004. "Aversive Discrimination." In *Emotion and Motivation,* ed. M. B. Brewer and M. Hewstone. Malden, Mass.: Blackwell.

Munro, K. 2006. "Safe to Shelter under a Mac?" *Infosecurity Today* 3 (5): 40.

Murphy, M. 2010. "Cyberwar: War in the Fifth Domain." *Economist* online, July 1. http://www.economist.com/node/16478792.

Myers, A., E. Ng, and H. Zhang. 2004. "Rethinking the Service Model: Scaling Ethernet to a Million Nodes." Third Workshop on Hot Topics in Networks, San Diego, November. *Proc. ACM SIGCOMM Workshop on Hot Topics in Networking.*

Nagl, J. A. 2002. *Counterinsurgency Lessons from Malaya and Vietnam: Learning to Eat Soup with a Knife.* Westport, Conn.: Praeger.

Najemy, J. M. 2004. *Italy in the Age of the Renaissance: 1300–1550.* Oxford: Oxford University Press.

Nakashima, E. 2008. "Bush Order Expands Network Monitoring." *Washington Post,* January 26.

National Intelligence Estimate. 2006. "Declassified Key Judgments of the National Intelligence Estimate 'Trends in Global Terrorism: Implications for the United States' Dated April 2006." In *National Intelligence Estimates.* Washington D.C.: U.S. Government Printing Office.

Nonaka, I., and H. Takeuchi. 1997. "A New Organizational Structure (Hyper-Text Organization)." In *Knowledge in Organizations,* ed. L. Prusak. Boston: Butterworth-Heinemann. 99–133.

Novak, J. D. 1998. *Learning, Creating, and Using Knowledge: Concept Maps As Facili-tative Tools in Schools and Corporations*. New York: Lawrence Erlbaum.

Nuwere, E., and D. Chanoff. 2002. *Hacker Cracker: A Journey from the Mean Streets of Brooklyn to the Frontiers of Cyberspace*. New York: William Morrow.

Nye, J. S. 1967. "Corruption and Political Development: A Cost-Benefit Analysis." *American Political Science Review* 61 (2): 417–27.

———. 2011. *The Future of Power*. New York: PublicAffairs Press.

Oates, J. 2008. "UK Gov Issued 250k Snoop Licences in Nine Months: Regulator Says System Working Beautifully." *Register* (U.K.), January 29. http://www.theregister.co.uk/2008/01/29/interception_communications_commissioner/.

O'Brien, K. A. 2003. "Information Age, Terrorism and Warfare." *Small Wars and Insur-gencies* 14 (1): 183–206.

O'Connell, R. L. 1989. *Of Arms and Men: A History of War, Weapons, and Aggression*. New York: Oxford University Press.

Olson, B. D. 2002. "Applied Social and Community Interventions for Crisis in Times of National and International Conflict." *Analyses of Social Issues and Public Policy* 2 (1): 119–29.

Oren, A., and D. Newman. 2006. "Competing Land Uses: The Territorial Dimension of Civil-Military Relations in Israel." *Israel Affairs* 12 (3): 561–77.

Palen, L., and P. Dourish. 2003. "Unpacking 'Privacy' for a Networked World." *Proceed-ings of the ACM CHI 2003 Human Factors in Computing Systems Conference*. Ft. Lauderdale, Fla., April 5–10. New York: ACM Press. 129–36.

Palmer, B., Jr. 1984. *The 25-Year War: America's Role in Vietnam*. Lexington: University Press of Kentucky.

Palmer, D. R. 1978. *Summons of the Trumpet*. San Raphael, Calif.: Pesidio Press.

Pan, X., C. S. Han, K. Dauber, and K. H. Law. 2007. "A Multi-agent Based Framework for the Simulation of Human and Social Behaviors during Emergency Evacua-tions." *AI & Society* 22 (2): 113–32.

Panagiotou, G. 2003. "Bringing SWOT into Focus." *Business Strategy Review* 14 (2): 8–10.

Paret, P., G. A. Craig, and F. Gilbert. 1986. *Makers of Modern Strategy: From Machia-velli to the Nuclear Age*. Princeton, N.J.: Princeton University Press.

Parks, T. 2005. *Medici Money: Banking, Metaphysics, and Art in Fifteenth-Century Florence*. New York: W. W. Norton.

Pasman, W., and J. Lindenberg. 2006. "Human-Agent Service Matching Using Natural Language Queries: System Test and Training." *Personal and Ubiquitous Computing* 10 (6): 393–99.

Patton, G. S. 1947. *War As I Knew It*. New York: Houghton Mifflin.

Pearl, J. 1999. "Probabilities of Causation: Three Counterfactual Interpretations and Their Identification." *Synthese* (Dordrecht) 121 (1–2): 93–149.

Pech, R. J. 2003. "Inhibiting Imitative Terrorism through Memetic Engineering." *Journal of Contingencies and Crisis Management* 11 (2): 61–66.

Pech, R. J., and B. W. Slade. 2005. "Imitative Terrorism: A Diagnostic Framework for Identifying Catalysts and Designing Interventions." *Foresight: Journal of Future Studies, Strategic Thinking and Policy* 7 (2): 47–60.

Perez, E. 2005. "Identity Theft Puts Pressure on Data Sellers." *Wall Street Journal*, February 18. B1.

Perrow, C. 1984. *Normal Accidents: Living with High-Risk Technologies*. New York: Basic Books.

Petraeus, D. H. 2006. "Learning Counterinsurgency: Observations from Soldiering in Iraq." *Military Review*, January–February.

Petrusic, M. 2006. "Enemy Combatants in the War on Terror and the Implications for the U.S. Armed Forces." *North Carolina Law Review* 85: 636.

Pew, R. W., and A. S. Mavor. 1998. Modeling Human and Organizational Behavior: Application to Military Simulations. Washington, D.C.: National Academy Press.

Platias, A. 2002. "Grand Strategies Clashing: Athenian and Spartan Strategies in Thucydides'" History of the Peloponnesian War"." *Comparative Strategy* 21 (5):377–99.

Pluchinsky, D. A. 2008 "Global Jihadist Recidivism: A Red Flag." *Studies in Conflict and Terrorism* 31 (3): 182–200.

Plumb, J. H. 1961. *Penguin Book of the Renaissance*. London: Collins.

Poindexter, J., R. Popp, and B. Sharkey. 2003. "Total Information Awareness (TIA)." IEEE Aerospace Conference, 2003, Big Sky, Mont. *Proceedings*, vol. 6. Piscataway, N.J.: Institute of Electrical and Electronics Engineers.

Porch, D. 2006a. "French War Plans, 1914: The 'Balance of Power Paradox.'" *Journal of Strategic Studies* 29 (1): 117–44.

———. 2006b. *Wars of Empire*. Cassell History of Warfare series, ed. J. Keegan. London: Collins.

Posen, B. R. 1986. *Sources of Military Doctrine: France, Britain and Germany between the World Wars*. Ithaca, N.Y.: Cornell University Press.

———. 1993. "Nationalism, the Mass Army, and Military Power." *International Security* 18 (2): 80–124.

Powell, A., G. Piccoli, and B. Ives. 2004. "Virtual Teams: A Review of Current Literature and Directions for Future Research." *DATA BASE for Advances in Information Systems* 35 (1): 6–36.

Powell, R. 1987. "Crisis Bargaining, Escalation, and MAD." *American Political Science Review* 81 (3): 717–36.

———. 1993. "Guns, Butter, and Anarchy." *American Political Science Review* 87 (1): 115–32.

Pritchard, D. 2007. "How Do Democracy and War Affect Each Other? The Case Study of Ancient Athens." *Polis: The Journal of the Society for Greek Political Thought* 24 (2): 328–52.

Proctor, G. 1844. *History of Italy: From the Fall of the Western Empire to the Commencement of the Wars of the French Revolution*. London: G. B. Whitaker of Ave Maria Lane.

Puchala, D. J. 2005. "Of Pirates and Terrorists: What Experience and History Teach." *Contemporary Security Policy* 26 (1): 1–24.

Ramírez, E. 2008. "Comparing American Students with Those in China and India: Americans Watch Grey's Anatomy While Their International Peers Study Longer Hours." *U.S. News and World Report* online, January 30. http://www.usnews.com/education/articles/2008/01/30/comparing-american-students-with-those-in-china-and-india.

Rashad, H., M. I. Osman, F. Roudi-Fahimi, and P. R. Bureau. 2005. *Marriage in the Arab World*. Cairo, Egypt: Population Reference Bureau and Ford Foundation in Cairo.

Record, J., and W. A. Terrill. 2004. *Iraq and Vietnam: Differences, Similarities, and Insights*. Carlisle, Pa.: Strategic Studies Institute, U.S. Army War College, U.S. Government Printing Office.

Reed, J. R. 2001. "The Savage Empire: Forgotten Wars of the Nineteenth Century." *Victorian Studies* 44: 164–65.

Rheingold, H. 1993. *Virtual Communities: Homesteading on the Electronic Frontier*. Reading, Mass.: Addison Wesley.

Rich, J., and G. Shipley. 1995. *War and Society in the Greek World*. London: Routledge.

Rinaldi, R. 2005. "Princes and Culture in the Fifteenth-Century Italian Po Valley Courts." In *Princes and Princely Culture, 1450–1650*, ed. M. Gosman, A. MacDonald, and A. Vanderjagt. Vol. 2. Leiden, Netherlands: Brill.

Robinson, C. P., J. B. Woodard, and S. G. Varnado. 1998. "Critical Infrastructure: Interlinked and Vulnerable." *Issues in Science and Technology* 15 (1): 61–67.

Robinson, E. W. 2001. "Reading and Misreading the Ancient Evidence for Democratic Peace." *Journal of Peace Research* 38 (5): 593–608.

Robinson, J. A., and R. Torvik. 2005. "White Elephants." *Journal of Public Economics* 89 (2–3): 197–210.

Rochlin, G. 1997. *Trapped in the Net: The Unanticipated Consequences of Computerization*. Princeton, N.J.: Princeton University Press.

Rodgers, N. 1984. "The Abyssinian Expedition of 1867–1868: Disraeli's Imperialism or James Murray's War?" *Historical Journal* 27 (1): 129–49.

Roe, E. 1998. *Taking Complexity Seriously: Policy Analysis, Triangulation, and Sustainable Development*. Boston: Kluwer Academic.

Rogin, J. 2007a. "Attack by Korean Hacker Prompts Defense Department Cyber Debate." *FCW.COM (Federal Computer Week* online), February 9. http://www.fcw.com. Available at http://www.mail-archive.com/isn@infosecnews.org/msg00977.html.

———. 2007b. "Cyber Officials: Chinese Hackers Attack 'Anything and Everything.'" *FCW.COM (Federal Computer Week* online), February 13. http://www.fcw.com. Available at http://www.grc.com/sn/files/fcw_on_%20cyber_warefare.pdf.

Romney, G. W., J. K. Jones, B. L. Rogers, and P. MacCabe. 2005. "IT Security Education Is Enhanced by Analyzing Honeynet Data." *Information Technology Based Higher Education and Training, 2005.* 6th International Conference on ITHET 2005, Provo, Utah, July 7–9. F3D/10–F3D/14. Piscataway, N.J.: Institute of Electrical and Electronics Engineers.

Ronen, S., and O. Shenkar. 1985. "Clustering Countries on Attitudinal Dimensions: A Review and Synthesis." *Academy of Management Review* 10 (3): 435–54.

Rosen, L. 2008. "Faith, Charity, and Terror." *Contemporary Islam* 2 (2): 139–45.

Rosse, J. W. 1859. *An Index of Dates in the History of the World in Two Volumes.* Vol. 2. London: Henry H. Bohn.

Rowe, N. C., and E. J. Custy. 2006. "Deception in Cyber Attacks." In *Cyber Warfare and Cyber Terrorism*, ed. L. J. Janczewski and A. M. Colarik. New York: IGI Global.

Rowley, C. K., and J. Taylor. 2006. "The Israel and Palestine Land Settlement Problem: An Analytical History, 4000 BCE–1948 CE." *Public Choice* 128 (1): 41–75.

Rubin, B. 2007. "Saving Afghanistan." *Foreign Affairs* 86 (1): 57–78.

Ruggiero, V. 2005. "Brigate Rosse: Political Violence, Criminology and Social Movement Theory." *Crime, Law and Social Change* 43 (4): 289–307.

Russell, B., and D. Russell. 1996. *The Prospects of Industrial Civilization.* 2nd ed. London: Routledge.

Russell, F. S. 1999. *Information Gathering in Classical Greece.* Ann Arbor: University of Michigan Press.

Russett, B., and W. Antholis. 1992. "Do Democracies Fight Each Other? Evidence from the Peloponnesian War." *Journal of Peace Research* 29 (4): 415–34.

Safire, W. 2002. "You Are a Suspect." *New York Times*, November 14. http://www.nytimes.com/2002/11/14/opinion/you-are-a-suspect.html.

Sagan, S. D. 2004. "Learning from Normal Accidents." *Organization and Environment* 17 (1): 15.

Sagan, S. D., and K. N. Waltz. 1995. *The Spread of Nuclear Weapons: A Debate.* New York: W. W. Norton.

Sageman, M. 2004. *Understanding Terror Networks.* Philadelphia: University of Pennsylvania Press.

Sanchez-Burks, J., F. Lee, I. Choi, R. Nisbett, S. Zhao, and J. Koo. 2003. "Conversing across Cultures: East-West Communication Styles in Work and Nonwork Contexts." *Journal of Personality and Social Psychology* 85 (2): 363–72.

Sanger, D. E. 2009. *The Inheritance: The World Obama Confronts and the Challenges to American Power*. New York: Harmony Books.

——. 2010. "Iran Fights Strong Virus Attacking Computers." *New York Times*, September 25.

SANS Institute. 2008. "CIA Confirms Cyber Attack Caused Multi-City Power Outage." *SANS NewsBites* 10 (5) (January 18). http://www.sans.org/newsletters/newsbites/newsbites.php?vol=10&issue=5.

Sarker, S. 2005. "Knowledge Transfer and Collaboration in Distributed U.S.-Thai Teams." *Journal of Computer-Mediated Communication* 10 (4). http://onlinelibrary.wiley.com/doi/10.1111/j.1083-6101.2005.tb00278.x/full.

Satloff, R. B. 2007. *Among the Righteous: Lost Stories from the Holocaust's Long Reach into Arab Lands*. New York: Public Affairs.

Schmidt, D. 2007. "Anti-corruption: What Do We Know? Research on Preventing Corruption in the Post-communist World." *Political Studies Review* 5 (2): 202–32.

Schneier, B. 2003. *Beyond Fear: Thinking Sensibly about Security in an Uncertain World*. New York: Copernicus Books.

——. 2006. "Movie Plot Threat Contest: Status Report." *Schneier on Security (A blog covering security and security technology)*, April 22. http://www.schneier.com/blog/archives/2006/04/movie_plot_thre.html.

Schonhardt-Bailey, C. 1991. "Specific Factors, Capital Markets, Portfolio Diversification, and Free Trade: Domestic Determinants of the Repeal of the Corn Laws." *World Politics* 43 (4): 545–69.

Schulman, P., E. Roe, M. van Eeten, and M. de Bruijne. 2004. "High Reliability and the Management of Critical Infrastructures." *Journal of Contingencies and Crisis Management* 12 (1): 14–28.

Schulman, P. R., and E. Roe. 2007. "Designing Infrastructures: Dilemmas of Design and the Reliability of Critical Infrastructures." *Journal of Contingencies and Crisis Management* 15 (1): 42–49.

Sciretta, P. 2007. "Bruce Willis says 'Live Free or Die Hard' Is BETTER Than 'Die Hard.'" In "Reviews" at Slashfilm, May 4. http://www.slashfilm.com/bruce-willis-says-live-free-or-die-hard-is-better-than-die-hard/.

Selznick, P. 1984. *Leadership in Administration*. Berkeley: University of California Press.

Sepp, K. I. 2007. "From 'Shock and Awe' to 'Hearts and Minds': The Fall and Rise of U.S. Counterinsurgency Capability in Iraq." *Third World Quarterly* 28 (2): 217–30.

Settings, M. 2006. "U.S. Ratifies International Cybercrime Treaty." *Computer Fraud and Security* 2006 (11): 2–3.

Shama, A. 1992. "Guns to Butter: Technology-Transfer Strategies in the National Laboratories." *Journal of Technology Transfer* 17 (1): 18–24.

Sheehan, N. 1988. *A Bright Shining Lie: John Paul Vann and America in Vietnam*. New York: Random House.

Sheptycki, J., and M. Innes. 2004. "'From Detection to Disruption: Intelligence and the Changing Logics of Police Crime Control in the United Kingdom." *International Criminal Justice Review* 14: 1–24.

Shevtsova, L. 2007. "Post-communist Russia: A Historic Opportunity Missed." *International Affairs* 83 (5): 891–912.

Shooman, M. L. 2002. *Reliability of Computer Systems and Networks*. London: Wiley-Interscience.

Short, J. F., Jr. 2001. "Youth Collectivities and Adolescent Violence." In *Handbook of Youth and Justice*, ed. Susan O. White. New York: Kluwer Academic/Plenum.

Shroder, J. 2005. "Remote Sensing and GIS as Counterterrorism Tools in the Afghanistan War: Reality, Plus the Results of Media Hyperbole." *Professional Geographer* 57 (4): 592–57.

Simonde de Sismondi, J. C. L. 1847. *A History of the Italian Republics*. London.

Sinclair, R. K. 1988. *Democracy and Participation in Athens*. Cambridge: Cambridge University Press.

Skaperdas, S., and C. Syropoulos. 2001. "Guns, Butter, and Openness: On the Relationship between Security and Trade." *American Economic Review* 91 (2): 353–57.

Smallman-Raynor, M. R., and A. D. Cliff. 2004. *War Epidemics: An Historical Geography of Infectious Diseases in Military Conflict and Civil Strife, 1850–2000*. Oxford: Oxford University Press.

Smith, G. A., and R. J. Allison. 2007. "Fighting a War on Terror or, 'Our Country, Right or Wrong!'" *Reviews in American History* 35: 358–65.

Smith, M., and P. Warren. 2010. "NATO Warns of Strike against Cyber Attackers." *Sunday Times*, June 6.

Smith, T. 2001. "Hacker Jailed for Revenge Sewage Attacks: Job Rejection Caused a Bit of a Stink." *Register*, October 31. www.theregister.co.uk/2001/10/31/hacker_jailed _for_revenge_sewage/.

Snow, D. A., and P. E. Oliver. 1995. "Social Movements and Collective Behavior: Social Psychological Dimensions and Considerations." *Sociological Perspectives on Social Psychology*, ed. K. S. Cook, G. A. Fine, and J. S. House, 571–603. Boston: Allyn and Bacon.

Sobek, D. 2003. "Regime Type, Preferences, and War in Renaissance Italy." *Journal of Conflict Resolution* 47 (2): 204.

Speckhard, A., and K. Ahkmedova. 2006. "The Making of a Martyr: Chechen Suicide Terrorism." *Studies in Conflict and Terrorism* 29 (5): 429–92.

Spector, R. H. 1983. *United States Army in Vietnam: Advice and Support: The Early Years, 1941–1960*. Washington D.C.: U.S. Army Center of Military History.

Spence, I. G. 1990. "Perikles and the Defence of Attika during the Peloponnesian War." *Journal of Hellenic Studies* 110: 91–109.

Spencer, R. 2002. *Islam Unveiled: Disturbing Questions about the World's Fastest Growing Faith*. San Francisco: Encounter Books.

Sperber, J. 2005. *The European Revolutions, 1848–1851*. 2nd ed. Cambridge: Cambridge University Press.

Spiers, E. M. 2007. "Intelligence and Command in Britain's Small Colonial Wars of the 1890s." *Intelligence and National Security* 22 (5): 661–81.

Sproull, L. S., and S. Kiesler. 1992. *Connections: New Ways of Working in the Networked Organization*, Cambridge, Mass.: MIT Press.

Starr, H. 1992. "Democracy and War: Choice, Learning and Security Communities." *Journal of Peace Research* 29 (2): 207–13.

Stein, K. W. 1984. *The Land Question in Palestine, 1917–1939*. Chapel Hill: University of North Carolina Press.

Steinbruner, J. D. 2002. *The Cybernetic Theory of Decision: New Dimensions of Political Analysis*. Princeton, N.J.: Princeton University Press.

Stenmark, D. 2000. "Leveraging Tacit Organizational Knowledge." *Journal of Management Information Systems* 17 (3): 9–24.

Sterlicchi, J. 2001. "California Energy Network under Attack." *Network Security* 2001 (8): 5–6.

Stiles, K. W. 2006. "The Power of Procedure and the Procedures of the Powerful: Anti-Terror Law in the United Nations." *Journal of Peace Research* 43 (1): 37.

Stone, D. A. 1997. *Policy Paradox: The Art of Political Decision Making*. New York: W. W. Norton.

Story, L. 2007. "Mattel Official Delivers an Apology in China." *New York Times*, September 22.

Stowsky, J. 2004. "Secrets to Shield or Share? New Dilemmas for Military R&D Policy in the Digital Age." *Research Policy* 33 (2): 257–69.

Strachan, H. 1983. *European Armies and the Conduct of War*. London: Unwin Hyman.

Strassler, R. B. 1990. "The Opening of the Pylos Campaign." *Journal of Hellenic Studies* 110: 110–25.

Strauss, A. L., and J. M. Corbin. 1998. *Basics of Qualitative Research: Techniques and Procedures for Developing Grounded Theory*. Thousand Oaks, Calif.: Sage.

Summerton, J., ed. 1994. *Changing Large Technical Systems*. Boulder, Colo.: Westview Press.

Sunstein, C. R. 2006. "Irreversible and Catastrophic." *Cornell Law Review* 91 (4): 841–97.

Takahashi, C., T. Yamagishi, J. H. Liu, F. Wang, Y. Lin, and S. Yu. 2008. "The Intercultural Trust Paradigm: Studying Joint Cultural Interaction and Social Exchange in Real Time over the Internet." *International Journal of Intercultural Relations* 32 (3): 215–28.

Tanham, G. K. 2006. *Communist Revolutionary Warfare: From the Vietminh to the Viet Cong.* Westport, Conn.: Praeger Security International.

Thachuk, K. 2005. "Corruption and International Security." *SAIS Review* 25 (1): 143–52.

Thelenius-Wanler, E. 2008. "Riksdagen röstade igenom FRA-lag." *DN.SE (Dagens Nyheter)* online. June 18. http://www.dn.se/nyheter/sverige/riksdagen-rostade-igenom -fra-lag.

Theobald, R. 1994. "Lancing the Swollen African State: Will It Alleviate the Problem of Corruption?" *Journal of Modern African Studies* 32 (4): 701–6.

Thomas, T. L. 2004. *Dragon Bytes: Chinese Information-War Theory and Practice.* Ed. Foreign Military Studies Office. Ft Leavenworth, Kans.: Foreign Military Studies Office.

Thompson, J. D. 1967. *Organizations in Action: Social Science Bases of Administrative Theory.* New York: McGraw-Hill.

Thomsen, J., R. E. Levitt, and C. I. Nass. 2005. "The Virtual Team Alliance (VTA): Extending Galbraith's Information-Processing Model to Account for Goal Incongruency." *Computational and Mathematical Organization Theory* 10 (4): 349–72.

Thucydides. [431–404 BCE] 2006. *The History of the Peloponnesian War.* Trans. Richard Crawley. New York: Barnes and Noble Classics.

Tilly, C. 1992. *Coercion, Capital, and European States, AD 990–1992.* Cambridge, Mass.: Blackwell.

Toffler, A., and H. Toffler. 1995. *Creating a New Civilization: The Politics of the Third Wave.* Atlanta: Turner.

Tomikawa, R. 2006. "Mongolian Wrestling (Bukh) and Ethnicity." *International Journal of Sport and Health Science* 4: 103–9.

Tremonte, C. M., and L. Racioppi. 2008. "At the Interstices: Postcolonial Literary Studies Meets International Relations." *Pedagogy: Critical Approaches to Teaching Literature, Language, Composition, and Culture* 8 (1): 43.

Tuchman, B. W. 1978. *A Distant Mirror: The Calamitous 14th Century.* New York: Alfred A. Knopf.

Tung, R. L. 2004. "Female Expatriates: The Model Global Manager?" *Organizational Dynamics* 33 (3): 243–53.

U.S. Congress. House. Armed Services Committee. 2008. *HASC Roles and Missions Panel Report 1.* 110th Cong., 2nd sess., January 8.

U.S. Office of the Secretary of Defense. Department of Defense. 2007. *Annual Report to Congress: Military Power of the People's Republic of China, 2007.* Washington, D.C.: U.S. Government Printing Office.

———. 2010. *Annual Report to Congress: Military and Security Developments Involving the People's Republic of China 2010.* Washington, D.C.: U.S. Government Printing Office.

Van Doren, C. 1991. *A History of Knowledge: Past, Present, and Future.* New York: Carol Pub. Group.

van Evera, S. 1994. "Hypotheses on Nationalism and War." *International Security* 18 (4): 5–39.

Vo, N. G. 1970. *The Military Art of People's War: Selected Writings of Vo Nguyen Giap.* Ed. R. Stetler. New York: Monthly Review Press.

Voas, J. 2003. "Assuring Software Quality Assurance." *Software* 20 (3): 48–49.

Volgy, T. J., and L. E. Imwalle. 2000. "Two Faces of Hegemonic Strength: Structural versus Relational Capabilities." *International Interactions* 26 (3): 229–51.

Wagner, U., R. van Dick, T. F. Pettigrew, and O. Christ. 2003. "Ethnic Prejudice in East and West Germany: The Explanatory Power of Intergroup Contact." *Group Processes and Intergroup Relations* 6 (1): 22.

Waldrop, M. M. 1992. *Complexity: The Emerging Science at the Edge of Order and Chaos.* New York: Simon and Schuster.

Wales, E. 2002. "Your Money or Your Website?" *Computer Fraud and Security* 2002 (12): 7–8.

Walker, B., and D. Salt. 2006. *Resilience Thinking: Sustaining Ecosystems And People in a Changing World.* Washington, D.C.: Island Press.

Walker, C. 2006. "Clamping Down on Terrorism in the United Kingdom." *Journal of International Criminal Justice* 4 (5): 1137.

Wall Street Journal 2009. "Winning a Cyber War: The 'Soft Underbelly' of U.S. Security." *Wall Street Journal* online, February 21. http://online.wsj.com/article/SB123517477106837383.html.

Waltz, K. N. 1979. *Theory of International Politics.* Boston: McGraw-Hill.

Wamsley, G. L. 1990. *Refounding Public Administration.* Newbury Park, Calif.: Sage.

Wang, K. Y., and L. Fulop. 2007. "Managerial Trust and Work Values within the Context of international joint ventures in China." *Journal of International Management* 13 (2): 164–86.

Weber, M. 1991. *From Max Weber: Essays in Sociology.* New York: Routledge.

Weick, K. E., and K. H. Roberts. 1993. "Collective Mind in Organizations: Heedful Interrelating on Flight Decks." *Administrative Science Quarterly* 38 (3): 357–81.

Weigley, R. F. 1973. *The American Way of War: A History of United States Military Strategy and Policy.* New York: Macmillan.

Weimann, G. 2004. *www.terror.net: How Modern Terrorism Uses the Internet.* Washington, D.C.: United States Institute of Peace.

Wendt, A. 1995. "Constructing International Politics." *International Security* 20 (1): 71–81.

West, J. 2005. "The Fall of a Silicon Valley Icon: Was Apple Really Betamax Redux?" In *Strategy in Transition*, ed. R. A. Bettis, 274–301. Oxford: Blackwell.

Whelton, A. J., P. K. Wisniewski, S. States, S. E. Birkmire, and M. K. Brown. 2006. "Lessons Learned from Drinking Water Disaster and Terrorism Exercises." *Journal American Water Works Association* 98 (8): 63–73.

Whitby, M. 2002. *Sparta.* London: Routledge.

Whitfield, S. J. 1996. *The Culture of the Cold War*. Baltimore: Johns Hopkins University Press.

Whitley, E. A., and I. Hosein. 2005. "Policy Discourse and Data Retention: The Technology Politics of Surveillance in the United Kingdom." *Telecommunications Policy* 29 (11): 857–74.

Williams, H. S., ed. 1908. *The Historians' History of the World: Italy*. Vol. 9. London: Cooper and Jackson.

Willis, H. H. 2006. *Terrorism Risk Modeling for Intelligence Analysis and Infrastructure Protection*. Santa Monica, Calif.: RAND Corporation.

Willis, H. H., T. LaTourrette, T. Kelly, S. Hickey, and S. Neill. 2007. *Terrorism Risk Modeling for Intelligence Analysis and Infrastructure Protection*. Santa Monica, Calif.: RAND.

Wilson, J. Q. 1989. *Bureaucracy: What Government Agencies Do and Why They Do It*. New York: Basic Books.

Wilson, M. A. 2000. "Toward a Model of Terrorist Behavior in Hostage-Taking Incidents." *Journal of Conflict Resolution* 44 (4): 403–24.

Winer, J. M. 2008. "Countering Terrorist Finance: A Work, Mostly in Progress." *ANNALS of the American Academy of Political and Social Science* 618 (1): 112–32.

Wittkopf, E. R., and J. M. McCormick. 1990. "The Cold War Consensus: Did It Exist?" *Polity* 22 (4): 627–53.

Wolin, R. 2011. "The Chronicle Review: A Fourth Wave Gathers Strength in Middle East." *Chronicle of Higher Education*, February 9.

Woolbert, R. G. 1935. "The Rise and Fall of Abyssinian Imperialism." *Foreign Affairs* 14 (4): 692–97.

Wriston, W. B. 1992. *The Twilight of Sovereignty: How the Information Revolution Is Transforming Our World*. New York: Scribner.

Wylie, G. 1993. "Demosthenes the General—Protagonist in a Greek Tragedy?" *Greece and Rome* 40 (1): 20–30.

Young, R. 2007. "Hacking into the Minds of Hackers." *Information Systems Management* 24 (4): 281–87.

Yuravlivker, D. 2006. "'Peace without Conquest': Lyndon Johnson's Speech of April 7, 1965." *Presidential Studies Quarterly* 36 (3): 457–81.

Zegart, A. B. 1999. *Flawed by Design: The Evolution of the CIA, JCS, and NSC*. Stanford, Calif.: Stanford University Press.

Zetter, K. 2009. "Mossad Hacked Syrian Official's Computer before Bombing Mysterious Facility." *Wired Magazine*, November 3. http://www.wired.com/threatlevel/2009/11/mossad-hack/.

Zuhur, S. D. 2005. *A Hundred Osamas: Islamist Threats and the Future of Counterinsurgency*. Carlisle, Pa.: Strategic Studies Institute.

INDEX

accommodation against surprise, 35, 45,
46, 72–76, 81–84, 223, 224; historical
examples of, 106, 112, 115, 126, 152, 166

action, theory of. *See* theory of action

Africa (Western), economic development disasters in, 66

agency theory, 192n12

air gaps. *See* slack

alliances, hostile, 4, 12, 28, 96, 109, 195

anarchy, 10–13 passim, 23, 29–30, 281

anonymity, cybered, 202

Apple computers, focus on security in,
185–87

Archidamian War, 83, 88

asymmetric conflict, cybered: harm
of, on national economy, 180; by
nonstate actors, 180n3

asymmetrical warfare, 179

Athenian Golden Age, 87

Athens, 10, 12, 83–88, 90–95, 166–67,
174, 193

Atrium organizational model for cybered
world, 79–81, 226, 229, 237–38,
253–70

attacks, cyber, 179–81, 202, 205, 286

autarkic systems, 11, 13

avatars, 192n12, 217, 221–22, 261n18,
268–69

backdoors, 16, 268

backup, of computer system, 34, 74, 103,
152, 184

backward mapping, 66

bad actor, cybered, 1, 4, 7, 8, 16, 33, 35,
182–89, 233, 238, 251, 284; in city-
states, 22; embedded, 239–40; peer
group of, 214, 218, 219; potential,
50–51, 53, 244; rise in, 10, 14; in semigoverned nation-states, 19; Soviet, 135;
transnational, 18; in Vietnam, 148

badlands, 7, 14, 18, 20, 277, 280–81.
See also dysfunctional regions

behavior-based privacy, 245–52; and
Cyberspace Policy Research Group,
University of Arizona, 267; and
validation and appeal (V&A), third
element, 225, 228–29

beliefs: focus of constructivism, 38–39;
liberal institutionalism, 22, 28, 30,
33–34, 38–40

biological weapons, 25

blue screen of death, 184

borders: city-state, 14, 96, 101–6;
geographic, 48; national, 1, 3, 5, 9,
17, 35, 233–34, 243, 262, 277; porous,
11, 21; secure, 5, 289; strategic, 5;
territorial, 10; traditional, 226, 229

Bosnia, and cybered operations, 230

bounty hunters, in every culture, 211n18

Britain: lost CDs of (2007), 241; successes
of, in past insurgencies, 36

Britain, small wars of: Abyssinian War
(1867–68), 118; Ashanti War (1873),
118

British school, and international relations theory, 32n19
bugs, in Microsoft software, 124, 186, 189

California electrical grid system, 192
capital: and bin Laden, 60, 67; and drawbacks of trust and greed, 213; failures of (Algeria, Morocco), 209; as strategic disruption tool, 62
cascades of failures in complex systems, 19, 21, 44, 48, 184, 271, 274
cascading surprise, 20, 88
catastrophic surprises, 78, 197, 227
Central Intelligence Agency, in Guatemala, 136
centrifuges, 16, 274
chat rooms, 189, 191, 221–22
China: army doctrine of, 179; and cyber attacks, 202, 206–7, 215, 287; and imports, 11; and informationized war (1999), 279; model, 208; and opium trade, 126; Opium Wars of, with Britain, 272–73; sex ratio in, 64; U.S. relationship with, 6, 283, 288
city-states, 3, 4, 6, 9–21, 47, 79–98 passim, 102, 116, 119–20, 177, 183–87, 209, 254, 280, 293; Athenian, 4, 10, 87, 90, 118, 122, 124, 171–72, 188–89; medieval Italian, 95
civil society, global, 279; and uncivil cybered international system, 5
coercion: cybered, 198–203, 297; deep constraints on, 203; as disruption tool, 49–53, 57, 61–63, 68–71, 198; in Florence, 96, 106, 108, 112, 169; legal barriers to, 200; as strategic tool, 150; and strike-backs, 199; as undermining confidence, 70, 208–10; unintended

blowback of, 198; in Vietnam, 136, 146, 150–53, 163
co-evolution of social and technical systems, 253
cognitive need, human, 19, 48
Cold War, 4–5, 10, 23, 27, 32, 59, 63, 209; historical examples of, 112, 115–16, 134–57, 171; theories, isolation of, from domestic-level literature on conflict, 40
collaborative deliberation, 22, 34, 49, 76, 81, 112, 163–65, 170, 226–29, 253–59, 265–66, 277
collective sense-making, 48, 71–72, 115, 289
collective wisdom, 22, 38, 187
combined military arms, and collective problem solving, 256, 261
complex systems, 44–47, 271, 288; and reliability, 18, 44–47, 74, 260, 273. See also resilience; surprise: resilience to
complexity, 1; in Abyssinian campaign, 119; of global system, 21, 44–47, 76, 239; on the internet, 17, 184, 224, 290; in national security, 274, 289; theories of, 3, 44–47, 73, 253, 271
computer security, 200
confidence, and theory of action, 41, 42, 50, 51, 52
conquest. See city-states
constructivism, 3–40. See also international relations; syncretic approach
contrary information streams, 50
corruption, 18–19, 65–67, 160, 163
coupling, 8, 46–48, 73, 178, 280
critical infrastructure, 181, 184, 199–200, 238n4, 252, 276
critical knowledge, 44, 48

critical systems, 2, 18, 70, 191, 223, 274–76; resilience of, 43–44, 47, 73, 74, 80, 83, 289

cultural guidance, 55

culture: and affective communication, 55, 215–16, 219; change agents in, 56; cue-giving authority in, 56; of liberal institutionalism, 30–33, 38n26; and neutral communication, 55, 215–16

cyber command, U.S. model for, 76, 277–79, 287

cyber power, national, 283, 289

cyber proxy soldiers, 191

cyber proxy wars, as emergent, 207

cyber stealing, 4

cyber targets, 6

cyber vandalism, 15

cyber war, first, Israeli-Palestinian (2000), 195

Cyber Westphalia. *See* sovereignty

cybercrime, 8, 18, 188, 202, 293

cybered age. *See* cybered conflict

cybered attacks: Australia (2000), 182; Estonia (2007), 193; Iraq, 177; Muslim Hackers Club, 196; religious fanatics/terrorists, 195; U.S. TSA (2009), 182; various (2008), 197, 202

cybered conflict, 183, 233; advantages of, 2; age of, 290; and destruction, 3; fighting requirement of, 76

cybered success, 179

cybered world, 4–6, 14, 24; conflict in, 71; operational constraints of, 198; security challenges in, 18–20, 33–35, 267, 270–90 passim; and surprise, 76, 79, 224, 229, 237; weighted strategies in, 51

cyber-enabled attacks, 20, 211, 213

dampening, in accommodated surprise outcomes, 35, 42, 45, 51, 58

decoupling. *See* slack

deep institutions, 28, 35, 55, 78, 227, 247

democracy, 12–13, 67, 203–8, 236–39, 252, 267; historical examples of, 93, 106, 137–40, 145, 150–51, 169

dependencies, 5, 9, 13, 21

destruction, versus disruption. *See* disruption

deterrence, 25, 36, 40, 45; cybered, 27

deviant amplitudes, 45

DHS. *See* Homeland Security, Department of

disruption: in British small wars (1867–74), 115, 124; cybered, 219; Florence, 96, 105

distribution of resources, as perceived by humans, 39

domestication, 8, 12–13

drivers of violence. *See* theory of action; violence

dual use, 15, 17n19, 96, 179

dysfunction, sudden, 16

dysfunctional regions, 4, 6–7, 9, 11, 13n17, 14, 20–21, 240, 270

economic models, 21

economic prosperity, and liberal institutionalism, 2, 11, 29, 38, 31

Egypt, 7, 118, 172, 276, 282, 283

electrical systems and grids, 16, 181; and attacks on California, 192

empires. *See* city-states

encrypted, 249

Estonia, cybered attacks on (2007), 193–95, 279; Russian involvement in, 194

evolution, 12, 34, 38, 44, 55, 95, 269

exercises, and limitation for learning by organizations, 255

expected-utility curves. *See* liberal institutionalism

experience lessons, 55

failing state, 10, 18, 27, 67

false front, 17–18

false-flag deception, 217

financial linkage, 13

financial system, global, 13, 22; and U.S. mortgage meltdown (2008), 13

fixity. *See* borders

Florence, 76, 95–113, 168–69, 174

force, as focus of realism, 39–40

form or frequency, as known in advance, 19, 45–48, 75, 260

fragmented playbook, 34

framing story, 39

free fire at will, 11

frequency. *See* form or frequency, as known in advance

games, online, increasing role of, 222

games for organizational learning: and Atrium model, 259; avatars in, 192n12, 221–22; and virtual world, visualization, and conceptual mapping, 259

gangs, U.S., 53, 64, 70, 179

geolocational tools, and loss of anonymity, 202

globalization, 1, 5, 10, 20, 22, 33, 48, 78, 182, 229, 273–74, 280–83; and effect of population growth and youth bulge, 281

God, butter, and guns. *See* theory of action

governance, 6, 11n5, 87, 248

graceful degrade, 184

Greece, 12, 96, 244

grievance, 39, 42–43, 62–65, 191–93, 211, 221. *See also* dysfunctional regions

grievance farming, 13, 16, 76, 78, 184, 219

grievance narratives, 221

ground truths, syncretic approach to, 33, 38, 224

Guatemala, U.S. small war in (1950–54), 135

hacker culture, 194; thrills and money as components of, 218

hackers, 8, 71, 178, 186–95, 200–207, 217–21, 232, 275; and California electrical grid (2001), 192; careers of, in cybercrime, 190; skills of, 190

hacking, as social movement, 15, 178, 184, 189–90, 195–96, 202, 207, 218

"hearts and minds," 31–32, 59. *See also* liberal institutionalism; Vietnam War

Homeland Security, Department of, 76, 225, 235, 254

home-loan market, 20

honest consultation, 83–84, 92, 109, 130, 154, 252, 266, 273

honeypot, as cyber deception method, 210, 221

humans, as pattern-matching animals, 39

ideas, money, and force. *See* theory of action

ideas all the way down (liberal institutionalism), 30

information: as strategic tool, 214, 219; warfare, 60, 180, 278. *See also* theory of action

infrastructure, 16, 20, 86–88, 165, 180–86, 197–206, 211, 230, 239, 253, 277–78, 288; critical, 181, 184, 199–200, 238n4, 252, 276 in-group violence, 56, 59, 221

innovation, 35, 47, 107, 110n24, 183, 193, 236, 256, 262–67, 283–86; American engine of, 284

institutional adaptation, 76, 79, 228–29

institutional change, 175, 229, 234

institutional design, 4; for knowledge development, 78, 228. *See also* Atrium organizational model for cybered world

institutionalists, 27–31, 35. *See also* liberal institutionalism; syncretic approach; theory of action

interdependence, 11, 20, 33, 44, 249, 272, 288. *See also* socio-technical systems

international economic theories, 20

international flows, 10

international networks, 15, 208

international political economy. *See* liberal institutionalism

international relations, 20–23, 30–33, 35–36, 38–39, 50, 175, 224, 273, 277, 291. *See also* syncretic approach

internationalists, 13n6, 27

internettedness, 15, 180, 279, 283

interventionism, 28

Iran, 15, 177, 206, 219, 220, 274, 282; Stuxnet attacks on (2010), 10, 251, 275–78

Iraq, 32, 59, 61, 66, 146n48, 177–78, 211–16, 222, 231, 265, 273; Bush policy on, 27–28

Israel, 62, 195, 276, 279–80

Italy, 12, 96, 97, 98, 99, 100, 101, 105, 107, 135

jihadism, 7, 23, 60, 69, 180, 190, 195, 240, 277. *See also* grievance farming

joint consultation, 49, 81, 155, 225, 230–34. *See also* knowledge: nexus

knowable unknowns in complex systems, 45–48, 72. *See also* accommodation against surprise

knowledge: burden, 73, 107, 119, 147, 185, 255; and collective problem solving in Atrium model, 256–57; continuous, multilevel, and multiscaled, 34; critical, 44, 48; dampening, deterring, destroying, remediating, improvising, or innovating, 34; development, 57, 130; embedded, 46; expressed as structure (liberal institutionalism), 30; and knowable and unknowable unknowns, 48; lack of, 151; nexus, 2, 87, 234–38, 240, 243–47, 271, 277; poor development of, 135, 178; refinement in operations, 1, 92; shortcoming, 46

largescale technical systems (LTS). *See* socio-technical systems

lawyers, money, and guns. *See* theory of action

lead paint. *See* China

League of Nations. *See* liberal institutionalism

legitimacy: cue givers, 56–58; disrupting cybered, 219; and theory of action, 10, 36–68, 80–88, 91, 95, 105, 123–29, 148–66 passim, 213–21, 238, 256, 282–83; two acceptability tests of, 54

legitimated information, 54, 58, 60, 69

liberal institutionalism, 22, 28–33, 38n26, 39–40. *See also* international relations; theory of action

Linux, 187–89; as FOSS (free and open source system), 188; security resilience of, 188

Live Free or Die Hard (2008 movie), cyber war on U.S. systems in, 181

logistics, 15, 101, 127, 129, 136, 210, 214, 257

loss-aversion, 34

mafia: international, 17, 190; Italian, 14; Russian, 188, 194–95

males, overpopulation of young. *See* dysfunctional regions

malicious code, 17, 182

malicious software, 15, 274, 279

mercenaries, use of, 29, 97–101, 105, 108, 111, 142

"messing with the mix," 50–53, 116, 136

Microsoft, base system of, as insecure, 185–89

Milan, 95–112, 168; and Duke Filippo-Maria Visconti, 95–106

military and police distinction, 20

military force. *See* coercion; theory of action

"mirroring the mix," 51, 115

mitigation, in accommodated surprise outcomes, 45, 236

modernization, 5, 161, 252n14, 285–86

money: as focus of liberal institutional-ism, 39–40, 65–67; as key component of perceived needs, 39

mortgage, 13, 21

motivation, human, 30, 36, 52–53, 84, 126, 136–52 passim, 224

motivators, and theory of action, 36–40, 43, 49–52, 68, 149, 169, 198, 209, 233

multiple source failures, 47; and cascading surprise, 20, 88

Muslim nations, 36

national security, 1–5, 13–26, 32, 35, 43, 50, 71–79, 139, 154, 176; strategy, 48, 180, 198

natural experiments, in historical city-states, 79

need: and perception of "relative" or "subjective" deprivation, 39, 63; and theory of action, 37–41, 44, 49–51, 76, 81, 83, 106, 148, 152, 224, 229

neglected outcomes, 43, 45–48

neo-Nazi movement, 7, 189, 277

network-centric warfare, 278

new medievalism, 9 ·

New Orleans, 16

nonstate actors, 3, 19, 48, 178, 180

nuclear: arsenals, 10, 24, 78, 227; attack, 5, 25, 197; power plants, 15, 49n35, 183n4, 251, 274; targeting, 164; war, 34, 134; weapons, 25, 59, 135, 175, 279; "winter," 175

offense, 6, 224, 240

openness: of city-states, 17; of computer systems, 186–87; of Western society, 203, 225, 242, 245, 284

organization: cognitive and authority structures of, 55; military history of, 230; reducing contingencies via, 77, 227

organizational boundaries, 234

organizational design, uncertainty of, 230

organizational doctrine, 32, 34

organizational processes, 2, 269

organizations: domestic, 29n17, 79; hidden, 14; military, 2, 69, 81, 227; security, 50, 170; semicovert "gray," 17, 19; terrorist, 25, 50, 210, 217; transnational, 14. *See also* mafia

out-group, 56–58, 215; hate for farming grievances and violence, 57

"Pearl Harbor," digital, 175

Peloponnesian War: First, 85; Second, 83, 86, 91, 167

Pericles, 19, 85–95, 113n25, 118, 166–68, 171, 174–75
"pile on," 21, 239, 274; and third parties (Brazilian, 2000), 195
post–Cold War, 4, 27, 32n19
precision. See scale, proximity, and precision
predictability: in complex situations, 39; in the environment, 55
privacy: behavior-based, 78–79, 175, 225, 228–29, 236–52, 266–67, 277; cybered, 19, 202–6
proximity. See scale, proximity, and precision
pseudonyms, 248–49

radicalization, 24, 39n28, 190n9, 212n19. See also grievance farming
rapid collective response, 48
"rational peasant," 31, 163–64. See also Vietnam War
realism, 11, 22–40, 47, 222n26, 272–73. See also international relations; syncretic approach
receptivity, to new information, 55
reconstitution, in accommodated surprise outcomes, 45
reductionism, 23
redundancy, 46n33, 73–76, 113n25, 115, 289; as essential to resilience, 2, 55, 82, 84, 91, 122–24; in Gulf oil disaster of 2010, 73
redundant system, 73
relative knowability, of surprise outcomes, 45
resilience: of Athens, 95; during British small wars, 115–31, 134; and continuity of operations, 71; of Florence, 101; and graceful degrade, 184; and Linux, 187–88; societal, 237; of Sparta, 193

resource distribution, as perceived by humans, 39
riots, 41, 52
risk-avoidance, 34
rogue outcomes, 46, 48, 72, 75, 265, 271, 272n3; unknowable unknowns, 47, 88
role maps, 55
role-playing games, 222
Russia: corruption and new wealth in, 67, 171, 195; cyber military forces of, 279

Saudi Arabia: corruption of, 67; Western female business executives in, 54
SCADA electrical grid key nodes, 181
scale, proximity, and precision, 6, 51, 224, 266–67, 270, 281. See also cybered conflict
scenario, 15, 95, 163, 206n16, 207, 210, 258, 260, 263, 268–69
security: in Athens, 92; in British small wars, 119; constraints, 60n40, 71, 198, 287; dilemma, 5, 23, 25, 27; in Florence, 111; four resilience strategy processes of, 49, 81, 83; historical examples of, 78–83 passim, 95, 115, 166–73; institutional adaptations needed for resilience of, 76, 183, 226–28, 236–38; by obscurity, 180, 289; organizational structures needed for resilience of, 252, 267, 273, 283; resilience strategy of, 33–37, 48–49, 71, 178; in U.S. small wars, 135; utopian belief in, 185
selective engagement. See realism
semicovertness, 14, 17
sensitivity analysis, 73, 82
September 11, 2001, 57, 60, 146n48, 197, 251; actions taken due to, 49, 183–84nn4–5, 203, 210–11, 235, 242, 247; pre- and post-, comparisons, 233, 269

Shaka Zulu, 53
shared daily practices, 35, 48, 59, 230, 255
slack, 48, 73–76, 97, 115, 276, 289; as essential to resilience, 2, 57, 84
SMS, text-based, 220
social construction, 35, 50, 185, 191, 218, 262
social contract, 275, 279
social movements, 24, 26, 28, 34, 63, 65, 78, 180, 189–92, 228, 239
social trust, 48, 214, 245, 263
socialization, 14, 32, 36, 72, 168, 170, 183, 252, 255
sociopolitical relationships, 9n4
socio-technical ensemble theory. See socio-technical systems
socio-technical knowledge competition, 284
socio-technical systems, 44n32, 46, 75, 265, 271; computerized, 285; large-scale, 43, 75, 289
sovereignty, 10, 98n10, 146, 208, 230, 273–76; realist support for, 29; rising, in cyberspace, 277
Spain, 8, 266
spam, 18, 193
Sparta, 12, 19, 83–95, 167–68, 193
state, failing, 10, 18, 27, 67
strategic buffer, 4, 20, 174, 201
strategic disruption, 37, 68, 71, 153
strategic response framework. See security: resilience strategy of
Stuxnet worm, in Iran, 15, 251, 274–78
suicide bombers, 15, 25, 59, 69, 191, 212
superpowers, 2–5, 20, 23, 40n29
surprise: accommodation against, 19, 35, 46, 112–15, 126, 152, 166, 223–26, 253, 262; cascading and disabling, 4, 20, 22, 24, 46, 72, 197; cybered, 4, 8,

175, 226, 229, 237, 281n6; overload, 34; resilience to, 3, 35, 46–48, 72–94 passim, 224, 261; sources of, 1, 4; unaccommodated outcomes of, 45
Sweden, 234–35, 279; 2008 law in, 204
syncretic approach, 3, 28n16, 33, 38n26, 40; security, 34
Syria, 177, 195n13
system change, 24

tacit knowledge, 226, 229, 253–54, 256, 259–60; and Atrium model, 79, 237, 262, 265, 268; as critical for surprise, 257
tailored disruption, 37, 50; strategic use of, 34, 37, 43, 49–51, 53, 58, 59, 62, 71, 73, 218, 237, 240
tailored weighted strategies, 51
tainted toothpaste. See China
technological design: early focus on, 186; unsecure by 1990s, 184–85
technology, 24, 44, 50, 72, 153, 183, 185–86, 213, 216n21, 221–22, 239, 242, 284; Atrium, 269; information, 179; modern, 243; older, 16, 181; simulation, 268; theft, 207
terrorism, 24, 169, 190, 204, 241, 242, 266; global, 22, 34, 36, 146n48, 234; religious, 25, 60n40, 233, 240
terrorists, learn from hackers, 217
text-based SMS, and neutral culture, 220
theory of action, 37–41, 44, 49–51, 76, 81, 83, 106, 148, 152, 224, 229
theory of surprise, as key to resilience, 46, 82, 83
threats, chronic, violent, "gray," and cybered, 34, 245
tightly coupled, 1, 13, 20, 44, 48
topology, 8, 9, 20, 76, 224, 231, 266, 276, 278

Total Information Awareness (TIA), 241, 247

trading partners, 11

transformation, 13

transnational, 9, 14, 17, 18, 26, 34, 220, 240

trial and error, 69, 73, 75, 76, 84, 173, 260, 266, 289

trust: broad-spectrum, 216; critical, 172, 192–93, 213–22, 243, 246, 256, 257, 261–63, 265–66; cybered, 192

Tunisia, 7, 275, 281, 283

uncertainty, 19, 46, 63n42, 72, 93; Roman army measures, 77, 108, 227, 231

undersea cables, 14, 283

ungroundedness. *See* strategic buffer

United Nations, and liberal institutionalism, 9, 28

unknown outcomes, and complexity theory, 48

unknowns, 54, 56–57, 81, 231, 240; knowable, 45, 47, 48, 72; unknowable (rogues), 45, 47, 72

Vietnam War (1954–65), 11n5, 31–32, 59, 116, 134–38, 145–66, 169–71, 221, 239n6

violence, 41, 42, 50, 51, 52, 56, 70, 196; and cognitive dissonance, 56, 163; and immigrant out-group hate, 57–58; threshold decision for, and theory of action, 37–41, 43–44, 49–52, 76, 81, 83, 106, 148, 152, 224–26, 239; among young males and modern British army, 64; among young males and relative deprivation, 39, 65; and youth bulge (in Asia), 64

virtual black market, 190. *See also* hackers

war: Athens-Sparta, 83, 85, 86, 91, 167; Florence-Milan, 95–112; history of, 33, 68, 83, 265; and theory of action, 68

warfare, network-centric, 278

water control systems, 15

weapon. *See* cybered attacks; nuclear

weapons, biological, 25

websites, 8, 15, 43, 49, 178–79, 183, 188, 193–96, 199, 210, 238, 282

weighted drivers, for theory of action, 40

WikiLeaks, 280–82

world system, 8, 22, 28, 37, 283

World Wide Web, 15, 184, 202, 266, 275

"youth bulge," and unemployed Arab youth, 281